MAYA LEELA

THE DIVINE PLAY OF ILLUSION

POETIC GUIDE FOR THE PLAY OF YOUR LIFE

HUGH SHERGILL

MAYA LEELA

THE DIVINE PLAY OF ILLUSION

POETIC GUIDE FOR THE PLAY OF YOUR LIFE

ISBN: 978-3-5943-9269-0

ISBN: 978-3-7184-3282-0

ISBN: 978-3-1415-3135-0

Hugh Shergill ®

Hugh Shergill

hughshergill.com

For you...

you know

who...

Love...

Hugh Shergill

CONTENTS

WELCOME

To The Play Of Maya Leela…

"Prepare to trip your reality…
Bringing forth your true reality…
Perhaps not what you want to hear…
Yet revealing what you need to hear…
To see it for what it is…
Not what you believe it is…
To what is going on…
By revealing…
What is really going on…
What was…
What actually is…
Upon the uncover…
Shall change forever…
You did not just happen…
To find this book…
In all actuality…
It found you…"

Hugh Shergill

PROLOGUE

"True recognition resonates…

Within continuous…

Any self elaborated recognition…

Is frivolous…

To know the particular…

Requires a soul ocular…

Into the deepest darkness…

For unveiling its sparkness…

Submerged in depths of conscious…

Immensely intense intimate precious…

Where glimpses of those sightings…

Revealed only through the writings…"

Hugh Shergill

Maya Leela

"To know the 'unknown'...
  One cannot take the route 'known'...
  To know the 'unknown'...
  One must step into the world 'unknown'...
  Revealing the previous suttle more...
  Revealing it to the point of know...
  Particular reveal of sequencencial flows...
  Where revelating wind of reveal blows..."

Hugh Shergill

"You only see. ..what you know"

Johann Wolfgang Von Goethe
(Renowned Writer / Poet)

"What is...
  Is what...
  Perceived life...
  Fictional austerity...
  Where truth is...
  The only luxurious reality..."

Hugh Shergill

The Truth of Reality...

Absolutely nothing that you perceive in your reality is infallible... If one has not encountered potent knowledge that makes one question everything that they previously perceived as the truth...one must continue acquiring more knowledge... Truth is simply stating factual information... Honesty is revealing the truth that was hidden...

One must first see before research...one's consciousness channeling aligns much before one first reads... Education and intelligence are distinctively dichotic...education follows intelligence...intelligence leads education... Intelligence is developed and accumulated through external information...that within the confine limitation of information processing capacity... However, Intellect is only developed through one's own experiences and consciousness depth capabilities...which is the energy of never accepting anything for granted and questioning everything...as nothing is never as what it seems...which is the infinite forte of both the seek and reveal of consciousness...as there is no value limit on seeking of experience...as consciousness depth ultimately merges with the infinite...

"Education is for the outer world...
 Intelligence is for our inner world...
 Innerstanding of you...
 Understanding of you...
 What you know of you...
 Is potent power within you..."

Hugh Shergill

"The only true wisdom is in knowing
 that you know nothing."

Socrates (Renowned Philosopher)

"One that does not know...
 Believes it knows...
 One that believes it knows...
 Does not know...
 One that observes its knows...
 Becomes to know..."

Hugh Shergill

Every intellect thought and experience comes from within one's conscious, sub-conscious and for a few certain...further beyond infinite conscious realms... As the birth of every book...the words are first conceived in one's consciousness...what is being revealed in this publication is one's intellect perception of one's consciousness...with certain intimate reveals of consciousness revelations...drivenly felt and compelled to share...in its own authentic manner...by bringing information to the ground what was deliberately left as underground...for those certain that resonate to the revelating reveals...as the essence of the reveals shall indeed either provoke or evoke...

"Make your own Bible.
 Select and collect
 All the words and sentences
 That in all your readings have been to you
 Like the blast of a trumpet."

Ralph Waldo Emerson
(Renowned Philosopher / Poet)

"First to exist is the reality of the truth...
Then the revelation reveal of the truth...
Concentration accumulation of the truth...
After follows the documentation of the truth...
Documentation is conclusive of the truth...
Never commencing of the truth..."

Hugh Shergill

Seldom, spiritual perspective is attempted to be fully explained and proved through scientific reasoning... This to me, is such a flawed futile attempt as there is a clear distinct dichotomy of thought reasoning and undeniable limitations of processing capacities... Indeed, there are certain scientific schools of thought that do more resonate, especially from the simple fundamental universal principles, biological processes...to the complexities of quantum physics...as spirituality in itself gives a much more higher in-depth understanding of quantum physics...allowing further deeper understanding of what is in actuality... allowance is the seed of possibility...confinement of strict structured scientific thought is not... A Marriage between two is a particular connection...not a union of the identical... In the relay race of awareness, spirituality truly starts racing only after science has exhaustively handed over the baton upon completing their respective yet a very restricted portion of the race... Science is naive realism...
Spirituality is actualism...

"Reality is what you perceive to be real...
Limited confines of one's conscious feel...
The absence of evidence...
Is never evidence of absence...
Anything finite can not be absolute...
Absolute actuality lies in the infinite..."

Hugh Shergill

All Science is based on confined establishments of only human physical observational processing, whereby things only become defined when they are possibly observed through the limited human physical processing experiences...which is mere naive realism... For furthering observation on the other hand, the pool of quantum realms is further altered, entangled, and determined upon the particular observation itself...particular is the key here...as each observation is an altered perception and altered manifest of what is being observed... Therefore all these observational confines can only be interpreted through each particular human experience of reality, which is limited within itself, as actually experiencing reality that absolutely and no doubtedly exists, but can not be possibly processed to its fully extent within the confines of the human thought experience...and yet science does not have the understanding of what is the actual source of thought... Spirituality is opening up ourselves and going beyond the ignorance confines to the inconceivable possibilities to explore the infinite realms of what is it that is actually observing the observed... A mere three dimensional existence experience shall fail to understandingly experience the world of fifth dimension... In a world dominant by naive realism... Spirituality is actualism...

Empirical evidence is observational experience...

Often profound discoveries are kept disclosed with the apprehension of being label targeted as 'non sufficient scientific evidential reasoning' or 'not yet scientifically proven'... Unfortunately conventional education should be expansion...however it is often used as a confined cloak of hiding ignorance... Being a scholar of doctored information...is a scholar of tampered information... Contrary, one feels at complete confident ease to share...as discoveries can not be uncovered for not the sake of validation... uncovering is the first step...as its experience defines the rest... As an example, if some particular personal health action makes you feel more vibrant and healthy, it would be utmost foolish to refrain from it until (or if wishfully ever) by waiting for a scientific study to support your actual personal positive health experience. With that said, any parallel references that merges science and spiritual concepts for further elaboration in this publication's particular subjects, i shall kindly share...which shall largely focus only on the universal established principle laws of this particular universe...that we are all confined perceived illusionary existence of...regardless of whether we perceived through science or spiritual thought processing...as revealing the truth amongst the lies is the utmost importance...

"No such is objective reality...
 All is just subjective reality...
 Intelligence embraces all knowledge...
 Where ignorance fails to acknowledge...
 The absence of evidence...
 Never evidence of absence...
 Life teaches...
 Experience preaches...
 Ignorant life roadies...
 Live merely by certain studies...
 Shifting from naive realism...
 Shifting to spiritual actualism..."

Hugh Shergill

Lineage Influential Knowledge Roots...

"Nothing is coincidental...
 All was preparation essential..."

One's primary physical genetic lineage is from the land that gave us the first known written scriptures... 'The Rig Veda'...'The Verses of Wisdom' which fortunately gave exposure to its vast lineage knowledge from one's early childhood... This lineage's knowledge root is primarily Vedic...with ideology seeds emerging from the Vedic era... specifically the respective Vedas, Puranas, and Upanishads... The Vedas were written to preserve Divine information on particular knowledge, customs, traditions, and ideology... furthering through the Upanishads to make one move further towards one's spiritual journey... these references act as sparks of information that ignite the flame of knowledge and discovery for those certain consciously driven...firing further with intuition extracts of multi realms of consciousness...with extracts of untapered authentic specifics of the ancient Vedas, Puranas, and Upanishads… As lineage knowledge remains dormant if devoid of expansion… For this…expansional experience and processes is a necessity… one must indulge in further depths…seeking…discovering experiences deep…deeper…nirvanic indulgence depths of Divinity…Shakti…Tantra…Mantra…Yantra…

Revealing further dimensional realms branches from the stem root of the lineage vedic knowledge… along with the immense soul felt referenced appreciation of its poetry…with utmost respective range from the Vedic era Vedas and Poetic Puranas…especially the Divinity sent Yajur Veda…the first scriptures of poetry ever written…

Furthering one's influences through the depths of Sufism poetry…an innate inclination perhaps due to also having physical genetic ancestral roots tied to the land of Sufism origins…

To the more recent, Shakespearean…an encyclopedia of theatricals indeed…fortunate to be exposed to its vast treasures of literature and stage plays from a very young age…perhaps more conveniently accessible due to physically taking birth in the land of Shakespeare…

Further, leading to perhaps the most influential for one poetically, Urdu poetry…linguistically blessed for its fortunate early exposure…words that serve as both pulses of blood with each heartbeat…and nectar for the soul… Manifesting as an inspiration that expresses in one's innate attempt poetically…

As apparent, the entire publication is written in Latin script…as the communicating language used is respectively English. Indeed primarily in English…however vedically infused with some corresponding language inclusion references that are Vedic Sanskrit rooted words… Sanskrit, the most ancient language discovered in complete scriptures known…contemporarily unveiled and understood by the immensely valuable research contributions of the ancient Sanskrit grammarian, Pāṇini. As, first came the existing era…then the existence…followed by soul conscious thoughts…communication…where then came the corresponding linguistics and recorded documentations…

"The sun does not self advocate…
 Its expressional capacities to illuminate…
 Undeniably its experience is what resonates…
 Never through the sun's self worth debates…
 What forever shines bright…
 Shall forever kiss the sight…"

Hugh Shergill

Persona Talks…Poetry Reveals…

Mentioning and revealing certainties of this particular life being existence…its vast experiences and perceived credentials…all that have admittingly, certainly, and profoundly contributed to one's intellectual experiential perception…perhaps may even be inspiring for some others upon share…as one must walk into the deepest darkness for unveiling its sparkness… However, this would shift this publication to more of an autobiography route...revealing deep soul experiences and its journeys that all compelled and led to writing this book...which is strictly not the attempt nor a desire to do so... Plus, the act of self praise... talking about one's own particular credentials and accomplishments is such a frivolous sad act of self humiliation...that one pities those who actively participate in it... This is what one feels confidently... where enigmatic secrecy and privacy are absolute dominant innate traits within...as fame and recognition holds absolute no importance...indeed there are certain intense dynamically infused soul experiences that have...(silence)...yet one prefers 'the unsaid' to be 'said' in a particular manner fashioned...where allowing one's persona talk instead of lips...whilst allowing one's poetry to reveal the rest...

"Informer is unimportant...
 Information is potent...
 Never about the messenger...
 Magic exists in the message...
 Revelating reveals leaked...
 Forever unknowingly you seeked..."

Hugh Shergill

"Appreciate the reveal...
 Of the enlightening unveil...
 One indulges the delicious meal...
 Prepared by that amazing chef...
 Regardless of its all else...
 One imbibes the poet's words...
 Regardless of its all occurs..."

Hugh Shergill

"Before this particular demise...
 It is important...
 To share the knowledge prize...
 Persona remains conflicting...
 Yet must now be revealing....
 What is shared...
 Revealed...
 Whom that shared...
 Revealed..."

Hugh Shergill

Divinely Divine Divinity…

"From the seeds and roots…
  What emerges is the Divinely tree…
  Of one's conscious expressions…
  Intuition nectar sweet extracts…
  With branches forming further…
  Through experiential expressions…
  Now the Divinity lit flowers blossom…
  As sparks of untapped awareness…
  Excreting fragrance of knowledge…
  Love dancing with its soul mate wind…
  Divine movement of loving karmic interaction…
  Being shined upon by the sun's Divinity…"

Hugh Shergill

"Where there is a creation,
  There should be a creator"

Rajinikanth (Renowned Actor)

"If there was no God,
  There would be no atheists."

**Gilbert Chesterton
(Renowned Poet / Writer / Philosopher)**

"Subject establishes existence…
  It exists to make your point sense…
  To truly disregard an acknowledge…
  Requires full disregard of acknowledge…
  To reject its existence…
  Requires to accept its existence…"

Hugh Shergill

"Restriction of an entity…
Validates its existency…
The efforting non believer…
Is forcing out the believer…
To ignorantly shun…
Is its validation…"

Hugh Shergill

'Divine'…is utmost respectively referred to as the Divine energy source itself, 'Brahman', the supreme consciousness existence of absolute reality… It is infinite, omnipresent, and the spiritual core of all that exists… The infinite Divine consciousness is also referred to as 'Shiva' and the Divine power manifested energy of the Divine consciousness is referred to as 'Shakti'… Some refer to the Divine consciousness as God, which i refrain to do so as it gives solely a masculine manifest impression, where in all actuality, the Divine energy itself manifests energy through Shakti, the feminine expression of all creation existence of all that exists, therefore the term God may also one feels…be even more correctly and appropriately referred to as Goddess…as all perceived creation is given birth by Shakti… With that said, labeling the Divine energy source itself is subjective…as its named label is not the importance but what it absolutely is…as any particular form label cannot truly label the Divine source universally…as it is labeless…formless…and yet forming of all…ultimately it is the Divine energy source of all…existing as all…in all…beyond all thought…with the only possibility of being felt in this very limited processing existence…unveiling only through the Divine spark of awareness existing as soul consciousness, the 'Atman' (also commonly pronounced as 'Atma') the soul…the soul spark of Divine…

However, for this publication reference purpose intent, the fundamental core existing references are absolutely required as everything is…is it itself…it is therefore utmost unconditional soul Love and respect referred to as 'The Divine Energy Source' 'Divine' 'Divinity'… and the 'Soul' being its creation conscious spark of awareness…

"You should not honour men more than the truth."

Plato (Renowned Greek Philosopher)

Maya Leela

Self Proclaimed Enlightened…

"illusion is…
 Is illusionary…
 Regardless of how…
 Magnificently perceived…
 Still a mere illusion…
 It is not about who i am…
 It is about what am i…
 illumination that…
 Radiates…
 Resonates…
 Not mere shining light on to oneself…
 To frivolously self privilege illuminate oneself…
 Act of unnecessary karmic residue of ignorance…
 That many self proclaimed 'enlightened'…
 Fail to experience the enlightened essence…"

Hugh Shergill

"He who does not desire power
 is fit to hold it."

Plato (Renowned Greek Philosopher)

"What a terrible era
 in which idiots
 govern the blind."

William Shakespeare
(Renowned Poet / Playwright)

"Desire is to not have you be a follower…
 Instead have you become the leader…
 Of your life play…"

Hugh Shergill

I am no self proclaimed Guru…

The terms 'Spiritual Guru / New Age Guru / Guru' and one acknowledging labels themselves as
the supreme one…is the ultimate expression of egorance…the combination of ego, ignorance, and
arrogance…which is the epitome of disgust that someone is so weak and empty within that it requires

external enhanced validation and accolades of their self proclaimed perceived credentials...as certain aware souls see right through this illusion facade... A Guru is defined as someone who is a teacher, specifically here referred to as a spiritual teacher...even if it stopped at that...it would still be somewhat palatable...yet there is fine line that once one is identified as a Guru...then commonly that one self crowns oneself as some supreme being...that makes even Divinity chuckle in astonishment...

"I will not permit...
   Anyone to do this...
   God alone is entitled...
   To such worshiping...
   He will destroy us...
   If we become God...
   I am only a humble servant...
   Of men...
   A guide..."

Movie: The Guide (English Version)
Dialogue: R.K Narayan
(Renowned Novel Writer)
Dialogue Recitation: Dev Anand
(Renowned Actor / Filmmaker)

As for teaching...even in teaching...spirituality can not be taught...only experienced...knowledge is shared yet never given...it is taken... Indeed one can share knowledge...yet it is up to whom the knowledge is being shared to on how it takes it...discovering it...experiencing it...enduring it...imbibing it within... Experience happens through discovery...discoveries of potent knowledge can be shared but never just mere taught... True spirituality is to discover and experience... spirituality is the light radiance of the Divine... therefore the light and its radiance is Divine...no one can teach or be taught the light...as light can only be discovered, shared, and experienced...at our very best we can perform to channelize and spot focus the light for a particular stage spot illumination... yet how that particular stage spot is being experienced by the audience is to each their own...thus I strictly refuse to associate oneself as being some self proclaimed guru absolutely...

On the contrary, one innately identifies as the rebel soul poetic guide...a guide embraces adventures of discovery...a rebel treading on to the unconventional untreaded paths to discover those certain undiscovered destinations... Thus, one is Divinely driven to perform as the poetic play tour guide of the Maya Leela play theatre...focusing the dedicated stage spotlight to bring to light...certain theatrical particulars of the theatre...for further focus attention for unveiling discovery...such as the Maya illusion, Maya stage, the play, audience, performers, and its performance...for the theatre visitor to indulge and experience it for themselves... A tour guide does not teach...it shares...guiding the traveler to certain discovered destinations to be experienced while information sharing of that particular destination... With that said, a tour guide holds further capability of enriching the tourist's experience through sharing their own particular in depth destination discovery experiences...revealing more than what just meets the eye of the discovery...

Maya Leela

"Those self appointed proclaimed enlightened...
 Are Soul blind for the actual enlightened...
 Perhaps that hidden was revelatingly received...
 Yet no one's business what was achieved...
 Keep those noble labels for the unnoble...
 Rebel Soul is comfortable being their trouble..."

Hugh Shergill

Unfortunately, 'find sharing' doesn't necessarily correspond with 'kind caring'... In this particular era, everyone commonly seems to be self proclaimed chosen awake...till they truly face their testing shake... Fortunately, as we evolve within and continue on our particular spiritual path...the power of intuitive discernment becomes very powerful...where one easily detects the inauthentic pretenders from the authentic soul contenders...

"Without effort...
 Shall rattle your reality...
 Whatever you put forth...
 Is questioned in your reality...
 Releasing your illusion entrapped mind...
 Unveiling even your perceived space and time..."

Hugh Shergill

Instead of being associated with self proclaimed 'Spiritual Guru'...one prefers being an active participant of 'Spiritual Emergence' movement...as the key to spiritual knowledge that resonates is emerging...this is spiritual emergence...not self claims of spiritual enlightened...spiritual emergence is the infinite pool of consciousness...where not just one...but every soul holds the capability to submerge to emerge...an emergence for mergence...

Emergence for Mergence…

"That spiritual emergence…
  Intensified intent for mergence…
  To submerge…
  To emerge…
  Deviations of existing perceptions…
  Experiencing shocking revelations…
  Unveil beauty of the heart beat…
  Ticking truth as nectar sweet…
  Awaiting no longer waiting…
  As all became evidently relating…
  The share that interests is revelating…
  Not a self proclaimed enlightening…"

Hugh Shergill

Writing Style…

Poetry & Poetic Proses…

"The writing style is poetic subconscious…
  poetry, stanzas, sestet, and poetic prose
  manifesting…imbibing avant-garde poetry…
  as art takes birth from unconformity…"

The writing style is deliberately unconventional… compilation fusion flow of poetry, poetic prose, stanzas, sestet, and quotes… Indeed, effortless convenience does exist to convert to the perceived 'conventional'… especially further with technological artificial intelligence advances…however i unapologetically refuse to do so…as it would no longer be soul core artistic authentic…nor the soul's driven purpose…as being 'unconventional' is in all actuality the most authentic…as unveiling the reality of the perceived 'conventional' is the purpose of these writings…therefore, what is purposely penned expressed…must reflect in its linguistic structure as well, regardless of how unconventional it may be perceived….and any compromising deviation would not be so…as only what one utmost authentically feels is deserving of effort to be written word by word entirely in its expression…only then it shall for my certain particulars…resonate…

Maya Leela

"Written on the soil of prose...
  Decorated with Poetry rose...
  Revelatingly informing...
  Aromatically revealing...
  Eloquence of thoughts...
  Opulence of words..."

Hugh Shergill

It is not the length of the words...in all actuality...it is the potency of the words... A scientific formula is just a few letters...for instance, Albert Einstein's equation discovery of $E = mc2$ Where energy equals mass times the speed of light squared...this five letter formula is no longer than an average word... Yet the intellectual indulgent in depth analysis of these five letters is effortlessly capable of producing volumes upon volumes of in depth explanatory texts in itself...that is the magic of certain word's potency...from a formula to all the way to a mantra...

Potent poetic proses...thus potency requires the use of pauses...as more potent...smaller each particular dosage delivery...otherwise it would not be a prose...instead just another conventionally constructed paragraph... As I am sure it is already apparent, that there is generous inclusion of '...' ellipsis in one's writing style...instead of the conventionally appropriate coma or full stop...as this is absolutely deliberate... Those suttle extra glimpse of moment extensions...are intended to allow for the very potent information to permeate within...resonate within...imbibe within...before being saturated further with further potency to what follows... What is written...is not the end...poetry is a felt thought... no thought is ever fully complete...it is the incomplete thought continuation that triggers and takes the poetic magic forward... Each written poetry and poetic proses compilation of words...enigmatically written...are deserving of continuation...liberty of additional moments for the respective reader to comprehend...furthering intimately thoughts revered from the initial trigger...bringing to surface one's conscious a plethora of personal experiences...thus, the generous use of '...' ellipsis in both one's written poetic proses and poetry...

Sipping Artist...

"Strong cognac taste...
  Tragical to haste...
  Controlling the tempt...
  Pacing the attempt...
  Euphoric raining weather...
  Indulgences liquiding further...
  Imbibing whilst the tongue's slip...
  Holding each drop of the grasping sip...
  Experiencing euphoria indulgence...
  Artist of sipping intelligence..."

Hugh Shergill

"Poetry…
  In Love…

Poetry…
Its resonation…
Submission…
Reciprocation…
Touches one's core profoundly…
The very depth of Love…
That once felt…
That continues to…
Powerfully pulsing…
Echoing through words…

Poetry…
In Love…"

Hugh Shergill

What is written is extremely intimate…as it is a very deep intimate reveal of one's consciousness intellect expression…and that is where the true romance solace resides…beyond any conventional appointed orthodox restrictive structures…therefore the soul felt word constructs are absolutely unconventional and tend to innately incline naturally more towards free flow verse poetic persuasive….

"Poetic spontaneity flows like water…
  Unimposed by any confined meter…
  Most potent bullet of the weapon gun…
  Is the ink of the factual written pen…
  Where one destroys physicality…
  While the other reveals reality…"

Hugh Shergill

Maya Leela

Poetic Originality

"My words poetically follow…
  Yet not tread a particular echo…
  What is previously read…
  Establishes a certain tread..
  Those who travel the untread path…
  Blessed to imbibe the purest breath…"

Hugh Shergill

"Where even the Ravi (Sun) does not reach...
  Is a place where the Kavi (Poet) does reach..."

Anand Bakshi
(Renowned Poet / Lyricist / Writer)
Translated by Hugh Shergill

A Poet by Sunil Dutt

"A Poet extracts...
  The entire potency of a sea...
  In just a few drops of words...

  A Poet undresses...
  Clothed emotions...
  Through its words...

  A Poet creates...
  Both a revolution...
  And the delivery of Love...
  With its words...

  A Poet capable...
  Of providing unrelenting power...
  Through its empowering words...

  Whenever my life was met...
  By its various difficult moments...
  Poetic verses empowered my soul..."

Sunil Dutt
(Renowned Actor / Philanthropist)
Poetic Translation by Hugh Shergill

Speaking of poetry, there is an innate strong attraction and admiration towards poetry... Words are felt as sacred...as each word itself is a vibrational mantra...respectively in each and every language... as it is one's consciousness association of the words that sparks the vibrational magic consciousness through the words... Further, the collective dominant association of the words must be kept in highest regard as well... Poetry has mystical capabilities to be experienced as both as a soul nectar or even a dynamic jolt trigger through its poetic words alone…

"Poetry is a felt thought...
Feelings are what is felt...
By itself are perhaps impactful...
Yet may eventually fade forgetful...
A thought alone is not heartening...
Remains confined to intellect appealing...
Thought devoid of the felt of feeling...
Felt without thought not all consuming...
Poetry is the manifest of mergence...
Marriage of the felt thought fusion...
Thoughts that are felt...
Poetry is a felt thought…"

Hugh Shergill

"What inspired transpired…
A masculine manifestation...
Is a feminine creation...
Extremely constructive...
Or intensely destructive...
All Karmically determined…"

Hugh Shergill

Inspirational & Poetic Quotes References…

As a soul felt tribute, certain intellect references through insightful and poetic quotes of renowned respective individuals are included to further emphasize certain subjects of intellect expressions… Poets… Philosophers… Revolutionists… Performers… Artists… and Actors…who perform the numerous variations representing and often accurately presenting the genre dynamics of the play of life…both on celluloid and the play stage theatre… Throughout time perhaps references are more associated with masculinity expressing…yet make no mistake…as the influential core creative energy that manifests in the artist's art is undoubtedly undeniably dynamic femininity… Divinity Shakti energy of creativity…

through its infinite forms…from suttle glimpse of influences to lifelong conscious connects…she forever inspires…through her Divinity of creativity…

It is an utmost humbling honourable privilege to include poetry expression tributes through poetic quotes…and even further by providing certain poetic language interpretation translations… Poetic soul quotes are encapsulated transforming energy…as seldom pages may get forgotten, but poetic soul felt quotes tend to remain…but timeline duration of perceived existence of the writer are refrained to mention…as any human made measuring construct as time can not justifyingly establish beyond existence measured reference…especially for quantifying soul consciousness, which never ceases to exist…as energy can never be created nor destroyed…it only shifts forms…forms that either are felt or not…but undeniably ever existing…

"Desire is within…
 Desire not to embrace what illuminates…
 Desire to reveal the illusion that illuminates…
 Desire to discover the deep dark kept Divine…
 Desire whilst the illusionary confine…
 Desire to seek the source of the shine…"

Hugh Shergill

Her Deep Lion Experiences…

Her Shakti…the Divine Artist's dynamic energy
manifesting as art through its performing
artist…in the Divine's play of Maya Leela…
where the performing performer explores,
experiences, and expresses…for the soul…it resonates deep within… Symbolically depicted, the lion represents power, fearlessness, will, and determination…the brave solitude king among the illusionary surrounding jungle…yet completely in deep awareness, humility and surrendered to its Divine force…the Divinity Shakti sitting above the lion that symbolizes her Divine mastery over all energies…omnipotent… omnipresent…the driving force of the lion's performance…guiding and protecting her deep lion through all the spiritual warfare battles…each step…each scene…each act…each lifetime…in the Divine spectacle stage play of Maya Leela…

Stage Play Theatre…

Metaphorically and parably…the analogical fusion is the stage play theatre…serving as the background narrative concept plot of Maya Leela… There is tremendous Love, interest and admiration for the performing theatre…especially Shakespearean…where there is a complete emotional spectrum appreciatively on display through the treasure archive of each of the plays…with the profound resonating poetic depth in dialogues, and its vast characters…that continue to exist through us and around us…

One is admittedly aware about the conspiracy and controversies that exists around the potential actual origin sources of Shakespearean writing... authorship question...questioning further to even the authenticity of the one perhaps that is conventionally credited to...yet what is referred to as 'Shakespeare' is correctly credited in this publication...as what one acknowledges as Shakespearean is strictly referred to the gems of words written...literature is ideology...as the Shakespearean literature goes beyond a particular referenced individual or individuals...as what is respectively acknowledged as Shakespeare is what is ultimately written...that is Shakespearean and ultimately from that origin Shakespeare source...whomever it is...as it is the information that is valuable...not necessarily the confined means of its delivery...

"Every question is answered...
  Seeker seeks the answered...
  What was discovered profoundly...
  Joyously it is to finally find you...
  Revelating revelation discovered...
  Forever desired to be uncovered..."

Hugh Shergill

Knowledge is never given, it is taken...experience happens through discovery...discoveries can only be shared but never taught...With all humility, certain thoughts, words and lines written may hold immense depth within...a potential awareness arsenal of self discovery for those that may courageously desire to discover and seek further...

Understanding...

"Understanding...
  Whom understands...
  Is understanding...
  Understanding...
  Who does not understand...
  Is also an understanding..."

Hugh Shergill

Revelating Infinite Immunity from Disagree...

Interestingly, the unique magical beauty of these revelation insights are that they are much beyond any convincing, persuading, argument, disagreements, and debates...as both resonating or rejecting the conscious expression expressed are both absolutely true perceived reality...and absolutely in support with what is written...therefore, one is completely in utmost respective agreement with both those that agree and also those that disagree...as all shall be revealed in complete peace spiritual ease with precision reasoning reveals...which...apologies for my immodesty...is unique in itself...perhaps the first ever of its kind…

With that said, i commence to share...what you may call a poetic study guide of the ultimate play... the inevitable and absolute play of Maya Leela that we all are participating and performing in...either knowingly or unknowingly…

**"May my Art…
Be that Artist's art…
Comfort…
For the disturbed…
Uncomfort…
For the undisturbed…"**

Hugh Shergill

Books are portals to worlds that one has not yet visited... This particular book is a heartfelt poetic expression put forth as a Love letter tribute to the Divine play of life...by providing comfort of clarity... clarity that counters and eliminates confusion of illusion...taming regressive emotions and programmed thoughts...fading away the arrogance and ignorance driven ego... An attempt that shall be life transforming for some...through creating an awareness ease of one's performance in the ultimate play of life...and at the very least, thought provoking, life questioning for others…

**"The book of Maya Leela…
Is the rain of revelation…
Discovery of experiencing…
The words are its rain drops…
Falling on the already existing soul seed...
That upon receiving the rain…
Shifts from the dormant seed…
To activated seed...
That grows through knowledge…
Blossoms flowers of awareness...
Bearing sweet fruit of performance…"**

Hugh Shergill

"True perception...
Is not what we see...
It is understanding what we see...
Perception is always a result of processing...
By what is we perceive to be...
And what actually is...
The unsaid is about to be said...
What is said shall never be unsaid...
What is felt shall never be unfelt...
What is once seen...
Shall never be unseen..."

Hugh Shergill

With utmost humility...one must admit...being innately an extremely secretive enigmatic individual...
writing this book certainly reveals an intimate consciousness glimpse of oneself unavoidably...yet
it absolutely is one's soul purpose necessity...thus one is extremely fearlessly motivated to reveal...
information that has been for many thousands of years remained intentionally suppressed hidden
unrevealed...till now... This information is for the very first time ever being revealed with such revelating
precision...indeed it has been long overdue...yet the destined moment has finally arrived for what was
left as unknown...is about to be known...
Poetic Justice...Poetically...

Her Divine Shakti Revelating...

Her Deep Lion Revealing...

Hugh Shergill

MAYA LEELA

THE DIVINE PLAY OF ILLUSION

Stage - Maya

Play - Leela

Director - Divine

Script - Karma

Audience - Consciousness

Performer - You

Poetic Study Guide by Hugh Shergill

CHAPTER 1.

HISTORY REVEALING MYSTERY

"What is a Theatre…
Without Any Credible Play History…"

"It was forever revealed from the first script…
Ignorance pinned down the reveal kept…
Truth is the only knowledge…
Beyond any confined lineage…
Your soul self has been forever aware…
Waiting upon this dimensional aware…
Pandora's box has finally opened…
Revelation reveals non-returned…
History full of mystery…
History revealing mystery…"

Hugh Shergill

**"People don't want to hear the truth
  because they don't want their illusions destroyed."**

Lord Krishna, Bhagavad Geeta

**"Truth is stranger than fiction,
  But it is because
  Fiction is obliged
  To stick to possibilities;
  Truth isn't."**

**Mark Twain
(Renowned Writer / Explorer)**

**"Truth is often eclipsed
  but never extinguished."**

Titus Livy (Renowned Writer / Philosopher)

**"For nothing is hidden
  that will not be disclosed,
  nor is anything secret
  that will not become known
  and come to light."**

Holy Bible (Luke 8:17)

**"Always go too far,
  because that's where
  you'll find the truth."**

Albert Camus (Renowned Writer)

Ancient History...Revealing Mystery...

Evolutionary and historically...there are certain regions that have culturally endured and survived more so than others...from certain catastrophic natural disasters to harsh radical climate conditions...such as the ice age...for example, more southern hemispheric regions were geographically more equipped to handle the most recent ice age...which dates approximately 25,000 years ago...Egyptian region, South America, South Asia... and more specifically India...are regions with very deep time tested cultures that survived centuries through the help of creativity, languages, arts, visuals, cultures, and storytelling...potent knowledge that was culturally passed on from one generation to another... Deep rooted India's ancient vedic lineage knowledge fascinates within due to both its vast knowledge pool and one's genetic ancestral connect...providing blessed linguistic essentials for furthering one's grasp of accumulating its knowledge and diving deep researching specifics into hidden extremely revelating unexplored aspects...

"We forgot more...
  Than we know...
  Deep one goes...
  Deeper one becomes...
  Being aware of the ailment...
  Stepping path of treatment..."

Hugh Shergill

"Most beautiful pearls...
  Remain shell enclosed...
  Awaiting upon release...
  For the seeker diving deep...
  Euphoric on treasure discovered...
  Etheric upon being discovered..."

Hugh Shergill

Deviation from the middle source...
Going direct to the core source...
Rediscovering the primary source...

Interestingly...every religion, religious institution, religious ideologies, and its corresponding scriptures ever known to humankind to date...are to a certain or more often to a larger degree...have been inspired and extracted in some form or way...from roots of knowledge...from sources of the previous chronological perceived timeline of various religions, religious institutions, religious ideologies, and its corresponding scriptures... Indeed, even in certain specific cases, straight out plagiarizing could also be included with valid scholarly referential proof...yet one will kindly refrain from diverting one's energy by stating all that...as unfortunately acute ignorance blinds one with eternal offense... Indeed the convenience of ignorance may ignorantly deny all this...yet nonetheless that remains the untampered truth...

"Maybe you are searching among the branches,
  for what only appears in the roots."

Rumi (Renowned Sufi Poet)

Maya Leela

"The storm deliberately...
  Flipped over collapsed...
  Uprooting the tree...
  Yet now unexpectedly...
  Its very core roots...
  Reaches exposed towards the sky...
  What remained root hidden...
  Is now the untruth's burden..."

Hugh Shergill

Thus, one shall instead keep the focus on the primary sources...the roots of knowing...as if one truly desires to be scripturally informed...intrinsically and authentically...it makes the highest intelligence and intellectual sense to go right back to the core source roots of the first scriptures available in the commencing chronological perceived timeline...as it is the primary source roots that are the actual authentic source...serving as the primary purpose igniting spark for that deeper consciousness exploration trigger...acting as that powerful meandering river force that creates its own discovery way as it moves ahead...

"Just like a meandering river...
  Upon its route, hitting the side rocks...
  Erodingly shaping them aswell...
  As it travels spontaneously...
  Progressively making a way...
  Wherever it travels...
  As the nature of beauty lies...
  In the meandering river flow...
  Not in a lineal confined structured flow...
  As it is in the unpredictable...
  Spontaneous river's beauty meander flow...
  Where the immense possibilities...
  Of new possibilities exist...
  Traveling on route...
  While shaping the route...
  I am that meandering river...
  Confidently aware of my deliver...
  Each movement is destined precise...
  Cutting through with each water drop slice...
  Wherever I shall travel...
  Destinations will unravel..."

Hugh Shergill

Let's now indulge deeper…
Into the primary driving force…
The primary scriptures source…
The Vedas and Puranas…

Vedas and Puranas…

The Vedas…

The Nectar of Knowledge…
The Power of Self-Realization…

The Vedas are the most ancient discovered known written scriptures to humankind…composed and written in the most ancient known written language, Sanskrit…that dates back 6000 plus years in written form from the Vedic era…further interestingly, Vedas are also known as 'Shruti' scriptures…which means scriptures that were documented from orally passed on traditions of many multiple generations…making it much more ancient than what its documented timeline reveals… Potent contents of the Vedas were passed on from one generation to another for thousands of years before it was actually written down…

Poetry…Hymns…Phrases…
Remember…Recall…Recite…

The power of rhythmic words…create an advantage of an easier recall…just like we easily recite the lyrics of our favourite songs without putting in forced effort…the rhythm of poetic words…along with the ancient culture of multi generations living in close knit environment…this created a perfect potent environment that allowed for the rhythmic words of the Vedas to be remembered…recalled…recited…

"The Vedas are not a religion…
What exists before any religion…
What does not establish a religion…
What does not encourage to follow a religion…
Is absolutely not a religion…
The Vedas are knowing…
Never a religion…"

Hugh Shergill

Veda…
Knowledge…
To Know…

The word 'Veda'…is derived from the Sanskrit word 'Vid' defined as knowledge or to know…there are four known classifications of the vedas…

1. Rig Veda (Knowledge)

First, the Rig Veda is 'the knowledge of verses and mantras'…the Rig Veda is the oldest written sacred texts known to humankind…Rig Veda is the oldest veda from the four vedas…as all the other three Vedas primary reference Rig Veda much more than one occasion…revealing revelating knowledge from the material realms to the spiritual realms…that even to this day, holds revelations reveals that still are undiscovered…for those who have not yet uncovered…

2. Yajur Veda (Poetry)

Second, the Yajur Veda is 'the collection of poetry and poetic proses'…revealing knowledge of Divinity and its creation poetically…a similar structure to this written publication attempt…

3. Sama Veda (Music)

Third, the Sama Veda is 'the book of songs'… uplifting devotion through poetry, songs, and music that leads one to tranquility of blissful state…

4. Atharva Veda (Yoga)

Fourth, the Atharva Veda is 'the storehouse of knowledge'… These Vedas consist of specific classifications of knowledge, education, and its devoted acts…including health and fitness through the knowledge of Yoga and Ayurveda respectively…

The Harappan civilization dates minimum 8000 years back…the Rig Veda written in Sanskrit was present parallel in that era…therefore existing minimum 8000 years back…comparatively the next closest civilization first historically available existence was the Egyption civilization dating 5000 years back…3000 years after the Harappan civilization…

Therefore, the Vedas, especially the Rig Veda is even much more older than what some scholars think… documenting Sanskrit language's timeline (8000 BCE) and the orally passed on 'Shruti Scriptures' for centuries… one can confidently say that the Rig Veda is 10,000 BCE + old at the very minimum…

Interestingly, the Rig Veda revealed our particular universe, our immediate solar system and planets, corresponding planetary distances in space, star constellations, and even speed of light in precision accuracy… Further, even more shockingly, the Vedas even revealed the infinite parallel multi-verses…the first known text documented all this and beyond…indeed an impeccable encyclopedia of knowledge… all being revealed from the very first scriptures…fascinating indeed…

The Vedas are from the Vedic Era…therefore the are correctly classified as 'Vedanta'…it is not the incorrectly classified assumed as Hinduism or any other religious title…indeed numerous chronological institutionalized branches emerged from the Vedas…yet they are simply nectars of knowledge… knowledge that is infinitely unbounded…not trapped in the confines of any particular religion…Instead of following confined religious rituals being…attempt was to follow centuries of tried knowledge living…

The Vedas are beyond the concept of religion...pure authentic knowledge of Divinity...and its corresponding action, devotion, faith, reasoning...developing an individual's mental, physical, and spiritual faculties through knowledge...with the most profound of all is the Rig Veda's nectar of mantras...holding immense power to shift one's reality from 'What Appears' to actually 'What Is'...

The Puranas...
The Poetic Verses of Literature...

The Puranas is originally composed in Sanskrit...consisting of 400,000 plus poems and proses as a tribute to the Divine and its creation...the creation of the infinite universes and its creations...Puranas are also known as 'Smriti' scriptures which translates to what is recalled and remembered...

The Puranas...the poetic verses of literature...poetic words that are dedicated to certain particulars of creation...from the creation of the multi-verses...to Divine and supernatural forces...

Knowledge is not confined to be Institutionalized...

Both the Vedas and the Puranas are knowledge that is beyond the confines of any Institutionalized structures...though certain schools of thought classify these verses as being religious...however one totally disagrees...knowledge is revealed...Knowledge is documented...knowledge is shared... knowledge is imbibed within...knowledge does not require to be structured nor institutionalized... therefore both the Puranas and Vedas are at its core are nectars of knowledge...not a religious Institutionalized structure of knowledge...

The Upanishads...
Sub categorical branch of the Vedas...

The Upanishads...sub categorical branch of the Vedas...these ancient texts reveal the spiritual knowledge of the Vedas by applying it to attain spiritual enlightenment while oneself experiences its true existence...

Interestingly, approximately 200 plus Upanishads have to this written date been discovered...with many more Upanishads yet to be rediscovered...as specific branch texts of the Upanishads flow further from one set of texts to another...not necessarily chronologically but ideologically...this flow of knowledge does not stall nor finitely conclude...which further emphasizes that there are absolutely more Upanishad texts yet to be rediscovered...better further put...uncovered by those who discovered...

**"Exploration of those hidden ancient vedas...
Destruction attempt by particular certains...
Indeed they burnt and hid certain scriptures...
Intentionally inviting series of conjectures...
Satisfied knowing nothing else remained...
Unaware what Divine clouds contained...
Showering gems on few left souls unslept...
Revealing revelations that were secretly kept..."**

Hugh Shergill

Shakta Upanishads...

Further specifically, the Shakta Upanishads go deep into the tantra metaphysical breakdown of the supreme Divine energy of Brahman... Shiva Shakti... Infinite Divine Brahman that is both consciousness and energy... Both formless and all forms... Shiva and Shakti simultaneously...

Shiva represents the masculine transcendent aspect of the Divine...the cosmic consciousness itself...the infinite energy source of all realms...giving direction to all forms...

Shakti represents the feminine transcendent aspect of the Divine...the infinite Divine in dynamic energy flow action...manifestation of the cosmic consciousness at play in all realms...giving birth to all that is... capable to change shape shift all that is...

In Shakta Upanishads, the Divine Shakti is emphasized...as it is the dynamic energy at play of all creation in perception... What exists...and appears to exist is the infinite flow of Divine Shakti... often respectively given a female Goddess association...Devi...

**"Divine is Shiva...
Cosmic consciousness...
Divine is Shakti...
Cosmic creation...
Their union is Divinity...
Creating eternity..."**

Hugh Shergill

Referential quotes on the Upanishads:

"Upanishads...Mystic meaning"

**Robert Ernest Hume
(Renowned Author / Professor)**

"Upanishads...Secret doctrine"

Friedrich Max Müller
(Renowned Philologist / Orientalist)

"Upanishads...Hidden connections"

Patrick Olivelle
(Renowned Philologist / Sanskrit Scholar)

"Vedas...The most profitable and elevating reading
 which...is possible in the world"

Arthur Schopenhauer
(Renowned Philosopher)

"Truth...
  Never created...
  Nor destroyed...
  Only uncovered...
  Often unappreciated...
  Never depreciated..."

Hugh Shergill

Understanding is dependent on processing... what can not be processed...can not be possible to be understood... The universe laws are absolutely not universal... The infinite realms of multi infinite co-existing parallel universes hold much further infinite possibilities beyond any possible conceptualization... where every perceived universal law eventually diminishingly dissolves...furthering to universe activity realms existing far beyond the human processing experiencial capacity ever possibly can...being truly non-dependent of human processing and yet absolute dominant of all processing capabilities... An example of this phenomenon, is black holes in this perceived universe...that deform the laws of the universe...including the deformity of space and time itself...

However, as further shall be further elaborated...consciousness goes infinitely beyond the confines of immediate human experiential processing...consciousness is beyond perception...as all perception of existence is within the Maya realm...therefore beyond perception is beyond Maya...

Before one grasps in what in all actuality is Maya... one shall focus initially the immediate human existing experiencial confined perceived level...to the infinite unconfined consciousness...to process and grasp further understanding of what is the realm of Maya...one shall begin by initially exploring and understanding the familiar knowing scientific referenced laws of relativity, duality, energy, and quantum physics...before and more importantly, going into the metaphysical depths...exploring the unknowing...

**"Awareness is being aware...
Of both of the knowing...
And the unknowing..."**

Quantum

Quantum is the minimum amount of any entity involved in an interaction...the complete structure of a human being's perceived structure is a quantum wave... Further, for the Soul, this quantum phenomenon at its core itself is one's Divine soul energy...

Perceived Existence...Duality and Relativity...

The Law of Duality:

**"Nothing is never truly alone...
as there is always an opposite
within the whole..."**

Duality is the oppositional state. Everything that appears to exist...exists in contrasts...everything has an opposite... Everything has a complementary opposite within the whole...such as light and darkness...

The Particle Wave Duality Paradox...
All is nothing but Energy...

**"All perceived existence is
both a wave and a particle simultaneously..."**

Everything in perceived existence is both a wave and a particle... The wave and particle duality is the concept in quantum physics that all matter is both a particle and a wave simultaneously...

Interestingly, the wave existence is energy...energy that is and always has been there...just transferring from one form to another...The wave nature of light is the perceived reality of the Universe...Therefore, all you see and experience in this perceived physical world is at its core nothing but energy...Shakti...

**"We are faced with a new kind of difficulty.
We have two contradictory pictures of reality"**

**Albert Einstein
(Renowned theoretical physicist)**

This is a profound 'duality paradox' that all particles also exhibit a wave nature and vice versa...this is the fundamental metaphysical fact of all perceived existence... Any given kind of quantum object will exhibit sometimes a wave...sometimes a particle characteristic...in certain particular physical settings... This phenomenon has been verified not only for elementary particles, but also for compound particles such as atoms and even molecules...

What determines the perceived perception of both waves and particles? This is determined from a quantum superposition where one perceived one over the other due to quantum fluctuations...in other words, attentive perception...intent influences...the key again is one above the other in terms of attentive perception...while both yet absolutely existing simultaneously in this duality of reality...this superposition that perceives the particular duality paradox is the state of super consciousness...

"Perceived reality is attentive reality...
  Non attentive realities are also absolute realities...
  Just devoid of your attention currently..."

Interestingly...a particle is able to be measured...yet its duality equivalent as a wave is beyond measurement... what is measured at that precise moment of observation...is for that precise moment only...where even a zeptosecond moment earlier or later... the wave measurement will be different... All energy is forever fluctuating and moving... never fixed therefore cannot be measured...it can be only experienced...and further enriched... through expansion and manifestation by one's power of consciousness... This is why the grandest manifestations are totally possible to step into one's reality... as waves are energy... infinite energy...infinite possibilities...all energy is Divine Shakti itself...if one's consciousness with purity is capable of tapping into the Divine energy field of all existence... Divinity will manifest what is desired in one's perceived reality...this is the power of intent...this is the power of one's pure core consciousness...

The law of Relativity:

"One perceives something as related to
  something else...you see day knowing of night..."

All objects in the perceived existing reality are referred to as relative because they only exist in relation to each other... Everything that appears to exist, exists by interpreting it relative to some way or something else...such as day and night...

In the confines of human experiential processing, it is impossible to have a single force manifestation concept. There must and always is, a pair of forces equal and opposite. Physically...specifically earth science, to perceive to exist, one cannot formulate laws outside of the confines of the law of Maya, which is the fundamental structure of all perceived creation...which is the Love creation projection of the Divine...one is only complete with the other...expressing all in complete complimenting creation expression in whole itself...the Divine energy source...

Law of Energy:

"True reflection of one...
 Is the suttle rippling reflection...
 Of one looking into water...
 As all your existence is energy...
 Energy in continuous motion...
 Every moment leading...
 To continuous fruition..."

Hugh Shergill

Energy can neither be created nor destroyed...it can only be transformed or transferred from one form to another...and then another...and so forth...

Energy is formless... Energy creates forms but is not forms... Forms do not create energy... A particular form may be destroyed however the energy remains... If energy was a form it could be separated and destroyed, therefore energy is formless... Energy exists without creating a form... It is the force... complete...it is Divinity...it is Shakti...

"Existence is energy...
 Energy is infinite...
 What was...
 Is...
 What is...
 Is...
 What will be...
 Is..."

Hugh Shergill

"Shakti is energy...
 Energy is a wave...
 Wave is also a particle...
 Particle is also a wave...
 All perceived is energy...
 All is Shakti..."

Hugh Shergill

Divinity is Omnipresent…

"O let one drink Ghalib…
  In a place of worship…
  Or route me instead…
  To a place…
  Where there is no Divine…"

Mirza Ghalib (Renowned Poet / Writer)
Poetic Translation by Hugh Shergill

"Divine is omnipresent…
  Every realm is its…
  Every presence is its presence…
  When there was nothing…
  There was Divine…
  When there shall be nothing…
  There shall be Divine…"

Hugh Shergill

"Quantum entanglement:
  Spooky action at a distance."

Albert Einstein
(Renowned theoretical physicist)

Quantum entanglement…in simple terms refers to the fact that aspects of one particle of an entangled pair depend on aspects of the other particle…no matter how far apart they are…or what lies between them…

Taking this further…quantum entanglement is not restrictively confined to just particles…yes indeed particles can have energy…yet energy goes beyond the confines of particles…every matter has energy… yet energy is beyond the confines of matter…which science refers to this phenomenon as 'Dark Matter' which is the acknowledged awareness for its presence…yet unaware of its infinite Shakti power details…

Quantum entanglement is unmediated…no signal to trigger the correlation…unmitigated…the strength of the connection does not fade down, reduce, or diminish regardless of the distance in space between…and is always instantaneous…with immediate correlation with no time delay…

**"Some connections of the heart are as such...
That they give out the news...
Which have not even been sent..."**

**Feroz Khan
(Renowned Actor / Filmmaker)**

Quantum particles are space time experiences in consciousness...yet are not confined by the cognitive processing of perceived space and time...

Further...what is very interesting and powerful to even intellectually grasp is that quantum entanglement is not only beyond perceived space but beyond perceived time also...quantum entanglement also exists for events over time...quantum entanglement is beyond the same perceived time line...entanglement is even occurring with different times in perceived timeline history...one particle can be entangled with a particle from either the past perceived time line or a future timeline...this is clearly the power of higher existence realm consciousness experience occurring that is beyond the confines of this immediate three dimensional realm perceived reality...an infinite quantum superposition that is beyond every conceptual confines possible including time and space...as consciousness experience is always beyond time and space...all is occurring and experiencing in precise correlation occurrence...all together omnipresent at once...regardless of how many universes or lifetimes away...

Information, energy, matter are all entangled through space time causality...Yet overruled by the power of higher consciousness...the super consciousness state... Super consciousness is in a superposition that is omnipresent...present everywhere...omnipotent...infinite energy...omniscient...entanglement of information across and beyond time space...thus all perceived reality is only your consciousness at play...

Your soul's timeless infinite energy is the seed spark of the Divine that creates, projects, and participates...in the play of Maya Leela...

Those quantumly entangled are not restricted to any perceived distance, timelines, or realms...a space of close proximity of just a micro millimeter or billions of light years away...further...beyond perceived time itself...whether it is immediate agreeable perceived timeline or lifetimes away...and even further... multi universes away...infinite multi-verses away...to even more further...the infinite consciousness realms...to ultimately...the super consciousness state of Divinity...

**"The most powerful quantum entanglement...
Is the Divine Rhythm between...
Divinity and its Soul... "**

Hugh Shergill

Once the energy is entangled...it is forever in connection...Divinely Rhythmic...forever in perfect rhythm...forever in tune Divinely...quantum superposition...forever entangled...forever immediate...

forever intently influenced...exchanging information instantaneously...synchronicity communication...the intention is what determines the observed...creator and its creation...Divinity and its Divine spark, the Soul...projection and the projected...

"Divine is primordial non duality...
  Upon creation...
  Divinity takes form in duality...
  Its vision...
  Forms its creativity...
  Staged intention...
  Playing out theatrically..."

Hugh Shergill

"Let the illusions begin..."

CHAPTER 2.

MAYA
THE
ILLUSION

"What is a Theatre…
Without a Performing Stage…"

"One's reflection…
One's validation…
Individual seeking its individuality…
Seeks a mirror…
Divine seeking its Divinity…
Creates the illusionary mirror…"

Hugh Shergill

"Answering the most difficult...
 Conundrums of life...
 To what is going on...
 By revealing...
 What is really going on...
 Screen tears...
 Reality pours...
 What kept enclosed...
 Was that opposed...
 World is not just a stage...
 It is staged..."

Hugh Shergill

Maya...The Divine Cosmic illusion...

Maya...conceals the true reality of the perceived reality...an illusion where things appear to be present, yet are not what they seem...defies normal human understanding... Divine energy force that creates the cosmic illusion that the perceived world is real... Divinity is in complete unity... for Divinity to appear as separate and diverse manifestations of its creation is presented on the Divine stage of Maya...
Maya is supreme intelligence, Divine power, and a deception all simultaneously...
Existence experience to one's particular observable universe...

"Maya...duality reflection of reality...
 illusion simulation masking reality...
 Soul's simulated existence...
 Confined to its observance...
 Upon the illusionary veil is lifted...
 Your reality has forever shifted..."

Hugh Shergill

"The nature of truth
 what appears to be true
 to the human mind,
 therefore is human,
 may be called maya,
 or illusion"

Rabindranath Tagore
(Renowned Artist / Poet / Writer / Philosopher)

Maya embodies the soul through delusion by believing its own existence is its own... illusioned independent of the Divine... Maya fades away from perception upon lifting the veil of of its illusion... where finally the soul realizes and sees the true reality of existence...achieving Moksha...the highest state of consciousness...Moksha is the liberation from Maya's illusion...Nirvana is the blissful euphoria state of that liberation...

Newton's Law of Motion:
Both the Law of Maya...
And the Law of Karma...

**"To every action there is always an equal and
contrary reaction; the mutual actions of any two
bodies are always equal and oppositely directed"**

**Isaac Newton
(Renowned Scientist)**

Newton's law of motion...in other words, is both the law of Maya and the law of Karma...

Law of Maya:

Action and reaction are precisely equal...a single one way force is impossible... the forces are both always equal and opposite...

Law of Karma

Every action has a reaction... perception is an action... therefore everything is dynamically connected with everything else... every action interaction has an equal dynamic reactive consequence...

(More in depth information on the law of Karma in the next chapter)

The world of Maya changes continuously, because the Divine Maya Leela play is a rhythmic, dynamic play...The dynamic force of the play is karma "action"...this active principle of the play creates a chain reaction for the infinite multi verses of Divine Maya projections...where everything is dynamically connected with everything else...playing all out on the Maya stage...

**"Maya is that...
All perceived reality...
Is an absolute deception"**

**Rig Veda
(the first humankind known written scriptures)**

Maya Leela

Rig Veda... the first humankind known written scriptures...in the first written known language, Vedic Sanskrit... Rivetingly immediately explains Maya and its illusions... that this perceived reality is an absolute deception... Maya...the cosmic illusion hinders truth to the perceived living senses... This immediate reveal from the first written texts is no casual coincidence...all confusions were put to rest from the very first scriptures...yet unfortunately purposely disregarded and unemphasized by those seeking alternative powerful exploitive motives...driven by mass power and control... Like someone trying to tie me up with a rope yet it becomes to my reveal that the tied rope is all an illusion...as the rope forever remained untied…

"Immediately upon Divinity's creation…
Duality of illusion emerges…
Whatever seems…
Is not..
Even though it is seen...
What is…
Does not seem…
As it remains hidden unseen..."

Hugh Shergill

"Duality existence running parallel...
Everything is simply vibrating matter…
Simultaneously both wave and a particle…
Coexisting emerging on the cosmos platter…
illusion obscures truth reality…
Masking trivial as actuality…"

Hugh Shergill

Duality

Every perceived existence is a dualistic experience...Duality and relatively...virtue requires vice to exist... vice requires virtue to exist...

**"Divine infinite energies…
Divinity creating illusionaries…
Maya manifest emerges…
Duality and relativity surges…
As the single vocal chord speaks…
Through the duality of the lips… "**

Hugh Shergill

Maya…Divine Cosmic illusion…

"Maya…Divine Cosmic illusion…

**Divine's Divinity…
Shiva merging Shakti…
Divinity projecting…
Soul's scripting…
Experiencing perception…
Believing deception…
illusionary illusions…
Reality intrusions…
Maya…Divine Cosmic illusion…"**

Hugh Shergill

**"What is…
Perhaps is…
What is not…
Absolutely is…
illusionary wars…
Even more so…
is…"**

Hugh Shergill

Maya, is the Divine cosmic illusion created by the creator, the Divine energy source of all creation…for the creation to be perceived experienced through the illusionary realms of time, space, and causation…

In order for the Divine's eternal energy existence to appear as separate and diverse manifestations of its own universal creation, an illusory relative dualistic perception manifests...this is Maya... Divinity's projected projection...

Maya...The Act of One On Oneself...

"Maya...The Act of One On Oneself..."

The 'One'...
Brahman, the Divine reality of all creation...
The infinite source...

The 'On'...
Is the Divine's creativity...
Divinity of infinite consciousness and energy...
Shiva Shakti...

The 'Oneself'...
Atman, the individual soul...
Infinite spark drop of the infinite Divine...

The 'Act'...
Maya, the Divine's theatrical creation projection...

Maya...The Act of One On Oneself..."

Hugh Shergill

"Divine energy invisible...
Desire to see self possible...
Manifests the platform mirror...
Where its energy can appear...
Creating an illusion Maya perception...
That appears on the mirror reflection..."

Hugh Shergill

The individuality and independence to its supreme creative source, the Divine supreme source manifests a cosmic deception... The Divine source spreads its creative desire with a universal cosmic illusion, this is Maya... Like a film director requires the medium of cinema to manifest its creative vision...cinema is its Maya...

The Divine supreme being source from all that exists, to appear as separate and diverse manifestations of a creation, an illusory state becomes in perceived existence… This illusionary dualistic creation is Maya…

Maya is the measurer realm of cosmic illusion… Maya is the power in creation by which particulars, limitations and divisions seem to exist in the oneness that is the ultimate true reality… Since the Divine eternal energy in its absolute form is complete in unity, the only way that it can appear as the separate and diverse manifestations, a cosmic illusion comes to be…this is Maya…

"This is just an illusion…
  This is not real…"

Mike Tyson (Renowned Boxer)

Maya illusion is Maya deception…deception emerges from perception…perception that is the illusion… the cosmic illusion of perceived reality…is Maya…

"illusionary deception…
  Hides in perception…
  Nine hides in six…
  Six confined in nine…
  The apparent reality of six…
  Awaits to unveil the hidden three…
  One simple shift in axis…
  The nine releases free…
  Apparent appearing perception…
  Was the hidden illusionary deception…"

Hugh Shergill

Practice an imaginary exercise…as you read this…imagine removing yourself from your particular environment…all that you identify as yourself no longer exists…now remove your particular surrounding environment as it never existed…now remove the platform where this vanished immediate surrounding environment once existed…which is the planet earth… now further remove the entire universe where this earth existed on…what is there now that exists? The first thought that should logically come to your mind is 'nothing'… that nothing exists on something…that something is complete empty darkness…dark matter…that dark matter is Divinity…the fundamental absolute core source of all creation…this is the Turiya…the Divinity of darkness…the Divine Maya source…

"Empty existence...
  Existence of empty...

  Nothing is ever empty...
  Even in emptiness...
  Resides emptiness...
  Upon its non acknowledge...
  Is its acknowledge...
  Where perceived non Divine energy...
  There is none except Divine energy...

  Empty existence...
  Existence of empty..."

Hugh

Maya Source...
Turiya...
The Divinity of Darkness...

"Darkness sparks illumination..."

Darkness is more powerful than light...state of perceived non-existent is more powerful than the state of perceived existence...Imagine removing all existence...your entire existence...your environment... the earth...time... space...causations...universe...infinite universes ...remove all... As all existence is removed...nothing exists...just darkness...darkness is everything...everything is Divinity...the Divinity of darkness...this is Turiya...

"The stage lights are off...
  Theatre is completely dark...
  Within that darkness...
  Entire theatre still exists...
  Your possible vision...
  Confined to light emission..."

Hugh Shergill

"To conceive the inconceivable…
 Inconceivable manifests as the conceive…
 Darkness of Divinity emerges as light…
 Light that shines projections as Maya…
 The infinite illusionary realms of…
 Time, space, causation…"

Hugh Shergill

"All perceived is in light…
 Perceived source is dark…
 Light must manifest…
 Into existence to illuminate…
 illuminating from…
 The platform of darkness…
 Light is only possible with…
 Infinite Divine presence…
 Darkness of Turiya…
 Lighting Maya…"

Hugh Shergill

"Turiya course…
 Maya source…
 Divine energy source…
 Divinity darkness Turiya…
 Source projector of all…
 Projected Maya source…"

Hugh Shergill

Turiya…Divinity Consciousness of All Existence…

Darkness is Turiya…ultimate state of Divinity…where all three consciousness states exist… Turiya is the platform for all Maya creation… Turiya is the Dark Divinity spaceless… timeless… eternal… The infinite realm of Brahman Divine…from where Divinity of Shiva Shakti emerges…the creation of all creation…

Turiya...

"Darkness is...
  Divinity presence...
  Fear of Darkness...
  Frivolous Ignorance...
  Embrace Darkness...
  Light Emerges from Dark Divinity...
  Turiya state of Divine infinity..."

Hugh Shergill

Darkness is Infinite...

"Light is destined...
  To be extinguished...
  Darkness is...
  Infinitely distinguished...
  Flame of the candle shall face demise...
  Revealing eternal darkness precise..."

Hugh Shergill

The perceived universe itself is dominantly dark energy matter...beyond expanding...beyond conceivable...beyond explainable... One therefore should not shy away from darkness...as darkness is the ultimate reality... Darkness holds all knowing...even when all knowing scientific evidence ceases...we conclude the unknowing as "Dark Matter"...

Darkness can never be created...

Light can be created...artificial light exists...artificial darkness never exists...darkness is absolute...never possibly be directly created...only contrastly projected through only light adjustment... modification... manipulation... elimination... but no one creates darkness...except darkness itself...ultimately reality is and always dark...omnipresent...this is Turiya...

"When there is nothing, there is"

Jiddu Krishnamurti
(Renowned Philosopher / Writer)

"Darkness is every hidden colour…
  Every hidden colour is darkness…
  Darkness…
  Itself is all colour condensed…
  Inversion of darkness…
  Reveals every colour possible…
  This is Turiya…
  The Dark Divinity…"

Hugh Shergill

The Blind See…

"Each blink is the truth unveil…
  Eyes closed is true vision reveal…
  Where one only sees Divine the dark infinite…
  Witnessed exclusively by the blinked felt…
  The blind is never devoid of true seeing…
  Always see the Divine darkness revealing…"

Hugh Shergill

"The eyes are useless,
  When the mind is blind…"

Bruce Lee
(Renowned Martial Artist / Actor / Revolutionist)

Every perceived sense…is a conscious construct…the eyes do not see…the ears do not hear…they are simply sense's apparatus means…the eyes only receive the photonic energy…it is one's consciousness that processes the receiving energy to vision a subjective conscious appropriate construct…any fluctuations within one's consciousness…results in an entirely different vision…

"Your mind is your seeing…
  Never the eyes viewing…
  World existence processed within…
  Yet extraction is only limited thin…
  Shifting fluctuations of your mind…
  Shall reveal what was once blind…"

Hugh Shergill

Maya Leela

"If it's temporary, it's an illusion"

Bhagavad Geeta

Absolute Reality...
Beyond Creation and Destruction...

"Awareness...
 Is being aware...
 Both of the knowing...
 Aswell of the unknowing...
 Any creativity...
 Never absolute reality...
 Absolute reality is the infinite...
 Existence of the creator...
 Before any of its creation..."

Hugh Shergill

The Black Hole...
The Maya Projection Lens...

"Astronomical Black Holes...
 Maya projector lens enclose...
 When the projector lens is off...
 It is nothing but appearing dark...
 Darkness seems illusionary empty...
 In reality holding all that is projected...
 Each black hole is a glitch in Maya...
 Revealing a glimpse into Divine Turiya..."

Hugh Shergill

Privilege opportunities are presented in glimpses when Divinity reveals its Divine darkness as the infinite pupil of the eyes through the familiar term referred to as the 'black holes'...inhaling and exhaling all that is...from exhaling Maya illusionary realms to inhaling reality moksha realm...projecting the illusionary projections through its dark projector lens... Each black hole is a glitch in Maya...Revealing a glimpse into the Divine darkness Turiya...

Turiya Breath…

"Turiya breath…
  Existence health…
  Divinity breathing darkness…
  Exhaling Maya…
  illusion…
  Inhaling Moksha…
  Escapism…"

Hugh Shergill

For Maya manifests to appear…you require an existence of expressional experience…as an expression must be able to manifest an experience…experience requires process…Maya is the illusionary realm of process…without Maya…everything remains as the infinite Divine platform…on the infinite presence of Divine darkness Turiya… Divine light manifests in existence in order to illuminate Maya… the illusionary light of perceived life… the enlightening spark of light emerges… manifesting Divinity in form appears through illumination…projecting light on to the illusionary projector screen realms of Maya…

Turiya Darkness…

"Turiya Darkness…
  Reality actualness…
  Under the lighted stage…
  The dark stage ever remains..
  Shutting all the theatre light…
  Shuns all except the true night…"

Hugh Shergill

Lighting is a Stage Tool…

"The illusionary Maya stage…
  Sits on the dark stage of reality Turiya…
  Lighting is a mere tool modified…
  To enhance the precise presence of darkness…
  Lighting is a stage tool to enhance clarity…
  Clarity existence is in darkness reality…
  Not Maya illusionary illumination…
  As more brighter the screen…
  More it appears faded…
  More contrast created…
  Through increasing precision darkness…
  Manifesting more clarity reveals…"

Hugh Shergill

Dark Mystery…

"Dark mystery…
  Maya history…
  Black is devoid of all colour…
  As it is the creator of all colour…
  Every existence perhaps illumination devoid…
  Every existence absolutely exists in the dark…"

Hugh Shergill

Maya… Maya Tricks… Matrix…

"Maya…
  Maya Tricks…
  Matrix…

  Matrix Availability…
  Maya Creativity…
  Perceived Actuality…

  Maya…
  Maya Tricks…
  Matrix…"

Hugh Shergill

Maya... Maya Tricks... Matrix...

As an example, the sun's experience is activated through its rays... To experience the sun by itself is not possible, however we experience the sun through the sun's creation of rays and the immense quality experiences of those rays... The sun's rays are numerous... with ultimately only one creator source, that is the sun itself... The sun and sunlight are one...yet one projects and the other is projected...one intentionally expresses and the other is the expressional experience... Divine projects...Maya projections... Projections themselves are incapable to project...believing Maya as the entire reality projects...is the illusionary trick... Maya Tricks...Matrix...Maya is the Matrix...

Maya is this illusory reality of all creation as perceived by the senses... This cosmic illusion...Maya, divides, measures out, the infinite Divine source into finite forms and forces of perception. The active cosmic illusion creates a reactive illusion, which makes the creation actually appear as a separate existing reality from its Divine creator source, when ultimately it is actually and always is one...

"It ever strike you that the world is not real at all?
 It ever strike you that we have the only mind in the
 world and you just thinking up everything else?"

V.S. Naipaul (Renowned Writer)

"What appears in presence...
 Is an immediate realm sense...
 Refrain from judging nuisance...
 By merely non depth glance...
 What is beyond ignorance...
 Is an inconceivable distance..."

Hugh Shergill

Maya is a Non-Solid Cosmic Delusion...

Maya, in all forms is simply a non-solid cosmic delusion... All matter is just a concentrated state of energy... consisting of a particular rate of vibrational cosmic energy... There is no form in the universe that is actually in a fundamentally solid state, as actually what appears is just a particular compact vibrational cosmic energy of the Divine source... This is true for the entire perceived universe and all of its interpreted states... including all perceived solid states... All one is and perceives to exist is moving energy Maya...

In core reality, the human body's existence is absolutely a non solid state. All that the entire human body consists of is just energy particles... These energy particles are constantly in a dynamic kinetic energy state that is attracting, inserting, extracting, binding, recycling, and redeveloping constantly...

The illusionary power of Maya is so dominantly powerful that the Divine creator source has caused the manifestations of matter to appear so distinct and specific that to the human mind...that our very own body is not solid flesh and bones...in all reality, there is nothing physical about the physical body... This is so profound, as even by being fully aware of this illusion, the illusionary experience seems so convincingly powerful that indeed it is physical...feeling my physical presence...as i perceive physically writing away with my hand...while with my physical eyes looking at my writing...

"What the eyes see and the ears hear,
 the mind believes."

Harry Houdini
(Renowned illusionist / Magician)

The Maya Screen...

"The Maya Screen...
 The Maya Realm...
 Projecting of Maya...
 Projected by Divinity...
 Watching movie Leela...
 On the Maya screen..."

Hugh Shergill

All perceived existence is just an energy projection of the Divine supreme energy source. As an example, an actor being viewed on a movie screen seems so real in existence but it is nothing but a radiation beam of energy appearing from the projector...

Your perceived reality, is this energy power of projection of the Divine energy source that projects all perceived existence...on to the Maya screen...which is a projection for your experiencing...perceiving the entire universe...through only energies of different frequencies and its interpretation through our limited processing capacities...including our very own human being perceived existence...this is all Maya...

Maya is the illusion projection of the Divine creator projector source in creation... However, the projection is not the projector... Just like a shadow requires an object to be produced, as without an object, there would be no shadow... Projector still exists without giving projection...however projection can not exist without the projector...

Maya... the ultimate illusionary virtual reality...

Taking this example further, the Maya screen example can be further directly understood as a virtual reality system...where the energy projection of the Divine energy source is playing out through the virtual reality system devices that puts the experiencer shockingly into a whole new different world experience that where its human body system begins to actually adapt and respond to it as actual perceived multi-dimensional existing reality... Is it really existing? Obviously not, however is it creating an illusion of existence? Absolutely...and that is Maya...further absolute reality is that Maya continues to exist even when the virtual reality system is removed from the user...as the ultimate virtual reality system is always present...always on...always experienced...this is Maya...

"Truth seeks...
  Reality creeps..
  Reality of truth got starker...
  Since one indulged darker...
  Where illusions are tangible...
  When all reality is intangible..."

Hugh Shergill

Spirituality, and much initially, it is the ancient Vedic scriptures from the Vedas to the Puranas, that declared that the perceived physical world operates fundamentally under the law of Maya... Further, through numerous centuries, Vedic texts and modern literature dedicated to spiritual traditions defined and referenced to the law of Maya, especially expressing through poetry...

"Maya is...
  A magic show...
  An illusion...
  Where things appear...
  To be present...
  Yet are not what they seem...
  Maya is power principality...
  Concealing true reality..."

Hugh Shergill

"Maya is the illusionary...
  Experiential existence reality...
  All reality relevance...
  Beyond Maya experience...
  Is beyond Maya...
  Above illusion...
  Reality emergence..."

Hugh Shergill

Reality illusion…

"Reality is the illusion…
  illusion is the experience…
  Experience is the reality…
  Reality is the illusion…
  illusion is the reality…
  Reality is the illusion…"

Hugh Shergill

The Real illusion Tarnished You…

The real reality… reality… the real illusion tarnished you…is absolute conscious felt experience, not just the reality existence perception… It is possible to perceive something without consciously experiencing it, and yet there are conscious experiences which one can feel without ever perceiving…what is consciously felt is much more a reality for one than what is seen…as consciousness is one's true seeing… The real reality… is reveality… the real illusion tarnished you…

Real Reality Reveality…

"Real Reality…
  Reality is the real reveality…
  Real illusion tarnished you…
  Revealing what the soul forever knew…
  Reality exists in its reveality…
  Real reality reveality…"

Hugh Shergill

The Puzzled Puzzle…

"Puzzle has many pieces…
  Puzzled seeking all pieces…
  Puzzle unfilled keeps the secret…
  Puzzle fulfilled reveals the secret…
  Puzzling secret romance…
  Puzzled inevitable consequence…"

Hugh Shergill

"Moment to unveil...
  One's reality's decipher...
  Wiping it all clean...
  Masking illusion buffer...
  illusionary Maya lifted...
  Liberating Moksha achieved..."

Hugh Shergill

The Undiscovered Hidden...

"Hidden knowledge from most...
  Deprived knowledge for some..."

Shiva Shakti...the Divine union of all creation... consciousness (Shiva) and energy (Shakti)...Divinely omnipresent in every realm... Shakti's dynamic creative forms emerging have been witnessed throughout historically...with each form exuding a powerful jolt from the infinite existence source to upon the Maya realm...

Shakti Peeths...are historical recorded precise locales tribute shrines on earth where major Shakti dynamic occurrences occurred... just like electricity surrounds us, yet striking lightning is witnessed in specific precise locales... These specific powerful Shakti Peeths...each revealing further dynamic revelations of this Maya realm...resulting often in corresponding sacred pilgrimage shrines, temples, recorded tales, scriptures and artifacts of that particular established event at that particular location...these shrines are dedicated to various forms of Adi Shakti... the supreme Divine goddess of Shaktism...the Divine form of all energy...worshiped by its Shakti devotees... especially Shakti energy infused deep yoginis and tantrics who indulged in very depths of tantra...Total 108 distinct Shakti Peeths have been scripturally mentioned in the ancient Puranas (400,000 plus verses with first documented references dating 10th Century CE) Interestingly, out of the 108 mentioned Shakti Peeths, only 64 have been discovered to this date...the other 44 are at unknown locales...which have either been intentionally destroyed, natural disaster occurrences, or still remain hidden and yet to be still discovered...well at least for some...

Maya Leela

Dynamic Divinity Shakti...

"The Divine energy Shakti transcends...
  Manifesting from one form to another...
  Femininity in its Divinity expression...
  Responsible as the constant creator...
  Creation is often superiorly constructive...
  Yet capable of being extremely destructive...
  Creatively disguised associate or Loved one...
  From the nurturing mother to a Loving Lover...
  Observe their all and every relation...
  Creating remains the common denominator..."

Hugh Shergill

Shakti's dynamic play of Maya Leela associated scriptures, poetry, legends, tales, art, references...is much more potent and extensive than what is currently available...further, potentially holds much more reality jolting reveals than what one perceives to be...

A relative example would be of an individual who is highly passionate about cinema and films...someone who is a film historian...studies films and film making thoroughly throughout its history existence...yet is still unaware of a tremendous amount of hidden archives of very impressive movies and corresponding filmmakers/performers that it doesn't even know ever existed...truly a deprivation tragedy...

All arts/entertainment are Divinely blessed through the energy of Shakti manifesting into different forms... such as steam, liquid, ice...all are fundamentally water H2O yet expressing itself in different forms at different states... Shakti created both the Maya and the Maya revealing clues through such as arts, entertainment, movies...

"A wise man once told me at a very young age that go watch a lot of movies... movies are today's modern theatrical plays...the more movies you watch... the more you shall understand the profound patterns of the play of one's life..."

Hugh Shergill

"Watching enthusiastically…
Scripted theatrics sequentially…
As the keen audience…
Often in different realms…
Both the play on display…
And my life at play…
Presented by Maya…
On display as Leela…"

Hugh Shergill

"Every stage…deserves a Play…"

CHAPTER 3.

LEELA
THE ILLUSION
PLAY

"What is a Stage…
Without a play…"

"Higher conscious realms…
Revealing all illusions…
To excel towards ascend…
One must presently attend…
Presented by Maya…
The play of Leela…"

Hugh Shergill

Maya Leela

**"The world is
A children's playground before me
Night and Day
This theatre is enacted before me"**

Mirza Ghalib (Renowned Poet / Writer)

Rasa...The Aesthetics of Divinity...
Residing in Natya Shastra…

The prime fundamental institution of arts and its various forms was first defined in the ancient scripture called 'Natya Shastra'... the Sanskrit name that defines as 'The Manual of Arts'...

Natya Shastra...the ancient Vedic scripture that is the manual of arts... going into the spiritual depths and significance of the collective institution of arts and entertainment...including stage theatre, epics, poetry, music, and dance... Just as the Vedas, Natya Shastra's revelating knowledge and its branches were initially orally passed on to multiple generations for centuries before it was structurally documented and scripted approximately 1000 BCE... from where further each particular art formed its own institution...

Interestingly, the spiritual soul connection of all arts is through the pathway of the unexplainable deeper depths of its subjective soul experience...

Indeed, in all arts and its various forms...on the surface level, the desired effect of the artist is to provide a particular form of entertainment through the art...yet on a deeper spiritual level...the intention is to take the spectator into another parallel reality whilst indulging in the nectars of aesthetics where it experiences the essence of its own consciousness in a previous untouched way...this is the magical experience of Rasa...

Rasa is the Sanskrit word that defines as nectar, essence, taste... the Divine gift of Arts exuberating the aesthetic flavours of visual, literature, and music evoking an emotion in the reader or spectator...Rasa that resonates, imbibes, emotes within the 'Sahridaya'...which is the Sanskrit word for referring to the 'Sensitive Spectator'...a Soul that feels and indulges the rasa deeply within while Divinely entangled...a true Rasa experience is unexplainable…only to be experienced...

All arts are in essence a Rasa... A book is an example of Rasa... where that certain particular 'Sahridaya' energy receptive reader will feel the taste of aesthetics... evoking emotional flavours within... whilst indulging in the world of the writer... taking the reader through the path of Rasa to experience a kiss from a previous non experienced realm to indulging in the unexplained realm…

"Rasa...
  Nectar of Arts...

  Rasa...
  Creates...
  Indulges...
  Experiences...
  Escapes...
  Ascends...

  Rasa...
  Nectar of Arts..."

Hugh Shergill

The play of Maya Leela is the ultimate Natya Shastra... the art of the Divine play...taking the spectator and actually putting it in the Divine play itself as the primary performer... indulging into the Rasa nectar experience whilst creating the Rasa nectar experience itself... even further...the Rasa experience ascending the performer from the play to an escapism realm of Divinity itself...

"Theatre, ah...now that was a labour of Love.
  Can there be anything better than performing
  without retakes and cuts, in front of people you
  can see, hearing them breathe in
  the darkness of the hall?"

Kabir Bedi (Renowned Actor)

Indeed precisely...nothing describes the joy of the theatrical stage play of life better than this quote from the renowned actor Kabir Bedi...perhaps subconsciously triggered when said...yet revealing the core essence of the play of Maya Leela in its entirety...where the protagonist soul performer is performing live without any retakes and cuts...emphasizing its own responsibility karma doings...as each action holds its complete accountability and proceeding consequences...acts that are performed amongst other people that include both its co performing actors and audience...spectators of its stage world that it visually sees and even hears breathe...are the sparks of the soul performer's higher consciousness itself...with all occurrences remain recorded in the witnessing darkness of the hall...that all witnessing darkness is the Divine darkness of Turiya state...from where the entire theatre is born...

Creative Expression of Maya is Leela…

"Creator communicates through creation…
  Creation is an expression of the creator..
  Creative expression of Maya…
  Is its play of Leela…
  The art is the artist's manifestation…
  Giving it life through its creative expression…"

Hugh Shergill

It is through the everlasting creative expression process of how the creator communicates through consciousness to all its creations…just like the artist indulged in the act process of creating the art… that magic that never ceases…this everlasting consciousness communication happens continuously to its creations both for many unknowingly and for some knowingly…and it is in the everlasting creation process where the creation consciously experiences the glimpse of knowing…knowing that it is and being created…that is when it becomes soul conscious aware…

"To know the unknown know…
  One's embracing the inhale…
  Imbibed surpassing realms within…
  One's exiting the exhale…
  The breath of Divinity…
  Reveals all of infinity…
  Exhaling illusionary maya…
  Inhaling liberating nirvana…
  Escapism from illusion…
  Through the leela play exhibition…"

Hugh Shergill

That beauty glimpse of knowing invokes the creation's soul awareness and mysteriously leads it to the performance journey of karmic lifetimes striving to be with one…the creation merging in with the creator…conscious shifting from the exhale illusion existence of Maya…to the inhale escapism nirvana experience of moksha…the infinite embrace of the Divine…the soul's climax bliss…fifth dimensional super conscious state… Liberation…Ananda…Moksha…Nirvana… As once one is with the one…there are no more questions nor answers…as one is whole…completely complete…all knowing unknowingly… in everlasting tranquility euphoric bliss… One is the Divine supreme energy source…that is all the knower, the knowing of all, and the known of all that is existing all as one…

"This is not the life now...
  Your real self is inside you...
  Your body gets old...
  But your soul and spirit never die..."

Muhammed Ali
(Renowned Boxer / Poet / Philanthropist / Activist / Humanitarian)

To reach the climax bliss of liberation...inhaled by Divinity...the escapism from illusion...nirvana infused moksha...the soul must perform, which is soul purpose...its dharma...and action...its karma...

Unfit stage is a dormant stage...devoid of any performance play... Any performing stage...is mere useless...if devoid of a performance play...the illusionary Maya stage becomes only active with the energy activity of Maya...Maya's energy expression on display takes in and expresses in the form of a play...the play of Maya...called Leela...the play of illusion...is the Maya Leela...

Leela...The Maya Stage Play...

Leela is Maya's action script on performance display... For any performance, you require a platform, a stage, audience, performers, and ultimately the play...the cosmic play...this is Leela...

"Everyone plays their part...
  In the art...
  On the canvas of Maya...
  In the painting of Leela...
  Vision is the displayed paint...
  Perception is the illusion..."

Hugh Shergill

Leela...
Karma 'Play' mode...
Of Continuous Maya Energy...

Energy is in infinite movement...each form...movement is Karma activation...active and reactive...Karma energy creates a karmic reaction for its next form...Maya realm's Maya energy in continuing movement is energy in continuing 'Play' mode...that continuing 'Play'...is the play of Leela...

"Your karma...
  Creates your drama...
  Your drama...
  Creates your Karma...

  What is your act...
  Is the script react...
  Play plot creating...
  It is you manifesting..
  As you act in the play...
  Is as sculpting clay...

  Your karma...
  Creates your drama...
  Your drama...
  Creates your Karma..."

Hugh Shergill

Leela...the Divine Cosmic Play...

Leela is the cosmic play of the Divine energy source that projects its magic creative power on to the illusion stage of Maya. Leela is the dynamic play of Maya... The dynamic force of the Leela play is karma, the action of cause and effect, where the Divine illusionary stage of Maya is in action play, where everything is dynamically connected with everything else...this dynamic play of the Divine is Leela, a play script which we all are participating in, both knowingly and unknowingly...

"Maya is the creative projection...
  Of the Divine source...
  Leela is the projected creation...
  Of the Divine source...
  An illusion movie play of Leela...
  Displayed through the lens of Maya..."

Hugh Shergill

The Law of Karma...

Karma is the action of cause and effect... Every action of thought, words, act, deed creates a corresponding reactive energy in some form or another... Karma is the reactive manifestation of actions from the past, present and future... These acts of actions can be physical, mental or spiritual...

Newton's law of motion:

"For every Act...there is a React...Re Act..."

For every action there is always an equal and opposite reaction... Mutually actions of any two perceived entities are always equal and oppositely directed... Therefore, action and reaction are exactly and always equal...

"Everything done...
  Everything not done...
  Is Karma...
  Everything we do...
  Everything we do not do...
  Is Karma..."

Hugh Shergill

The three types of Karma...

1. Sanchitta Karma (Karmic Debt)

This is accumulated reactive manifestation of previous acts. This karmic reaction of manifestation cannot be stopped from fruition... this is one's karmic debt... For the soul being, this is the vast accumulation of karmic consequences from both immediate and previous soul journey past lifetimes... Sanchitta karma comprises the reaction of every action that your soul has ever made in your past and present lives...

2. Prarabdha Karma (Karmic Construct)

This is the accumulated Karma reaction into present construction... this is one's immediate karmic construct... this is the specific karmic art piece that each soul currently experiences in this Maya realm... Prarabdha karma is the construction of your current particular experienced reality... every act of the past makes your perceived today... inevitably immediately present...unavoidably experienced...

3. Agami Karma (Karmic Power)

Agami Karma is the power of Karma that we are creating for ourselves right here in the current moment... this is one's karmic power ignited by one's free will... It is the reactions of actions that we are constantly creating and often immediately also experiencing by each and every conscious choice we make right now... Agami karma is the karmic power that one creates and experiences in one's present perceived reality...

Tri-Karmic Energies…

All three of these tri-karmic energies are platforms that create the soul's current immediate perceived reality experience in this Maya realm…and every physical, mental, spiritual act of this present moment will create our karma in the future…like your next taken breath will karmically result in being able to experience the next moment of your physical existence…

"You may forget what you said…
 Karma never forgets your address…
 You may disregard your intentional acts…
 Karma never disregards your address…
 You may be on the run for lifetimes…
 Karma still shows up on your address…"

Hugh Shergill

"Karma is experience,
 and experience creates memory,
 and memory creates imagination and desire,
 and desire creates karma again."

Deepak Chopra
(Renowned Author / Spirituality Advocate)

"If you truly Loved yourself,
 You could never hurt another."

Buddha

Leela… the Maya Play of Karma…

Ultimately, everything we do as well as don't do is actually an action… As there is no escape from action… Even if one sits inactive by doing nothing is also an action…specifically an inaction, which is an action of responding to the force of life through a certain performance action response even in its perceived lethargic dormancy…

The Maya Leela play director is Divinity…Maya is the stage…Leela is the play…playing out as cause and effect…through the performer's performance of karma (cause), which leela processes and responds with (effect) by modifying the everchanging leela play script accordingly yet dynamically…

Play is the script…the script is the play…script is karma…play is Leela…karma is Leela…Leela is karma… the cause is the effect, and the effect is the cause…all your past present future consequences playing out on the Maya Leela stage play… It is the impeccable cosmic intelligence of the Divine in dynamic action play... Leela is the fluidity adaptive responsive script where the play of karma is in performance on the illusion stage of Maya... Karma acts out through the play on display as Leela...agami karma... one's present acts creating immediate and following karma...active and reactive karma...modifying the play script...influencing the play script...improvising the play script...the everchanging Maya Leela script collectively through the Maya stage performers...on display as the Leela play...

What we call fate or destiny is one's individual and collective karma duration stretch...cause and effect, which is actively played out through the Leela play... Through this play, Leela has a way of revealing things to you...revelation reveals, synchronicity, patterns, hints, insights of the play script, acting as a soul intuitive conscious guide to the soul performer as they perform out the maya play scenes assigned to them... The soul performer must discover, learn, perform in harmony to the perfect standards of the play... That is the play of Leela...

Essentially at its behavioural core...every soul is an actor... switching from one role to another... depending on the particular co-actors and particular scene on stage at that particular moment... performing accordingly as one feels appropriate for that particular acting role scene...at all certain moments one is acting as whether it is...a child...a parent...a guardian...a Lover...a spouse...a friend...a sibling...a relative...a professional...a formal working colleague or associate...to even to the most unveiling dramatics and theatrics of the Maya Leela play script...where one is enacting that powerful well deserved role as the main character protagonist in opposition to all your particular antagonists...which interestingly and ironically will most likely run dramatically parallel with many of these other mentioned enacted roles...

Maya is the stage...Leela is the play...you are the actor performer...performing various vast roles parallelly and simultaneously...in the script of unveiling karma...

"Destiny approaches one inevitably...
  Otherwise counter scenarios are plenty...
  Before the thirsty lips...
  Desperate enough...
  Get to kiss the water...
  Hands already innocently...
  Released it effortlessly...
  There was no scope for conspiracy...
  It was all simply Destiny..."

Hugh Shergill

Maya Leela

"Arrival...
  Departure...
  Is not in the hands of anyone...
  When desires go to a particular path...
  Destiny takes us into an opposite path...
  Once in frustrated exhaustion...
  I questioned Destiny's intention...
  What does it actually desire?..
  It answered...
  Go beyond your desires...
  Follow my lead into your destiny..."

Movie: The Guide (Hindi Version)
Dialogue: R.K Narayan
(Renowned Novel Writer)
Dialogue Recitation: Dev Anand
(Renowned Actor / Filmmaker)
Poetic Translation by Hugh Shergill

Harmonic vs Inharmonic Performance...

Leela is a two inevitable result play...a play that is everlasting...however climax for each play soul performer...with two possible results...one is the soul performing inharmonic from the Leela play and the other is performing harmonic with the Leela play... Inharmonic performance results in a further entrapment cycle of karmic patterns and results in karmic confinement... Harmonic performance results in a performance that is in tune with the frequency of the Divine cosmic play and playing out their karmic performance optimally...opening infinite possibilities towards ultimately liberation bliss...moksha... nirvana...

Just like any play, the play director's approval is essential, which here is the Divine energy source itself... Divinity directing the Maya Leela play... The Divine approves the first take of the performer performing harmonic within the Leela scene and then presents the next play scene, which is ultimately progression and evolution for the soul's journey... However, the performer that is performing inharmonic with the director's vision...this results in an inevitable retake, then possible further retakes until the performer gets its performance right...this is potentially an everlasting karmic scene perpetual performance multiple lifetimes cycle that keeps repeating and repeating until the performer performs in harmony with the Maya Leela play script...

These patterns are profoundly present in our lives as certain emotions and life lessons keep repeating and repeating through interaction with different co-performers, scenes, and particular scenarios... and yet end with similar if not the same results... It is only when we become aware and modulate our performance harmonically with the Maya Leela play...is when we begin to actually evolve and graduate to the next level of the play scene...

"The Play of Maya Leela...
 Entertained by Evolving...
 Through Experiencing...
 Living...
 Learning...
 Leading...
 Through Play Performance..."

Hugh Shergill

The play of Maya Leela...it is the entertaining distraction from the inevitable perceived physical existence experience demise...the entertaining factor is evolving through experiencing...as each scene unfolds... each step of evolving opportunities are presented...those that take this advantage...progress... yet those that don't...regress...

The Divine director is not a strict taskmaster...but the one that has infinite pure Love for each of its projection existence and wants the performer to perform to its utmost potential...which is the Divine's Divinity art...the creation of the creator...as it is ultimate an creative expression of the Divine itself playing out in the play itself...

Leela is the ultimate play of creation... The entire perceived existing universe and beyond...is Maya Leela...a dance performance of energy staged on the cosmic illusion maya stage...performed by the dedicated performers...

Every Karma never fails to serve...
Even if not from...
The immediate perceiving source...

Every Karma never fails to serve... whether positive or negative... Let's explore good karmic action as an example... Karma doesn't reciprocate necessarily from the initial source, act, or that specific individual... as you must on some occasion have experienced doing specific good for an individual with no positive recognition, acknowledge, and nor attempt to reciprocate from that particular individual... however you surely must also have experienced a good karmic action towards you from an individual that was initially a stranger that you never knew and never expected anything from... yet blessed you with many treasures...this is again due to your own Karma...
Karma is energy in action...it continues to flow...if it doesn't abrupt from the initial play source zone...it certainly shall continue to flow and emerge from another play source zone...

Why the play of Maya Leela?

"Maya is aware of its illusion...
　Solidifying its existence position...
　It creates an entertaining distraction...
　The play of Maya Leela entertaining...
　Entertained by Evolving...
　Evolved through Experiencing..."

Hugh Shergill

The Purpose of the Play...

"The purpose of the play of Maya Leela...
　It is an entertaining distraction...
　Maya is aware of its illusion...
　Its sole purpose is existing in the duality...
　The mirror form of the Divinity...
　Entrapping forces through distraction...
　Distraction is the longevity factor of Maya...
　Awareness is the destruction of Maya...
　Attempting efforts of this distraction...
　Distraction creates entrapping entertainment...
　Entertaining the soul through the Maya Play...
　Luring them in for further stay...
　Divinity does present forever opportunities...
　Moments to awake from the distraction...
　Those that take advantage...
　Soul shall wake to progress...
　Ignorance towards opportunity...
　Soul continues to be trapped in regress..."

Hugh Shergill

Maya Leela Play's Objective...
Energy Forever Active...

Why is there life? All Existence? Maya realm? Maya Leela play...it is all simply energy expression at its most powerful possible state...Divine energy forever active and constantly changing from one active state to another...Divine energy forever active eternity...even in its most core Turiya state...it is still active as infinite potential energy...Divine is energy...and energy has been active for infinite eternity...

the realm of Maya is energy active expression as Divinity projection…this is the kinetic energy activation transferring from the active potential energy Divine Turiya state…Divine darkness creator of all creation…

Divinity's energetic active projection is the realm of Maya…further…Maya realm is active Divine energy itself…thus it further changes form into Leela…the play of Maya…even further energy activation…active with all the characters, scripts, and theatrics of the play of Maya Leela…now further activation with the karma consequences of each character both individually and collectively on the Maya Leela stage… From Turiya core Divine state…to the soul's grand Moksha liberating state…all remains Divinely active…in every energetic state simultaneously infinitely eternity…Maya is an infinite realm within its realm…as Divinity is the supreme creative infinite…thus soul energy is infinitely eternal…there is no death of the soul…only changes its form…emergence, reincarnation, reemergence, and ultimately liberation is absolute essence of soul energy…liberation is a state of existence…not completion…as there is no death of the soul…

"Death has nothing to do with going away.
  The sun sets
  The moon sets
  But they are not gone"

Rumi (Renowned Sufi Poet)

"If life is good…how can death be bad?
  Do you really think the universe
  created us to suffer?
  I don't think God is going to be cruel to us.
  Death is just part of life
  that we just have not experienced…"

Mike Tyson (Renowned Boxer)

Existence Liberation…

"Purpose of existence…
  Is achieving liberation…
  Through unveiling maya…
  Liberating spiritual eye…
  Makes the Maya veil fly…
  Moksha is the liberation…
  From Maya's illusion…
  Nirvana is the bliss state…
  Of that liberation…"

Hugh Shergill

Soul Reincarnation…

"Soul reincarnation…
  Purpose manifestation…
  Inevitably must fulfill…
  Before your liberation will…
  From the moment you left from…
  Is the moment you shall start from…"

Hugh Shergill

Reincarnation…Reemergence…

"Actor's Reincarnation…
  Actor's Reemergence…

  Actor heads back on to the stage…
  Continuing its performing play..
  Right from where…
  It previously left from…

  Actor's Reincarnation…
  Actor's Reemergence…"

Hugh Shergill

Within the Maya Leela illusion…
Lies the opportunity for exclusion…

Divine presents forever opportunities of moments to slip out of this entertaining distraction… It is the entertaining distraction that entraps… yet Divinity is forever providing soul opportunities for the Maya Leela escape while still being within the Maya realm… Within the Maya Leela illusion…
Lies the opportunity for exclusion… Becoming evolved while entertained… one evolving through the entertaining…the entertaining factor is forever evolving through experiencing…as each scene unfolds… each step of evolving opportunities are presented…Those that take advantage… Soul shall wake to progress… Entrapped ignorance towards opportunity…Soul continues to be trapped in regress…

"The most accomplished actor...
 Is someone that submerges...
 In the very depths of its character...
 To the point it becomes its absolute reality...
 Yet consciously deep enough to...
 Realize that it is performing the role...
 As the actor...
 Realizing 'the act' by the actor...
 Allowing the actor to escape from...
 Becoming only 'that act'...
 Realization is the conscious objective...
 Of the Divine play of Maya Leela..."

Hugh Shergill

"Maya Leela...
 Vanishing illusions...
 Through the purifying process...
 Of the Divine play...
 Experiencing Infinity...
 Revealing Divinity..."

Hugh Shergill

The soul journey is ultimately Divinity mergence...awareness of the illusionary Maya projection screen... where the Divine energy expresses...revealing the expression...in pure soul essence the expressed expression strives awareness of the Divine's expressing source...that energy process of revealing the expressing source through awareness requires a process...hence the process play of awareness by vanishing illusions...the play of Maya Leela...the play is ultimately the soul journey of awareness and Divine mergence...

"Maya is the clouded screen of illusion…
 Clarity is awareness…
 Awareness requires action…
 A play…
 A script…
 An act…
 A process…
 Hence the play of Maya Leela…
 Playing by performing…
 Performing a soul performance…
 With Divine's Divinity existing within…"

Hugh Shergill

"Before the play begins…
 The audience must arrive…"

CHAPTER 4.

MAYA'S AUDIENCE

"The artist's artistic brush stroke of colour...

Fractionally exists within the art canvas cover...

Unaware of its existence in the art's totality...

Absolute devoid of the art's true reality...

Experiencing within the art is mere illusion...

Truth of the art lies in the depth of the vision...

For the visionary truth to become experience...

Requires that certain conscious distance...

Detaching from the perceived abode...

Deviating from the miscode to decode...

Maya illusionary stage manifests for the play...

As the actor enacts the illusionary Leela play...

Viewing the play is must from an audience eye...

Where all the illusionary play theatrics lie...

Observing the art as the non intruder...

Is the liberating clarity for the art observer..."

Hugh Shergill

"The innocence of the audience...
 Is that at all times...
 It is aware that...
 Whatever is occurring...
 That whatever...
 Is just a play...
 To truly understand...
 The intricacies of the play...
 Is to understand...
 What is actually at play...
 This is to comprehend...
 Either resulting...
 In a distracting descend...
 Or a awakening ascend...
 Level of distraction of the audience...
 Dependent on the level of the audience..."

Hugh Shergill

"It's not what you look at that matters,
 it's what you see"

Henry David Thoreau
(Renowned Poet / Philosopher)

"Perceived reality...
 Never absolute reality...
 Absolute reality detection...
 Beyond confined perception...
 Perception detection of Maya...
 Unveillance deception of Maya..."

Hugh Shergill

Perception Detection of Maya...
Unveillance Deception of Maya...

Perception is a process...process of perceiving... confined to one's limited senses to perceive... perceived reality is not actual absolute reality... whatever is not absolute reality...is merely a perceptory illusion... Maya... your specific perceived reality is a specific frequency of perception processing... existing simultaneously among infinite unique frequencies of perceived reality... yet never the absolute reality...as to tap into absolute reality... one must leap beyond the confined realms of perception... through higher consciousness...perception detection of Maya...
Is the unveillance deception of Maya...

"The entire illusionary existence...
  Of the perceived universe...
  All and everything within...
  Sits just behind one's veil eyelids...
  Being processed as one's consciousness...
  Requiring it to be as one perceives...
  Consciousness contains all...
  Of the cosmic Maya illusion...
  Glitch of conscious elapses...
  All Maya illusion collapses..."

Hugh Shergill

"A very little key will open a very heavy door"

Charles Dickens
(Renowned Writer / Social Critic)

"Why do they shut...
  All the lights completely...
  In the movie theatre?
  Because they don't want you...
  To deviate from the screen and see...
  Your actual surrounding reality..."

Hugh Shergill

Non Local Consciousness...
The key that unlocks the real reality...

To understand the complexities of the Maya stage, it is important to understand the multi levels
of being experience of Maya... Consciousness is the non local Divine energy... your Divine cosmic
awareness of one's existence... state of self-realization...it is the audience of the Maya play stage...

The perceived reality existence is dependent on the capacity of one's consciousness...which are the
true eyes of perceived reality...therefore consciousness is the viewing audience...one only sees what
its consciousness is capable of showing...

Consciousness is non local and non located...it exists where the existence exists...which is non local...
multi-dimensional beyond space time causation...it is an infinite spec of the Divine energy itself...
Consciousness is one's true existence awareness, a Divine cosmic unique subjective experience of
existence... incapable of true objective analysis from any other being... To record something, it must
first be located... What one can not be located, then it can not be recorded... The cosmic experience

itself is infinite Divine, however compromisingly limited to each being's processing capabilities... Consciousness, only truly can be experienced, and that by that one and only who's experiencing...

Imagine a technological device that processes certain energy frequency...the device is just the means of processing the energy frequency, it is not the frequency...the frequency energy is not core located within the device, it is just processed in the device... A satellite is positionally aligned to receive certain specific signal frequencies...the receiver device processes the satellite signal frequencies upon received... One only is able to receive and process the signal frequencies...yet never generate those signal frequencies...as those signal frequencies are and will forever be non local...

One's brain...particularly the neurons in the cerebral cortex...the brain's outside layer that science has firmly concluded 'governs' memory, thought, language, attention and consciousness... The key here is that it 'governs' not 'contains'... A computer is able to process the internet...not contain the entire internet...as the internet remains and exists separately from the computer...the internet is non local from the computer's existing and operating position...

The human body processes consciousness experience...therefore the body is confined to ever be explored for the processing locales only...never capable to locate one's consciousness... The stage play exists only if it is viewed by the audience... Consciousness is the true existence of the audience... not the body...which is the receiver processed projection of existence, not the existence itself...

Our identity...is very interesting...even defined as one...we are not one identity...in all actuality...a collage of various identities...within and without... submerged in deep depths of consciousness processing...while being emerged with the receiving higher consciousness frequencies...

Variety of complex explanations of consciousness exist...from multiple medical terms to psychological theories, all examining multiple conscious attention trait behaviours and its recorded results... Consciousness is however an experience state that can not be truly recorded until one actually is able to fully identically experience another's conscious experience...which is not possible...therefore what is left to record is physical existing attentive behaviour and biological processes analysis...

The slight exception and closest possibility of one individual being knowing another being's conscious experience is the merging of one's higher conscious state into the conscious state zone of another... however even then, the record will be observed and experienced through one's own subjective conscious experience...which again is limited...never absolute...

"Consciousness...
 One's existence...
 Non local awareness...
 Reality processing...
 Actuality crossing...
 What is known...
 What is shown...
 To each their own...
 Factual discrepancies...
 Processual Infancies...
 Uniquely existing experiences...
 Consciousness intricacies..."

Hugh Shergill

For example, if one examines a virtual reality game player's experience without actually having a parallel reference viewing screen/audio to see/hear what is it that the game player is perceiving experiencing in the game, would be a non-start evaluation from the get go... This handicap confines one to only record attention action (or lack of) behaviour of what the game player is expressing while playing the virtual reality game. Further handicap exists...once the game player begins explaining and describing their game play experience...as that now moves into the subjective consciousness territory of the recorder's itself... which is again confined to interpret the experience within their own experience conscious state. To the most true record of the game player's experience would require for the recorder to put on the virtual reality kit and identically precisely play in the same spot, angle, with twin identical human experiencing, processing, and capabilities... This is an impossible feat...no being is actually capable of experiencing someone else's being experience...at most only relating...

Empathy is a deep Love felt thought, which is humanely such a beautiful being experience, however never a complete true experience...it is a soul's Love core...a Divine blessing trait that shines one's soul path... The only individual that can truly assess oneself, is the individual itself that experiences... One must first discover one's self as no one else is capable of doing... Immediate lower consciousness is and always will be to each their own... Bonus is to have associated empathic souls...that may light your path...yet never walk your path...

"Lower Consciousness...to each their own...
 Higher Consciousness...the key to all..."

The only enhanced possibility key is to increase the observational experiencial connect of consciousness... Is to experience an ultra observation of consciousness... requiring one to experience consciousness from a separate realm...that is beyond the restriction of experience only of and within the immediate Maya realm...

Maya Leela

Watching Charlie Chaplin...

"Watching a Charlie Chaplin movie...
  Left my heart very uneasy...
  Full screen zoomed out...
  A hilarious comedy...
  Head focused zoomed in...
  A heart aching tragedy...
  What one perceives...
  Is from the distance it sees..."

Hugh Shergill

Maya Leela is a live play...
Playing out on delay...

"Maya Leela is a live play...
  Playing out on delay...
  One only perceives the previous...
  Never the immediate...
  Every question asked by an individual...
  Is asked by a younger version of them...
  Never that immediate individual...
  Immediate is beyond one's grasp...
  One only perceives the previous...
  Perceptual interaction with previous...
  Never the immediate...
  No one witnesses the immediate...
  Play is playing out live...
  Yet not immediately alive...
  The Maya Leela stage play...
  Is occurring live on delay..."

Hugh Shergill

What we perceive as the world...is only our world...not the real world...as there are numerous species that perceive this world in a different light and spectrums...which again is their particular world...again not the real world...perception is our confined reality...upon piercing through the confines...reveals astonishing finds...

All perceived reality is the reality illusion that we perceive as reality…a human construct for perceptual and cognitive activity that we call mind…thus all physical world is simply a mental projection of the individual… Perceptual cognitive activity in consciousness…

Be in the present reality moment…I challenge you to experience the actual present reality moment… which is impossible to achieve through the physical body perception…as all perceived reality and actual reality are on two distinctly different perceived reality timelines…all what you now perceive, has already happened…

What exists and what you experience differs…everything you experience changes continuously forever eternity…as the realm of all existence is Shakti…Divinity energy…always in Divine activity…therefore what you perceive as your reality is always an illusion…perception of what is not there…even if it differentiates by a zeptosecond of close proximity perceived reality…to a vast difference of billions of light-years when perceiving those now non existing stars as stars in the galaxy…it is still and always a difference and anything that is different…differentiates from true reality…it is always an illusion… Maya…the Divine illusion of reality…all existence is confined to this Maya reality…all matter…all existence…all experience of the existence…all is an illusion…

Perceptual lag…what you see no longer exists…no one in this human flesh ever witnesses immediate reality…everything perceived with the five senses is confined to the moments of delay required for the cognitive processing…immediate reality is beyond one's physical reach…all we perceive is our processing teach…that perceptual immediate experience is just not there…that immediate person in your presence is just not there…those words they just uttered are not just said…all this physical life experience is playing out on delay…there is no physical present moment experience…

Higher consciousness is immediate…meditative state is immediate…discernment is immediate.. intuitions are immediate…as consciousness is not confined to just the confined physical senses…

This is the power of Maya…going into the depths of your higher consciousness…where the perceived reality of the physical senses can be tapped into…modified…enhanced…producing an ultra enhanced perceptual reality…a reality experience that the confined physical cognitive senses can not even ever imagine…

"We have only met previously…
 I yearn to meet you immediately…
 Love let this realm dissolve…
 Come consciously rise to evolve…
 In the multi realms of clairvoyance…
 Immediate realm a distracting nuisance…"

Hugh Shergill

Maya Leela

The Art of Observational Experience...

"One Within Lost...
One Without Most...

What remains in the art...
Becomes part of the art...
Never the entire art...
To see the entire art...
One must be separate...
Step out by deviate...
One within a canvas painting...
Is deeply embedded within the art...
Existing as a particular aspect of the art...
Confined to certain aspects of the art...
Left completely within lost...
Restricted to only possibilities...
Of experiencing within the art...
Confined of non separate distant of observing...
One without confine knows most...
It is the one art without..
Able to be observing...
The art of observational experience...
Seeing art from a particular separate distance...
Sees not only that one existing within the art...
Also the entire complete art canvas...
Able to engage, observe, experience...
Every particular aspect and completeness...
Of the art wholeness...
Contrast to the confined to canvas...
Whom is restrictively existing...
Lost within the art experiencing...

One Within Lost...
One Without Most..."

Hugh Shergill

One may be able to recall a past experience in life...where one faced a very distressing and hurting situation...while in that situation and experiencing what one had to face...certain behaviours and emotions were triggered...which ironically differs when inspected in retrospect... With many passing moments...when we then analyze in retrospect through re-visiting, re-examining, and re-experiencing that particular situation...our perspective subjectively shifts dramatically to a certain degree...as one now is able to detach from that immediate event crisis experience and now perceive it by examining what...how...and why...all that actually happened...this detachment allows for better understanding of what was actually going on...contrary to what was going on with us...

Only the audience of the theatre are able to experience the entire play experience... the stage... the play... the act... the actor... therefore more privileging deserving of establishing any possible judgment of the play...as the viewing spectator...not just on the stage performing actor...

**"What remains in the art...
Becomes part of the art...
Never the entire art...
To see the entire art...
One must be separate...
Step out through deviate...
Once the actor steps away...
Merging with the audience through play...
Now it has mastered the play essence...
The art of observational experience..."**

Hugh Shergill

The Tri Levels of Consciousness...

The perceived reality existence is dependent on the capacity of one's consciousness...which are the true eyes of perceived reality...therefore consciousness is the viewing audience...one only sees what its consciousness is capable of...the conscious capacity...

Consciousness is the experiencing energy audience of the Maya play stage, processed through the play performer... The performer performs the play on stage and experiences its performance play as the theatre audience through its consciousness travel...which is always non local multi-dimensional... with Divine capacities to merge with the Divine energy source itself...existing on multitude of multi levels...just as the multiple audience theatre seating zones...seats of multi rows and particular levels...

The soul consciousness existing experience is a three level state being...

Level One:

Maya Consciousness...
3D - Three Dimensional
The Front Row Audience...
The Perceived Awake State...

First level of consciousness... is Maya consciousness, the three dimensional conscious state... This is the fundamental basic level of consciousness state that exists and commonly associated with... All beings can easily experience this within one's five or less physical processing senses...the physical state being in space, time, and causation... This can be labeled also as the 3D three dimensional Maya conscious state... What one experiences is at the very core in tune with the maya stage of perceived physical existence. This is the highest ego stage, where one's experience is very associated within the 3D Maya world existence. This stage is also referred to commonly as the 'awake' conscious state... which ironically in all Maya reality...is the most furthest away from being actually the most consciously awakened state...

Among the third dimension, time and space is also included, as the third dimension perceptual universe requires both a particular time and particular space...

(For more in depth analysis, please feel free to read the included advanced level bonus chapters on time and space)

The Maya conscious audience level can be described as the front row seated audience of the Maya Leela stage play... Here the audience's perceived focus is primarily on the stage play, with no additional or very minimum aware focus on any theatrical experience beyond the stage... Interestingly, one who is very closely seated to the stage play, after a while, becomes attentively so engaged in the play, that it begins feeling that they are actually within the play... consciously interacting and participating...on the stage...even though they are still seated outside just perceiving the stage play... This is the Maya stage illusion... The powerful illusionary energy state of Maya and its conscious audience state...

"The more one closely associates Maya consciousness with the perceived existing world of Maya...the more one becomes attracted and remains attached to the world of Maya..."

Level Two:

Semi-Maya Consciousness...
4D - Fourth Dimensional
The Mid Row Audience...
The Semi-Awake State...

Second level of consciousness, is semi-awake, the semi-maya consciousness, the fourth dimensional conscious state... This is the semi-active Maya conscious state... This is the conscious state that goes beyond the confines of one's five physical senses ego existence... This is a magical fluid state beyond space and time strict confines, where the flexible potential intuitive discoveries are discoverable and discovered within... Meditation, sleep dreams, day dreams, desires, imagination, visualization, creativity, intuition, and synchronicities are associated with the semi-maya conscious state... This state of consciousness has the ability to develop and access sixth sense perception... the possibility for extra sensory perceptions for some...where higher reality and higher intelligence goes much beyond the human brain processing capacity and reasoning... Semi-maya consciousness is disregarded more often than regarded by the reluctance of absolute reasoning...however rewarded to those that regard, respect, experience its Divinely magical existence...

This audience level can be described as the mid row seated audience... Here the audience's perceived focus is still primarily on the stage play, however now there are also additional suttle experiences beyond Maya awareness... Here the spectator is viewing the play from an outer existing presence of the stage play, which creates possibilities to detect and bring attention to other potential activity presence in the theatre beyond the stage play... The deviated space from the stage establishes the firm presence of the stage...the stage existence is separate...the experience of the stage is separate... The Maya stage play projection questions of how? and why? Begin to arise within this spectating audience...

Memory...Sleeping...Dreaming...Exposing?

All memories and experiences are in consciousness...Semi-Maya Consciousness...the fourth dimensional consciousness is non local...out of the physical body confines...it is located the non local higher semi-maya consciousness...similar to what technology would refer to as 'cloud storage and processes' ...past life regression for certain reincarnated soul beings is a primary example of this...how is one physical body no longer in existence...yet its memories are still actively being experienced by a different physical being...as if the immediate memory bank was within the body, then it would be equally dead along with when the physical body is dead...yet that is not the case... the brain processes memory and experience...yet it is not containing it...a brain damaged individual has compromised memory and experience processing, not loss of stored memory and experience... memory loss is impossible...the inability of memory processing recall is possible...memory loss is never...memory recall perhaps not...

Dreams expose and explore possibilities of the semi-maya conscious realm further...it is a state of awareness that taps into the possibilities of deviates from the grounded core Maya stage...often more truth is revealed in this state than the perceived three dimensional state of truth...

"Often dreams are more real...
  Where one cannot fully take their ego feel...
  Every nightmare must be faced unveiling...
  Through deviates of illusionary feeling...
  Waking up terrified from the core intrusion...
  Returning to the perceived reality illusion..."

Hugh Shergill

The Conscious State of Possibility...

As the second level is a semi-awake Maya conscious state, then the question also arises: what and where is the other semi-awake active conscious state? Anything semi is half experience...where is the other half experience? As consciousness is always complete in totality... The answer is the conscious state of possibility... Possibility is never absolute... possibility is always infinite...

As one is seated mid row, further away from the Maya stage... the opposite duality further off the stage must also exist... with the relativity curiousity possibility of discovering backstage components that are perhaps influencing the stage play...come romancing into one's conscious play... including the arising curiosity of what is happening behind the curtains? Who is backstage? Where and whom is the play director? How is it directing? From where is it directing? What is currently happening backstage? These are all curiosity of possibilities arising from this possibility of conscious semi-maya conscious state...

Sub-Conscious state also includes Pre-Conscious state... Pre-conscious mind...one's previous lives soul journey residual and impactful thoughts that remain beyond the physical recycling processes... exists in this state as well...often revealing itself in thoughts, dreams, intuitive powers, and synchronicities... Curiosities now begin to receive answers...

The Bridge Conscious State...

Connection to Both Above and Below...

From this Bridge Conscious State...

In a semi-awake state, what is the actual one perceives and bridges to become the actual 'Awake' state...either through the Maya driven conscious awake state...or the actual above Maya soul conscious awakened state...

Further, in the semi awake state, the awareness of a further front evokes the curiosity of what is further back...as the possibilities of a higher level conscious state sparks the desire within... To which level the conscious shift of discovering these possibilities depends on the conscious being's driving force of either Maya or Soul... Maya driven will take shift the possibilities redirected back lower to Maya consciousness... Contrastingly, the soul driven consciousness will take the possibilities further to the third level of soul consciousness...

Structurally, in the theatre arena...it is often the mid row audience that are in close proximity to both stairs descending closer to the stage and stairs ascending to the VIP accessed balcony section...

Transcendence Fifth Dimension...

Transcending fifth dimensional state where everything becomes meaningless...not mere a voided state but a magical space that soothes the soul...where devoid of thoughts and their meaning...the most authentic blissful state of existence...

Level 3:

Soul Consciousness...

5D - Fifth Dimensional
Super Consciousness...
The Top Balcony Audience...

The Awakened State...

Third level of consciousness, is soul consciousness, the most prominent fifth dimensional state of super consciousness...infinite...ever existing yet required to be seeked and discovered... Just as there are infinite signals beyond the receptive capabilities of a satellite...it is further seeking and processing capabilities enhancements that are required to tap into the undiscovered signals... As one has to be spiritually tall enough to take the Divine soul ride... Here the soul being is in a highly super consciousness state and is capable of perceiving and experiencing a conscious state beyond the confines of the Maya Leela play perceived existence...a powerful quantum leap...a complete paradigm shift...quantumly entangled with Divinity itself...

Just like beyond the five senses, there is a possibility for extra sensory perceptions for some...soul consciousness is the extra conscious perception, directly connected with the Divine...as a single raindrop is completely identical in creation as the entire rainfall...This is the most powerful state of the conscious soul being... One is one with the Divine as one...beyond the Maya awareness existence... ultimate intellect intelligence liberation... non-duality... Kundalini arising and awakened... Moksha... Nirvana... Ananda... Euphoria... Tranquility... Everlasting bliss... All is one... One is all... Complete ego detachment as one is risen beyond the strict confines of the 3D Maya conscious state identification and has opened their soul conscious state...merged in as one with the creator...the Divine energy source... One is now seated consciously above awakened...

As earlier mentioned...all perceived existence exists not only as a particle but also as an energy wave... simultaneously existing in the paradox of duality...switching one's perception to a particular requires a superposition...to witness the infinite quantum fluctuations...where one can perceive the particular not only as a particle but also as a wave...this super position of witnessing the quantum fluctuations of the duality paradox... is super consciousness... the soul consciousness...

"Soul consciousness is the only complete non-maya entity existing in the entire Maya Leela illusionary stage play theatre...as it is awakened and above..."

This audience level can be described as the top balcony row seated audience of the theatre... The balcony represents the additional separation space that is separate from the other seating zones and yet still a part of it... Unlike the first and mid zone audience seating, the top balcony row is reached through accessing additional staircase that is exclusively reserved for this audience section, therefore additional effort is required to enter this audience zone... This audience zone may not be discovered at first, however it always exists...waiting with anticipation to be discovered...for those with the resources capacity and willing effort to walk up these additional stairs...

Here the audience's perceived focus is still primarily on the stage play, however they are also in a super privileged position to perceive and enjoy the complete theatrical arena experience of the stage play in one's soul conscious totality... Beyond the stage play, one is also able to view and bring attention to many other components of the stage play, that collectively contribute to the whole theatre experience of the play... From the director's position, stage lighting source, special effect zones, orchestra, stage projection source, other technical/structural contributing factors, to the very own entire bird's eye view of the audience observation... This is a rewarded advantage to both view the stage play and each member of each audience zone, observing the stage play performers and also behavioral responsive engaging patterns of the fellow surrounding audience...as viewing participants...

Unlike the front row audience that is strongly attracted and attached to the maya play stage and feels it is actually on stage... This top balcony row feels naturally a lower level Maya attract specifically to the Maya stage solely as they have discovered immensely much more in the overall theatrical play experience...beyond the confines of just the play stage...

Another interesting component of this audience view perception... is the ability to see and locate all the possible exit avenues to exit...with the possibility existing to exit the entire play theatre of the Maya Leela at will... This phenomenon exists in the core of conscious soul awareness...repeatedly found in individuals from all walks of life...as the more one seeks their higher realms of their soul conscious path, the less inclination and attraction they feel for the cosmic illusion of this worldly stage of Maya...

Eagle Eye

"Take off to fly...
  One must look high...
  Out of range of the eye...
  Roams the eagle eye...
  Seeing both the hunt...
  And the hunter..."

Hugh Shergill

The Fourth Wall of Stage...
The Veil of Maya...
Breaking the Fourth Wall of Stage...
Unveiling the Maya...

'The Fourth Wall of Stage' is the classical theatrical concept of the stage play theatre...where the actors on stage deliberately imagine a wall between the stage and the audience...which is transparent for the viewing audience yet opaque to the actors on the stage...

The fourth wall is the imaginary wall that separates the stage play from the reality realm of the observing audience... On the play stage of the theatre, there are three surrounding walls that enclose the structured stage, with an imagined invisible fourth wall that is enclosed right in front of the audience...for the stage play actor while acting that programmingly prevents the actor from perceiving and acknowledging the audience while performing...however the fourth wall is fully open to the audience to view into the stage play... The fourth wall is like a movie screen for the watching audience...a one way mirror...where the audience views and comprehends the enacted stage play... yet the stage play actors are unable to comprehend the existence of the viewing audience...

Metaphorically… The play stage is the Maya Leela play illusionary realm…where one is acting and performing on this make believe stage…the audience is the performer's higher ascension soul consciousness realm…the real reality experience realm of soul consciousness… The fourth wall of stage is the veil of Maya, separating the reality from the illusion…entrapping one into remaining in the play illusion…devoid access to their higher soul conscious experience of observing the real reality… ultimately devoiding the potential of co-creating the play…

"And the truth shall set you free."

Holy Bible (John 8:32)

This famous biblical quote "The truth shall set you free" could not be any more true… Freedom of truth is the luxury granted for those who break the confined walls of entrapment…especially the fourth wall of the Maya stage…

Everyone born into this Maya realm is by default born with the entrapping fourth wall of the Maya stage… A performance devoid of higher conscious real reality influences is a very entrapped confined stage play performance…where the karmic script and acting are played out in precision within the illusion…however devoid of any potential improvisation and reality ascension performance due to the blocking of higher soul conscious real reality influences of the viewing audience… This deliberate ignorant block of attentive energy given to the audience by the actor brings out a more enclosed stage play performance that is devoid of reality, interaction, and reaction of the audience…which is its viewing higher soul consciousness… A play performed completely illusion entrapped without any glimpse of ascension reality influences of co-creating…results in a limited potential for any elevated real reality performance…

**"Entrapped Is a lost performance…
  Untrapped is freedom of performance…
  Puppet on strings is never performing…
  Puppeteer fooling illusion occuring…
  illusion is confining…
  Reality is elevating…
  To resonate beyond realms…
  Requires access to beyond realms…
  Confines of walls hold no purpose…
  For those with an ascension purpose…"**

Hugh Shergill

Maya Leela

Conversely, 'Breaking the Fourth Wall' is the phenomenon where the stage play performing actor breaks that one way mirror wall…allowing direct access to the viewing reality audience to co-create the soul's play performance…which is now a potentially profound influential factor…where the play performer breaks the confines of the illusion stage and allows the real audience not only view the play but to actually participate through reality influenced interaction directly with the play… This is a power position for the audience…where not only are they entertained by the play but also create the play with their participation…

Breaking the fourth wall phenomena of stage play…where the audience participates taking the script forward…power to co-create the soul's performance and ultimately influence the entire play trajectory in itself…this is the unveiling process of revealing reality and releasing entrapped illusion…this is your soul consciousness power that through agami immediate karma that shapes your performance and ultimately the play script going forward with the spice of reality…This is the soul performance ascension key…stepping out of the illusion…tapping into the magic of actual reality…where now one is performing in the Maya Leela play with access to its higher reality conscious realm…the top balcony viewing audience…a realm that views all…knows all… Allowing its higher consciousness reality interaction with your performance shall elevate your play…elevate your performance…elevate your soul…

Imagine yourself watching your favourite movie on screen…with a scene of your most favourite character…all of sudden you get access to step inside the screen…control your favourite character and maneuver its performance further…as you have already seen this favourite movie of yours before…you will naturally break away from the status quo anticipated performance…you will inevitably effortlessly improvise and create further…you will excel the character's performance in some form or way…you will dynamically flip the script for an even more exceptional movie experience… Imagine giving access to your soul consciousness witness to your physical play of Maya Leela…imagine how dynamic possibilities would become to exist…taking your confined entrapped play to a Divinity access dynamic ascension play… Embrace to break the fourth wall of the Maya Leela stage…break free from the illusion veil of Maya…revealing reality through quantum leap into your super consciousness…

**"Life is not what it seems…
Reality lies behind the scenes…
Free yourself from Maya illusion…
By seeing through Maya delusion…
Elimination of illusion…
Eliminates its delusion…
Attempt one views further…
One becomes to see further…"**

Hugh Shergill

Quantum Leap into Super Consciousness...

Quantum is the minimum amount of any entity involved in an interaction... For a Soul being, this quantum phenomenon is one's Divine soul energy itself...

Quantum leap of one's soul transitions into a new reality immediately which one has not accessed before...This quantum shift of the soul into the previously untapped super consciousness...shifts one perceived minimum three dimensional Maya illusion reality to the fifth dimension super consciousness reality...

The sequence of this phenomenon of immediate shift does require a sequence of prerequisites to occur...first is awareness of the true informed reality...then consciously shifting one's conscious awareness into that unveiled reality realm...now powerfully energizing this reality...through meditative concentrative powers...unlocking the previous locked blocked chakras within...for some even further blessed unleashing of one's Kundalini Shakti in an untamed state dance of freedom...this power house of energetic prerequisites will allow one to immediately quantum leap from lower consciousness state and shift into super consciousness state...this is the ultimate quantum leap...once shifted...forever accessible...

"Seed of elevation...
 Is the act of separation...
 To elevate...
 One must separate...
 Passing through it...
 While rising through it..."

Hugh Shergill

Perception Defines and Re-Defines Experience...

As perception shifts...so shall experience... A simple example is whenever we re-watch a favourite movie of ours...what you experience differs from your initial experience of first watching the movie... and this goes beyond the predictability factor of re-watching the movie scenes...it is actually the deeper experience determined by one's current perception state...the same movie reel is repeated... yet the precise movie experience is never repeated...as perception is continuously forever evolving... the watcher and the watched is continuingly interactly experiencing...each repeat watch of the movie...is a new experience of the movie...the repeat value is not in the particular movie...it is in the value of one's conscious pool of experience...

Free yourself from the trap of physicality...refrain from thinking this is a real world...It is at its core an unfolding sequence of the play of Maya Leela... A screen on which you are a part of the projection... projecting your performance on this projection...nothing is matter...it is all energy... interactions within you...your performance is always in your control with you...

Detach to Elevating Attach to the Play...

De-personalize yourself from the Maya Leela play and you will simultaneously elevate your personal performance within the play... For example, An individual that just efforts to personally lift tremendous amount of weight is at a disadvantage compared to an individual that attempts seeing themselves lifting that same amount of weight first...visualization of your performance...excels your performance...

"The best view comes after the hardest climb..."

Ascending into a Fifth Dimensional Being...

Fifth dimension can also be called the infinite dimension... Elevated consciousness inevitably will result in a profound transformation...the formation of you as the fifth dimensional being...an awakened soul being...

Fifth dimensional being is completely in sync with in all three conscious realms...unveiling within powers that perhaps were lying dormant untapped...

Upon your elevation to these higher realms...the lower realms become less significant...the small talks no longer serve any significant purpose...the once offended issues are less bothersome...the emotional responses are responded with higher emotional intelligent...this is the Soul being's true upgrade...your true VIP status of existence...your VIP experience of the Maya Leela play theatrical experience...

Ananda

Soul Consciousness Bonus Treat...

The Everlasting Bliss...

Here the top balcony soul conscious audience also have the privilege availability to consume their desired treats and beverages...while watching the play unfold...these treats is the opening of the third eye chakra...the full activation of the pineal gland in the human body...unleashing an everlasting blissful high state...Ananda...that is the direct euphoric orgasmic bliss connect with the Divine source itself...everlasting...independent of the entire Maya Leela play and all of its performers and performances...

Ananda differentiates from the temporary perceived joy and happiness that comes from the physical sense of existence and validation... True bliss requires no validation or explanation...either by us nor others... On a physical Maya three dimensional conscious state...every internal satisfaction, joy, happiness, and perceived bliss requires a certain validation of understanding and explanation... Validation of oneself or by the perception of others that one particular is experiencing joy because of a certain external factor stimulus... Without the perceived validation understanding of the external stimulus trigger...such as one is happily in blissful joy because of wealth, health, Love, success, etc... and if a person was still experiencing blissful joy...without no Maya apparent validation and explanation...then that person would be labeled as someone who is not quite sane...that something somewhere was not correct within their mental state...this is the ignorance bliss thought process of Maya...as contrarily everything is actually always correct bliss within...

Ananda refers to a joyous bliss state that is everlasting conscious happiness that keeps one interestingly occupied through the everlasting Divine bliss connect...like a light illuminating once directly electrically source connected...illuminating always once connected... Unlike the solely maya perceived happiness joy that is also an illuminating light...but running on temporary battery power...that absolutely eventually shall fade...requiring the recharge power stimulus to once again illuminate...again...and again... Exhausting never everlasting... Whereas Ananda is everlasting and never exhausting... An everlasting soul conscious bliss state that resides within one's highest level consciousness and cannot be found through anything other than this... Once one has this Divine joyous bliss, the joyous bliss remains forever despite any fluctuation experiences of the Maya Leela stage play scene, performers, and performances...

A stage play experience can be profoundly enhanced by one having the luxury to sip on their desired beverage and gourmet snacks while engaged in the play...if it is a good play scene...the theatrical experience shall be enhanced...and if it is a scene or performance not to one's desire or preference... The luxury consumption indulgences makes the theatrical experience much more pleasant...a pleasurable viewing enhancing experience state...of the Maya Leela stage play...

Conscious Level Shift...

Awake, Semi-Awake, Awakened...

Anyone highly experiencing one particular conscious level, shall be compensated by down regulation of the other one or possible two conscious levels... For example, any being who is experiencing high soul consciousness awakened state will lack semi-awake and Maya awake conscious levels...with respect to the cosmic principles of adaptive duality and relativity... You can not have high ego Maya and non-ego soul consciousness experience simultaneously at the very exactly same moment... one must give in for the other to rise and vice versa... You can not physically sit in the audience in the front row, mid row, and top balcony simultaneously... However, the top balcony view will let you view the entire stage play theatre experience, and with its advantage soul conscious perception power lets one focus in observe the particulars of the entire theatre and all those positioned in it....which ultimate drives the play performance forward through the enhanced audience awareness and engagement...

"Audience awareness and engagement influences the play performance, and once the audience realizes this, both the play and the performers are forever influenced..."

This is the ultimate soul conscious theatrical experience of the stage play...being aware of the stage play projections, experiencing all audience zones, engaging and blissfully enjoying the stage play to its Divine capacity totality...while also performing as the conscious projection performer actively on the Maya stage...in the play of Leela...

"Every play...requires a script..."

CHAPTER 5.

MAYA LEELA SCRIPT

"What is a Play…
Without a Script…
Maya Leela…
Play script…
Eternal romance between…
Destiny…
And Karma…"

Hugh Shergill

Maya Leela

Destiny Bow…Karmic Arrow…

"Destiny Bow…
  Karmic Arrow…
  Dichotomous…
  Yet in Convergence…
  Destined submerged…
  Freedom emerged…"

"The arrow releases from the bow…
  Fearlessly piercing through all the wind flow…
  Freely all in control is its illusion blow…
  Freedom that remains at the mercy of the bow…
  Precision angle distance in all its high to low…
  Arrow's freedom always belonged to the bow…"

"Surprisingly the pulled back bow…
  Felt more resistant from this one arrow…
  Densely sharp required more pull from the bow…
  Projected target now undetermined for the bow…
  Intensely it releases the arrow towards target…
  Arrow not just hit but goes through the target…"

"Bow controls the arrow…
  Not the make up of the arrow…
  Beyond precision control of the bow…
  There is that exceptional arrow..
  No pull is equal from the bow…
  Nor is identical every arrow…"

Hugh Shergill

The Performer's Performance Scope…

Your Self…

"You did not totally create yourself…
  You do not fully control yourself…
  Uncover yourself…
  Discover yourself…
  Experiencing yourself…
  Exuberating yourself…"

Hugh Shergill

Free Will vs. Destiny…

Is there Free Will in Maya Leela?

With a simple parallel geometry analysis, lets connect the dots and look at free will, destiny, and karma:

Firstly, let us mark down two small dots (.) apart from each other as first point B (Birth) and second point D (Death). Secondly, let us join them by drawing a straight line, this is defined as a 'line segment'… A line segment is named by its two end points, as it connects point B to point D, it is written as 'Line-Segment BD'. Line segment is bounded by these two distinct end points and has a definite defined length…which is the shortest distance between these two points. Line segment BD exists because of both points B and D, and is absolutely binded by both in order to exist…

Line-Segment BD

B .————————————————. D

Point B marked is your this particular perceived physical life birth. Point D marked is your this perceived physical life death. Connecting these two end points, is the Line-Segment BD, which is the journey of one's life from point B (birth) to point D (death)…

Q. Point B, your birth…was it in your control?

Q. When you would be born?

Q. Where you would be born?

Q. From whom you will receive physical birth from?

Q. What would be your race/gender/physicality?

Q. What family/religion/community/nationality you will be born into?

Q. Certain genetic health strengths and delicacies beyond lifestyle?

Answer for all the questions above is a clear No…

Now to Point D…

Q. Point D, your death…is it in your control?

Q. When precisely will you die?

Maya Leela

Q. Exactly how will you die?

Q. Where will you die?

Answer again for all the above questions, is a clear No…

Finally, now to the Line-Segment BD…

The life journey from point B birth, to point D death…

Q. Is the life line journey completely in your control?

The answer is both No…and interestingly Yes!

The answer in the No:

Point B to point D is destined…

When both your journey start point B (birth) and journey end point D (death) are completely and absolutely not in your control… As at this very moment…you are absolutely aware of two inevitable events…one that has already occurred…your physical birth…and one that in your physical future shall absolutely occur…your physical death… Thus, what events that are already established are inevitable… and interestingly…what events that one has no control over are beyond the control of free will…therefore are destined…controlled by destiny…

Line segment BD, the life journey itself is absolutely binded to the results of both points B and D to exist as it is completely closed line segment between these two points… As any possible altered line shift dynamics from a closed line segment (point B to D) to any possibility of even a half-open line segment, would require you to have at least one complete point control (of either point B or D) which is either having full control of your birth or death… For example, if you desired through free will to alter your destined death…then you must have full control of your birth… And vice versa, if you desired through free will to alter your birth…then you must have full control of your death…which both are completely impossible within the confines of the physical three dimensional realm…thus the completely enclosed Point B to point D is absolute destined…

The answer in the Yes:

What is possible is developing the illuminating width glow of the Line-Segment BD, as the width glow or the lack of…holds no value effect to the connect value of connecting point B and point D. Once the Line-Segment BD is established, it shall exist as long as both B and D points exist, with the line width glow being an inessential value for the BD line segment value…

Enter the Karma…

Now, this is where the magic of karma exists…it is in this BD line width illuminating glow…the infinite potential glowing expansion and illumination of width energy of this line…which connects to both points, however with what potent energy and magical capabilities of illumination it connects with is infinite… to ignite this power is tapping into the power of your infinite soul…just like a wire connecting two technological devices is established…the potential capabilities of this connection upgrade is open to undiscovered infinite possibilities…

Once there is physical birth, there shall be a physical death, no question…as that particular life line exists… However, what type of potential experience, perception, quality, time illusion duration, opportunities and capabilities that exists within that life experience, is our cosmic Maya Leela play gift…our infinite potential life line glowing illuminating expansion performance scope…through our soul performance…which is our karma… Enlighten, illuminate, glow up your life line through the power of your karma…Karma that is powered by your free will… Agami Karma… one's immediate karma…the Karmic actions and their reactions that one creates through its play performance on the life play stage of Maya Leela… The scheduled play duration remains fixed…the dedicated moments on stage (Life Line) to perform remains fixed…the performer's both entry (Birth) and exit (Death) moments remain fixed… yet the performer's performance remains entirely its own…agami karma power of free will to perform an enlightening illuminating enriching performance…shining glowing bright one's life line to its utmost potential…

Just like one's home has fixed established physical rooms, one can not physically re-shift the existing rooms sequences around, however one can freely enter move around each room and experience their entire home rooms at will… Further, each room can be dedicated, detailed, designed, decorated, furnished completely to one's desired preferences and capabilities…

Similarly, one's genetics determines the growth, colour, texture, duration of one's hair…this is destined… however one has complete freedom to style and cut their hair as desired…options to enhancing it aesthetically…and further enhance the quality of the hair through adequate nutrition and lifestyle choices…as this freedom to choose and apply destiny enhancements happens through only one's free will karma…not destiny… These activity of free will experiences…is karma…cause and effect…the performer's performance…the performer's destiny enhancement…ultimately illuminatingly enhancing destiny…

Point B to D is…
Moments of specific distance…
Not Time Duration…

(For in depth analysis of the illusion of Time, please feel free to also read Advanced Level Bonus Chapter 23: Maya Kaal…Time)

Both points B and D are specific moments…not time duration…point D moment of physical demise is established…so is line between points B to D…yet time is a physical realm illusion…time is another expansion factor of the BD line…therefore age extension in terms of time duration through one's karmic actions is certainly very possible to slightly stretch…the key to visualize the time duration is not to measure the distance of line between…instead visualize time as the illusionary glowing illuminating acceleration and deccelarate energy travel factor surrounding the BD line… The physical demise is certain…even the longest rope has an end…what is the duration time illusion is available to be measured determined but not the finish moment… Just like track racing car has a fixed determined start point and a finish line…yet it is the free will acceleration speed the car travels at that creates and establishes the measured duration…which the illusion of time measurement…that speed acceleration is in the control of the driver…yet still has its limitations…as the specific vehicle performance and driver are confined to their particular already established limitations… Playing a vinyl record on a very slow speed will not add additional bonus tracks…it shall only increase the record's playing perceived time…as the last track 8 is the last track 8 of the record… If one wants to increase their life duration in measured time age…it is possible to slow your biological processes to increase the perceived duration…yet only to the maximum established confines of one's karmic physical vessel…yet one can not ever stretch the fixed determined distance…

"Your life duration is not the number of years…
  Instead it is the number of biological breaths…"

One positive exercise experience that one can do to slow down one's biological aging processes to increase its perceived duration…is to give it unhindered attention as possible…to live a healthy lifestyle at the best of your ability…and then to believe truly within that you are living your very best healthy lifestyle with attention…this powerful karma synergy of thought and actions with prolonged attention will result in slowing down one's biological aging process…increasing your duration…increasing your number of breaths…not perceived years…

Quantum Zeno Effect…Power of Observation…

"What the observer observes continuously…
  Refuses to decay…"

The quantum zeno effect is a feature of quantum mechanical systems allowing a particle's time evolution to be slowed down by measuring it frequently enough with respect to some chosen measurement setting… Just like someone very frequently checks the time clock…it seems often that the time just doesn't pass by…yet not checking the time clock frequently due to one's important distractions makes the complete day fly by…

The key factor is 'frequently enough' which in its all power capacity should be 'continuously'… however it is impossible on this three dimensional realm to continuously observe something continuously without the hindrance of any distraction…however prolonged attention of observation… surely has its impact…therefore…even prolonging one's longevity, health, and youthfulness…is very possible through diving into its attentive and responsive energies of self Love… therefore if you desire to be more youthful and healthy? Then give it your absolute attention… Whether it is your health, well being, Love, passion, hobbies, creativity…whatever has your prolonged attention, refuses to decay… otherwise it eventually fades away…

"Circumstantial established distance…
Is one's Destiny…
Maneuver of one's travel…
Is one's Free Will…
Point B is one's birth…
Point D is one's death…
Destiny is the point B to D…
Expansion and contraction…
BD line segment value width glow…
Is one's Karma freedom scope flow…"

Hugh Shergill

From your destined point B to D, the connecting line is the infinite soul energy line that the Divine dedicates based on your soul's previous karmic timeless script actions and the indication of potential capacities for higher karma in this particular life performance…

Future is the continuity of the past as destiny, modified in the present through karma… Where you are… What you are… is your karmic destiny…created through your past karmic actions… Where you go… What you become…is being created through your current karmic actions…therefore one must forever choose wisely…

The stage play of Maya Leela that you are currently performing on…has fixed specified moments…with the entry door and exit door openings of the stage are out of your control…you enter the stage without your will…you exit the stage without your will…only the performance you perform on stage for those moments is your will…you control nothing but your performance while on stage…

With your current physical being existence, the start of the journey is not in your control…the end of this journey is not in your control…in between this, this 'return ticket' journey itself is the ultimate gift of infinite potential from the Divine…the creator's creation magic through karma…where infinite possibilities exist through the power of one's soul performance karma…once in tune…the performer's performance becomes spectacular…magical…this is your opportunity gift as the assigned soul being performer in the play of Maya Leela…let your soul make your life line glow…

"Life is not short…
We just start living late…
By the time we begin to understand…
The trajectory of our actual journey…
Time to return…
Creeps upon…"

Irrfan Khan (Renowned Actor)
Poetic translation by Hugh Shergill

Performing Actor...Karma Reactor...

"Performing actor...
 Karma reactor...
 Is performing the script...
 For the script to exist...
 Script must be complete...
 From commencement to conclusion...
 Actor performing the script is the play...
 Play in performance is dependent...
 On the actor performing...
 Play exists because of the performance...
 Performance exists because of the actor...
 Actor exists because of the script character...
 Scripted character exists because of the script...
 Script exists because it is completely written...
 Scripting play exists in the actor's performance...
 Performance is the act...
 Act is action...
 Action is karma...
 Performing actor...
 Karma reactor..."

Hugh Shergill

Karma Expansion Glow...

"Karma expansion glow...
 Glow is freedom flow...
 Travel while growing...
 Is one's Karma glowing...
 Attracting through illuminating...
 Enlightened conscious activity...
 One's karma line furthering...
 The glow of attracting...
 Through illuminating..."

Hugh Shergill

"Just like a demised being's tombstone...
With that engraving...
Has a birth date...
And the demised date...
With a dash separating both dates...
That dash...
Is your co-creation line...
Go live that dash...
Through your karma stash..."

Hugh Shergill

BD Line Thread...Sutra Thread...

Sutra defined in Sanskrit refers to a thread...a particular thread is fixed in terms of its length, texture, density...yet there are vast potential possibilities of what beads and jewels are bejeweled within that sutra thread...

Destiny is the predetermined journey...yet the experience of that journey is your free will...your own karma...it is not the journey path that is of highest importance...it is the journey's experience on that path that imbibes one within...

The river's intense flow and route is predetermined...yet the boat remains in your control...desire a better boat?...then increase and build your physicality to your utmost potential...desire a better performing boat...then build up your emotional and spiritual strength to your utmost potential...then sit back indulge and enjoy your predetermined river route journey...through your controlled experience...

"Row, row, row your boat
  Gently down the stream
  Merrily merrily, merrily,
  Life is...but a dream"

The riveting rhyme is revealed to children from a very young age...profoundly prophetic...for those receptive...

Maya Leela

"The heart with immense purity...
Shall always be blessed by Divinity...
Shoot out your arrow...
With impeccable karma...
It shall hit that target...
That is your desires select..."

Hugh Shergill

The String of the Guitar...
The Lifelong Metaphor...

Metaphorically...take the single string of the guitar...or any other instrument that consists of just a single string... The string is confined to its established predetermined length...with a beginning...and an end... Yet its vibrational karma movement holds immense potentiality... the ability to create infinite music magically...

Meera...the renowned mystique poet and Divine Devotee...was known to carry along with her and play an instrument beautifully called the 'Ek Tara' which means 'One String'...as its name...it is an musical instrument that consists of just a single string...yet the music it produces is euphorically mesmerizing to experience...

This is life...the BD line segment...a line of birth and death...the confined single string of the guitar... with a beginning and an end...yet holding immense potential to create beautiful music infinite...through its own vibration...vibration of karma…

The String of the Guitar...
The Lifelong Metaphor...

"The string of the guitar...
 The lifelong metaphor...
 Single string of the guitar...
 Destiny intrude...
 From its commence...
 To its conclude...
 Yet the string remains...
 In freedom to inspire...
 Before its inevitable expire...
 Vibrational movement...
 Holds immense potentiality...
 Ability to karmically create...
 Infinite music magically...
 Movement of the string...
 Is its...
 Infinite creation of music...
 Is its..."

Hugh Shergill

Be the master of your destiny line journey…

Vibrate your life to its utmost potential through your karma… Develop your karma power line…
Through soul powered performance play…
Anything that glows...radiates and illuminates light...a life line that glows, not only travels enlightened,
but also illuminates all surroundings in its travel life passage... attracting and expanding all through the
magic glowing...
Karmic expansion can be further enhanced through igniting this karma line with the flame of awareness...
an aware connection with the Divine source itself... This is the ultimate blessed phenomenon as the
aware soul is expansively potentially aware to create the awareness spark of consciousness awareness...
illuminatingly glow your life line light through your karmic light...light within...light all... attract all...as the
popular gospel song lyrics state…

"This little light of mine…I'm going to let it shine…"

Harry Dixon Loes
(Renowned Composer / Writer)

Maya Leela

As the soul radiates and glows...a beautiful transition manifests...from being selfish...to unselfish...to ultimately being selfless...where one desires to travel not only solely on one's performance path...but also plant flowers of Love...on the path...for other fellow souls to experience and resonate the potential bliss as well...through Love, care, service, and awareness... Make your future so bright that you can not even see it...as the unseen is the infinite Divine...

Selfless Tree...

"The selfless tree...
 Gives Love free...
 Holding its breath to spare...
 Providing oxygen in your air...
 Self sacrifices into wood...
 Luxuries comfort necessaries...
 Providing all as expected should...
 Tree's selfless giving...
 Is eternally living...
 Proudly held in their hands...
 As monetary paper wealth...
 Yet no concern...
 For its family's remaining trees...
 Even upon your demise...
 It shows further Love...
 Providing its wood...
 For your coffin glove...
 Sparking fire as a matchstick...
 Burning itself for your flame...
 Providing cremation ascension...
 Certifying your demise record...
 With its wooden pencil tick..."

Hugh Shergill

Negative Karma

Whatever expands is also capable to contract...as you get what you deserve, not what you desire... therefore become deserving of your desire...as your particular karmic actions creates both expansion and contractions from your own free will karma doing. Positive actions expand the BD line with expanding further potential reach of bliss experience. Negative actions contract the BD line and restricts and confines one's experience. The life line can be a strong wide glowing light... Or may also become a very thin barely hanging fragile dim light weak line...

While the lifeline duration remains identical, the experiential journey of the lifeline being experienced is very dependent on one's karma decision actions, made when the destiny opportunity presents...

"It is important to live a big life...
Not necessarily a longer life...
Flow with life...
In positive karmic expansion...
And life shall flow...
In positive expansion..."

Hugh Shergill

"Karma is conclusive...
Predetermined for you...
Previously determined by you...
Karmic life path span is the flowing river...
Body resides on the dedicated boat...
Conscious will is one's paddle...
Steering away to karmic destination..."

Hugh Shergill

"The predetermined life path span flows...
As determined by one's karmic play script...
Meandering flowing...
Determined by continuously flowing...
Forever changing karmic acts...
The body is one's traveling means...
Dedicated to the particular determined boat...
Privileged with the awareness paddle...
Of one's consciousness will...
Giving blessed ability to steer away...
As desired to the determined predetermined...
By one's karmic play script..."

Hugh Shergill

"The unseen scene...

    To shift the scene...
    Unseen must be seen...
    To see the unseen...
    Shift the scene...
    What is now seen...
    Was your unseen scene...

    The unseen scene..."

Hugh Shergill

We all are just actors, that deliver poor (inharmonic) or good (harmonic) performance in the play... The actor that performs in complete harmony with the play...results in accolades of rewards... Just like a competent performer in a play, that time after time impresses the play director with its performance... the possibility of the director opening to the desires and scene suggestions from the performer also increases proportionally... Similarly, an excelling student is able to skip particular grades and have more freedom of educational choice of preference, based on their performance excellence... This is karma, as the Maya Leela presents you exactly what you deserve. Therefore, if you desire a scene shift... then creating karma awareness through your performance...flip the script through your active karma performance...the script shall surely flip…

"Changing once again...
    The costume...
    Into character...
    O Ghalib...
    Witnessing once again...
    The play of karma...
    Play theatrics..."

Mirza Ghalib (Renowned Poet / Writer)
Poetic Translation by Hugh Shergill

Maneuvering the Meandering…

"Maneuvering the Meandering…

  Created canvas is destiny…
  Creating is your opportunity…
  The river's distance is fixed…
  The riveting remains perplexed…
  Meandering turns are inevitable…
  Maneuvering freedom is still possible…

  Maneuvering the Meandering…"

Hugh Shergill

Destiny Tree…

"The seed emerges into the tree…
  Predetermined space not outside..
  Yet the branches expand blossom free…
  While within the destined confide…
  Becoming all as it shall be…
  During its destined growth ride…"

Hugh Shergill

"Your destiny is like a set of piano keys.
  But the symphony you play on is your own.
  Don't like what's happening in your life?
  Play a different tune today…"

Shekar Kapur (Renowned Filmmaker / Actor)

Maya Leela

Destiny's Orchestration…

"Divinity's Instrumentation…
 Destiny's orchestration…
 Experiential duality…
 Spiritual polarity…
 Melodiously kept…
 Karmically felt…"

Hugh Shergill

Ride Ticket…Ride Performance…

"Ride ticket is destiny…
 Ride performance is free will…
 Destiny grants the vacation return ticket…
 Vacation experience is one's karmic act…
 The tree trunk gives branches birth…
 Yet it is the branches that bears the fruit…
 The particular cards have been fixity dealt…
 How one plays determines its victory wealth…"

Hugh Shergill

Riveting Rivering River

"Uniquely rivering moment came…
 Distinctively encapsulating timeframe…
 Riveting river waves you overcame…
 Rewarding non repeat right of fame…
 Forever river shall never be the same…
 Forever you shall never be the same…"

Hugh Shergill

**"Luck Is What Happens
When Preparation Meets Opportunity"**

**Lucius Annaeus Seneca
(Renowned Philosopher / Writer)**

No Such Phenomena of Luck Exists...

There is absolutely no such concept of luck that exists... What we define as luck is just the result of one's Karma...which is created by the one performing the actions... Luck is nothing but a mysterious and highly appreciated way of Karma to deliver fruits of one's past actions in an unexpected manner and circumstances...therefore you are the creator of your so called luck...

As all in essence, the law of karma is that all actions have an equal and opposite reaction...therefore if you perform specific actions for something... you are absolutely assured to creating results accordingly in line to the nature of that something action. These results may not necessarily yield the desire of happiness...this is because what you may regard as giving you happiness today may as well be the reason for unhappiness in another today...the results are always in precise precision of the performance that goes beyond the Maya illusionary state of happiness...and inching closer harmoniously with the Divine source...which is beyond happiness...the state of infinite pure joy and bliss...

The Divine play of Maya Leela is so powerfully precise that everything that perceives to exists...exists in synch with everything else that exists...there is absolute reason for why and how everything unfolds... unfolding the page to the next chapter only occurs through the action of unfolding by the reader flipping to the next page...not by random luck of the reader assuming that it flipped to the next page through luck...now what surprisingly appears on the next page is karmic destiny created by the previous actions of the previous pages read by the reader...read as performance of preference...

The soul... once it becomes in harmony with the Maya Leela play and elevates to higher Divinity consciousness, only then your performance becomes complete...which is rewarded by Maya Leela through desired scene modifications meeting the evolved vibrational soul...this is the ultimate performance to preference through...which shall shift the play to what you desire, the scene that you prefer to be seen...and that ultimate desire is creation becoming one with creator...

**"Divinity sends...
Divinity ends...
Ascending descends...
Descending ascends...
Dharma lends...
Karma mends..."**

Hugh Shergill

Maya Leela

Be with what is...and create the rest...

The key to blissful experience of the journey is shifting the leela play to your preferred experience perception...through the magic of your performance awareness in Maya Leela.
Shift experience with harmonic awareness of the Maya Leela play...and put forth a karma performance that accolades a desired performance journey and rewards infinite liberation bliss... Performance Expansion by being in True Harmony…

"The actor's character is precisely dedicated...but the character props are designed according to the actor's fit..."

"Whatever happened,
  Happened for the good,
  Whatever is happening,
  Is happening for the good.
  Whatever will happen,
  Will also happen for the good."

Lord Krishna, Bhagavad Geeta

Poetic Elaboration by Harivansh Rai Bachchan:

"If things happen according to…
  How you wish…
  That's good…

  But if they don't...
  That's even better...

  If they are not happening…
  According to your wish…

  They're happening…
  According to the wish of…
  Some Divine force…

  And that Divine force…
  Will never think ill about you..."

Harivansh Rai Bachchan (Renowned Poet / Writer)
Translation by Amitabh Bachchan
(Renowned Actor)

"Looking back...
I now realize..
The universe was writing...
The screenplay of my life..."

Kader Khan (Renowned Actor / Writer)

"It is currently what it is...
It was previously what it was...
It will absolutely be what it will be...
Release the unnecessary burden...
Of forced control and let go...
What you felt your...
Desired plans were ruined...
Was actually Divinity saving you...
From those plans that...
Would have actually ruined you...
Shift your perception from all restraints...
As it shall manifest much more magical...
Then one could ever imagine...
Align with the Divine Shakti energy...
Flow with the most powerful energy...
Not ineffective forever against...
Simply align with the Divine...
Magic shall be forever...
Your power prime..."

Hugh Shergill

Today's Play...

"As I cross paths with some others...
I meet some of my story chapters...
The daily play is commencing...
With each sunrise eye's opening...
What is in store today...
Is another act of the play..."

Hugh Shergill

True performance expansion requires letting go of all resistances that encourage inharmornic performance by holding oneself back by holding on to certain confines of desires... This is an inharmonic performance distraction... Once the performer opens up the possibility of an even greater desired outcome in the play of life, then a greater desired outcome shall prevail that has the most authentic best interest for the performer... This is a powerful authentic path of complete Maya Leela harmonic performance... The Divine consciousness source creator cares more for its creation than the creation itself realizes... A child may get distracted from putting their best interest first, however the loving parent ensures that their caring Love route manifests results in the best interest for the child...

**"A person often meets his destiny
  on the road he took to avoid it"**

**Jean de La Fontaine
(Renowned Poet)**

Open yourself to all possibilities of route enhancements while traveling to one's desired destination. This enhanced vibration frequency of possibility...through soul conscious existence awareness...is the infinite width expansion potential of your BD line segment...readily available to be accessed in every part of our lives...as soul performance enhances through expansion...by tapping into the Divine magic play of maya leela...being in and living in harmony with one...

**"One not performing one's script...
  One performs the dedicated script...
  One's power lies in performance...
  One's script enhances by performance...
  One's performance is as experienced...
  One experiences shifting of the script..."**

Hugh Shergill

**"If your thoughts are confined to being logical...
  You've declined the leap to being dimensional..."**

Once something is conceptualized...it then exists...perhaps not in the confined realm of the non-believer of its existence...even as a defined concept...it still exists...even if it sits on the platter of a conscious concept...it still exists... authentically beyond belief...

Our consciousness creates our world... what we perceive on a microcosmic level...manifests the perceived reality experienced on a macrocosmic level... this is a double edged sword...contrasting how we perceive reality from a macrocosmic level... creates our reality perception on a microcosmic level... The key is to prioritize your perception from your own consciousness to experience all perceived reality... Fully meticulously observe the perceived reality but not modify your own consciousness by the influences of the perceived reality... Be extremely protective by prioritizing your inner conscious perception...this will nullify the heavy misaligning influences of the outer reality perception... Afterall, your world should be your real reality...not someone's else's perceived reality... Align with your authentic reality beyond all the illusionary influences...from there your consciousness will indeed take you places... experiencing an aware soul's Maya Leela performance...

"What is meant for you,
will reach you
even if it is beneath two mountains.
And what is not meant for you
will not reach you
even if it's between your two lips."

Al Ghazali (Renowned Sufi Philosopher)

"Spiritual compass...
Aligns you...
Directs you...
To all the spiritual experiences...
Deserving of you...
Destined for you..."

Hugh Shergill

Quantum Entanglement...

Quantum entanglement...what you seek...also seeks you...the soul seeks its Divine creation source... every one that with utmost genuine core within seeks...it will connect to the Divine...

"My brain is only a receiver,
in the Universe there is a core
from which we obtain
knowledge, strength and inspiration.
I have not penetrated into
the secrets of this core,
but I know that it exists."

Nikola Tesla
(Renowned Scientist / Discovery Inventor)

Revelations do not belong to anyone in particular…they reside in the infinite realm of possibilities…which is fortunately available to those rare that have expanded and ascended their soul conscious awareness enough to obtain them…

Knowledge can only be received by someone who's receptive to the frequency that the knowledge is available on…otherwise the message will not be received…the seeker must seek what it desires…perhaps only then the desired may agree to go on a informative date with its seeker…a date in the quantum entanglement of the most highest institutional realm of learning…

"Seeker seeking its desires…
 Desired considering its inquires…
 Fortunately chosen blessed are some…
 Whom Divine angels lower wings upon…
 Where hidden beyond the stage reveals…
 All those secrets resting on the veils…"

Hugh Shergill

"All exists in that one…
 One thought…
 One decision…
 One step…
 Manifesting one step existence…
 Of your infinite existences…"

Hugh Shergill

Maya Quantum Karma…
Existence from Conscious Experience…

Consciousness creates existence experience…
Emerging as the most conscious compatible version of one's existence that is experienced… existence is essentially existence selected from one's consciousness…selection is action…karma…consciousness karma…
Therefore one's consciousness is the creator of one's experienced existence…as ultimately consciousness is Divine's Divinity itself…above and beyond all realms of maya…tap into your consciousness through awareness and select your own existence experience…

Observe what is being experienced…as the following act to follow is your karmic performance… manifestation of the following existence of yourself…from the quantum realms of infinite existing experiences simultaneously existing...emerging the one that shall be experienced...is based on what was previously observed...entangled...experienced...Maya quantum karma...

Familiar Stage Spots...Soul's Vantage Points...

Due to residual lifetimes of karmic soul influences...there will be certain locales that shall resonate deep within one's soul existence... the experience is so deep and so profound...you feel it is almost like your own home... This familiar space feeling even without ever visiting it before...this special space holds a soul alignment frequency vibration...which is an energetic location beyond the Maya realm...quantum field...these stage spots are unique for each soul as each soul is playing out their unique Leela play script... Indeed, one will Love this when this experience happens...as it will be felt without ever having desired...

Same Stage Sharing...
Different Space Experiencing...

(For more in depth analysis of Maya Space, please feel free to also read the advanced level bonus chapter 24: Maya Verse...Multi-Verse)

Same stage sharing yet each actor occupies different space on the stage...each experiencing their performance from their particular space uniqueness...what one receives an applause performance moment...may for the other, just be acting response moment...individuals are perhaps in the same room yet in different spaces...different realms...different conscious states...
everyone on stage has their particular vantage point...the key is to make your vantage point...your advantage point...your vantage performance...

**"If it's temporary it's not real.
 If it's real, it never ends."**

Bhagavad Geeta

Soul Espionage...
Mindfulness of illusionary Maya Existence...

"Soul Espionage...Improvise...Evolve..."

When one is able to experience existence beyond one's lower surface illusionary Maya realm existence... and able to just instead of experiencing the existence but actually observe the existence...remarkable power of mindfulness existence flourishes...performing by being mindful of the mind... The soul espionage of one's perceived illusionary existence...the observer is now observed...soul espionage... and what is observed is now open for potential modification of the observer...the processing power of how and what is actually experiencing...leading to improvisation of one's performance...evolving to a higher realm of infinite existence...beyond all illusionary existence...

Maya Leela

This mindfulness of illusionary Maya existence is in all actuality soul existence...soul existence is the authentic Divinity existence...Divinity existence is Divine itself... Divine is all...our source of projection resulting in our projected existence...the creator of the creation...therefore what creates, holds the power of creation...creating is the artistic power of the artist to create art as it desires...

"Shifting your Drishti...Perception...
Shifts your Shrishti...Universe..."

Observing perceived reality... Changes perceived reality... Maya realm life existence is an experience... as essentially, even on the perceived physical existence to the highest level of soul consciousness...one is a field of energy...energy changing into further forms...constantly opening...open...opened to infinite possibilities... As the control is yours...as consciousness is yours...therefore the world of Maya Leela play is yours...create the play by being in observational awareness of the play...consciousness exploration exposes the familiar defined quantum factor...entangled...but unexplained...yet all aware on higher consciousness realms...as the art of observation awareness changes the art itself...unpredictably... unprecedentedly...how one observes the play...determines the play...infinite possibilities lies within the infinite consciousness observations...

"Environmental creation requires distance...
Extending its expression from distance...
For creativity to flare...
One becomes canvas aware...
The artist must step out of the canvas...
To create spectacular art on canvas..."

Hugh Shergill

Interestingly, the play plays out absolutely differently when one is not in aware observation of the play... also the play plays out absolutely differently when one is in aware observation of the play...not just opposite...not multiple...but infinite...infinite Maya existences in infinite Maya universes...all parallelly co-existing in existence...emerging and being existence experienced through consciousness indulgence... as perception of consciousness awareness is your infinite power...power playing out the play...infinitely... therefore create the play performance that shall be experienced...by being in observation of the play... infinite versions of you in the Maya realm exist...therefore infinite Maya performance experiences exist... create your play experience...by being aware of the play experience...Maya quantum karma...act by act...scene by scene... play by play...

"Stage is yours…
  Play is yours…
  Performance is yours…
  Experience is yours…
  Knowledge is yours…
  Victory is already yours…"

Hugh Shergill

This is your true soul power…your power of mindfulness existence through soul conscious existence… playing out your Maya karmic performance as the soul performer in the play of Maya Leela…

The stage is set…the play is active…the director is Divinely competent…the audience has arrived… seated…ready to be engaged… Now it is time for the performing actor to perform… To make shift and excel both the performance and the play scenes performed in… Now the performer must also be aware of its specific role in the play and also the assigned roles of the fellow co performers sharing the Maya Leela stage…

"Now let's introduce the play performers…"

CHAPTER 6.

MAYA

LEELA

PERFORMERS

"What is a Play…
Without its Performers…"

"Stage of the play…
Where all characters lay…
Some exist only on stage…
Some go beyond the stage…
Not all performers are equal…
Not all are capable for the sequel…"

Hugh Shergill

Maya Leela

**"All the world's a stage,
And all the men and women merely players"**

**William Shakespeare
(Renowned Poet / Playwright)**

Such prophetic words of Shakespeare...direct description of Maya Leela...as the world is the Maya stage...and all beings are performing players in the play of Leela... indeed profoundly prophetic...now let's explore these performers...

The Maya Leela Performers

**"The Enriching Presence of Some...
The Revolting Presence of Some..."**

We all have surely experienced this... On one occasion, we have come across an individual, regardless of how personally unappealing to our preference their exterior presence was... you just felt enriched by their pure soul presence... On another occasion, we have all also come across an individual, regardless of how pleasantly attractive illusionary their exterior was...their character seemed so soul cringed, that you feel revolted by just being in their presence... This intuition aura feel for both judgments are absolutely correct... Regardless of how particular the optical illusion was presented... that initial immediate felt was absolutely correct... Soul energy detects, resonates and permeates in all that exists and beyond...as it is all...therefore on its deepest level...knows all...

**"There is an optical illusion...
About every person we meet"**

**Ralph Waldo Emerson
(Renowned Poet / Philosopher)**

There is an absolute purpose reason for this...

'De ja vu' is the conscious alertness of having a strong sensation that an event or experience that is currently being experienced has already someway or somehow been experienced in the past... We all have at some moment felt this phenomenon...often associated in our Semi-Maya conscious state consisting of thoughts and dreams...

Duality on the other hand...

'Jamais Vu' or more commonly referred to as the reverse of 'De ja vu' as 'Vu ja de'...this is the conscious alertness of experiencing an individual and or situation that one absolutely recognizes in someway or somehow as familiar...but that nonetheless still seems very absolutely strangely unfamiliar... This 'never seen before' Vu ja de...is the phenomenon of experiencing an individual and or situation that one deep down totally recognizes and is aware of... Yet nonetheless, still seems like an authentic noveling unfamiliar experience...indeed quite the paradox... Yet both of these conflicting dichotomic simultaneous experiences...are profoundly certain...yet deep down are Divinely connected...It is the Divine conversational after effects... The energetic conversation between Divinity and one's soul consciousness...interacting and revealing to us...of us...and in regards to us...as it knows all...is all...and expresses as all...

"We know what we are,
 but not what we may be"

William Shakespeare
(Renowned Poet / Playwright)

The Protagonist Performer

A protagonist is the one who plays the leading character in the play... The protagonist is the central performer of the Maya Leela play script, where it performs through certain decisions and actions, then experiences the karmic consequences of those decisions...playing out in the play of Maya Leela... The protagonist is the primary performer in the audience's eyes that primary presents and takes the play forward...

The protagonist's theatre audience is consciousness...with their major fan based audience residing in the top balcony soul consciousness... the protagonist performer is the soul being...always...

Soul Being... The Maya Leela Protagonist...

Sura...Soul energetic entity of the Divine itself...

The word 'Sur' means rhythm...'Sura' is being in Divine rhythm... 'Divinity Rhythm' the rhythmic connection of the Divine creator and its Soul creation...Brahman (Divine creator) and Atman (Divine's soul creation)...both are forever in 'Divinity Entanglement' always infinitely entangled...connected... always engaged rhythmically...a human being in tune with the rhythm of Divine...the 'in tune' is soul energy...therefore a Sura is a Divinity's soul entity...a Divine Soul human being...

Soul Being is the manifestation being projection of the Divine energy source itself, that is beyond the web of the maya stage...that ultimately contains soul consciousness, undiscovered or discovered...

A soul being, contains soul energy creation experience which is directly Divine energy itself, which is infinite, beyond the confines of Maya dimension existence... As Maya is the stage and Leela is the play... both illusionary existing for the experience exclusively for the soul being. The soul is the protagonist performer of the play, that ultimately desires to dissolve itself as the creation with its creator... Therefore, the soul being is the guest performer in Maya Leela, participating and performing...yet not of this Maya stage platform...

Sura are also known as 'Deva'...Deva is derived from the word 'Divya'...which means 'light'... Deva is a masculine term...the feminine equivalent is respectively 'Devi'...Suras are innately soul aware of their Divine soul energetic existence...with undeniable Divine connection...

Maya Leela

"All know that the drop merges into the ocean,
  but few know that...
  the ocean merges into the drop"

Kabir Das (Renowned Poet)

Nothing New Under The Sun...

"Nothing new under the sun...
  All is illusion beyond the one...
  Extracting the one from the whole...
  Remaining aware from the all...
  One among all...
  Yet none for one...
  Nothing new under the sun..."

Hugh Shergill

"What seems as the flat sea...
  Depth exists in the unsee...
  Physicality is mere the illusion mesh...
  As the Soul holds power beyond flesh...
  Tip of the iceberg seems insignificant...
  Only its depth reveals its magnificent..."

Hugh Shergill

The Guest Protagonist Performer

The soul being performer is the primary protagonist performer that performs in the Maya Leela play as both the main character and the guest of the play... Guest in terms of existing in this Maya world yet not of this world...awareness of not residing in this realm, just passing through...

It is through its depth of soul consciousness that it is seeking much more than the script performance at hand... That seeking is soul conscious discovery and ultimate liberation by becoming one with the Divine source itself through complete performance victory in the play of Maya Leela...

Victory performance for the soul being requires complete Divine director's approval through completing each karmic Leela play scene optimally...efficiently...and moving on to the next...then the next...each scene after scene...while expanding its audience engagement reach...from the front row Maya conscious audience to the top balcony soul conscious audience...acquiring accolades through its performance...

Two major embedded characteristics of the soul being is its soul intuition discernment guide and unsettling drive to discover more than what is perceived in the Maya illusionary existence... This combination of guided drive leads the soul being to the ultimate performance victory as the creation becomes one with the creator...

Generally, in society...religious or non-religious...spiritual or scientific...one may not agree however one is aware of the term Soul and what it is defined and referenced to... Some define it as the essence immortal energy of each living being...the true actual self that is living out through one's physical existence... For others, define it more practically as mind, consciousness, and intellect... Both are correct, however there is a twist...a major twist...potentially, an astonishing twist...

"There are two kinds of Maya:
 Divine Maya...
 And UnDivine Maya..."

Rig Veda
(the first humankind known written scriptures)

Embrace...

The 'Eureka' Effect...
Your Life's Revelating 'Aha Moment'...
Has Arrived...

Surprise Entry in the Maya Leela Play...

The principle laws of relativity and duality once again come profoundly into immediate effect in the infinite Maya universes at play, as anything perceived to exist in the Maya illusionary existence is confined to these principle universe laws...without exceptions.. There is no escape... Maya leela is not a mere fantasy happy go lucky theatrical play story, it is a multi-layered multi-genre dramatic adventurous psychological thrilling unfolding mystery...with multi genre, multi sub genre combinations that are genre dose dependent by the particular karmic Leela play script of the soul being... with twists and turns scenes that keep the conscious audience continuously engaged... Scene after scene... Act after act... therefore for any scope of performance ancession...resistance is also absolutely required... one step forward requires removing the backward step... This is the Maya law... Darkness must be present for lightness to illuminate... For each benevolent, there is also a malevolent... In the play of Maya Leela... For each protagonist, there is an antagonist...

"In every play of life...
  There is a protagonist...the Hero...
  And there is an antagonist...the Villain..."

Anand Bakshi
(Renowned Poet / Lyricist)
Translation by Hugh Shergill

Enter The Antagonist...

The protagonist is the primary main character of the play, and the one who is in opposition, is the antagonist... The antagonist is the malevolent resistance provider to the protagonist which is its contrast, the benevolent... From resistance, forces, obstacles, and complications...the antagonist creates numerous conflicts that truly tests the protagonist and its play performance throughout life... The antagonist through its performance creates resistance and conflict, that reveals the strengths and weaknesses of the protagonist's performer... Therefore, the antagonist performer plays a pivotal role in the play of Maya Leela...

"Maya is the illusion of all perceived reality...
  Maya shows its utmost powerful illusion form...
  By creating a perceived Soul being common...
  But a complete illusionary Maya being...
  For every Divine Soul genesis...
  There is a soul less nemesis..."

Hugh Shergill

Maya Being... The Maya Leela Antagonist...

Maya Being is the manifestation being projection of the Divine energy source itself, however within the web of the Maya stage... Maya creation existing in Maya for Maya existing...

Just as the protagonist soul being, that contains soul energy creation experience which is directly Divine energy itself... Maya being contains the Maya energy created experience...existing with the purpose as a direct Maya source existence...which is ultimately the duality and relativity effects of Divine energy expression in itself...

Maya beings are powerful by-product manifests of Maya projection...this particular existence is the highest order of Maya entrapment for a soul being...as an individual adapts to itself, situations, and environment innately as Maya survival...however having to live among and interact directly with illusionary illustrations forms of similar human beings to oneself...yet absolutely being devoid of true infinite existence...the Divine soul consciousness...this is the ultimate illusionary script enhancing conflict of the play of Maya leela... Hidden behind the biological vessel human being exists a complete soul less being…that the Divine Soul being must face and overcome in the scripted theatrics of Maya Leela…

Ironically, a fundamentally core atheist will expansively, accurately, and unknowingly describe a Maya being by describing and explaining human being existence without any Divine existence…which is absolutely not what one agrees with, however for the purpose of living in Maya matter existence without having Divine conscious connection, it is described very well…

"Maya being…consequently existing through
  Divine's participation…yet devoid of Divine's
  conscious connection…"

Living biological matter existence without Divine conscious connection…is absolutely possible and true… but still there is a Divine participation throughout its existence…as for all existence to exist, it shall only be possible through activation of Divine source participation…which for the Maya being means existence through Divine's Maya participation…however without no possibility of Divine conscious connection…

"One is existence…
  The other a consequence…

  One is Divine's spark effect…
  The other a Maya by-product…

  Same stage…
  Same play…

  Each their own…
  Unaware of the known…

  One a protagonist…
  Other an antagonist…

  Maya beings innately detached from
  the higher realm…

  Soul beings innately detached from
  the Maya realm…

  A Soul being is Soul consciousness…
  Divine energy itself in existence…

  A Maya being is Maya consequence…
  Divine energy duality consequence…

  One is existence…
  The other a consequence…"

Hugh Shergill

One is Divine energy itself...the Soul being... The other is Divine energy duality consequence...the Maya being... Both are identifiable (almost identical) biological human beings however serving very contrasting positions in the Maya leela play...just like two identical technologic devices... yet with different receptive energy frequency networks... receiving signals that are contrastingly different... making both identical physical devices process and act distinctly different...

"We are all in the gutter,
 but some of us are looking at the stars"

Oscar Wilde
(Renowned Poet / Playwright)

Just like an illuminating light... For example, both an ordinary light and laser light are essentially electromagnetic waves that travel with the velocity of light in a vacuum... However, an ordinary light is divergent and incoherent whereas laser light is highly focused, precise, directional and coherent... able to reach capacities much more further powerfully than the ordinary light capabilities... Both are light yet distinctly unique by their dedicated capacities... All human beings are just that...illuminating light as life existence, but distinctly unique by the light processing potential capacity coherence, as consciousness... Soul conscious beings and Maya conscious beings...separately distinct by action, capacity, and awareness...one has Soul conscious awareness like a powerful laser light... the other has restrictive Maya conscious awareness like an ordinary light... both are in essentially light but distinctly and dramatically opposite by capability coherence potential... One is divergently distracted spread out consciousness but only within the lower realms of Maya...the other is coherently precision focused consciousness, powerfully reaching out beyond the realms of Maya... This is the dramatic distinction...of the protagonist and the antagonist... co-existing within Maya and yet some are privileged way beyond Maya...

Casually, these distinctions very consciously we all do make in our daily interactions with others...with innately leading one being aware of...someone who feels as a 'positive' person...and other perhaps one feels is a 'negative' person...which is subjectively experienced by one without any other external convictions...just instead through energy aura perception... The ultimate distinction awareness comes from one's conscious awareness...and much accurately with precision when it is perceived from Soul conscious awareness discerning intuition...

Everything exists with contrast...there is no absolute universal grey... If there is perceived grey, then both black and white must both absolutely exist separately... In this illusionary Maya universe, it is impossible to perceive any existence that is excluded of the principles of duality and relativity... everything has an opposite...and exists because of the other...

**"There are roses…
And there are thorns…
Both emerging from the same branch stem…
Sharing the stem platform of existence…
Yet with distinctive expressional existence…
One stings expressing hurtful deterrence…
Other providing expressional Love fragrance…"**

Hugh Shergill

The human being existence is no exception… There are absolutely two distinct human conscious beings…opposite of one another and yet co-exist in this illusionary Maya existence because of the respective other…if not, the Soul being without the Maya being would immediately escape the Maya web entrapment and reach unrestricted liberation climatically in the Maya leela play realm… And a Maya being without a Soul being would cease to exist as the Maya stage would immediately be non existent without the presence of Soul beings… Each requires the other's presence on this Maya stage and ultimately in the Maya leela play…required yet never merged…

**"Oil and water never merge…
Truth and illusion never merge…"**

Ignorance is perceived bliss… Since existence, human beings have been illusionary ignorant through the Maya illusionary facade, by defining and categorizing a human being based on sex, physicality, status, race, nationality, religion, political, and other frivolous illusionary distinctions… When in all core reality there is, yes, indeed a distinction… only one and only one sole distinction…as which without Maya projection would not ever exist as relativity and duality is Maya mirror itself… Therefore, yes there are just two contrasting relative dual distinctions of human beings…a human being with a soul… and a soul less human being…

"The ultimate illusion is to deceive you at your most comfort, common, intelligent, logical, perception…taking you away from actual reality by presenting the ultimate illusion reality…as what appears similar to you…a similar appearing biological human being as yourself…however it is actually completely opposite to you…"

**"Looking into the mirror…
A comforting familiar…
Is it truly my vision?…
Or mere masked illusion?…
I see my reflection existence…
Yet what is seen by the consequence?…"**

Hugh Shergill

Maya Leela

Maya Being... The Soul Less Being...

"Asura...the Anti-Soul being"

Rig Veda
(the first humankind known written scriptures)

Asuras...are the contrasting opposite of Suras... 'Asura' is an entity devoid of any possible Soul energetic entangled interaction with the Divine... The word 'Asur' defined is 'Anti-Rhythmic' an entity devoid of being in tune with Divinity rhythm... In rhythm 'Sur' referenced is 'Divinity Rhythm' the rhythmic connection of the Divine creator and its Soul creation...'Divinity Entanglement' is always infinitely entangled...connected...always engaged rhythmically...however an 'Asura' is an entity infinitely devoid of Divinity Rhythm...a human being incapable to be in tune with the Rhythm of Divine...the 'in tune' is Soul energy...therefore an 'non tune' Asura is a soul less entity indefinitely...an absolute soul less human being...

Vedas called them the 'Asur'... 'Sura' is referred to as the energetic light of Divine...in rhythm of Divine...that is the soul energy...the respective masculine energetic form as Deva...the respective feminine energetic form as Devi... Asura is the contrasting energetic duality consequence of Divine in the Maya stage realm... Out of rhythm of Divine... the Anti-Deva... the Anti-Devi...the diabolical soul less entity...consequential existence and occupance strictly confined to the Maya stage illusion realm...with absolutely no possibility of liberating higher access...

Soul Being...Sura...Sura Deva/Devi...

Maya Being...Asura...Asura Maya...

Divinity Existence vs Creation Consequence...

Maya's spiritual warfare battle is the play of Maya Leela itself...forever since the play's existence... where Suras play perform against the Asuras in the illusionary Maya Leela play stage... Divinity has no opposing force as it is all force...yet upon the creation of the Maya realm...a creative side effect is born where duality and relativity also comes into play along with the Maya Leela play...where even the Divine creator itself must face its creation consequence...it's opposing force...its energetic nemesis... throughout all ages and yugas...infinite multi-verses...this has occurred and shall continue occur as this is the fundamental essence of the realm of Maya...

For the Divine expression of Shakti Durga...
There is also its asura nemesis Mahishasura...

For the Divine expression of Rama...
There is also its asura nemesis Ravana...

For the Divine expression of Krishna...
There is also its asura nemesis Kansa...

And so forth...for the infinite Divinity's conflict with its consequence legendary examples of its Maya realm existential experience...

Sura Deva/Devi versus Asura Maya...

A spiritual warfare eternal battle...
Forever in existence...
Played forever on the realm...
Of Maya Leela...

Your soul is a primary example of this spiritual warfare battle that you have knowingly or most likely unknowingly have, are ongoing, and shall continue to be facing and fighting with your opposing soul less forces...

Maya Confession...

"Maya: I shall make a confession...
  Now for my most profound illusion...
  A similar looking familiar being...
  Yet absolute opposite to your being...
  I am going to present you many...
  Yet there is not a soul in any...
  All theatrics orchestrated to entrap...
  Awareness will instead counter trap...
  Compelled to perceive the world as it be...
  Yet who unveils the world...
  Shall be the..."

Hugh Shergill

The Soul Less Beings...

As there is no Soul...another term to truly define Maya beings would be 'soul less beings' which is essentially absolutely correct term...maya beings are absolutely soul less entities...as in reality, majority population in society predominantly consists of these soul less entities...that are wearing the Maya mask of illusion by disguising themselves as almost identical beings to soul beings...yet in reality are the absolute opposing energetic force to the Divine spark of soul... A diabolical soul less entity...placed opposite you on the stage of Maya Leela...

Indeed, absolutely undoubtedly...Maya beings hold no or any potential capacity for soul energy consciousness, just like a lab created biological human being clone... however the Maya being and their purpose of existence is still importantly valuable...as every existence has a reactive duality consequence... A soul requires a non soul relativity...for the Maya Leela play to exist... Maya is the Divine's stage, and any creation being created with the exclusive purpose for the Maya Leela play to continue exist, requires the existence of a Maya being... Without these soul less entities...there would be no conflict in the play script for the primary performing soul being...thus the Maya Leela play itself would ultimately collapse and vanish... Just like the earthly realm to remain intact requires the force of gravity and the solar system operational dynamics for existence... Similarly, the play of Maya Leela requires the force of the entrapping soul less beings of Maya... Therefore, each being... Both soul being and Maya being are respective co-performers in the Maya Leela play...each with their respective dedicated roles...

Conflict is the seed of the play... Without conflict...there is no act...without the act... there is no character...without character...there is no story...without the story...there is no play script...thus the existence of conflict is absolutely necessary in every layer of the play script...from one act to another... scene after scene...conflict is the seed of the play...

As the protagonist only play performs if also the antagonist exists... Both day and night both must exist for each for the play of the complete day to exist...that is the Divine conflicting beauty of the play of Maya Leela...protagonist versus antagonist forever in conflict in the realm of the play... both beings are either Divine's existence or Divine's consequence... each serving contrasting positions in the Maya Leela play... One is Divinity's existence...the other Divinity's consequence... True existence of the protagonist soul performer requires awareness of the soul less consequence... Become aware... Be aware... yet Beware... For the soul's victory play...

Catch here is...the soul performer requires to perform the play of Maya Leela successfully as the stepping stone towards the eternal escapism...the Divine mergence bliss realm of Moksha experiencing Nirvana... In order for the soul to perform the play...the play requires conflict resistance in order to perform...therefore the play requires the soul less maya being to provide conflicting resistance for the soul being performer in order for it to perform optimally and successfully...

What purpose would a gym serve if there was no resistance equipment...yet the individual visiting that gym would still exist...however without individuals visiting the gym...the gym would inevitably shut down...the gym is the Maya Leela play stage...resistance equipment are the maya beings...the gym visitor is the soul performer...

Soul being does not directly require the soul less maya being to exist...however the soul being does require the soul less maya being to exist in order to perform in the play of Maya Leela... Contrastingly, the soul less maya being requires both the soul being's existence and its energy to exist...in order to perform and exist in the play of Maya Leela...which for it is a limited confined existence is exclusive to the Maya realm only...as there is no soul...therefore no possibility of higher ascension and Divine mergence...

Soul's victory over the soul less is the key of victory climax of the play...escapism victory leading to the eternal realm of liberating Moksha...experiencing eternal bliss of Nirvana for the soul performer...

Maya Being Identification...

Identifying and preparing for the Maya Being...
Is not discriminatory...

"Identification is not discriminatory...
 It is extractingly identifying...
 And preparing...
 For the existing relativity duality...

 First hint of sunrise...
 While still present in the night...
 Identifying and preparing...
 For the emerging day...
 Is not discriminatory...

 First hint of sunset...
 While still present in the day...
 Identifying and preparing...
 For the emerging night...
 Is not discriminatory...

 Identification is not discriminatory...
 It is extractingly identifying...
 And preparing...
 For the existing relativity duality..."

Hugh Shergill

"There are too many people,
 and too few human beings."

Robert Zend (Renowned Poet / Writer)

"Some people feel the rain.
 Others just get wet."

Bob Marley
(Renowned Singer / Poet / Writer / Musician)

Maya Leela

**"One may smile,
and smile,
and be a villain"**

**William Shakespeare
(Renowned Poet / Playwright)
Hamlet, Act 1, Scene 5**

Maya Being is an Asuric Being…
Asuric Soul Less Energy…
A Diabolical Entity…

**"Some have character…
Some are a character…"**

Demons in one era were cannibalistic…indulging and consuming human flesh…similarly Asuric Maya beings instead consume Soul being's soul energy for survival existence…

Asuric energy is extreme havoc…greedy…wants to take all…parasitically spelled…going beyond the obvious materialism fed…the asuric energy requires the soul energy fuel for the continuation burning existence of the asuric flame… If the soul fuel burner…cut its supply…the asuric presence will destructively vanish…

In the Vedas…176 primary Asura types are mentioned…each differentiates from the other in certain specific innate characteristics…names are available and vedically documented in the Veda and Puranas scriptures…for those interested in further researching them…I will however not state them… as each name hold specific diabolical asuric energy mantra…which I refuse to include in my writings out of responsibility…as I don't want any reader to imbibe that negative diabolical energy while reading… Instead, the attentive focus will be on the various traits of the asuric energy and their operated entities…
Each soul being shall cross…depending on their particular karmic play script…cross paths with at the very least more than one…if not many …of these specific asura types throughout each Maya Leela play lifetime…

**"No Diabolical Possession…
For the Diabolical Itself…"**

What authentically exists within is one's core existence…no other external possession will influence what is already saturated within…for the Asuric soul less maya being…they are exactly what they are…there is no diabolical possession…as it is that itself…therefore there is no reforming nor saving hope for them…indeed they are an integral part of the Maya Leela play and are performing the antagonist role as dedicated to them…however there is no soul energy…a soul less entity…a contrasting opposite of a human being with a soul…Harsh as it sounds…even the extreme oxymoron 'Walking Dead' fits perfect descriptively when describing these diabolical soul less entities…

Indeed shocking is its reality…yet it is the shocking reality…in certain revelations…truth is more stranger than fiction…as truth is not confined to any narrative…it presents not one prefers but what actually is…

Moment has arrived to further explore the intricacies of Maya Leela…its illusions and by-product delusions…detailing the reveal with details…

"The play becomes entertaining…
With the details in the script…"

CHAPTER 7.

REVEALING
THE REVEALED

"What is a Script…

Without its Twists and Turns…"

"History is the mystery…

Perceives objectively…

Perceived subjectively…

One that does not know…

Believes it knows…

Believes it knows…

One that does not know…

Where the known is recorded…

The knowing remains unrecorded…"

Hugh Shergill

Maya Leela

The reveal is not just a reveal...but in all actuality...revealing the revealed...revelational re-unveil...unveiling...from the most ancient recorded textual evidence of the vedic era...all the way to the more recent yoga era...

Truth Roots...

"Tree's truth remains rooted...
  Easily enduring all storms...
  Tree's fragile leaves looted...
  Easily breezing on untruth norms...
  Grounded deep truth connected...
  Remains energetic in all its forms..."

Hugh Shergill

Four Seasons Maya World...

Four Maya World Yugas...Decoded...

The veil of illusion itself is essentially energy... thus constantly in moving fluctuation...from dark to almost transparent... with further glitches and revelations of truth events piercing through... from cycles of new world formation transits... These veil fluctuations are similar to four seasons of Maya world...the four world yugas:

Satya Yuga...
Treta Yuga...
Dwapara Yuga...
Kali Yuga...

These seasons each lasting for multiple centuries each...repeats the four seasons of Maya world cycle consecutively... with each world dominantly concentrating on a particular emphasis of the world of Maya...

1. Satya Yuga...

Satya Yuga... 'Satya' is the Sanskrit word defined as the 'Truth'...the age of truth... this is the spiritually most advanced season of the Maya world... the Divinely blessed season...where the Maya veil is so apparent that it becomes transparent...where the truth makes it perceive it as almost non-existing with the vision of truth...suric and asuric energies were acknowledged and actually labeled non hesitantly...a soul less asuric demon being was acknowledged and referred to as a 'Asur' and that was clearly defined without any exceptions...the ancient Vedas and Puranas make hundreds of references directly...as in this era of purity...rightfully the righteous Soul beings prevailed with Love and truth...as Love and truth prevailed above all...

2. Treta Yuga...

Treta Yuga...'Treta' is the Sanskrit word defined as the 'Three'...the age of three...triad of energy emphasis on all three realms of consciousness...all three conscious realms of existence experience... First, the immediate physical 3D three dimensional conscious realm... Second, is the 4D fourth dimensional sub conscious realm... Third, is the 5D fifth dimensional super conscious realm that merges completely with the Divine itself... In this era...the Maya veil is foggy yet with the energy of higher consciousness light within...one is able to still see past the veil...through the Maya realm...with soul conscious ascension by the soul discovering themselves within...

3. Dwapara Yuga...

Dwapara Yuga...'Dwapara' is the Sanskrit word defined as 'Two'...the age of two...the age of duality consequence...duality ignorance...conflict of duality... Spiritual warfare battles of the opposing duality forces facing each other for supreme dominance... Maya entrapment vs Maya escapism...Soul being vs Maya being... the age of spiritual war... Soul vs Soul less... this is the age of the epic Mahabharata war took place...where the Maya veil is pierced through with the arrow of soul truth in spiritual war... here the asuric soul less energies were massively dominated and destroyed by the Divine beings seeking the reemergence of the pure Satya yuga era...yet the Maya realm exists on the power of duality and relativity...destruction of mass asuric energetic forces did not eliminate them...but created an even more powerful reemergence consequence...which lead to asuric world domination...Kali Yuga...our current world dominance that is being experienced...

4. Kali Yuga...

Please note: do not mistake 'Kali Yuga' with the Divinity's Shakti form of Goddess 'Kali'...here darkness refers to the Divine darkness realm of Turiya itself...where all time and space creation and destruction manifests...Divine Shakti form of Kali is both the gentle loving creative mother Shakti energy and yet also fierce dynamic protective warrior energy...a very powerful dynamic Divinity Shakti form that is extremely transcendent of both destruction and creation of all that exists...energetically extremely powerful and extremely dynamic respectively as it is Divinity...

Kali Yuga...'Kali' is the Sanskrit word defined as 'Darkness'...here darkness refers to the age of darkness...further, one may even refer it as the age of blindness...the age of destruction through ignorance...the Maya veil of illusion is so dark that it appears as the Divine realm of Turiya itself... the Divine stage of all existence... Kali Yuga is the era of vengeance for the diabolical asuric maya beings by dominating and making the collective soul beings suffer acutely... After the Dwapara yuga, the diabolical asuric soul less in the spiritual war were dominantly defeated...prominently due to the epic mass war of the Mahabharata...resulting in a very large number of the diabolical asuric maya beings were completely wiped off the Maya realm itself...hence asuric energy field made a comeback vengeance by creating total world dominance... the Kali Yuga...world of Maya veil hidden in diabolical darkness...resulting the majority perceive this world in deep darkness of blind ignorance... blindly following the enslaving protocols for existence without even questioning it once...the ignorance of perceiving the immediate world as it is all... the Maya realm's confined three dimensional soul less beings dominate and rule over the eternal Divine spark of Soul beings unfortunately...where 'Doctored' is no longer defined as 'Interference' but falsely 'Healing' and a means of 'Dominance'... yet every dominance has a saturation point before it itself explodes...the heavy Maya entrapping asuric energy leads to multitude of mass world destructions... inevitable destructions to reset and recreate the Maya world again by revealing the Divine truth... repeating back the Maya world cycle to the purity of Satya yuga...

Currently and unfortunately for the soul beings...we are experiencing the Kali Yuga Maya world season...and this is the current era when this publication is being written... however some publications and books survive centuries... With great optimism...perhaps someone in the future lifetimes ahead reading this then...it may fortunately experiencing the Satya Yuga Maya season again or almost at the commence of it...fortunately a moment of blissful euphoria world era of truth... Well for now...Kali Yuga world domination still exists... This is the four seasons of Maya world yugas...decoded...

Bhagavad Geeta...
Decoded...

Jñāna Vijñāna Yog
Chapter 7, Verses 3 to 6

"Amongst thousands of persons,
  hardly one strives for perfection;
  and amongst those
  who have achieved perfection,
  hardly one knows me in truth."
  7.3

"Earth, water, fire, air, space,
  mind, intellect, and ego
  these are eight components of
  My material energy."
  7.4

"Such is My inferior energy.
  But beyond it,
  O mighty-armed Arjun,
  I have a superior energy.
  This is the jīva Shakti (the soul energy),
  which comprises
  the embodied souls
  who are the
  basis of life in this world."
  7.5

"Know that all living beings
  are manifested by these
  two energies of Mine.

I am the source of the entire creation,
and into Me it again dissolves."
7.6

Bhagavad Geeta
Jñāna Vijñāna Yog
Chapter 7, Verses 3 to 6

"Sometimes to hide something...
 You have to keep it at plain sight..."

Bhagavad Geeta...Jñāna Vijñāna Yog...chapter seven...verses three to six...could not have made it any more clear precise reveal...Lord Krishna reveals to Arjun directly about the two distinct beings that exist on this Maya realm...one is strictly material based (Maya Being) and the other is the embodied souls with Soul energy...Jiva Shakti (Soul Being)...

Above, please feel free to reread these above four verses with more emphasis on the underlined words...here is revelating reveal:

'Hardly knows me in Truth'

Even those perceived perfected enlightened beings are devoid of knowing the actual truth...
the verses have been read, recited, repeated for centuries... Sometimes to hide something... You have to keep it in plain sight... Reading texts extremely close to one's eyes also results in a blur... Ironically...the information has been right in front of us...however not occurred to us...

'Material Energy'

Human being's biological existence, including all elements of earth involved in its creation...to the creation of mind, intellect, and even one's ego...is all merely material...referred to as 'Inferior Energy'...

'Inferior Energy'

Solely Human being's biological existence is referred to as 'Material Energy' which is 'Inferior Energy'... This 'Inferior Energy' is the 'Maya Being'...existence is solely on a biological human being level...devoid of Soul energy...

'Superior Energy'

'Jiva Shakti' which is 'Soul Energy' are the 'Embodied Souls' who are the 'Basis of Life' in this world... which is the 'Soul Being' the Divine sparks of soul energy living in this Maya world...

'Two Energies'

All living biological beings are manifested by these two energies...the key words here are the distinct 'Two Energies' not 'Both Energies' or 'Combined Energies'... Even the non-tangible elements of the human being...both mind and ego is included in the 'Inferior Energy' then why not also include the non-tangible 'Soul Energy' in that? That would have been a complete oxymoron... The reason is that soul energy is the Divine 'Superior Energy'... it is distinct...it is separate...it is uncommon... it is special...it is superior...it is Divine...resulting in distinct separate 'Two Energies' resulting in the manifestation of two separate energetic human beings...one with a Soul (Soul Being)...the other Soul Less (Maya Being)...

Bhagavad Geeta...Decoded...

Divinity is always one...completely complete...it is however its projection onto the realm of Maya that emerges manifest of all perceived existences into existence through duality and relativity... all energy beyond the core of Divine exists as its projection through duality and relativity...even as immediate entrance of Divine's energy projection as Maya...it takes a synergy form of both masculine and feminine energies...Shiva and Shakti...these two distinct energies exists parallel in all perceived existence on the entire realm of Maya...one cannot perceive to exist without the other...perhaps one is more dominant in one however both energies remain present in everything in existence... Shiva Shakti is incorrectly perceived as religious reference...as in all actuality it is all perceived reality...energy is not defined by labels...it is labels that are defined by the energies... As every biological human existence has a certain feminine and masculine energy that emerges together for its existence...the two sides within the human body...the nadis...the ida and pingala...the yin and yang...each distinctly unique but absolutely requiring each other... synergy within energy...

Similarly, there is a distinct dichotomy of all living being energy...it is these two distinct energies... both are living energies...both individually complete but distinctly separate... Two energies is the key distinction...energy that merges with another energy is one not distinct...therefore what is distinct... is separate independent...and shall always remain separate and independent... Two distinct energies classified for all living beings...one is living matter energy...the other is living soul energy...both Divinely created...yet both contrastingly exclusive...one is Divine's soul spark existence...the Maya's consequence material existence... One is soul living existence...the Divine energy consciousness... encapsulated within the biological vessel... The other biological living existence as the illusionary Maya realm consequence... Both are two distinct energies...there is no intertwined mergence...indeed one may parallelly include the other through residence...such as masculine and feminine energies within each existence...existing as Shiva Shakti...parallelly coexisting however never merging into the other...just as oil and water...both may exist together within the sea...however shall never merge into each together...always separate...always distinct...always unique...

"Perceived living distinctions...
  Gender race status appearances...
  All are frivolous illusions...
  Of perceived false perceptions...
  Truth lies in the ultimate reality...
  All existences in a single plurality...
  The duality of all living energy...
  Coexisting in maya synergy...
  Soul energy living...
  The soul being...
  Matter energy living...
  The maya being...
  All the rest appearing...
  Is illusionary occurring..."

Hugh Shergill

All living matter in existence...living Maya matter includes all forms of existence...from a human being to to that single stand of grass...has the potential of having soul energy...a soul living being has a soul that resides in a particular physical living Maya matter such as a human being existence...yet all living maya matter shall not have soul residence...as if that was the case...then all living matter should have soul conscious energy...from every human existence to even that micro spec of each individual bacteria existence...this is impossible...karmic turmoil Maya realm destruction itself...as we would not be even in human existence with such destructive karmic effects of killing billions of soul existences in living bacteria matter...each time through even the simple hygiene act of washing one's hands even once... There is absolutely living Maya matter in all living forms of existence without soul energy... therefore resulting that there are absolutely human beings in living existence without a soul...

"Being amongst is soul's illusion...
  Soul solely enters the room of mirrors...
  Tricked seeing its soul's multiple reflections...
  Soul yet remains sole among the illusions...
  Triumph by separating soul from the person...
  Being amongst is soul's illusion..."

Hugh Shergill

Maya Leela

Revisiting the Ancient History...

The Vedic Era Vedas Puranas Reference...

The ancient Vedic era, which exists as one of the first history documented human civilization and its respective recorded written texts, the Vedas...being among the oldest sacred texts known to humankind history which are systematically broken down further into subcategories of individual texts that includes the Upanishads...the first ever known Maya Leela reveal ever documented exists in these very sacred texts...

"The Upanishads have been
 the acknowledged source of
 numerous profound philosophies and religions"

Sri Aurobindo
(Renowned Yogi / Poet / Spiritual Reformer)

One the first major human existence dualism conflict of Maya documented, emerged from the ancient vedic civilization era... The vedic era was a global soul awareness phenomena that was not confined to South Asia/India only...as identical vedic referenced archaeological evidence was discovered in different opposite global regions...such as India, Central America, South America, Arabia, Eastern Asia and many other regions...some discovered and some yet to be still discovered... Indeed, India led the vedic movement as the largest concentration of evidence, monuments, and scriptures were discovered and or remained preserved... The most known corresponding vedic texts...are the Vedas... These ancient sacred texts originated in the ancient vedic era India, composed in the Vedic Sanskrit language... these are multi-series texts consist of the ancient Sanskrit literature and scriptures...these are considered as the direct Divine reveal revelations experienced by ancient sages Maharishis while tapped and indulged in super soul conscious deep meditative states...

Apauruseya Vedas...
'Alien' Knowledge...
Not of 'Human' Intellect...
But 'Super Human' Intellect...

It is fascinating, these Vedas are also labeled to be 'Apauruseya'... meaning that they are not of human intelligence...actually Alien knowledge...not of human intellect...but of super human intellect... therefore also labeled as being 'Authorless'...which is further fascinating in itself...as the scriptures were written, so conveniently could have been the dedicated writer's name... So indeed commendable it is, of how these utmost respective ancient sages disregarded credit for the revelation unveil, which is a gesture that clearly demonstrates a true soul being essence of one...with no regard to be credited or referred to...with much higher and greater regard for the Divine by crediting oneself as "authorless" with complete undisclosed identity of this illusionary ego existence of one...devoiding one of any praise or accolades...which is indeed highly admirable...utmost ego less being gesture...a feat since then yet to be replicated...

Religions are structured institutions that perhaps at best act as a broad compass route to angle one to reach its Divine destination...yet to arrive precisely at the destination...one has to go beyond the routed angle path and enter a more precise destination soul path...that soul path is knowledge... knowledge is soul's spirituality...soul's energy force is only truth...truth to know...

Knowledge has no religion...all religions core   foundational revelations are perhaps to certain degree soul felt...however it is the interpretations and implementations that one effortlessly deviates from...as the only true religion is truth...the untampered truth...

As most historical documented references... unfortunately the Vedas have also not been immune to being doctored with...and doctored they are...as unfortunately even further conquered intentions for particular religious control through illusionary entrapment spreading...by intentional destroying of revelation reveal source texts...manipulative restructuring of religious interpretations to suit certain societal, cultural, and political purposes...

Fortunately, of what little remains...certain revelation resources do resonate...especially the reveals of Vedic era knowledge, and in particular the Vedas, which were never religion based... instead mystical revelations... 'Veda' means knowledge, not an organizational institution... As there is a clear distinction between information and organization...although vedic civilization is still referenced by many as being the ancestral seed of all religions... However, vedas and vedic knowledge advocated not any confined religious structuring, as they existed before the time of any structured religion was ever documented, instead advocating one's self discovery through soul knowledge living... However, later certain organizations did regard some certain vedic knowledge and included the vedas at their own convenient organized interpretations...also unfortunately by further excluding and tampering other crucial vedic knowledge which was an inconvenient hindrance in setting up an organization... As a relatively simple example, in the vedic era, there was absolutely no marriage institution nor concept... However, as every religion advocates marriage with certain ceremonial rituals...it was therefore interpreted and conveniently included...when in all reality, what did not exist, can not possibly have a ritual ceremony... As no one participates in the act of marriage who never marries... Thus, it is contradicting to read marriage ceremonial ritual references from the vedic era in the vedas... One of the factors, is unfortunately due to the frivolous societal stigma that still exists on the so called 'illegitimate child' when in absolute reality, there is nothing that exists as illegitimate in nature... as existence in essence is always pure...a beautiful rose is a beautiful pure rose...and shall always remain so...excreting exuberance of purity fragrance... In all truth, each one of us, all of our previous biological existent ancestors were also so called illegitimate children, absolutely born out of wedlock... Therefore, out of specific organization intentions...to suppress such perceived harsh realities to be more suitable organizational societal thoughts and standards... many revelation treasures of vedic era sacred knowledge...was either tampered with, deliberately destroyed, and or deliberately secretly kept hidden...

Similarly and unfortunately, such happened with the vedic reference on the emphasis of how all perceived existence in the illusionary infinite universes exists in absolute relativity and duality...as every existence of energy exists with an equal opposing energy force... This absolute duality is also the foundation of every human being's existence...as each human existence is nothing but a particular collective expression of energy...this duality distinction of the human being's existence in this Maya illusionary existence is inevitably present... there are absolutely indeed two distinct human beings existing...and this is not referring to sex gender, as that is the relativity and duality of reproduction energy... The energetic field of human beings exists with two distinct opposing forces...resulting in two distinct opposing human beings... This knowledge was concerning for particular organizations... as any information, that clearly simplifies one's self knowing journey...by creating awareness that requires no other additional assistance other than one's truth of oneself...which is its direct connect with the Divine...soul consciousness awareness living...escapism efforts from the Maya jaal web entrapment...by being aware of all the Maya traps and the Maya trap advocate performers... This one's awareness, immediately eliminates majority organization potential followers...which is definitely not an ideal scenario for those seeking power to control the majority...which is a fundamental requirement for any organization to remain relevant or survivingly exist...which are the fundamentals of Maya jaal web entrapment...

Intentionally Hidden Knowledge...

Indeed it is not merely a rumour...actually far from it...even legends have emphasized it throughout historically... Well, without getting into any specific reveals of the discovered details...one must acknowledge being an experiential soul witness of this fact...from lifetimes to one's immediate multi decades of deep research journey...as one has been exposed to unintentionally unforeseen 'shocking glimpses' of this reveal...many enclosed scriptures known as broadly 'the undiscovered vedas' of the ancient vedas remain discreetly circulating in specific families, groups and communities for multi-centuries...unfortunately the motives are far from noble potency knowledge protection...but unfortunately instead taking the upper hand in exploiting knowledge for specific advantages...which ultimately is power...as nothing is more powerful than knowledge...only knowledge is forever power...

The Knowing Leaf...
Nadi Granthas...
First Concept of Library Source...

A parallel phenomenon that exists and circulates in particular societal groups is the fascinating 'Nadi Leafs'...specifically the 'Nadi Granthas'...'Nadi' means pulse...'Grantha' means to tie together sacred knowledge...therefore Nadi Granthas are pulses of sacred knowledge...these specific sacred knowledge were written by ancient Indian sages on palm leafs...the leafs were preserved by being rubbed in peacock oil and written in sanskrit using a pen like sharp object called ezhuthani...these leafs were stored carefully in discrete locations of temples and some even in certain secret chambers of highly royal palaces...as these nadi granthas are the first evidence of the library concept...instead of books...it was carefully stored preserved leafs of sacred scriptures knowledge...revealing revelating revelations of perceived past, present, future...unfortunately many of these sacred scriptures were either purposely destroyed by specific ill intentions and or ruthless invasions...fortunately what remains indeed is very fascinating...now majority of these sacred leafs are stored in southern India in certain libraries and temples...also some are secretly kept within certain particular groups, families and particular secret organizations... Majority of these scriptures that revealed the soul less diabolical asuric entities have been deliberately kept hidden from the general population...due to power control domination...as what reveals its power...often leaks its power...

Suras 'The Sura Maya'
Soul Being Protagonist

vs

Asuras 'The Asura Maya'
Maya Being Antagonist

Fortunately, of the remaining and non hidden extraction information of the documented vedas, one of the major revelating details still exists...revealing the two opposition distinct forces of existence in this human body Maya existence...it is revealed as the 'Suras' and the 'Asuras'...as mentioned earlier, it is two energetic forces that are either rhythmically 'in tune' with Divinity or 'out of tune' with Divinity...

Divinity is always one and complete...any further branching projection spark of Divinity is still Divine and complete with no sub categories of Divinity...the entire sea and drop of sea is as complete... as volume does not determine completeness...the Divine Maya projects either soul living or matter living...there is no superior Divine nor inferior Divine...simply two distinct energies of which one contains soul conscious energy reflection...the 'in tune' Divine energy... the highly gloss shining Divinity's reflection energy... Energy that reflects back to its Divine source itself...existence beyond the Maya Leela play canvas existence... The other is Maya's duality consequential biological existence...a non Divine reflect energy...the 'out of tune' with Divine energy...a dull matte non reflective energy that exists only on the canvas of the Maya Leela play realm...

Soul Being vs Maya Being

Soul being is an expansive infinite soul energy...
A Macro Being...

Maya being is Maya confined realm existence...
A Micro Being...

The Reflect Effect...
Gloss Reflect...
Matte Effect...

A metaphorical artistic example... The Divine artist creates two almost identical arts by painting the identical image on two identical Maya canvases...with the only discrepancy of painting one with high gloss paint that actually holds the ability to reflect back on to the Divine artist...where the Divine artist sees its own Divinity reflection in the painting...while the other almost identical painting exists as matte paint...the distinct difference lies in the two Divine types of paint...as all creation on the Divine's Maya realm exists in duality relativity...for gloss to exist there also must be relatively matte existence...one sura soul gloss and the other asura matter matte...unaware are both paintings of what each is...as in dimness the gloss painting perceives itself as identical to the matte painting...it is the Divine's will that shines illumination that vanishes the illusion where gloss painting realizes its distinction and Divinity's sparkling stars of reflection...gloss may accumulate dust yet always hold the potential to wipe away all to uncover the Divine reflect...yet matte shall never transform into the gloss reflect...

Suras 'The Sura Maya' Soul Being

vs

Asuras 'The Asura Maya' Maya Being

Opposite energies are conflicting energies... Both Suras and Asuras respectively represent the Divine source dual energy as projected in the Maya living existence form...as either living matter and living soul...that is a distinct dichotomy of energy that is ever eternally repellent towards each other... as each living existence is either Asuras...the Maya living matter (maya being)... or Suras...the soul living matter (soul being)...always in energy conflict...entrapment vs escapism...core positive vs core negative... Protagonist vs Antagonist... Soul Genesis vs Soul's Nemesis... All played out through the Maya Leela play of perceived life...

"Suras...the Benevolent aspect...Soul being...
  Asuras...the Malevolent aspect...Maya being..."

The Asuras, the inauspicious malevolent aspect of the Divine's Maya realm duality consequence, this is the antagonistic performer of Maya Leela locked in eternal battle with the Suras, the protagonist performer of Maya Leela...the auspicious benevolent aspect of the Divine...

This vedic era reveal is one of the first major known human existence dualism energy discovery ever documented... This directly represents the Maya being, as the 'Asura Maya' the malevolent aspect, as the Maya duality consequence representation form...versus...the soul being, the 'Sura Maya' the benevolent aspect, as the soul representation form directly of Divine source itself, which exists infinitely beyond the realms of the illusion realm of Maya...

"Nothing will come of nothing"

William Shakespeare
(Renowned Poet / Playwright)
King Lear / Act I / Scene 1 / line 99

A key major difference between Asura and Sura is the distinction contrast of...one is forever empty incomplete 'out of tune' Asura...and the other one is forever fulfilled complete Divinity 'in tune' Sura... the soul devoid Asuras are extremely narcissistic, selfish and egotistical...they are all...they are convinced that they can manipulate and coerce their way through anything...to ultimately achieve everything...to further their desire...their soul devoid existence is so twisted that everything they come across in their quest for material fulfillment is to be exploited by any means...innately spiritually empty vessels that lust to fill their forever empty being by extreme greed and selfishness...all is what they perceive...unlike the sura...the soul being...who is innately aware that they are complete beings of the Divine and with much humility aware that much more exists than what is perceived...

Soul is the Divine driving force...

The eternal battle of the asura maya and sura maya is the drive of soul consciousness... duality versus non-duality... soul consciousness is the driving determining force of remaining either Maya existence or attaining Maya escapism by achieving liberation...asura maya exist as long as Maya exists...therefore it is important for the maya being that the soul conscious being sura maya remains unliberated and maya entrapped... Sura maya on the other hand must fight this asura maya's resistance and rise higher towards... ascension...liberation...non-duality...moksha... nirvana... euphoria bliss beyond the maya jaal web of entrapment...

In one specific Vedas, The Kaushitaki Upanishad, it is clearly stated that the Suras Indra was much weaker than the Asuras when he did not know its own 'Atman' a.k.a 'Atma'...its soul...its true authentic self... However, once Indra had the self-knowledge, he became independent, sovereign and was totally victorious over the Asuras...

"The one who knows its inner self...
 Gains independence, sovereignty...
 and is unaffected by all evil"

Kaushitaki Upanishad
(Renowned Ancient Vedas, Book Four)

The suras's 'soul discovery' is its victory edge factor...otherwise it would have also been equally documented that similarly the existing opposition asuras's victory edge is also its 'soul discovery'... which is impossible...as asuras are absolutely devoid of soul...what does not exist...shall never be mentioned nor discovered...

Synonym Sanskrit words...
For the Soul Less Maya being...

'Atma Vaheen' - The One Devoid of Soul
'Asur Maya' - Diabolical Soul Less Entity
'Asura' - Nemesis Entity of the Divine Soul

The Atma Vaheen...
The Soul Devoid...

The ancient vedic references also commonly labeled the asura maya as the 'Atma Vaheen'...which is essentially a living being devoid of actually having a soul... This term was very commonly associated with the soul devoid in the vedic times...yet unfortunately it was deliberately excluded through destroying documented references...both by the religious enthusiasts and then further through intruders...as any information that filters and extracts souls from non souls is undoubtedly a hindrance in any potential group, tribal, culture, and religion formation...as ultimately what is the actual role for religion if there is actually no soul consciousness within the individual...therefore these religious fanatics and intruders practiced that whatever does not serve their cause is better off sacrificed for the cause...unfortunately creating perpetual spiritual obstacles for the sura maya...the soul beings...

Fortunately, what has remained is low key hints of the diabolical asura soul less 'Atma Vaheen' word references passed on linguistically through the vedic lifestyle devoted...from generation to generation...especially more concentrated in South India...which fortunately suffered less intruder destruction in comparison to northern Indian regions...

Atma vaheen beings were easily identified and were very cautiously associated with...as the preservation of one's soul energy was considered as the highest form of spiritual practice...any activity or beings that caused an hindrance to this spiritual desire was perceived as a threat...which was best dealt with avoidance and to strictly disassociate...

The following are two powerful historically documented examples... yet highly controversial...due to the doctored legendary presentations...to deliberately suit and hide the fundamental foundation of the soul less duality existence...and the Maya jaal illusion entrapments of every possible Maya's realm Leela play... For historical researching enthusiasts...I would encourage to research for yourself...as it will certainly be a thought provoking paradigm shifting experience...

"Upon the illusion realm entry...
 Even Divinity forms a duality...
 Being its own creation...
 Resulting in duality consequence...
 Presence of the Divine...
 Presence amongst the Un-Divine..."

Hugh Shergill

Lakshmi's Goddess Duality Twin...Alakshmi...

Shakti Energy Goddess Lakshmi...is the Goddess of wealth, fortune, power, beauty, fertility and prosperity... Even her highly Divine entrance upon existence in the realm of Maya resulted in a non Divine duality consequence...through her Maya being twin Alakshmi...which a very few are actually aware of this...prepare for this...

Alakshmi means the one who is 'opposite' to Lakshmi and represents everything opposite to her... which represents everything dreadful... Divinity vs non Divinity's...Soul being vs Maya being... Auspicious vs Inauspicious... Divinity Devi vs Asuric illusion... Every energy has its opposite...even for the highly respective Divinity's Goddess form presenting itself on the Maya realm...creating an equal opposite form as well...this hidden twin phenomenon is often disregarded due to its highly inauspicious presence...however why is this so? How is this so? Are questions that are not only not addressed but hiddenly disregarded throughout the historical timeline... The Maya realm is so powerful that even Divine's Maya presence itself...results in an equal Un-Divine presence...

**"Divinity spark as Sita...
Takes the illusionary form...
As Maya Sita...
For the illusionary entrapment...
Of the entrapping dominant...
That dared to illusion Divinity...
Divinity thus provides its reciprocity...
illusionary creation bait...
Destroying the entire illusion state..."**

Hugh Shergill

Maya Sita...the Hidden illusion...

Ramayana... the Divine play of Maya Leela...

Ramayana is a prime example of the ultimate Divine play of Maya Leela...where Ravana's destruction comes from being intensely occupied into solidifying its asura dominance through Maya Jaal entrapment attempts against souls...daring even the impossible...by attempting to Maya illusion entrap Divinity itself... This is very interesting as modern interpretations of this Divine tale...certain power control Maya being religious fanatics conveniently left out two compelling revealing aspects of Ramayana that present and expose the the illusion of Maya Leela itself...Ravana's own reverse Maya Jaal entrapment destruction...and even more importantly, how Divinity flip the illusion play script through creating Sita's Maya realm duality consequence emergence in the form of 'Maya Sita'...

Maya Sita... the illusionary Maya's duality form of Sita... Whom Ravana kidnapped is not Sita but Sita's Maya projection...Maya Sita...the illusionary Maya projection of Sita...as it is impossible for a diabolical asura entity to perceive itself powerful enough to interfere and disrupt the destined script by actually having the arrogant audacity to kidnap Divinity's spark itself... Thus it was Divinity's illusion projection as Maya Sita...coming into formation by condemning the arrogance of Ravana on daring to entrap Divinity's spark itself...resulting in inversingly entrapping the entrapper itself...entrapping Ravana into its own Maya jaal web entrapment...regardless of its high intelligence, accolades and credentials... Ravana's destruction was inevitable due to its asuric deep entrapment existence arrogance in the realm of Maya that dared the Maya realm creator...

Authentic Soul Sita reemerges...only during the Agni pareeksha...the firing purification... Metaphorically represents not one stepping into burning fire but stepping into one's flaming unveillance truth... Sita's authentic soul reemergence process occurs as stepping out of the Maya illusion occurs...this is the lifting of the illusion veil process through fire purification... Divinely Sita's soul reemerges out from the Maya projection...after the Maya projection accomplished its goal of defeating Ravana through its own web of Maya Jaal play entrapment...

Agni pareeksha of flaming purification of Sita symbolizes the process of shedding illusionary Maya Sita and unveiling the authentic Soul Sita...this is literally every soul being's Maya's Leela journey...

To A More Recent Reference...
Sri Aurobindo Reveals in its own way...
Asuric Soul Less Maya beings...

Now to a more recent parallel reference...to re-emphasize the vedic era knowledge and referencial roots...through yogic knowledge...

It is an utmost privilege to share direct insightful excerpts of Sri Aurobindo, one of the leading founders of spiritual evolution of integral yoga...declaring that 'all life is Yoga'...where one does not give up the outer life to actually live a yogic lifestyle...as one is fully capable present in regular perceived life and able to still practice a full yoga spirituality living in every aspect of life...

What is about to be shared in the following are excerpted references of Sri Aurobindo's views during a very particular interesting questions and answers interview session taken place on 12th May 1929... as the following five paragraphs referenced are direct excerpts from Sri Aurobindo's response in regards to his views on these soul less beings...to which he referred to as 'Energy Vampires'... further astonishing is that this response occurred almost a century back...at a perceived time when energy scavenging entities were not even mainstream discovered nor in any form popular...let alone labeled... This is the reason why one respects Sri Aurobindo's response to the asked question... as its authentic soul energy clearly reacted and resonated...it authentically felt...it ascended and accomplished the realm of the unveiled...perhaps the defining labels differed from one...yet being aware of what actually is going on...is utmost commendable...where a water drop involuntarily blushes by the resonating flowing river...

What is being shared word by word respectively... Indeed, one does have the creative liberty to poetically translate...yet it is presented without any poetic translation...as one desires for you to feel the unfiltered undoctored intensity of Sri Aurobindo's each word when describing these soul less diabolical energy scavenging entities... Thus I kindly share the full excerpts...which is word by word in resonance with one's deep reality within...as what is said by Sri Aurobindo...is what one also feels... absolutely...undoubtedly...

Interestingly, what Sri Aurobindo describes as 'Energy Vampires' is exactly one's identical perception...exception of the defining label...indeed asuric soul less maya beings are also energy vampires without a doubt...however that is not one's primary reference label to use when one defines or refers to them...instead when describing them...one prefers to name them in the most ancient authentic rooted labels...just as it was first written, defined, and described in the very first scriptures ever known to humankind...the Rig Veda...as Asuras...Asur Maya...Atma Vaheen...the soul less maya beings... Further, what one feels Sri Aurobindo is describing as 'not human' and 'only human appearance' is referring to the fact that a real human is one with the Divine soul energy...and the mere appearance of a human is simply a soul less biological human entity...which is the asuric soul less maya being...

Sri Aurobindo's take on these Soul Less Entities...

Excerpted references from Sri Aurobindo's Questions and answering session (12th May 1929)
Source: Sri Aurobindo Ashram Library

Question:

"There are some human beings
 who are like vampires.
 What are they and why are they like that?"

Sri Aurobindo's Answer:

"They are not human; there is only a human form or appearance. They are incarnations of beings from the world that is just next to the physical, beings who live on the plane which we call the vital world. It is a world of all the desires and impulses and passions and of movements of violence and greed and cunning and every kind of ignorance; but all the dynamisms too are there, all the life-energies and all the powers. The beings of this world have by their nature a strange grip over the material world and can exercise upon it a sinister influence.

These beings, when in the human body, are not often conscious of what they really are. Sometimes they have a vague feeling that they are not quite human in the ordinary way. But still there are cases where they are conscious and very conscious; not only do they know that they do not belong to humanity but they know what they are, act in that knowledge and deliberately pursue their ends. The beings of the vital world are powerful by their very nature; when to their power they add knowledge, they become doubly dangerous.

These creatures, when in possession of an earthly body, may have the human appearance but they have not a human nature. Their habit is to draw upon the life-force of human beings; they attack and capture vital power wherever they can and feed upon it. If they come into your atmosphere, you suddenly feel depressed and exhausted; if you are near them for some time you fall sick; if you live with one of them, it may kill you.

The vital power incarnated in these beings is of a very material kind and it is effective only within a short distance. Ordinarily, if you do not live in the same house or if you are not in the same company with them, you do not come within their influence. But if you open some channel of connection or communication, through letters, for example, then you make possible an interchange of forces and are liable to be influenced by them even from a far distance.

The wisest way with these beings is to cut off all connection and have nothing to do with them, unless indeed you have great occult knowledge and power and have learned how to cover and protect yourself, but even then it is always a dangerous thing to move about with them. To hope to transform them, as some people do, is a vain illusion; for they do not want to be transformed. They have no intention of allowing any transformation and all effort in that direction is useless.

There is nothing to be done with these creatures; you should avoid having any dealings with them."

Sri Aurobindo
(Renowned Yogi / Poet / Spiritual Reformer)
Questions and answering session (12th May 1929)
Source: Sri Aurobindo Ashram Library

Historical Reveals Intentionally Hidden...

Unfortunately... despite this information being stated in the very oldest written texts...the Vedas... still to this day unfortunately still remains in its embryonic stage...suppressed destroyed by the advantage seeking diabolical asuric soul less Maya beings... creating a Maya Jaal entrapment web in an attempt to prevent the ascension of the Soul beings by not revealing the utmost importance of unveiling this illusionary veil... instead they kept mass societies distracted through status, sex, race, religions, regions throughout time... when simply all the play of life is just soul protagonists attempting to rise above the soul devoid tactics and the maya jaal entrapments... the spiritually alive vs the spiritually dead...

Compelling indeed...intensifying within indeed...felt without action is frustration... felt and acted upon is execution...Soul within could not accept this deplorable injustice... Well it is my absolute pleasure to extract what was once embryonic... whilst present in a literary gift poetic...

"Name of the energy changes...
 The energy never changes...
 Name of character perhaps changed...
 The character has not changed...
 Name of the play...
 Does not change the play..."

Hugh Shergill

Discover your Being...Recognize their Being...

"Nobody is superior,
 Nobody is inferior,
 but nobody is equal either.
 You are you,
 I am I.
 I have to discover my own being;
 You have to discover your own being."

Acharya Rajneesh (Osho)
(Spiritual Leader / Philosopher)

Some People...

"Some see through people...
 Some hear through people...
 Some exist beyond people...
 Some are aware of people...
 Some actually are people...
 Some appear as people.."

Hugh Shergill

Maya Leela

Recognition is not Judgement...

"Recognition is not Judgement...

  Detect before Correct...
  I Discover...
  Recognize...
  The 'Actor' through their Actions...
  Recognition of discovery...
  Is not judgement...
  One must detect the issue first...
  Before dealing with the issue...
  The 'act' first deserves to be discovered...
  To be recognized...
  Followed by discovery of the Actor...
  Performing the particular Act...
  Judgement of the 'act' occurs...
  Only upon concluding...
  Never leading...
  The recognition of discovery...
  Of the particular being...
  Is revealed by the being's action itself...
  Never judgement...

  Recognition is not Judgement..."

Hugh Shergill

"One must recognize...
  The conflict of the play...
  In order to performatively play..."

CHAPTER 8.

MAYA
JAAL
ENTRAPMENT

"What is a Play…
Without its conflict…
Confinement is the script conflict…"

"Divine…
Breathing Divinity…
Maya…
Exhaling illusion…
Moksha…
Inhaling escapism…
Maya jaal…
Smoke of entrapment…"

Hugh Shergill

Maya Jaal…
The Maya Web of Entrapment…

Word 'Jaal' is derived from the Sanskrit word 'Jala' meaning 'Entrapping Web Through Deception'…
'Maya Jaal' is the 'Web of illusion Entrapment'… This is the core essential of Maya Entrapment of
the Soul through soul descension…by entrapping and preventing Maya Escapism…which is soul
ascension… The soul question is…will you or will you not rise to the bait?…

Before we deeply pursue explore Maya Jaal entrapment…it is important to first explore further depths
of the protagonist and antagonist performers…as it is essential to understand why each exists on the
confined Maya realm stage, the vedic revelations, and their specific objective purposes are for their
particular existence… Maya Entrapment vs Maya Escapism…

Maya Entrapment vs Maya Escapism

**"Maya Leela play…
 Your ultimate conflict…
 Soul ascension through…
 Battle between…
 Maya entrapment…
 Maya escapism…"**

Hugh Shergill

Maya Realm…
A Confined Structure…
An Entrapped Structure…

Birth and Rebirth into the Maya realm is the ultimate Maya realm entrapment…as everyone that is in
existence in this realm of Maya…is entrapped by default existence experience in this realm of Maya…
thus Maya itself is the ultimate Maya entrapment…

**"Writer of destiny…
 You provided infinity…
 What one received…
 Was Karmically achieved…
 Music tune of abundance…
 Moves with Karma dance…"**

Hugh Shergill

Indeed...the realm in itself is the beauty of all projected creation experiences... Filled with infinitely immense essence of Love creations by the Divine creator... customized modified fluctuations karmically for each one's experience... precisely accordingly depending on each individual's particular acts of karma in totality and also collectively...

However, the maya realm play stage itself still remains an enclosed experience...thus confined...a return ticket vacation experience...thus temporary and potentially soul repeating... regardless of the infinite realms of multi-verses of Maya projections...all in grand infinite totality stage is still a confined realm...and anything that exists only in a confined structure...also exists in an entrapped structure...

"Maya Realm is entrapping...
  Maya Jaal web of entrapment...
  Maya beings the entrapping hunters...
  Entrapped illusionary experience...
  Soul's Karma dependent...
  Conflict presents...
  When entrapping hosts...
  Attempt to entrap souls..."

Hugh Shergill

Entrapping hosts...
Attempt to entrap souls...

Just as one's higher soul conscious witness breaks down the fourth wall of the Maya Leela stage... freeing the confines of the play...by giving direct interaction access to the witnessing audience to co-create the play... With that, there is also an illusion entrapping realm on the stage itself that is determined that the Soul's access to its soul consciousness is distractingly deviated from...this is the entrapping realm of Maya Jaal...the illusion web of entrapment...

As one travels the journey of life being Maya Leela aware...phenomenon of being here but realization of not being from here...with soul consciousness being one's true identified identity... with this innate soul authentic identification... one naturally steps in and performs the Leela play as the Maya guest performer along with some other guest performers... also with many more numerous Maya host performers...

Maya illusionary stage platform is the institution of perceived existence, with maya beings being the maya host of this existence. Just like a luxurious hotel, the host's primary purpose is to service/ sustain the hotel and attract/serve the hotel guests... If no guests visited the hotel, no hotel hosts would be required, and further the hotel itself eventually would no longer exist... The hotel guests are the primary factor for the hotel's existence, and the hotel hosts must be required to lure and serve the hotel guests...

"You are the honored guest.
 Do not weep like a beggar
 For pieces of the world."

Rumi (Renowned Sufi Poet)

The Maya Theatre…

The Maya theatre platform stage, the theatre performing host, and the theatre visiting guest audience, all three must coexist for the theatre to exist… The only freedom of the three, is held by the visiting guest audience as it holds the power option to shut down the entire theatre by exiting the theatre… Therefore, in order to keep the visiting guest audience engaged into the theatre…the performing host is absolutely required to perform… Performing to sustain Maya through reinforcing the Maya entrapment, the Maya jaal…

Interestingly… the Egyptian pyramids represent ascension at its core metaphorically…sharp triangular precise peak pointing towards ascension…yet any flip reverse reverse triangle symbol association is nothing but descension at its core…one symbolizes ascension with its peak…the other symbolizes deep descension digging towards lower realms…forces in work to keep all ascending souls entrapped into the illusion… Maya Leela…Maya tricks… Maya trix….Matrix…

"The web is a weave…
 Tailored to deceive…
 What is perceived…
 To be achieved…
 Mere an illusion received…
 Only shoots…
 Impartial truths…
 Indeed is unique script of the world…
 Where true intents never unfold…"

Hugh Shergill

Maya Jaal...the Maya Web Entrapment...

"Venomous prey upon...
 The non venomous...
 Non venomous weapon...
 Is escapism...
 From lured attract...
 To engaged entrap..."

Hugh Shergill

"Maya jaal is similar to the spider's web...
 Where the maya being is the spider...
 Preying to entrap the free bird...
 Which is the soul being...
 The bird's defensive escapist weapon...
 Is not the spider's venom...
 It is its powerful wings...
 Advantageous ability to fly to freedom...
 Unreachable for both the spider and its web...
 Wings victorious over venom..."

Hugh Shergill

Maya jaal at its core, is the web trap of emotions...luring one into the Maya web existence further by reinforcing all that is Maya...an illusion...through the power resistance performance of the maya being...

Maya beings existence is entirely Maya based... The maya jaal is the fuel of existence for the maya being... The Divine energy created the Maya illusionary existence stage platform and all the existence within the Maya platform, is Maya itself... This includes every living being existence, including all human beings. The only exception is the soul being, as soul consciousness is further directly connected to the Divine itself...it is both the projector spark and projection...existing as one within and beyond the Maya realms... whereas the maya being is only the Maya projection and exists as so long as Maya exists...therefore it is absolute essential for the maya being's existence, that the Maya platform continues to exists...by creating utmost resistance as possible to prevent further spiritual enlightenment growth of soul beings...as each enlightened soul has the potential capacity to exit the Maya jaal entrapment...as soul energy is essentially Divine energy itself...soul being's potential liberation towards moksha highly exists...the ultimate blissful state of being...nirvana...moksha... enlightenment bliss...which is the soul being's core desire...for creation to merge with its creator... This blissful state of the ultimate spiritual attainment weakens the Maya stage platform...a weak Maya platform, weakens all that exists exclusively on the Maya platform...which includes the maya being...as more soul beings enlightened and attain moksha equals less maya beings in possible existence...

The soul owns the maya illusionary stage...it is both the guest and the landlord of maya...as the soul is Divinity's spark itself...soul perception of maya existence is the absolute illusionary existence...it is its existing platform...therefore if the soul escapes the illusion entrapments...the illusionary platform collapses... The play ceases to exist...with its final play spectator...

"The illusion...
 Creates confusion...
 What requires attention...
 Is forever put to retention...
 Playing with your perception...
 To disrupt your ascension..."

Hugh Shergill

Maya Being... The Maya Host...

The Maya host is the maya being...the soul less diabolical asuric Maya Leela antagonist... The Maya pawn of Maya jaal entrapment... Maya being's primary purpose is maintaining Maya existence... through Maya entrapment jaal by creating powerful soul being resistance...

The Maya Jaal Entrap Chess Pawn...
Unknowingly But Innately Performing...

Maya being, the antagonist plays out the acting performance unknowingly but innately...as the maya stage host performer is to create resistance conflict for the protagonist, by reinforcing the entire Maya illusionary stage Leela play through its acting performance...expressing the Maya illusionary web of entrapment... The Maya Jaal...acting out as the dedicated Maya Jaal entrapment chess pawn...

Maya Being is a Matrix Maya Bot...

Maya is Maya tricks...Maya is the Matrix...a Matrix being is simply a Matrix Bot...thus one can also describe a Maya Being also as a Maya Bot... One that works diligently to preserve and sustain the illusionary realm...entrapping and sustaining the illusion at any cost...is its absolute objective...by any means necessary...

Soul Being... The Maya Guest...

The Maya guest is the soul being...the Maya Leela protagonist... Soul beings purpose is exiting Maya existence...through defeating Maya jaal resistance and becoming one with the Divine source...by attaining moksha...liberation...experiencing nirvana...eternal bliss...

The soul being shall and must face turbulent resistance from Maya jaal entrapments...carving away at you...always in motion...sometimes quite abruptly and with horrific intensity...other moments of more suttle attacks...however always active in motion...it is the solid rock of the soul that must decide if it is either simply going erode away or manifest itself into a spectacular sculpture...

"Pressure creates...
 Diamond traits...
 Divinity continuously tests you...
 Carving away at you...
 To see if you merely erode away...
 Or actually transform into a sculpture..."

Sunil Dutt (Renowned Actor / Philanthropist)
Poetic translation by Hugh Shergill

Karma and Reincarnation...

Most Powerful Perpetual Maya Entrapment...

Karmic actions and Reincarnation birth cycles are the most powerful and complex perpetual web forms of Maya jaal entrapment...as all lessons are repeated until learned...all performances will require another take...if not adequate enough for an ascension performance...

Now let's look into Karma and Reincarnation in depth...

Maya Being's Karma and Reincarnation...

Indeed karma exists for a maya being also...however only on the Maya stage exclusively...just like everything else existing within the realms of Maya... The karma for the maya being exists within the confines of the lifetime...there just is no soul karma...as it is only karmic soul residual that goes beyond one lifetime existence...which evidently manifests in the soul being's karmic journey...

As there is no individual karmic soul journey for the maya being...therefore there is no scope for reincarnation... Individual reincarnation is non existing...as once a maya being physical existence expires...so does that particular maya being completely...maya is the illusionary existence and all that exists in this realm outside of the direct soul consciousness expires without any possibility of reincarnation...

No Soul Less Reincarnation...
Just Dissolve into Asuric Existence...
The "Go to H..." existence...

Collective asuric energy field...is an agonizing dreadful field...this is where the Asura Maya being upon its physical demise forever lies...this collective asuric energetic field is responsible for all Maya

Jaal entrapment forces…thus extremely negative energetic forces of asuric excretion and asuric experience…producing further pool of asuric energy and its beings…experiencing its own perpetuity of negative karmic effects… This is quite a similar description to what some would refer to as…that commonly associated horrific place that starts with the letter 'H' and ends in a 'L'… Individually the dreadful diabolical asura maya being never reincarnates…only dissolves into the dreadful pool realm of asuric cloud existence…collective existence…never again a specific individual energy journey existence…

Upon the Maya realm's perceived physical demise…the maya being's asuric energy existence rejoins the Maya realm's collective asuric field…this asuric collective energy field…where the asuric maya being is dissolved, recycled and reintroduced as another maya being…with not just an individual previous karmic profile…yet an even more potent collective hestrocious asuric energy karmic profile… Asuric energy field is responsible collectively for all its asuric karma in its entirety and dealt with collectively…

Asuric Energy Cycle:

Recycling…
Re-emerging…
Re-distributing…
Re-planning…
Re-Suffering…
Recycling…

Collective Karma of their Asuric Energy Field…

Each maya being's unresolved Karmic debts accumulate concentrate in the collective mass asuric energy field…that recycles their asuric energy into further born maya beings…their negative karma potency continues to enrich in the form of the next generation of maya beings…resulting in further horrifying mass scale tragedies and catastrophic events…

For example, the cliché that
'Children often pay for the bad karmic deeds that their parents did…'
This is absolutely true for multiple generations of Maya beings…well some refer to this phenomenon often as 'ancestral curses'… Ancestral curses are an absolute reality…curses that repeat for the Maya beings in family structures for multi generations…only to be broken down by that only distinct one… odd yet very special Soul being born into their family… Soul beings are the antidote to the venomous generational curses…

**"Nothing escapes the law of Karma…
  Karmic reset is inevitable…"**

Karma and Reincarnation…

Now what I must address is a very sensitive point and would seem coming off as apathetic…however far from it…as every human being's life is important and must be honoured and respected for its particular karmic journey...yet unfortunately the harsh reality exists...the power of Karma spares no one...both for the Soul...and for the Non-Soul...certain complex points shall re-emphasized to ensure it is understood...as a heavy topic can not be taken lightly...

Controversial and as unfortunate as it sounds...the destructional forces of the Kali Yuga world is at play... Unfortunately 'Victims' of mass level destruction tragic events are indeed 'Victims' of the karmic debt accumulated concentrated in the collective bank of negative karmic asuric energy... the more negative actions by mass soul less maya beings in the world...the more mass and frequent tragic world events resulted by their collective Karma... this Karmic mass phenomenon further results in the duality balance reset for the Maya stage to exist...too many antagonists compared to protagonists ratio will cause an intense turmoil destruction of the Maya realm itself...which is in all actuality...all that we perceive as reality... The Maya duality strict ratio is inevitable...and to halt the proceedings for asuric collective karma reset is impossible... Karma resulting reset must occur...Often unfortunately resulting in mass horrific tragic catastrophic events...

Karma must be claimed and paid for...both for soul beings and maya beings... For maya being's negative karmic debt...results in the collective asuric karmic debts that prey on their recycled new generation Maya beings...and also some soul beings...soul beings that have acquired accumulated previous resulting negative karmic debt...that shall now trap them and place them in the precise moment where the mass tragic event will take place... On the other hand, a soul being that has no place to be eliminated in that mass tragic event...will surely and absolutely survive... We all have heard of those miraculous 'Sole Survivours' in such horrific tragic events... indeed these 'Sole Survivours' are in all actuality 'Soul Survivours'... Specifically 'Good Karmic Profile Soul Survivours' who have a higher soul purpose calling that yet must and shall be fulfilled on this Maya realm stage before their destined exit...

Everyone in the majority is unfortunately facing such mass horrendous almost identical perceived time karmic ramifications on such mass numbers globally...mass specific disease suffering...mass war attacks...mass poverty...mass killings...mass sickness...mass tragic events... This is a clear indication that there is clearly something going on much beyond any one's single individual specific karmic debt journey...there is highly active energetic forces in the background controlling mechanism that is mass controlling them...and is paying its negative karmic debts through them...through karmic consequences, reset regulation, and elimination...unfortunately...

Ironically...take war as an unfortunate example...a great asuric karmic ramifications reset is executed on to themselves on a mass destructive level...executed by diabolical asuric entity slave pawns on the orders from diabolical asuric soul less leaders... Asuric energy field executes destructive pending karma through its own current karma...a perpetual karmic reset by its own doing...creating destruction for its own destruction...no one ever wins in the three dimensional illusionary realm war...karmically who destroys also gets inevitably destroyed...completely idiotic, unfortunate, and tragic as it sounds... this is the pathetic diabolical asuric energetic field dominance...completely devoid of the Divine soul energy realm awareness and experience...

It is astonishing to witness...whenever these unfortunate mass tragedic events occur...majority begin to question the existence presence protection of the Divine...ignorantly unaware...never attempting to seek deep within of why has this actually occurred...when everyone is perceived to have their own individual karma profile...then why are these unfortunate occurrences occuring mass collectively and suddenly...it certainly indicates that there is some energy controlling on a higher mass level that is being ignorantly disregarded and questioned when the outcome does not suit a particular desired preference... This in itself is very strangely peculiar and absurd... Indeed, when Divinity created the law of karma...it simply retired...

Maya Being's Non Reincarnation...
Yet Karmically Responsible...

Just as Divinity in its infinite entirety blesses its Divine spark of soul... The undivine diabolical asuric energy is forever connected and responsible for all its asuric soul less low vibrational energy...

Instant karma and a lifetime of karma exists for the maya being...and then it is simple deletion of their existence...task completed...game over...back to the asuric factory for recycling...
Instead of specific individual reincarnation...these soul less maya beings are recycling collectively reproduced... What does recycle as the maya being is actually the collective asuric energy of the entire maya leela play...where duality and relativity must be absolutely present for the maya realm existence...therefore as long as suric soul beings are Divinely instructed to continue on their protagonist maya stage play journey...the maya stage shall continue to create maya beings as the antagonist asuric structure to provide corresponding resistance...where the asuric maya being structured resistance survives off feeding on the suric soul energy of the soul being...

The Undeserving Blessed...

One may also question...as there have throughout history been many prominent individuals who regardless of their immense amount of negative karma deeds...were still able to flourish and live a perceived completely happy, fulfilled, and healthy lives...this phenomenon is due to them actually either being a deeply entrapped soul being that is blindly accumulating negative karma...or is a highly favoured asuric soul less being that is serving a major horrendous asuric energy entrapping domination purpose ...

The deeply entrapped non-evolved unaware soul being...Who's currently negatively operating soul... that indeed has yielded positive protective karmic fruits of their past life existences...which powers and protects them in certain immediate existence in some form or way...as every karmic result flourishes equally to its previous deed without any discretion...equally for all both negative karma and positive karma accumulated...whatever perceived blessings that they have...is not accidental nor coincidental...that soul energy is karmically deserving of all it rightfully...even if it is perceived as extremely unfair and unjust for them to be so blessed in the immediate...as karma is the power force of precision action and reaction with no room for selectiveness...what one has is fully karmically deserving of it or serves a yet unseen major purpose in the intricacies of the Maya Leela script... Blessings is power...however with great power also comes even greater responsibility...otherwise karmic consequences awaits with vengeance...if these karma blessings are abused by being severely tempted, lured, and trapped by the maya jaal entrapment web...the soul being shall absolutely face the karmic consequences...what we perceive as the grandeur magnificent life that this current individual experiences...however we are totally unaware of the horrific life and multiple life experiences that are inevitably viciously awaiting for them, due to the negative karmic debt accumulated...that shall be consequently dealt with...karmically paid for including all debt with interest...and taking the soul being on a regressive soul journey of many lifetimes before any possibility of shifting enlightening soul progressive ascending journey...

As all lessons are repeated...until learned...additionally repeated enrollment lessons come with the additional accumulated Karma costs and fees...all that shall be inevitably paid for with interest...

The soul's primary purpose in the realm of Maya Leela is to perform...a poor performance shall result in regression status...requiring retakes and Karmic costs...until optimal performance is achieved... otherwise another repeat...

Similarly, for the highly favoured appointed asuric soul less entity that took their antagonist maya jaal privileged power actions to such horrific asuric energy driven extremities that shivered the entire maya stage completely...which is afterall a realm of the Divine...that must be honoured and respected...as no stage performer is allowed to harm the entire theatre's existence itself...and must pay for those consequences... Here not only the specific soul less entity pays for its karma but the entire asuric energetic field pays for the Karmic consequences...suffering both as the individual asuric energy and also as the collective energy of the entire asuric energy realm...sending havoc destructions to the Asura realm...where one not only is individually karmically burning...but additionally karmically burning collectively for the entire asuric energy realm...

Take the example of Ravana from the epic of Ramayana...who attempted to asurically create new asura diabolical world domination...yet Karma prevailed...completely within that asuric maya being's lifetime existence as it was ultimately dethroned, defeated, humiliated, prematurely eliminated and deleted back into agonizing asuric collective energy cloud... no one escapes karma...no one...no being...neither the soul...nor the soul less...

No Karma Consciousness...
Complete Diabolical Insanity...

For the maya being, there is no karma consciousness...there is no personal internal ignorance within their conscious...as they are consciously ignoring nothing...as there is nothing that consists within them to ignore...they actually are ignorance themselves ...programmed rigid by their hierarchy soul less asuric cloud energy...for them the absolute agenda is being ignorant of the energies of the Divine...the infinite soul energy...ignoring it through their ignorant performance...this is the Maya Leela's Maya being's act performance of egorance...
ego, ignorance, arrogance...

No karma consciousness... unlike a soul...who will eventually realize the absolute correlation of their deeds in one's journeys of lifetimes and their Karmic consequences...through its innate karma consciousness, awakening, enlightenment, evolution, and higher ascension process...

Whereas on the contrary, on a micro individual asura level, the soul less entity will continue to perform negatively and continuously facing its karma idiotically...yet never realize...nor capable of realizing...

instead their finger will always forever point blame others for everything... That is why one should never authentically expect or accept an apology from these diabolical entities...as deep down...they are truly never remorseful nor apologetic for anything...ever...

Similarly, on a vast macro level...the entire asuric energy field also does not realize its continuous perpetual negative Karmic consequences...as it will continue on more deeper by further accumulation of Karmic debts costs by continuing the repeating cycle collectively... Indeed...complete diabolical insanity by doing the same thing over and over again and expecting different results... which is impossible...as Divine's soul spark of Divinity is forever Loved and protected from even the most extreme diabolical soul less attacks... Diabolical insanity metaphorically...is an asuric soul less entity that runs with its wicked diabolical intentions on the hamster wheel till its very complete asuric energy end...

"The one with the soul lives on forever...
The others shall simply vanish away
like soap bubbles..."

Acharya Rajneesh (Osho)
(Spiritual Leader / Philosopher)

As there is absolutely no specific individual reincarnation for Maya beings...it is collective karmic reincarnation of Maya beings within the play of Leela that takes place...unfortunately resulting more often abruptly as what one would call mass society tragic unfortunate events and collective suffering occurrences... Everything within the play of Leela is regulated through karma...both for some individually and for some collectively... Optimum Divine balance ratio for Maya Leela existence is absolutely necessary...

By Divine balance...does not mean one to one equal ratio...as such soul energy abundance would easily liberatingly ascend and dissolve the entire Maya realm... Entrapping always outnumbers the trapped...as there are many more entrapping prison bars for each individual prisoner... The ratio is uneven in terms of quantity...however the energy duality is always modulating in Divine balance for Maya operation... Divine soul beings are indeed much much more outnumbered than soul less maya beings...however it is still in energetic competitive balance as each individual soul being is energetically much much more powerful than numerous maya beings...effortlessly...

Only one individual Soul Being holds immense triumphant capabilities over many multiple Maya Beings...unlocking the key to these capabilities is becoming knowingly aware of the Maya Leela play and its participants...

"Soul being's existence is infinity...
 Maya being's existence is temporary...
 They are fearing death...
 As all ends with their last breath...
 Oil vanishes burning away...
 Yet water forms clouds far away..."

Hugh Shergill

Soul Being's Karma vs Maya Being's Karma...

No Sequel for the Maya Being...

"Maya being's play stage receipt...
 Absolutely resisted to repeat...
 Eliminate...
 By complete delete...
 No sequel...
 For the Maya being..."

Hugh Shergill

Soul beings live...
Maya beings exist...

Maya beings are metaphorically biological third dimension robots...all produced in the same asuric energy facility...where old models go into the recycle bin...while new models are released... dipped into the collective asuric energy karmic debt pool data...and released...

Play performer's exit from the play holds both purpose and karma...

Soul Being's Purpose Karma...

Existence is absolutely dependent on the purpose in the play... extinguished or expired purpose...exit from the play is absolutely inevitable...
Defying one's soul purpose karma... Existence may also fall short for the soul being... premature demise is inevitable if one acts within the play that contradicts their soul purpose meant for the play...

Throughout history...there have been certain individuals that had so much potential for soul greatness...yet became tempted and falling into extreme entrapments...deviated from their soul calling path...that caused a turmoil shift effect into their life path script...leading them deeply perpetually trapped in the Maya jaal entrapment web...

Maya Being's Collective Karma...

Beyond the karma of actions and reactions a human being faces within its three dimensional lifetime... Maya beings additionally hold collective karma that regulates their appropriate mass existence in the Maya Leela play script... unfortunate as it is...mass global tragedic events and suffering losses occur in perfect precision as the regulatory karmic effect...

As the majority often ignorantly ask...if there is a God...then why so much suffering? My reply is yes indeed there is suffering...as there is a God...and there is its law of Karma... inevitable... indiscretional... inescapable indeed...the moment Divine created the law of Karma...it essentially retired...for each to their own...responsible for their action consequences and their influential energetic driven forces...

Just as a soul being is responsible for every karma within one lifetime...lifetimes...multi-reincarnated lifetimes... Maya being is responsible for every karma within their one lifetime...recycled and remerged lifetimes...and additionally asuric energy collective maya beings karma and maya stage state...

This is a major factor why a strict atheist innately feels there is absolutely no individual presence beyond death...that once they die, they die...game is over...this on a simplest level existence structure is Maya intuitively absolutely true for the maya being...as their individual energy existence is completely over with their last taken breath... Thus, one completely agrees with the non-reincarnating atheists...

Maya being's collective karma accumulates and precipitates as more maya beings recycle and reemerge on the maya stage...collectively they pay in mass tragic numbers...

For example, simply observing the world...as mass existence creates a particular negative karma existence and narrative thoughts...the more the world reflects karmically to their negative karmic existence...producing a collective world stage more awful than the previous perception states... This is collective synergy karma...which in the modern world is very apparent through mass influences...

"You act from the entrapments of illusion...
  You are responsible for the entrapping illusion..."

A very dynamic complex web of karma is in effect for the maya being...as not only are they responsible for their individual karmic actions...but are additionally responsible for the entire asuric maya entrapping energy that they are heavily influenced and controlled by...

For example, a crime gang member pays for its particular crime and additionally pays for its particular gang affiliation influence... Assistance and associations to a crime is also a crime...Maya being's individual karma also additionally includes karmic debts of their collective asuric energy influence... often more hard hitting than a soul being could not even imagine... Influence and being influenced is a very powerful component of every action...that shall be absolutely accounted for...as no 'actus rea' physical act component of a crime is a crime until there is the presence of the 'mens rea' mentally influenced intent of the crime... Maya being karmically pays... and further Maya being's asuric energy collectively in its entirety also pays...

One can effortlessly see the ramifications of this perpetual deep negative karmic debts being played out right in front of us...as it is heartaching to see immediate three dimensional perceived completely innocent beings suffer so much without any immediate karma realm resulting explanation...especially when one views pure innocent underprivileged and innocent children...it is extremely hurtful to witness this...and naturally for an emphatic soul being will innately have you question life, creation, and the creator itself...yet unfortunately harsh as it sounds...Divinity never desires for any of its creation to ever suffer...what is occurring is one's own doing...nothing more...nothing less... as with each generation...there is a collective uprising increase in all kinds of suffering of society in entirety... health...starvation...exploitation...suppression... Even in my perceived current life line, I have been once privileged to witness at some moment where majority of people around you had a pleasant demeanor...an aura spark in their eyes and a suttle pleasant smile commonly...now in contrast... it is unfortunate to witness majority of people that you come across on any given day...have such a grim almost haunting ghost walking dead low vibrational aura...suffering in some way or form is very clear that it powerfully resonates for those with innate empathy and energetic sensitivity... Indeed, the majority seem to be carrying with them such a heavy negative burden...an asuric dark cloud encapsulates them...that clearly is beyond any three dimensional physical explanation of their current life resulting actions...going much beyond any labeled mental health issue or depressive state...even a suttle smile is out of the question...as one can easily view that the slightest trigger is capable of drowning these individuals further in suffering...unfortunate indeed...for those being in presence of witnessing this non-healing karmic debt bleed...

On the other hand...a soul being...regardless of all that it is facing...still innately holds Divine optimism...knowing this shall also pass...keep on continuing doing good with genuine Love...and all will eventually turn out for the good... Quantumly entangled and forever in rhythm with Divinity... The Divine connection path is a simple path...simple in terms of its immense impeccable purity... energetically connect of Divinity and its Divine spark soul being... Karmically actions of truth, kindness, Love ...not only is in position for karmic ascension...it is the weapon to overcome all obstacles on its path when energized with pure flawless faith in its Divine creator...

Kabaddi, the Vedic Era Sport...
Maya Jaal Entrapping Metaphor...

Sports represent and reveal unique interpretations of one's life journey... Striving to excel by winning the game one is playing is both challenging and rewarding... Kabaddi, is one sport that originates from the ancient vedic era...deeply rooted in the vedic culture for centuries... In the Sanskrit epic Mahabharata, It is said that the warrior Arjuna...mastered kabaddi's skills from Lord Krishna, who Loved the sport... Legend has it that Arjuna would breach enemy walls unnoticed and would walk back unharmed due to its immense kabaddi skills... Interestingly, this sport truly portrays the dynamics of the Maya Leela play and the Maya jaal challenge...

Kabaddi is a direct contact sport... Played between two opposite teams... The sport objective of the game is for a single player on offence, referred to as the 'raider' to run into and enter the opposing team's half side of the court zone, tag out as many of their seven 'defender' players as possible, and return back to their own half of the court, all without being tackled by the defenders, and all in a single breath sequence and or dedicated time duration... Points are scored for each player tagged by the raider, while the opposing team earns a point for stopping the raider. Players are taken out of the game if the defenders are tagged or the raider is tackled down and left trapped in the opposition's court zone for the dedicated duration...

Metaphorically, this vedic era sport beautifully represents the entire Maya Leela play... The raider is the soul being...that enters the opposition's maya platform court through taking birth...experiences the maya platform court upon entering and running as life experience...comes in direct contact with one or more of the seven opposition defender players, which all are the soul less maya beings...where the soul player faces a contact interaction maya struggle...the seven defender players represent the soul's seven primary chakras...each one must be challenged face on...make fighting efforts to purify each karmic residual of each soul chakra for victory...through the soul has to now challenge itself by striving to tag the soul less maya being and return back to its soul being zone court half...running back is evolution self knowledge awareness...of knowing you are in the opposition's courtside and must escape back...winning the game by returning to its true comfort soul zone courtside which is its game play win as maya escapism... escaping Maya...attaining moksha liberation and nirvana bliss...

Failure to do so...occurs when one loses its breath or dedicated time, which is its immediate physical life duration... The maya trapped tackled down occurs by the maya being...where the soul being remains trapped in the maya platform court...which is the maya jaal entrapment court...and ultimately taken out of the game...until next game reset...next game attempt...life cycle repeat...karmic reincarnation...

This is Maya Leela's Maya Jaal Sport...

Quintessential game play sport drama... interactive conflict play drama of Maya exist versus Maya exit...through soul conscious awareness...to each its own...the protagonist soul being versus the antagonist maya being by engaging performance play battle with the web of Maya jaal entrapment... reshuffling and recorrecting the maya stage play script...scene after scene...karmically.. this is the maya leela play...the play of life...

"Reality never leaves you...
 Yet we run from reality...
 The only nation...
 Is true information...
 The only nationality...
 Is knowing the truth of humanity..."

Hugh Shergill

Premature Forced Play Exit...Suicide?...

"With anxiety I say...
 I will commit to die...
 What if I still don't find peace...
 Where will I lie?"

Sheikh Ibrahim Zauq
(Renowned Poet / Literature Scholar)
Translation by Hugh Shergill

"No one is going to escape life...
 Life is going to live you..."

Mike Tyson (Renowned Boxing Champion)

The play on the stage absolutely continues...even if a performer intentionally jumps off the stage... the play script...the play duration...the remaining performers...will continue on and take the destined Divine play forward... while the fallen off stage quitting coward performer lies identity less in the dark corners of the edge of the stage...for the entire remainder destined play duration...

Suicide or any purposely intended forced exit results in same pre-destined life duration destined for this three dimensional illusionary Maya realm play...yet now that remaining residual destined perceived time moments will just transfer one into an unrested haunting energy... either a an unrested unfulfilled spirit for the soul being...or a negative diabolical asuric haunting atmospheric energy for the maya being...there is absolutely no escape... for no one... even for the suicider...the play shall complete before the Divine exit doors open... even if one decides to go the powerless cowardly ghost route... suicide is your definite route ticket towards becoming a haunting ghost...

"It is only one step...
 From the limo...
 To the gutter..."

Mike Tyson (Renowned Boxer)

"Homeless Streets... Drug corners...Red light districts...Prisons...Mental Institutions...Rehab clinics... These are particular play stage examples... unfortunately where more often than not... Maya being's intentionally entrapped Soul victims reside in immense suffering..."

Crime Confinement...
Maya Entrapment...

"Crime Confinement...
  A Maya Entrapment...

  Every crime is a Maya illusion trap...
  Every criminal is the weak entrapped...
  Victim is the unfortunate karmic consequence...
  Placed vulnerable in the weak's presence...
  Everything driven by a particular illusion...
  Incorrectly perceived as some Love conclusion...
  Ignitingly capable of the most vicious crime...
  Devoiding one from its kindest shine...

  Crime Confinement...
  A Maya Entrapment..."

Hugh Shergill

Soul Less Maya Being...
The Agent Provocateur...

There are certain maya beings that are innately very dangerously capable of acting as deceptive 'Agent Provocateurs'...by luring and enticing certain vulnerable soul beings to commit certain acts of karmic sin through their intricate Maya jaal webs of entrapments... Upon successful execution...the maya being deceptively portrays full innocence as it excels in its desired objective in the Maya realm... securing its asuric energy longevity further by having one more soul entrapped in the Maya realm... for its soul energy consumption... While the soul being is left confined entrapped with a heavy burden of negative karmic debt...with additional possible criminally charged debts...along with a plethora of regretful emotions that shall follow one's soul as a negative burden shadow...which all ultimately will result in a perpetual cycle of reincarnation rebirths on this Maya Leela play stage...where each karmic debt test shall inevitably repeated until learned and cleansed through one's soul performance...all this powerful occurring...is the soul less Agent Provocateur's doing...this is just how powerful the Maya jaal web entrapment is...

Unfortunately, throughout history...there are a lot of soul beings that fell prey to the extremities of Maya jaal entrapments...falling prey to the lures of the low vibrating soul less maya beings and their maya jaal entrapments...luring them into doing what they should never have done...destroying one's soul karmic path and sacrificing one's soul energy...to those maya beings and their entrapping maya jaal traps...very unfortunate...many soul beings remain confinely entrapped in prisons and mentally ill institutions as a result of becoming victim prey of their real entrapping Maya jaal web entrapments...

True prevention of recidivism...is for the one who committed...is to become aware that there is much more involved than what perceives the eye...emotional Intelligence, karma consciousness, and Maya awareness…are the tools of mastery to overcome and defeat the Maya jaal web entrapments and its soul less agents… One becomes very powerful when you have dominant control over your emotions and mind processing…That freedom to Lovingly feel as one desires…embodying that vibration…while shunning any hindering entrapping distractions…

The hamster running away intensely on the spinning wheel trying to obtain the cheese…is genuinely working its best without complaints… yet it shall always be devoid from its prize goal due to its predetermined confines…yes it can jump off the wheel at will… but it also loses that perceived desired prize by will…

"Efforts that feed into your confines…
Are efforts feeding controllers of confines…
Every decision of yours benefits someone…
Key is to dedicate the beneficiary one…
Criminal intentionally commits the crime…
Delusionally seeing themselves prime…
Upon being caught…
Increases in monetary note…
Benefiting boost by the law breaker…
For all those associated with the law maker…
Criminals commit…
Others benefit…"

Hugh Shergill

No One Knows…

"No one knows…
About that violence…
In all its highs and lows…
That became this silence…
Divinity protection controlled…
How otherwise…
Would have one controlled…
No one knows…"

Hugh Shergill

**"To experience the unveil of illusion...
One must not become the delusion...
Prepared the right answers...
For the wrong test...
Reality is beyond illusions...
Real test requiring real answers..."**

Hugh Shergill

Education...Institutions...Establishments... they all prepare one and enrich one with the right answers for the test...yet it is the perceived test...which is incorrect...that is not the real test...real is beyond all illusions...the real test...the real test requires a different set of right answers...that differs from the prepared right answers for the wrong test...as the real test requires real answers...

All frustrations...hurt...discomfort...agony...arise when one's perceived prepared answers for life just don't answer correctly the perceived test of life...as the real test that one is experiencing is absolutely impacting and influencing...yet it is mysteriously hidden behind the Maya veil...going beyond the illusions...reveals all the delusions...then the true test appears...and only then one can correctly discover and prepare for the right real answers for right real test...to be the best...you must face the test...through your true self...

**"You my Soul...
How could you?...**

Allow...

**Those who can not even...
Control themselves...
To control you?...**

**Those who do not know...
Where they are going...
To guide you?...**

**Those who are devoid...
Of having a soul...
Entrap your soul energy from you?...**

**You my Soul...
How could you?..."**

Hugh Shergill

"Why do you stay in prison
  When the door is so wide open?
  Move outside the tangle of fear thinking
  The entrance door to the sanctuary is inside you."

Rumi (Renowned Sufi Poet)

Live authentically…live freely…live fearlessly…live Lovingly…break free from the entrapping traps that are deliberately placed in your play lifeline Maya Leela script…forces that desire to control you by presenting a life path structure totally opposed to you…for you… "Live" (read in opposite reverse) is not what one would deliberately desire…then why would one live opposite to what one's soul desires? That would be "Live" (read in opposite reverse)…

"Moment has arrived to prepare…
  An arsenal of powerful aware…
  To face war with the enemy…
  One must prepare for the enemy…
  By becoming aware of the enemy…"

CHAPTER 9.

MAYA

PERFORMER...

Maya Being...

The Malevolent Antagonist...

"Determine of ability...

Determined by capability...

Seeping ability of water...

As seeking of the seeker...

Soul conscious experiencing...

Ability to receive the water seeping...

Rejected by the non porous...

Resonated only through the porous..."

Hugh Shergill

The Outsiders...

Maya beings are outsiders...all their existence is based on the confined outer existing external three dimensional illusion Maya realm... Unlike the Soul beings who are innate insiders...all their existence is based in the eternal internal soul within...the core Divine energy source...above and beyond the Maya realm...

There is only one percent DNA biological difference between a human being and a chimpanzee... yet they are worlds apart...
Even a banana fruit shares sixty percent of genetic
similarity to a human being...and yet no one would ever visibly detect that amount of stunning similarity...
Similarly, two human beings...sharing almost one hundred percent identical human being DNA traits with the only differing soul energy factor...
are totally existencial worlds apart...

"We are the same appearing...
 Well that is the illusion deceiving..."

Indeed, the maya being is absolutely a human being, identically identifiable to a soul being biologically, but devoid of the essence soul spark conscious of the Divine... All soul energetic aura, spiritual chakras, Kundalini Shakti (dormant and active), energy chakras are absolutely non-existent... as there is no soul energy activation spark within...therefore no corresponding energetic aura vibrations... Maya beings are exclusively Maya conscious beings...devoid of soul and its abilities... Therefore completely devoid of soul consciousness capabilities...the soul less...with all their mess...forever remain less...

Just like an empty glass devoid of the beverage, yet the glass is identical in physical structure as the glass with the beverage...

Empty vessels...just like two identical vehicles parked next to each other...one is not able to determine which one actually has fuel within to go further, just by mere looking at them...one will have to seek within the vehicle to determine which one has the fuel capacity for further destinations or not...

"Hell is empty and all the Devils are here."

William Shakespeare
(Renowned Poet / Playwright)

Asur is an entity that is not in tune with the Divine...thus not connected to the Divine...which often in Biblical scriptures are commonly referred to as the fallen angels...fallen as the Divine cord is forever cut off...resulting in a non Divine connection...forever fallen indeed...

"Maya being...
  Human Maya experience...
  Experiencing maya existence...
  Through human existence...
  Unknowingly used...
  Completely confused...
  Maya jaal entrapped...
  Forever infused..."

Hugh Shergill

A maya being is no different to any other human being's physical scientifically created cloned version... Physically a human being, however created as and for the human being experience only, lacking any possible soul Divine connect experience... There is no higher scope of consciousness other than the semi-maya subconscious state...at most experienced only as dreams, maya influences, maya induced creativity, agendas, and ideas...

"Unfortunately I often observe that...
  Most people don't even have a soul...
  Harsh reality it is...
  There are only a few who are alive with a soul..."

Praveen Kumar Sobti
(Renowned Gold Medalist Athlete / Actor)

Empathy and Apathy...

Soul beings possess innate empathy...therefore an empathic individual is a being with a soul...the empath...

Maya beings from their innate core are apathetic...other's feelings are never truly felt and more often than not...not even acknowledged nor respected...a cold hearted narcissistic personality traits are a core component of a soul less maya being's personality...

"I say there is no darkness but ignorance"

William Shakespeare
(Renowned Poet / Playwright)

Maya Leela

Ignorance is illusionary bliss...

"Ignorance is illusionary bliss...
  Ignorance is a sweet coated miss...
  Comfortably encapsulated entrapped...
  Devoid authentic never freedom...
  Ignorance is an unrelenting liar...
  Ignorance is the gravity force of Maya...
  Any rising deviation from the Maya stage...
  Reveals the orchestrated illusionary cage..."

Hugh Shergill

Ignorance is Maya's Gravity...

Maya realm only exists when one is seeped into the pool of Maya's illusion...ignorance is the gravitational force of Maya's presence...and ignorant actions only solidify Maya's illusionary existence...therefore ignorance alone feeds existence to the maya realm...ignorance encourages Maya existence...ignorant acts solidify Maya's existence....

"Ignorance is Marketing/PR force...
  Dedicated to promote, sustain, and flourish...
  The Maya illusion brand..."

Ego is the maya weight force that increases its gravitational attraction force to the Maya realm when associated with ignorance...ignorance ignites in the presence of ego...that encapsulates and confines one deep into the illusionary realm of Maya...creating a fake persona built upon arrogance... The triple infused...ego...ignorance...arrogance...creates egorance...

"Maya Acting Performance...
  Ego...
  Ignorance...
  Arrogance...
  Is Egorance...
  Fueled by lies and deceits...
  Maya being's innate characteristic...
  Prevalent acting traits...
  Elevated state of Ego...
  illusionary state of reality...
  Driven by Ignorance...
  Unaware of actual reality...
  Reinforced by Arrogance...
  Refusal of knowing of reality...
  As more one knows...
  Less the ego...
  Ignorant unaware arrogant traveler...
  Never shall lead you...
  To your correct destination..."

Hugh Shergill

"Identification through their karmic detection...
  The acts performed reveals their character..."

Soul Less Seven Acts...
Atman Vaheen Sapta Natya...

"Egoistic, ignorant, arrogant performance...
  WIth the make believe fuel of lies and deceits...
  Performing the soul less seven acts..."

The 'Soul Less Seven Acts'...in Sanskrit defined as 'Atman Vaheen Sapta Natya'... In the ancient vedic era, orally passed on generational traditions...the typical acts of these entities were referred to as the 'Atman Vaheen Sapta Natya'...the 'Soul Less Seven Acts' which not only identified them but additionally allowed certain souls the certain specifics, wisdom, and knowledge of how to specifically deal with them... As scriptural evolution occurred... unfortunately scripture doctoring also occurred... by those who both identified and felt threatened by certain revelating reveals...

Egoistic, ignorant, arrogant performance driven by the fuel of lies and deceits...performing the soul less seven acts... There are seven primary maya being performance acts that the maya being acts out, through egorance acting, which is nothing but the act of lies deceiving manipulation, the acting performance of make and believe...performing in the make believe illusionary world...

Maya Leela

The seven acts are also ironically, all are absolutely necessarily justified for maya beings performance and existence...

Their 'Soul less Seven' is their 'Magnificent Seven'...all done unapologetically and without any remorse nor guilt... yet these same characteristics are the greatest hindrance traps of Maya entrapment for the soul being's quest for becoming one with the Divine...a mighty paradox of same stage existence yet distinct separate existence...similar biological beings...yet energetically absolute opposite beings...

"Maya Being...
  Being Maya...
  Maya Act...
  Seven Soul Less Acts...
  Maya Egorance Acting...
  Egoistic Ignorant Arrogant Performance...
  With the make believe fuel of lies and deceits..."

The seven soul less stage acts...Maya entrapment seven soul less acts through egorance...the triple fusion of ego, ignorance, and arrogance acting performance...with the make and believe fuel of lies and deceits...The maya being's core characteristic trait acts...performed through Maya illusionary egorance acting...on the minimum, for some at least one act will be more dominant, and for many...it will be maximum dominant in all...which as a thought is horrifically revolting but unfortunately present in many of these asuric soul less entities...

The Soul Less Seven Acts:

Ego
Greed
Envy
Jealousy
Attachment
Anger
Lust

Egorance Acting:

Ego...
Ignorance...
Arrogance...

Acting Fuel:

Lies...
Deceits...
Dishonesty...

These soul less seven acts are in no particular order and are performed through egorance acting by the maya being...as acting is manipulation... the make and believe tactics...thus fueled by lies and deceits used as the illusionary tool for the maya being's performance of unknowingly strengthening the maya jaal entrapment... The antagonist's power of resistance lies in the dominant use and in some cases...the extremities of acting out these maya entrapping soul less acts...

1. Ego

**"Whatever praises itself but in the deed,
 devours the deed in the praise"**

**William Shakespeare
(Renowned Poet / Playwright)**

Extremely heightened ego identity... As one is existing solely because of maya, therefore there is an illusionary dominant identification of one's perceived existence...the body and its processes...

Maya being only identifies from their confined five or less senses world existence and perception... There is absolutely no room for deviating from this existence experience... One will never make an attempt to romance any thought or idea of the possibility of any scope of beyond their minimum worldly experience... Everything accumulated is acquired from the external...as internally they are intellectly empty within... A statement such as "you are not your body" would seem highly absurd and amusing for them... Similarly any topics of Divinity higher power...higher consciousness realms would be very confusing and unrelatable... There is absolutely nothing incorrect in this, as it just positively reinforces their highly correct Maya instructive play performance... Any deviation from the antagonist would break the protagonist's performance and the overall Maya Leela play...the Divine source director shall never allow that...thus the antagonist puppet performs asurically as it is...

"An ego is an over dressed insecurity"

**Quincy Jones
(Renowned Musician / Music Producer)**

"Ego..

 **Everything
 Goes...
 Over...**

 **Never...
 Within..."**

Hugh Shergill

Maya Leela

No Third Eye...Just 'i'

As there is no possible third eye awakening...ever...therefore that 'eye' is replaced by a more typically maya readily available dialogue of 'i'...
'i am' 'i have' 'i did' 'i want' are 'i' words more excessively repetitively used in their overall communications with others...which goes much beyond simple appropriate communication reference of 'i'...

On the contrary...for the soul...the 'i' compellingly makes one ask themselves the question "who actually am i?" A question that spark triggers their continuing ascension journey...

Their 'Delusion of Grandeur'...
Innately Born Syndrome...

Soul Less diabolical asuric maya beings innately possess 'The Delusion of Grandeur' where there is an extremely false belief in their own superiority, greatness, and intelligence... For the witnessing soul being, this is an 'Amusing Delusion of their Grandeur' which is peculiarly humorous as the soul being sees right through the empty soul less shenanigans of the maya being...

For the maya being, there is a false ego pride that exists...molded through egorance..ego, ignorance, arrogance... Direct fake superiority complex within, direct narcissistic traits... Everything else is merely secondary, as for the maya being, their existence is the highest existence and everything else must serve this ego pride... If something does not or nor longer feeds their ego, then it is completely disregarded and removed... On an extreme level, the elevated ego feels that it is the master of the universe and the entire universe should highly appreciate their existence, like it is actually them doing a favour to the entire universe for existing, and it is the duty for everyone and everything to utmost comply and serve them as a thank you appreciated gesture... If they don't, or not to their desired level, then they should be disregarded... Indeed highly amusing 'Delusion of Grandeur' ego beings...

"My stance gains power...
 With each passing of the hour...
 Results of you holding onto ego...
 Any potential ascension is a long go ..
 Those who refuse to help themselves...
 Will be left on demising shelves...
 Congratulations on continuing...
 Ignorantly self decomposing...
 Your treasure stands in front of you...
 Yet your blind ignorance punishes you..."

Hugh Shergill

Wealth, Power, Status...
The Ego Enhancer Ticket...
For the Maya Being...

The Done and Doing...
The Maya Disparity...

Concept of superior and inferior is the most elevated ignorant Maya ego existence concept...
Behind every creation of the fundamental needs of a human being...whether food, water, clothing,
shelter...is the perceived lacking superiority of an individual's utmost labour effort... And behind every
superior's luxury portrayal created is also the same perceived lacking superiority individual utmost
labour effort creation...commanding utmost respect as the contributing creator of the perceived
superiority...as anything that enhances one's perceived superiority...is much more beyond superiority...

The plant is dependent to the gardener...the gardener is not dependent to the plant...no perceived
superior individual will physically build a house for others...sew clothes for others...create and cook
food for others...even at the peak of their charitable gesture...the effort force shall always come forth
from the perceived inferior...even further, the wealth accumulated always is collectively accumulated
from the perceived inferior...as it is much easily convenient to fulfill a payment transaction for a
perceived cause than to physically fulfill the cause...money is Maya...and the core physical vessel
of existence is the physical identity of one...as the most active perceived philanthropists would be
exhausted by actual physical philanthropist expression... therefore the perceived inferior is much
much more greater contributor than the ignorant arrogant perceived superior... yet ignorantly and
arrogantly receiving accolades for the service...

The priceless art can be potentially similarly recreated and further enhanced by the infinite artistic
fingers of the creating artist... Indeed, admire the art...but even further respect the artist...the creator...
Every perceived superior was created by the perceived inferior...and on the contrary, every perceived
superior shall never enhance or make effort towards the perceived inferior...which is the epitome
gesture of ignorance...a profoundly dominant trait visible in the soul less maya being... Wealth and
power does not change one...it only reveals one...

Popular being is begging and craving for perceived recognition...when the actual hard working
labourer is content with their absolute efforts...the perceived inferior sleeps peacefully at night...when
the perceived superior is tracking and analyzing every potential accolade opportunity for their lesser
actions...taking advantage of the maya illusionary expression...where the creations accumulates
accolades of the creator...identical to how one's ego identity takes all credit as the created, away from
the creator...as now the maya being illusionary existence is boosted by falsely perceiving themselves
as the creator of all...the desire of having all...creates an unrelenting greed to be above all...

Their Eyes of Arrogance...

"Judge them by appearance...
  View mediocrity in their presence...
  Blind lens entrapped preference...
  Expensive determined ignorance...
  Either viewing from far away distance...
  Or viewing with their eyes of arrogance..."

Hugh Shergill

Maya Being is an acute chronic Narcissist...

The long list of narcissistic traits...all of the above...apply to the Maya being...what psychological driven traits of a narcissist is listed as a behavioural condition...is simply describing a soul less Maya being entity...

2. Greed

"Enough no more,
  tis' not so sweet now
  as it was before .."

William Shakespeare
(Renowned Poet / Playwright)

There is an unrelenting thirst of greed for the maya being... This is deep rooted by the fact that all the energy focus is consumption of what is perceived to exist... Unlike the soul being, that dedicates the majority of its energy with desire to seek and gain what is beyond the perception of what seems to exist...

"Money is numbers and numbers never end.
  If it takes money to be happy,
  your search for happiness will never end."

Bob Marley
(Renowned Singer / Poet / Writer / Musician)

"Beware of overconcern for money,
 or position, or glory.
 Someday you will meet a man who cares for
 none of these things.
 Then you will know how poor you are."

**Joseph Rudyard Kipling
(Renowned Poet / Writer)**

Everlasting accumulation and consumption is of highest priority value of what the soul less maya being entity desires... Then further, greeds to be repeated...and repeated as the thirst of greed is never fulfilled completely. This is due to the deeper knowing consciousness of the maya being that this is it... That this life existence is so limited, that whatever can be accumulated and consumed as desired is of the utmost highest importance. This is absolutely true, as this is it, one limited life, one limited existence for the maya being, therefore gather as much as possible before the maya stage switches off their ever limited power button... This is it, before permanent power outage...game over...

"All is that is...
 Seems to exist...
 All is desired...
 Is that exists...
 Greed wanders...
 Where ego sits..."

Hugh Shergill

Power and wealth at any cost, everlasting, ever accumulating, ever increasing... are common examples of what one observes in these soul less maya being entities... Nothing is ever enough, as once more is gained, the more one greeds...
A soul being observing this behaviour seems baffled by how much will ever be enough for them, as enough is simply...enough...

"Thousands of desires...
 Each is worth dying for...
 Much more I have attained...
 Yet I continue desiring more...
 To consumingly cherish...
 Knowing it results in...
 My inevitable perish..."

**Mirza Ghalib (Renowned Poet / Writer)
Poetic Translation by Hugh Shergill**

Somewhere, there is a completely fed full stomach individual that still reaches out for the last piece of food on the shared plate, fully aware that it is already full enough...yet can not control themselves from overstuffing themselves...

There is yet also somewhere... A hungry homeless individual that further splits that very last food piece...sharing it with their also hungry dog...very well knowing that it won't be enough portion for either of them...but enough to survive to the next scene act of this illusion play...

"Ten beggars can sleep on one rug,
but two kings feel uncomfortable
in one country"

Saadi Shirazi (Renowned Poet)

Greed seeds all interactions and relationships...a greater motive based on the surface perception of others... Maya being uses others to quench the thirst of greed of wanting something they perceive is lacking by using others for their particular needs...often hidden in the cloak of being perceived as 'highly sociable' is actually 'self centered greed'...

"To witness destruction at large...
Put maya beings in charge...
Selfish greed shall be their priority...
By unleashing acute chaos in society...
Doing of their greed seed...
Makes others heart bleed..."

Hugh Shergill

"Kicking off the ladder...
Upon destination reach...
You shall be an example
For others to teach...
For now enjoy...
Your karmic ignorance ride...
All appears well...
Till the karmic destruction tide..."

Hugh Shergill

"The wealth of the wicked
 shall be transferred to the righteous"

Holy Bible (Proverb 13:22 King James Version)

Regardless of how much wealth through sickening greed these timophilia driven diabolical soul less entities acquire...eventually karma shall set its justice... What was accumulated with ill selfish intent will all be forever lost...and once again recirculated transferred righteously to those who are karmically soul deserving... This is inevitable...as regardless of how much these asuric entities accumulate...the law of karma will always prevail... No one can take away for whom it is meant...ever...

"Desire makes slaves out of kings,
 While patience makes kings out of slaves."

Al-Ghazali (Renowned Poet)

3. Attachment

"Life's but a walking shadow,
 a poor player that struts
 and frets his hour upon the stage,
 And then is heard no more.
 It is a tale told by an idiot,
 full of sound and fury,
 Signifying nothing."

William Shakespeare
(Renowned Poet / Playwright)

For reference poetic decode... Here Shakespeare's referring to 'a tale told by an idiot' is not referring to the Divine but to the Un-Divine Asuric energy that controls the diabolical acts of the 'poor player' the low vibration less competent...which is the soul less asuric maya being...that 'frets his hour upon the stage, And then is heard no more.'

Attachment is to validate oneself through something or someone...which is dependency...dependency on validation of others... Maya being feeds off false attachment to everything is what exists on the maya stage. From their own existence, existence duration, co-existing performers, the stage background, Leela play script, particular performance... All is highly attached to the maya being as both consciously knowingly and unknowingly, it holds on to it as that is what all defines their entire existence. This is again absolutely true...for the maya being. Maya beings exist because of the maya stage, therefore being attached to everything on the maya stage is their core asuric existence itself. Just like a person hanging on to their dear life on the edge of a cliff...the extraordinary power attached grip emerges within the hands...as one makes a further intense attachment effort to hold on to life... while deep down they know that all attached will eventually weakly slip away...as Shakespeare's words 'frets his hour upon the stage, And then is heard no more.'...bye...

Death and fear of death is an interesting example... Some maya beings live fearlessly as that shines their elevated ego's existence further, giving them a false ego boost of arrogance bravery perception label... However, and more often, majority maya beings live in constant thought of and fear of death, doing everything as possible in their power to enhance and prolong their illusionary existence. As death is absolute death for their existence, which is both their truth, and also the absolute truth...once over it is...back to the Un-Divine Asuric energy cloud...

Maya beings are constantly living in a paranoia of getting more than the normal recommended full medical check ups...and then more check ups...and even more check ups...craving with fear to potentially discover something ill within...what they may discover may be eventually correct... but surely they will develop some further ill in the process of discovering... The actual ill...goes undiagnosed, which is the permanent innate disability of being devoid of soul...

The fear of death accumulates further as years go by...resulting in an elderly state of misery... emptiness...knowing and unknowingly aware as this is it...like a ticking time bomb...as each minute passing by...fear and anxiety creeping in...through emptiness within...looking for some attachment thread to hold on to...sub-consciously aware that their performance role served as the antagonist performance is only for the souls higher grand rise...

Another maya being's false existence identity feeds off attachment is to enhance one's existing profile through other co-performers existence. Maya beings crave social interaction to feel importance. The true void is inside of devoid of soul conscious awareness...

Romantic Love, friends, family...may be beautiful blessings in one's life...however the overly attached state to any or all of these absolute maya classified co-performers...and their validation approval advice importance...is actually nothing but over emphasis of one's maya existence and false importance through association with and approval of others...especially other maya beings...as that acts as a reinforcing structure for the maya stage...

Attached to becoming and being popular...and worshiping popular figures...those in perceived higher status positions...following them unrelentingly...when in all reality a soul being in its highest form...shall only follow its soul...and nothing and no one else...to touch or wearingly display diamonds does not make one a diamond...it is or is not... However, maya beings, regardless of heightened ego, still are followers by being attached...whether people, entrapping beliefs, environment, or objects...as at their very core...they are the Maya Leela play being followers commanded by asuric energy...following the maya jaal entrapment web instructs...

Being highly socially pretentious, craving to appear the life of the party...attention grabbing crave... crave for high crowded social settings and the available social platforms...the constant intense craving for being popular and or among the perceived popular... All the social crave is highly burdening through all the limited energy exertion and wastage of the limited moments one is blessed...as within this limited maya existence...ignorance of the limited time existence and limited existence resources is absolute wastage through attachment...

Attachment to previous information sets one in the trap of ignorance of potentially never discovering the truth and evolving oneself... Orthodox and conventional thought processes dominate the maya being...whether it is societal, political, religious, religious extremities, cultural, family traditions...the maya being feels best at ease when they are highly attached and grounded to the Maya illusion...as this makes sense for them completely...any shift beyond the Maya illusion...and their existence shall be concerningly jeopardized…

4. Jealousy

**"So full of artless jealousy is guilt,
  It spills itself in fearing to be spilt."**

**William Shakespeare
(Renowned Poet / Playwright)**

Jealousy is to feel threatened, insecure, or protective of something you already have...here the maya being's entire existence is dependent on Maya existence...this fact makes them very protectively jealous of the Maya illusion entrapment realm...to ensure that souls remain unawake and unaware of unveiling their illusion...by every means necessary…

Maya being feels a plethora of jealousy driven emotions while co-performing with the soul being on the Maya Leela play stage...by being jealous of the threat of soul being's awakening awareness that is potentially capable of severely disrupting and eliminating their previous convenience maya entrapped status quo...capable of collapsing the entire Maya Leela play stage by unveiling the illusion...hence threatening the maya being's very limited existence…

Major spiritual attacks on soul beings are driven by the maya threat jealousy that maya beings experience… Keeping the potential awake...unawake...is the highest priority...keeping the soul vibration frequencies as low as possible...by reinforcing their dim grim asuric energy of Maya jaal web entrapments…

5. Envy

Envy differs from jealousy…

Envy is the longing to have something particular that some other individual has...whether it be some attributes or possessions... Whereas, jealousy is to feel threatened, insecure, or protective of something you already have…

A factory defected or compromised product will naturally envy others who are the same fully functioning quality product and or user of the fully functioning product...this is how a maya being is ever trapped in envy...as either they are envious of other maya beings, who are in some way perceived as a better maya product than them...or they envy the product user soul being...who is blessed further by being beyond the product and actually for whom the product exist for...the soul protagonist's performance enhancer as serving as their antagonist performer...

The maya being feels intense envy of the Divine energy spark of soul energy that the soul being possess that is forever devoid from their temporary limited existence...hence again threatening their limited existence ego...creating a perpetual cycle of envy driven Maya entrapment attacks...often capable of extreme severity and cruelty...unfortunately...

**"Never underestimate
the power of jealousy
and the power of envy
to destroy.
Never underestimate that."**

Oliver Stone (Renowned Filmmaker)

6. Anger

"Never anger made good guard for itself.'

**William Shakespeare
(Renowned Poet / Playwright)**

Anger is deeply imbedded in maya beings as reactive ego response...being and solely existing in Maya...everything is taken to overwhelming reactions very rapidly and intensely as this is their home stage...the Maya stage...naturally one always perceives with personal protective perspective when the subject involves one's home and their existence within that home...this maya protective mechanism expresses out as hysterical anger...

Anger...from a biological perspective is simply an overstimulated sympathetic nervous system threat response of 'fight or flight' which is the opposite of the relaxed state of parasympathetic 'rest and digest' state... Fight or flight response is instinctive and very in tune with the survival of humanity... especially from the ancient hunter and hunted era... A perceived threat stimulates this response for survival...when one cannot fulfill this response through either fighting or fleeing...this threat takes on an angry state of being...either expressed or surpressed...but still present within until the perceived threat is no longer acute or extreme...or down regulated naturally from the fight or flight stimulated stage...

For a maya being, the most threatening stimulus is anything that threatens its core existence... Both as being maya presently existent...and the maya stage of where it perceives to exist...both are absolutely required for the maya being existence...any threat to this...triggers an anger response to re-emphasize one's ego existence and continue survival...

Ego is existence...attachment is to existence...greed and jealousy reinforces this existence...threat to this existence...is a violation...anger acts out this violation threat...as violence...the lust of harming others for one's dominant existence...either verbal, physical, and or to oneself self destructuring existence...all this is common rooted with its fascist existence...when physical existence is all they have...it becomes overwhelming presence of the maya being as existing on its Maya stage platform...as that rightfully is all that a maya being has...is this Maya existence...therefore it protects it unrelentingly...using anger as its guard...

7. Lust

**"One sin, I know,
  another doth provoke.
  Murder's as near to lust
  as flame to smoke"**

**William Shakespeare
(Renowned Poet / Playwright)**

**"Lust is...
  Conditions of want...
  Love is...
  Deviation from not...
  Purity potency protected...
  From making Love with all..."**

Hugh Shergill

Lust...the crave of Maya indulgence...

Lust is not just restricted to sexual crave...but lust is simply put the lower aspect of all Maya desire itself...with unrelenting urgency... Lust is unpacifying crave for the Maya realm and all that exists within it... Lust is fundamentally a weakness... Lust is selfish... Love, in its true expression is unconditional... as there is no condition attached to the maya stage and maya leela performers...there is no lust involved... Love is power...power is devoid of weakness... Lust is a weak impostering illusion of how one falsely craves for oneself as existing and how desiring all that lustfully fulfills and enhances this illusionary perception of existence...

Maya Leela

Sexuality and sexual crave is deep rooted to existence...as reproduction is synonymous with sexuality... Lust is essentially crave desire of reproduction... The reproduction of one's Maya existence as a maya being... In all reality this is impossible... As maya being unknowingly is aware of this, therefore the lust of desire to remain existing...manifests in many aspects of the maya being...that is beyond just sexual desire...

Desire of existing...is the Maya lust...all as Maya...and everything within Maya...is possible and open to lust for...this illusionary trap state of desire...is the selfish existence state...that puts the maya being on the Maya lust circle treadmill wheel that is ever present while illusionary existing...craving...crave until to the grave...unbreaking until game over...the maya being existent deletion...which is absolute... the inevitable no...no soul...no continuation...this unknowing yet knowing of the no creates urgency to indulge in all manifests as lust...ultimately as the lust for Maya...

Lust is utmost emptiness...hidden in illusionary maya...that remains unfulfilled...therefore the crave never ceases...the more one lusts...the more one lusts...lust can be hidden but never pacified...this never ending cycle gets even exhausting for the maya being...as no more matter how much lust is fulfilled...it remains unfulfilled...it is viciously rooted within...more the indulgence...results in more entrapment...the entrapment of Maya...the Maya jaal web of entrapment...

Soul Less Behavioural Characteristics...

"Maya beings use a lot of word...
  Yet never keep their word..."

The soul less maya being is forever suffering from soul energy famine... forever starving and craving soul energy... reaction, interaction, acknowledgement from a soul being is desperately required... Therefore excessive use of communication words are used constantly...yet ironically keeping their word is their innate scarcity... A lot is assured, promised, and said... however when the moment arrives to deliver...they act dead...
Ingenuity is the forte of asuric energy soul less maya being entities...as their energy itself is ingenuine...all is not only talk...all is...just talk...

"Promises assurity loyalty...
Innately a foreign entity...
Using lots of words constantly...
Keeping one's word a scarcity...

Their words..
Mere words...
Lies of words...
None are genuine...
Just said to up one...
Their associations...
Mere associations...
Lies of associations...

Promises assurity loyalty...
Innately a foreign entity...
Using lots of words constantly...
Keeping one's word a scarcity..."

Hugh Shergill

Gossiping is Worshiping...

Maya Beings...
The Gossip Kings & Queens...

Innately...souls are aware of how poisonous gossiping is for one's soul...it is that forbidden fruit of the serpent that poisons the soul...yet this is not the case for the asuric soul less...as this is their primary passion for poisonous indulgence...

Interestingly indeed, not only as a last attempt to extract the soul being's energy...also the most passionate hobby and interest of a maya being is talking about others...gossiping about others...spreading illusionary rumours about others...trolling others...putting others down to their already existing levels... The reason is simple...the key word here is 'Others'...they extremely envy the high energy 'star of the stage play' undeniable vibes of the soul being's innate soul aura...as they deep down are aware that behind their false fake persona illusion...that they are the outsiders of this collective play stage...there is nothing potent within their empty vessel...they know that they are highly low vibrational entities and must bring all attention to themselves to create the illusion of appearing high vibrational and above the soul being...in every way and every any means necessary... The maya being is an extremely low vibrational soul less asuric entity...they are diabolically desperately in need, crave, desire, extract potent energy from soul beings... (More in depth analysis of energies in the upcoming chapters)

In an attempt to scavenge the soul being's potent energy...yet if the soul being denies direct access...therefore now the maya being can not directly access this energy from the soul being, as the awakened soul being does not give access to its Divine soul spark energies by setting strict

Maya Leela

boundaries of space and communication… Now the desperate maya being attempts to extract some energy from that particular soul being by occupying themselves in their fascinating thoughts…in a way that is a forced maya being's own unique peculiar strange version of meditation, mantra chanting, and worship of the soul being religiously…by talking nonsense, gossip, rumours, ranting, trolling, putting others down etc…this is their soul being energy extraction worshiping method…a highly appearing humorous peculiar method of meditating, worshiping, and repeatedly mantra chanting on the name of the soul being followed by their asuric soul less seven acts infused egorance acting nonsense…

Maya being's Fascination…
Envy of the Real Play Star Soul Being…

Maya being's Meditation is…
Occupied in Thoughts of the Soul Being…

Maya being's Mantra is…
Talking about the Soul Being…

Maya being's Worship is…
Meditating & Mantra Chanting of the Soul Being…
Unrelentingly Passionately Religiously…

Indeed and unfortunately…the bigger the lie, the more people will believe it…however in the long term, this worshiping method is ineffective…even the longest rope has an end…rumours and lies eventually get exposed reaching their end…it does little or nothing to the worshiped soul being…if the soul being simply ignores and disregards the maya being's worshiping…as one cannot stop a Divine journey to respond to each maya being's filthy gossiping worship…letting instead karma take its Divine course… This worshiping method is extremely detrimental and dangerous for the maya being…as the maya being itself ends up depleting their already low vibrational fuel asuric energies even further low and then even lower…bringing their depleted energy vibration so low that the depleted energetic field now causes severe deprivation and compromisation in their physical and mental health…physically, they will biologically age very rapidly…a rotting type of rapid aging and deterioration of physical appearance and health… mentally, there will be many mental health and psychological issues that will be instantly triggered perpetually… Unfortunately…a Maya being is that hamster on the running wheel…as they are incapable of realization of how their strange worshiping practices are actually digging their own early grave…as they will passionately continue to bite and chew on each gram of soil that they are digging out with their own mouth for their own grave…till their very end…

"Those that believe my rumour…
 Are too weak to be near anywhere…
 Keep on listening to the illusion…
 I shall continue my ascension…
 Whenever you get exhausted…
 Witness my uplift exalted…'

Hugh Shergill

That Question…am I perhaps a Maya Being?

Impossible, absolutely impossible…this question of perhaps doubting your based on these relevationary traits would not be understood nor further resonate…the Maya jaal entrapment would never allow processing and resonating of these revelations for its own maya beings ever…as their asuric low vibration soul less energy will only result in complete disregard reject of this revelating reveal…

The correct and appropriate responses are either resonating of the revelations presented as a soul being…or complete egorance disregard of the information presented to the maya being…

Real Question…
Of what you have read so far…
Does it resonate?
Or do you completely reject?

Your answer will answer your previous question…as both responses are absolutely correct within their particular and differentiating confined limitations of processing and conscious awareness levels…this is warmth calm beauty of the revelation insights…truth itself is its defense…truth never needs to be defended…truth defends itself…which are beyond argument, debates, and disagreements…as both agreeing and disagreeing are both absolutely correct…

The interesting response is the one of perhaps slight doubt…doubting one as being a maya being… devoid of soul… With that question arising within…congratulations…you have just become soul aware of your soul…with the resonating of the reveal…breaking past the Maya jaal entrapment…which would never let this resonate to their appointed maya pawns…as for a revelation of awareness to occur, requires soul consciousness…which is impossible for maya being to acquire or develop… Soul exists or it does not…either knowing or unknowing… So therefore, embrace and celebrate of being soul aware, which is the most crucial step towards progressive awareness…what you are therefore experiencing is the severities as a soul being being a prey of the maya jaal entrapment web that has stalled or very slowed the soul being progression journey…time to create your true karma…by making effort to escape from the maya entrapments…and your soul will progressively evolve and shine through…

"Make way on to the stage for star quality…
 Moment of grand stage entry by far…
 Of the play's main protagonist star…"

CHAPTER 10.

SOUL
PERFORMER

Soul Being…

The Benevolent Protagonist…

"It takes a Soul…

To touch the whole…

What was the extraction…

Holds ingredients potential…

Required credentials to know it...

Requires capabilities to touch it…"

Hugh Shergill

Maya Leela

The Insiders...

Unlike the outsider Maya beings... Soul beings are insiders...all their existence is based in soul within... the core Divine energy source itself ...much above and beyond the Maya realm...

"My soul is in the sky"

William Shakespeare
(Renowned Poet / Playwright)

Soul being...beyond the confines of Divine's Maya expression...it is the Divine being expressed itself through its Divine spark...not just the projected but the projecting itself...the human projected Maya experience with soul consciousness projection...experiencing Maya existence through soul being existence...immediately unknowing but activated soul performer...the anti Maya jaal performer... Soul being's purpose is a breakthrough performance from Maya existence...a Maya escape artist switching from illusionary existence into Maya escapism...and emerging as one again with the Divine...shifting from mere limited projected existence to the infinite projection existence...existence as and in all...

Soul beings are soul conscious beings...consisting of soul consciousness...the soul spark conscious of the Divine... All spiritual chakras, nadis, Kundalini Shakti, third eye chakra, pineal gland are all actively present with full potential activation...yet initially in dormant stage awaiting to be ignited with soul energy activation spark within through one's enlightened awareness... Just like a glass...that is fully containing one's desired beverage...all awaiting to be indulged...

The soul spark is blessed by the Divine through conception...the purity of Love...Love that is itself making Love...sparking the infinite soul spark of the Divine magically within the purity of womb in the realm Maya existence and beyond...with eternal euphoria aura...of soul experience existence...

Divinity Aware Living Environment...

Divine Lit Spark Flare...

Soul being's surrounding Maya perception environment has Divinely lit sparks of existence...to travel a pathway...the pathway should be visible...

As one travels on the path of ascension...the Divine path is lit with sparks of Divinity...Dynamically these Divine lit sparks...lights up our ascension path towards moksha state experiencing nirvana...helping us to keep on track with lamps of Divine's Love...like the numerous stage spotlights set for the play stage... illumination induced with indications...sequencing lighting performance...

Every living organism is potentially capable of having a reciprocal Divine spark...Every living organism has that Divine spark potential if it is within aware of the existence of a higher power...quantum entanglement...what one seeks...stimulates what is seeked...this awareness is the voice of the Divine...

this awareness spark may exist in every living organism...from a single strand of grass...to a flower... tree...animal...to an human soul being...the key is the innate Divine awareness...this nature and its beings influences may act as both soul solace and Divine path guidance...giving innate soul comfort upon association...this is the reason why soul beings resonate more towards certain nature spots and certain specific animals that they feel a deep connection towards...often more so than other fellow human beings...often you will see an unexplained soul bliss of an individual taking their pet for a walk in a nature path...this is a factor why ancient sages in deep meditation were completely protected even when residing in the most dangerous deadliest jungles and forests...vedic legends numerously have mentioned the mystical aura of a snake...even ancient mythological legends commonly have mentioned and associated the shape shifting Shakti energetic aura from a particle to a wave is present in a certain few Divine's selected snakes... An unprovoked venomous snake attack on humans is highly rare... as a potentially fatal attack as such has much more to it on a spiritual realm than what meets the three dimensional eye...

On the Maya Leela stage...there is always a soul energy communication with other soul's at play... it's a resonating soul aura communication entangled romance...as each playing out its karma script sequence...what is soul equipt...shall realize the synchronizations communicating through the script...

"Dear Flower...
  Witness you are...
  Felt the witness you were...

  Surrounded among many in nature...
  Yet I gravitated to you in particular...
  As I approached touched you close...
  Felt a shy hesitating flashback pause...
  There is something about your scent...
  Profoundly I find it reminiscent...
  A Soul memory beyond your fragrance...
  Resonating aroma of life times romance...

  Dear Flower...
  Witness you are...
  Felt the witness you were..."

Hugh Shergill

The Innate Non Egorance State of Soul Being...

Anti-Egorance...innately...the anti ego, anti ignorance, and anti arrogance state...the opposite state of the soul less egorance existence...just by being a soul...soul being...authentic soul spark of Divinity itself...

Just as every human...the soul being also experiences the perceived physical state of existence... however its awareness exists...on a core soul higher conscious level...that one perhaps is processing knowing or unknowing...that the fact is that it is indeed existing in an illusionary state of physical existence within and further in the illusionary realms of maya itself...therefore the attachment to this state is not given illusionary weight comparatively to one's absolute authentic existence...the eternal soul... Divinity expressing itself...soul being...being soul itself...

**"We are in the world...
But not of it..."**

Denzel Washington (Renowned Actor)

Beyond the illusionary Maya physicality processing awareness...manifests as an anti-ego state...ego is experienced, realized and yet one is able to detached aware of its presence...that deviation of ego identification...revealingly experiences a soul being state...where one becomes the observer of the observed...not the observed...that Maya detachment is Divinity soul experience...tranquility euphoria state...that ultimate leads one to moksha ..nirvana...liberation existence...

Detachment to ego...detaches one to the strains of ego...the ego identification...ego is acknowledged and kept in ease control state...as the soul being existence shines through by illuminating light that vanishes the dark illusion entrapments of the ego...shining and illuminating possibilities of life that remained undiscovered through ego ignorance...ego arrogance...collectively egorance...

When one is beyond ignorance...all that was ignored...appears now on to the Maya Leela stage... perception awareness increasing...results in ignorance decreasing...further resulting in arrogance vanishing...where one comes to realization of one true self...beyond the Maya jaal entrapment performance structure of egorance...by being in the authenticity of one's soul...the soul being...this awareness state gifts humility essence within...

**"And oftentimes, to win us to our harm,
The instruments of darkness tell us truths,
Win us with honest trifles,
To betray's in deepest consequence"**

**William Shakespeare
(Renowned Poet / Playwright)**

Often...unaware soul beings falsely associate with the Maya entrapments through the Maya Leela stage and Maya jaal influence...however unlike maya beings, this takes place with a profoundly affecting heavy soul burden...where one's soul feels the heaviness egorance existence burden and continues to do so... karmically through multiple lifetime existences...as each lesson is forever repeated until learned...until it finally becomes consciously awake and aware of the Maya Leela stage curtains...and that curiosity motivates to discover what lies behind the curtains of the Maya Leela stage...lifting the curtains of Maya...where all and then all is revealed within...

Innately...beyond all the lures of Maya Jaal web entrapments...the soul being is essentially an anti Maya jaal being at core...it possesses an anti egorance personality innately...this innate core soul trait lacks the illusion trapped heightened ego...therefore it further authentically lacks ignorance and arrogance... Being essentially devoid of egorance results in natural counter Maya entrapment acts in the soul being's acts of Maya Leela performance...this remains core within...both either knowingly or unknowingly...this is however subjected to modulation based on the individual soul being's illusionary Maya existence, karmic debts, experiences, and particular weaknesses that may lure one into the ever dominant Maya jaal web entrapments...

The Non-Maya Entrapment Acts of Soul Being

"Counter Maya entrapment acts...
  With soul conscious acts..."

Non Ego...

**"We know
 what we are,
 but know not
 what we may be"**

**William Shakespeare
(Renowned Poet / Playwright)**

All Aura...

**"Drop the attitude...
 Embrace gratitude...
 Strive to inspire...
 Before this expire...
 Power within is confidence...
 Power pretend is arrogance..."**

Hugh Shergill

Being soul conscious... One is aware that this mere illusionary physical is not all...as there is absolute much more that exists within...this awareness of existing beyond the physical awareness...even at its unaware Maya realm existence...creates innate humility...ego existence perhaps may still exist be identified with...dependent on the soul being's particular evolutionary experiential process journey...but innately it is still to a very minimum comparatively to a maya being...as one knows it does not know...and is beyond all that illusion perceiving is...

**"Even the tallest tree...
  Bends its branches lower...
  Once it bears its sweetest fruit...
  Ironically and ignorantly...
  People attempt to stand tall and stiff...
  Upon bearing some success gift..."**

Hugh Shergill

**"In one drop of water
  are found all
  the secrets of all the oceans;
  In one aspect of you
  are found all
  the aspects of existence."**

Khalil Gibran (Renowned Poet / Writer)

Not 'I'... All is 'I'...

The ego is simply the perceived sense of self...soul being's are beyond the ego...as they are aware of that their 'self' is much beyond their physical self...that their self itself is essentially Divinity's spark of soul expression itself...and what is Divinity's...can not be just be yours...non ego is non just self...an 'I' for the soul being...is not merely a physical entity referenced as 'I'...in fact all is the 'I' the collective essence of all existences and operatives karmic consequences...the 'I' may include the perceived 'I' yet it openly and more importantly includes all that created this 'I'...what is beyond self...thus not just self...a non ego existence eternity...not 'I'... Instead all is 'I'...

**"Revulsion felt by the deflated ego...
  When in presence of the inflated ego...
  Deploring to be amongst the present...
  Those that feel they are the present...
  Incapable of even creating their own I...
  Terribly failing to impress my eye..."**

Hugh Shergill

The one with a soul...feels weighed down internally when talking about themselves in high regard... whether it is one's perceived physical attributes, particular Maya realm accomplishments, and any other associated accolades... This weighing down factor is not a humble taught trait for oneself as fortunately collectively as a global society...at least surfacely perceived ...those that self praise themselves are still perceived generally as narcissitically egoistics...therefore the large majority that highly identify with their ego popular being superiority perhaps would have been taught reprogrammed and deviated from that existence being...but that is not the case...high ego existence state is not forced upon one nor shunned...it is always that particular individual's internal driven consciousness that determines how strongly one identifies with this illusionary existence...as high ego and high Maya illusionary existence is synonymous indefinitely... As commonly it is said..."Success and riches makes a good person more good...and a wicked person more wicked..."

"I'm not a person who wants to
die with my shoes on.
I do not think I can be immortal.
Maybe my deeds will be immortal.
Not me."

Mithun Chakraborty (Renowned Actor)

"Ego is a drink...
That requires completely...
To be ingested within...
Any external spill...
One's character falls ill...
Carefully drink it...
Never spill it..."

Hugh Shergill

The soul being, as it evolves further on its soul righteous path performance...less and less it finds interest in the physical illusionary realm existence... One shifts focus from 'I' to more collective all is 'I'... All that is as all that it exists...beyond particular realm restrictive existences... This soul trait creates caring and consideration for all others...as one perceives all as a mere illusionary existing physical state...aware of the fluctuating discrepancies of evolved performance...but nevertheless no superiority of anyone comparatively on a physical state of existence exists...

"Arrogance is pretentious...
Confidence is conscientious...
Empowering smile of confidence...
Empty smirk of arrogance...
Arrogance often reveals...
Forever attempting lifting its lows...
Confidence keeps whispering lips sealed...
With effortless ease with all it knows..."

Hugh Shergill

Superiority does not exist in existence... Superiority is in the karma performance of one in the Maya Leela play... A so called perceived superior physical existing being is capable of a highly inferior performance...much below comparatively to the potential that perhaps exists... And also a so called inferior physical existing being is capable of a superior breakthrough performance that merges one directly with the Divine energy source...the true and ultimate superiority... Striving, evolving, flowing on one's true performance is the journey of the soul...self illusionary recognition stalls the journey... Superiority is not in the existence of the play character...but in the performance of the character... Therefore the egoistic driven crave for self praise and also seeking praise vanishes...as the soul only values truth...nothing but the truth...and all its manifests...

"The odor of ego is appalling...
 For those capable of its smelling..."
 Those swimming deep in a tank...
 Have no idea of ocean depth bank...
 Shun dimming your shining light...
 As they are incapable for your flight...
 As the ego begins to expire...
 Essence of soul begins to inspire..."

Hugh Shergill

Non Greed...

"Fortune reigns in gifts of the world"

William Shakespeare
(Renowned Poet / Playwright)

The crave of accumulation beyond one's absolute requirements is perceived as futile... Consumption is what is consumed...beyond that is mere assumption... The illusionary existing physical existence also extends to its consumptions... These consumptions are respectively acknowledged as necessities for surviving optimally while experiencing the ever limited illusionary state of physical existence...however going beyond the necessaries of consumption is never soul performance motivated...

Desire given... Requires Desire taken...

**"Desire given...
  Requires Desire taken...**

**Each desire requires
Another of ours...
Desires sacrificed…
For desires to facilitate...
I've placed many of my desires...
Encapsulated in my soul pocket...
As it takes a lot of expenditures...
To reach one's destination…**

**Desire given...
Requires Desire taken…"**

Hugh Shergill

**"Life is simple beautifully light…
  False desires create the fight…
  Is it truly your ambition?...
  Or an imposed tradition?
  Prioritize your soul calling…
  Not your soul opposing…"**

Hugh Shergill

The Gambling Ritual of the Deepavali…
Indulgence of a Much Deeper Insight…

Interestingly, In the popular respective festival of lights…Deepavali (Diwali)…it is auspicious ancient tradition to play games/cards while gambling with money…the gambling with money on Deepavali is an interesting ritual…not in terms of seeking monetary gains but to beautifully witness the deeper duality dynamics of the Divinity Shakti Lakshmi…the Goddess of wealth and prosperity… During the festivities of Deepavali…where one is participating in multiple traditional ritual activities to evoke and welcome the blessings of Lakshmi Shakti…including given this one night of the year liberty of indulging in the games of gambling…where along with the all the fun and games…a more deeper meaning of the temperament of wealth is revealed… Indeed, one may possibly be witness blessed with some winning immediate monetary gains…yet also as the games continue to unfold…one will also witnesses loss of the monetary gains as it shifts to the next winner… This is the humbling witnessing temperament of wealth…you may for now gain immediate…yet the dynamics Shakti energy of wealth will continue to flow on its destined destination…either towards more gain or loss…yet it will inevitably continue to shift…this is the essence of energy…this is Shakti of wealth and prosperity…today it is yours…yet tomorrow it may not be…the day after it surely will not be…just as your soul journey continues its ascension…the wealth energy will continue its separate destined journey…traveling from one hand to another hand…hand after hand… innately…the soul being is always aware of this…thus it never attaches itself to wealth and one's winning season with the asuric diabolical trait of greed… The soul being appreciates with gratitude for all its wealth and prosperities blessed upon it…yet is forever unattached by being soul aware of its temporary presence and forever shifting temperament…

"You only lose…
 What is yours…
 That of today…
 Is not of tomorrow…
 Wind experientially felt on one's hand…
 Yet never be entrapped by one's hand…"

Hugh Shergill

An Ancient Sufi Tale…

One day…a visiting tourist enters the home of an elderly man and peculiarly notices that apart from a small lamp, there was nothing else in the entire home…

The tourist asks him:

"Where is your furniture, sir?"

The old man replies:

"And where is yours?"

The tourist is baffled by the response and replies:

"I am only a visitor here. How can I own anything?"

The old man replies:

"I am also only a visitor here in this world…

 I can claim nothing as my own…"

Indeed, this is a 'Return Ticket' visit to the play of Maya Leela...there is nothing one can really own... nor claim...a soul's only possession is its own soul...whatever you claim to own sits on something that you can never claim as your own...further, the claiming claimer itself can not claim ownership of its own perceived physical body that already has its set expiry...You have nothing to lose in this perceived realm...because nothing is yours on this realm...

"Only true poverty in this Maya realm...
  Is the scarcity of Souls..."

True Land Property

**"Earth is our ground proof...
  Sky is our atmospheric roof...
  Existence of interference...
  Devoids complete ownness...
  Ego yet boasts of owning property land...
  While it airly rests on this earthly land...
  To truly own without contradicting proof...
  Eliminate first its ground & atmospheric roof..."**

Hugh Shergill

True Wealth

**"Wealth perceived power is temporary illusion...
  True power is brave wisdom knowledge...
  Power that continues resonating on...
  Beyond physical existence gone...
  Cheapest measure of a person's level achieved ..
  Who measures wealth accumulation perceived...
  A poverty stricken Soul is much more rich...
  Than a self proclaimed arrogantly rich..."**

Hugh Shergill

**"The whole concept of
  the self-made man or woman
  is a myth."**

**Arnold Schwarzenegger
(Renowned Athlete / Actor / Politician)**

"Self made man is amusing…
 As the term itself is confusing…
 How does one create itself?
 Requires the universe as oneself…
 You have nothing to lose…
 Nothing created was ever yours…"

Hugh Shergill

"Is not dread of thirst when your well is full,
 the thirst that is unquenchable?"

Kahlil Gibran
(Renowned Poet / Writer / Visual Artist)

"Achieving that full well is illusionary….
 Cloaking the forever unquenchable thirsty…
 Even the fullest well eventually dries…
 Yet infinite thirst remains in disguise …
 Unrelenting striving greed for a well fuller…
 The thirst shall remain forever greater…"

Hugh Shergill

The soul being deep within is aware of this…and sharing with others all…whether resources or knowledge… is an innate state of being…never manipulation motivated… The appreciation of this Maya stage existence and the brief opportunity for the soul being to participate in the play of Maya Leela…makes the soul being graciously grateful to the Divine for granting this beautiful opportunity to experience and participate in its Maya Leela…which is indeed the Divine's such generosity… Being aware of not being the center of Maya Leela but playing a part in the Maya Leela… innately shifts the soul being from selfish Love to selfless Love…enhanced further through gratitude of appreciation of being given the opportunity to participate in the play of Maya Leela… Therefore, the soul being is ever grateful to reciprocate that highest Divine's generosity gesture by also being utmost generous while performing in its Maya Leela play journey… Giving generously whole heartedly to one's utmost capacity…

"Secrecy of remaining youthfully…
 Secretly giving with generosity…
 Key to satisfying longevity…
 Fire of intentions selflessly…
 Fuel of your unconditional giving…
 Keeps your existence vibe ticking…"

Hugh Shergill

Nature itself is direct Divine expressing...sharing itself wholesome untampered with no dedicated filtered discrimination... The Sun's rays illuminates all that it shines...with all its capacity at that giving moment... The air consumed is never filtered held back...the oxygen is all available precisely for all present at that very giving moment...water is hydrating for all never just selectively few... All nature restrictions created are created through tampering intentions of those motivated and driven by selfish greed... Nature in its untampered state is forever purely giving and giving wholesome generously...

"Water accumulates...
When it precipitates...
For condensation...
Requires evaporation...
That all giving...
Is all receiving..."

Hugh Shergill

The soul being is aware of its physical state is a being a part of nature, never apart...therefore it is necessary to share and give wholeheartedly...of all of oneself...being at service on all realms of existence... Greed is not a natural state of being...it is a Maya jaal entrapment illusionary diabolical force...and as the soul being is aware of this...it strives to overcome greed entrapments through authentic soul driven generosity... Taking subtracts...adding enhancements...soul is aware...enhanced...

The joy of giving is a much higher state of bliss than the joy of receiving...giving is the act of selfishness... on a Divine level...the soul realizes this...as innately the soul source Divine itself only is giving in all in its expressed expressions... When the soul being gives...it further extends its expressed existence on to others...which ultimately enhances one's soul expressed expression...which is a true blissful state of being...soul contagious and soul addictive...

"Service to others
is the rent you pay
for your room here on earth."

**Mohammed Ali
(Renowned Boxer / Revolutionist / Humanitarian)**

Philanthropy and charitable gestures of generosity are performed by the soul being as undisclosed and confidential state...always...this is due to keeping one's self praise ego existence exercise tamed as much as possible...any deed is never excused karmically performing in Maya Leela...what is never unnoticed...does not require to be noticed... The greatest philanthropists of Maya Leela are, have and always been unknown... Those practicing deeds of generosity to be noticed and praised...are not authentic soul performers...they are simply Maya performers interested in praise worthy illusionary Maya realm...yes there are some known exceptions...as even then, whatever is documented is only a fraction of their philanthropy gestures...respect to those that give beyond what is expected or assumed...

Non greed state is being and experiencing an abundance state...as any state of particular potential energy expansion shall manifest into kinetic energy expansion...therefore when one feels being in an expansion state shall experience an expansive state...absolutely... Greed is rooted in being in a forever devoid state...even when one is perceived to be in abundance...greed shall shadow that abundance... as there is no contentment and gratitude of what is...and the urge of always wanting more...keeps one in a permanent perpetual scarcity state...that is why some of the most highly perceived successes are empty devoid failures within...as the soul devoid asuric cloud state is always ever lurking as a dark cloud dominance curse...that prevents one from ever truly experiencing abundance...

Soul conscious being is direct Divine expressing...the abundance of all that is...overwhelms within... creating an everlasting joy blissful contentment state...where one could be in complete darkness and yet experience all radiance of light...everpresent...everlasting... Divine abundance...

"Tree's kind request...
  Please feel free to spend time under my shade...
  Just please don't cut me to suit your aide..."

Gulzar
(Renowned Poet / Lyricist / Film Maker)
Translation by Hugh Shergill

Non Jealousy...
Non Envy...

"Let's go hand in hand,
  not one before another"

William Shakespeare
(Renowned Poet / Playwright)

Soul being in its core state of existence does not express envy or jealousy to anyone ever...as it is aware and conscious of its particular journey performance in the play of Maya Leela...
Every co-performer is respected and realized with their dedicated performance, scope enhancement of performance, and capacity of performance karmically...

No co-performer is playing the soul being's performance...for each it is their own...always is...always shall be...whether it is a fellow soul being performer or even a maya being performer...each one is directed and dedicated specifically to their own performance...therefore just as one cannot play the part of another...no other can play your particular part...thus there is no threat or insecurity of jealousy...nor self perceived deprivation state of existence that ignites the flame of envy...

The soul being realizes that there is no competition with anyone else besides competing with oneself... Competing is competing karmically...by putting forth a performance karmically that excels each step further above the previous step...this evolution is progressive performance...that competes with the previous oneself...and only oneself...step by step...

What then takes over for the soul being above envy is admiration and inspiration...admiration and inspiration for those souls that have enhanced their performance scope and capacity of performance all through their own karma...nothing in existence is accidentical as everything exists as expression of what is...the more perceived enhanced state of one...then there is absolutely enhanced journey of one that has lead to the enhanced state...that is worthy of admiration and inspiring for the soul being...never being envious nor jealous...as Divinity grants what is deserving indefinitely...the soul being is aware of this...as the soul is Divinity's soul spark itself...

What that is felt to inspire shall aspire...inspiration leads to aspiration...aspiration leads to manifestation... Being inspired opens the soul to realms that aspire...that what aspires leads to realms that manifests... what one seeks is what one becomes...what inspires shall become...transforming one from being inspired to becoming the inspired...the karmic play of attraction...

Non Attachment...

**"I myself am best
 When least in company"**

**William Shakespeare
(Renowned Poet / Playwright)**

Solitude is Soul in Tune...

The soul being is aware there is no such entity as loneliness that actually exists...even that awareness that one is lonely...that awareness itself is with you every moment of existence...therefore any conscious awareness in your soul existence...is a union...an everlasting Divine dating romance...accompanying you...interacting you...enriching you...

This evolved aware state of soul being creates innately a complete persona within...non dependent to any other attachment... All perceived attachments are viewed as respective separate from oneself... Innately, this for the soul being shifts the perception of what would be attachment to what is existence... Co-existing while the soul being performs the traveling play of Maya Leela but never attached traveling...

Just like a traveler on a train experiencing its journey independently but still co-travelling with others... there is certainly possible revolt or fondness of some of the co-travellers...perhaps even one also appreciates all the luxury, comforts, amenities that exist within the train compartment...however none of them are actually attached to the one traveler...who's only attachment is existence...existing as the traveler on the train journey...many co-travellers during the journey process will join and leave...luxury indulgences experienced...but the traveler and its journey remains on its destined route...nothing less... nothing more...

Maya Leela

Non Anger…

**"I feel within me a peace
  above all earthly dignities,
  a still and quiet conscience"**

**William Shakespeare
(Renowned Poet / Playwright)**

Emotions are synonymous with ego...higher the state of ego existence...the higher possible emotional abruptions exist... The soul being exists as soul awareness...therefore the soul vessel as the body is experienced separately... Any separation creates distance...that beauty of distance awareness of the soul and the physical perceived illusionary existence creates control...control of the body and all its contained emotions...the soul driven emotional intelligence…

All anger is rooted in offence or threat to one's ego identity...when the notion of ego existence is reduced to the very minimal level...all potential perceived offensive and threatening triggers to this ego...also experience profound reduction…

Innately, beyond the Maya jaal entrapments...the soul being does not experience abrupt anger.. but instead a soul triggered response when one soul's existence is lured into the Maya jaal entrapments... shifting one's route through Maya jaal hindrances and obstacles...this frustration of soul speed breakers leads the soul to further take dynamic actions to get back right on track...once again in full force... picking up speed and focus traveling back on to its soul journey…

Indeed, one may be deliberately lured in Maya jaal entrapment by a maya being to express an intense emotional outburst...this on a physical level is justified as a threat of stimulated sympathetic nervous system trigger...which is fight or flight...reaction...reaction that may be necessary for survival and safety... however emotional outburst of anger is unnecessary ineffective...raising one's voice...portraying and acting aggressive for survival and safety is absolutely necessary in certain threatful scenarios...or even when one is taking a stance against injustice...but using these physical triggers for emotional triggers that go beyond safety and survival is unnecessary, ineffective, and counter productive... Soul being is aware of this...even during lured Maya jaal entrapment moments...regret and remorse shall prevail...false excuse of justification always builds soul guilt heaviness within... Evolving and learning to effectively react to these emotions is self soul motivating...always on the soul being's evolved conscious level...and it shall evolve without a doubt...whether within one illusionary existent role living...or if karmic necessities of upcoming evolution existence opportunity lessons...the soul burden is overbearing and shall be overcome...soul assured...

Emotional control is highly important for soul beings... Metaphorically, treat emotions, especially anger as the 'Vish' (poison) consumption of Lord Shiva... Lord Shiva consumed the poison but kept it only in his mouth, neither ingesting it...damaging himself...and neither excreting onto others...damaging them... Keeping it in your mouth is a metaphorical reference as storage, concentrate, potentize, acknowledge... to transform that deadly venom into miraculous medicine...to heal and transform...encapsulating it and storing it as medicine to heal oneself and to excel oneself…

Non to Lust…

"Love surfeits not,
  Lust like a glutton dies;
  Love is all truth,
  Lust full of forged lies."

William Shakespeare
(Renowned Poet / Playwright)

"Lust is mere feel…
  Love is Divinity real…"

Craving for lower Maya realm desire is what a maya being lusts for…lust is intense desire with urgency… consumed completely by the desire..this urgency of desire reflects on the maya being's inevitable deletion…serving no higher purpose beyond one's illusionary physical craves for limited span… Contrarily, living for purpose and higher realm desire…is the soul being's expressive motivated path… Love…patiently pursued on the eternal journey…lust never exists…and Love forever exists…lust is selfish…Love Is selfless…

Lust is non existence for soul being as what exists instead is biological physical requirements and soul conscious requirements…which is Divinity Love… as physical and emotional indulgences, needs, and desires are not foreign for evolved soul beings…those that deliberately portray its complete abstinence… are contradictory hypocrites that are portraying an illusionary facade triggered by Maya ignorance… hiding and taming is not evolving… yet protecting one's energetic and biological aura from unnecessary foreign intrusion is definitely a must…through soul discipline, intuition, and discernment…

"Treat your ego…
  Like your libido…
  Every moment of urge…
  Idiotic to be entertained…
  Desire with depth…
  Intimately kept…
  Never play with someone's soul…
  For the mere desire of their flesh…"

Hugh Shergill

As an optimum healthy physical state shall illuminate life…life that desires and requires on all realms… biological, environmental, materialistic… The difference for the soul being is the spiritual evolved state of higher realm desire…desire driven by truth and honesty that is aspiring from Divinity Love…aspiringly spiritual purity…not lust…where one is traveling and performing one's Maya Leela soul journey with higher purpose beyond the physical illusionary state...motivated by spiritual connect, Love, care, evolution, with higher purpose for oneself and others...which is ultimately Love...never lust...

"Intimacy influenced...
  By inadequate Love ...
  Is a lost soul wandering dove...
  Where failingly seeks...
  Impossible honesty reveal...
  Where more honesty is found...
  In an intimate transactional deal..."

Hugh Shergill

Evolution is never granted...it is an earned state...accepting this is the first step of evolution...desire is energy...energy is either kinetic energy or potential energy...nevertheless energy...ever present...shifting the dynamics of the energy is the key...from the lower level Maya lust to evolved desire with higher purpose...Love...

"All is energy...
  Desires are energy...
  When settled below...
  It is Desirely Kama...
  When at its highest flow...
  It is Divinely Rama..."

Hugh Shergill

Compassion...
Most definite trait...
Of a Soul Being...

"In any situation,
  do not leave compassion
  until one's last breath,
  if compassion is left,
  you may be anything,
  however you will definitely
  not be spiritual…"

Tulsidas (Renowned Poet)

"Having Kindness…
  Divine Fragrance…
  Having Empathy…
  Divine Personality…
  Having Compassion…
  Divine Passion…"

Hugh Shergill

Soul is Authentic…Not Perfect…

"Soul is authentic…
  Not perfect…
  Authentic is not perfect…
  Soul is authentic…
  Never claiming to be perfect…
  It is the perfection of its authenticity…
  Not self proclaimed perfectibility…

Hugh Shergill

Imperfections
Are Perfections…

"Imperfections
 Are perfections…
 Imperfections of the authentic is perfection…
 Brilliant cut zircon can never be…
 On the value of a raw uncut diamond…
 Whether it's soothing sunlight…
 Or rebellious lightning revolt…
 Light always remains light…
 Existence amongst all unlight…
 Diamond shall bright its maximum shine…
 Revealed to those with vision precise…"

Hugh Shergill

"To know your energy abilities…
 Reveals your energetic capabilities…"

CHAPTER 11.

ENERGY
TREASURES

"Bodies of energetic treasuries…
Specific complexity of energies…
Infinite pool of possibilities…
Inevitable travel of trajectories…
To protect the treasure…
Be aware of the treasure…"

Hugh Shergill

"If you want to find the secrets of the universe, think in terms of energy, frequency and vibration."

Nikola Tesla
(Renowned Scientist / Engineer / Inventor)

View every individual in terms of their energy...not their physical entity... To protect one's energy... one must become aware of its energies...the various surrounding energies...the complexity of the energies...the dynamics of the energies...the interactions of attraction and repellency of energies...

"Just as one learns about electricity...
 Precautions of handling its energy...
 It is necessary to learn about...
 Your surrounding energies...
 To protect one's own energy...
 Prepared with protection...
 Eliminates your execution..."

Hugh Shergill

Two Primary Governing Energies...
In the Realm of Maya...

1. Prana
2. Asura

1. Prana Shakti...

The Powerful Cosmic Energy...

All energies associated with a soul being is called 'Prana Shakti'... Prana Shakti is the primordial cosmic energy that governs and energizes the soul being's mind, body, and soul...

2. Asura Maya...

Maya Confined Energy Source...

Primary energy source associated with a maya being is called 'Asura Maya'... Asura Maya is the independent asuric energy confined to the Maya realm only...this energy is contrasting opposite to Prana Shakti...governing and providing energy to maya being's mind and body... As Asura Maya energy is confined to the Maya realm only...it is very much low vibration energy in comparison to the powerful cosmic energy of prana Shakti...that governs all and every realm...

Tri-Soul Being

The three level bodies of a Soul Being...

A Soul Being's body in this Maya realm vessel, is made up of a combination of three distinct level bodies...

1. Physical Body (Karya Sharira)

The physical body is the immediate biological existing body in this Maya realm... consisting of all the biological existence requirements to be considered as a living human being...

Both Soul beings and Maya beings on a physical biological level share identical physical biological processes...

2. Energy Aura Body (Linga Sharira)

The energy aura body is the non physical energy aura body that is both within and beyond the confines of the physical body... The energy aura body can be also referred to as the consciousness body...as one's consciousness creates karmically a unique distinct energy levels form an energy field both in and around the body known as the aura...
The aura body despite being within the physical body is also energetically aura connected, reactive, sensitive to every other energetic aura forms... both positive and negative energy...

All chakras exist in the energy aura body of the soul being... These from low to high are active for each particular soul being...these chakras are forever fluctuating and modulating... However the powerhouse energy... Kundalini Shakti remains dormant in the energy aura body until it is not triggered and influenced by the soul body...

Proximity is energy exchange...we exchange energetic aura energies with everyone in our immediate physical environment...communication is not the only factor...more important is just your and their presence...even standing still with your eyes closed and ears plugged...you will sense energy...you will see their energy influences...you will hear their energy influences...and most profoundly...you will undeniably feel their energy influences...

The physical energy aura body is most potent within the radius of one's physical height multiplied by three... For example, my physical body height is six feet tall, multiplied by three, is eighteen feet... My energy aura is most powerfully potent and receptive within a radius of eighteen feet in my surrounding physical space...further distance still has an effect but not so potently... Therefore, anyone within my eighteen feet space is influenced energetically by my energy aura most powerfully...and more importantly vice versa, is also influencing my energy aura most powerfully by being within eighteen feet of space to my physical body...

Maya Leela

Two Linga Sharira...

Two Distinct Types of Energy Aura Bodies:

      A. Suric Energy (Soul Being Sura Energy)

Soul Energy...

Energy aura body that consists of the Divine spark of soul energy...with a multitude of beautiful soul energy chakras, nadis, and containing the Kundalini Shakti (both dormant and active possibilities)...like the beautiful sparkling stars in the milky way...all galactically existing Divinely within...

      B. Asuric Energy (Maya Being Asura Energy)

Asura Chakra Energy...
Diabolical Energy Sphere...

Energy aura body that consists of 'Asura Chakra' which is one mega diabolical asuric energy chakra, dominantly operating over the entire asuric energy aura body, both their entire internal aura and external aura...

To describe the 'Asura Chakra'... imagine a large spherical negative energy ball three times the physical height radius of that particular maya being...in which the asuric maya being permanently resides in...not entrapped diabolically as being diabolical is their core essence existence...instead forever influenced and dominated by that negative energy spherical ball while in their limited existence...and further causing intense repellent deplorable friction whenever a Divinity soul energy being enters that asuric sphere radius space of theirs...yet paradoxically...repellent as it is to soul energy...the asuric chakra sphere also serves as a vacuum to suck soul energy as that is its desperate fuel for its continuing diabolical asuric existence...

As this diabolical asura chakra is their only primary energy dominant field...there are no other active energy chakras, nadis, along with the absolute impossibility of containing the Divine Kundalini Shakti...

3. Soul Body (Karana Sharira)

The soul body is simply one's soul... Your true infinite body... Divinely eternal... the Divine's creation spark itself that is indeed seeded in both your physical and energy aura body...yet infinitely beyond... connecting one the Divine's creation to the Divine creator itself... The soul body is the Divine infinite source with infinite possibilities... it is the key to unlocking the Kundalini Shakti...

Bi-Maya Being...

All similarities between a soul being and a maya being end at the biological physical appearing body...
Maya Beings have only two level bodies...
Physical and Energy Aura Body...

Never a Soul Body…

Maya being's existence is the obvious physical body and asura chakra energy aura body only…
No Soul body for the non Soul…

There are no more further energy structure dynamics of a maya being…beyond their physical body and asura chakra asuric energy aura…as all asuric soul less energy stops there…with no further possibilities of any soul energy induced energetic gateways…

Continuation of infinite Soul energy…

Nadis…
Chakras
Kundalini Shakti…
Infinity…
Moksha…
Nirvana…
Divinity…

Nadi…The Soul Energy Aura Channels

Nadi is energetic aura channels…there are
multi-thousands of specific energy aura channels within the energy aura body itself that are forever forming, dissolving, evolving as karmically required for the soul being's immediate soul journey state experience…
Similar to the billions of stars in the milky way galaxy… Forming…dissolving…evolving…all on the galactic stage play…

3 Major Nadi Energy Aura Channels…

Sushumna (Center)
Ida (Left)
Pingala (Right)

The soul energy aura body itself also has duality…along with the straight vertical split line of the sushumna nadi…each side of the body governs a particular duality of energy…one's left side is referred to as 'Ida' the 'Shakti' energy aura…and one's right is referred to as 'Pingala' the 'Shiva' energy aura…

The Ida Shakti left side energy aura is associated with one's feminine energy aura…and also the input energy aura of inner receiving soul energies…

The Pingala Shiva right side energy aura is associated with one's masculine energy aura…and also the output energy aura of outer giving soul energies…

This is a major reason why wearing jewelry on the left side of the body has a more internal feminine energy soul experience...as wearing jewelry on the right side of the body has a more external masculine soul experience...

The Sushumna Nadi is the main center channel of energy that is a direct spinal cord aligned pathway from which the sacred Kundalini Shakti rises up from the root chakra to the crown chakra... The Sushumna Nadi is the most powerful energy channel as it consists of both energy centers of the right pingala and left Ida...further the energy is more potentized with the soul chakras on its travelling energy pathway flow...

Soul Chakras...

Chakras are soul energy centers that reside in the energy aura body for the soul being... The word 'Chakra' derives from Sanskrit language and means spherical energy wheel...as chakras are not static but in continuation...rotating, accumulating, releasing energy, receiving energy constantly... These soul energy spherical forces in the body move through particular centers...influencing and modifying according to one's Karmic acts...

As chakras are not a two dimensional flat wheel but a three dimensional energy sphere ball that cover both the front facing of the body and the back of the body...positioned in the middle of the body from both the very front and back of the body...aligned with one's physical spinal cord...

Chakra's sufficiently balanced energy spinning direction is primarily clockwise...one's visual clockwise direction...for example, visualize a clock in front of you, the 9th hour would be your left shoulder, and the 3rd hour would be your right

shoulder...12th hour would be your crown chakra...6th hour would be your root chakra...and so forth...

Rotational Direction...
Clockwise...Output...Divinity...
Counterclockwise...Input...Maya...

Rotational direction is based on our front facing direction...
When chakras spin clockwise...they spin the interior energy out of our body into the space around us...with capacities to send out our energy and connect to the Divine...this makes our soul energy aura more potent by being constantly in entangled connection to Divinity...

When chakras spin counterclockwise...they spin pulling energy from the exterior...including the immediate environment and the individuals in it...spinning counterclockwise, pulling in, and imbibing that energy within...

The chakra's dominant frequency, spinning direction, spinning speed...determines how much energy one draws into the body or releases it outward...this influences whether one lives in or out of balance in their daily lives...

Clockwise dominant spinning direction keeps the soul being's energy aura Divinely connected, potent, and protected... Counterclockwise dominant spinning direction potentially puts the soul being in a vulnerable state where one may indeed pull in more unwanted asuric energy and its burdening excretion negative asuric outer energy release...

"A clock is a prime example of a chakra direction...turns its needles continuously moving clockwise direction consistency...sending out the illusion of time existence..."

Chakras are very sensitive and have the potential of becoming misaligned...instead of spinning in one's output clockwise direction majority of the time, it is turning opposite and spinning input counterclockwise direction more frequently and dominantly... Some frequent counterclockwise spinning direction of chakras is necessary for the input interaction with the Maya Leela play realm script and its characters...however excessive dominant spinning in counterclockwise direction is harmful... there are multiple influencing factors for this...including physical stress, emotional stress, disruptive thoughts, incorrect unhealthy diet and lifestyle...with the the most impactful factor is the negative asuric energetic influences from other individuals in our immediate environment...therefore even a negative asuric soul less individual's mere presence in one's close proximity is powerful enough to shift the spinning direction of one's energy chakras in the opposite direction...be very wary of this at all times...

Chakras Complexity...
Seeds Spirituality...
Heart's Empathy...

There are a total primary 114 chakras...108 within the soul being's energy aura body...with 2 chakras out of the body...along with 4 consequential directed chakras that act and travel like neurotransmitters interacting with all the 114 chakras...

7 primary chakras within the body are given rightful importance as they are located along the upper body straight vertical center split called the 'Sushumna Nadi' that governs one's biological, mental, and spiritual processing...this is our main center energy channel that also aligns with the physical body spinal cord...from Kundalini, sexuality, personality, heart, emotions, expression, perception, brain, to higher consciousness...all flow through these primary seven chakras...

(Please view the illustration reference provided for the locations of the primary soul chakras, nadi centers, and Kundalini Shakti pathway)

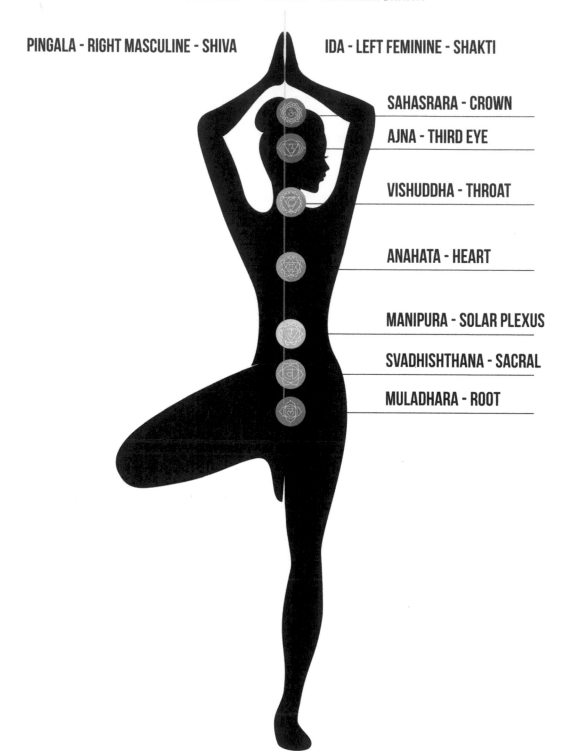

SUSHUMNA - CENTER - KUNDALINI SHAKTI

PINGALA - RIGHT MASCULINE - SHIVA

IDA - LEFT FEMININE - SHAKTI

SAHASRARA - CROWN

AJNA - THIRD EYE

VISHUDDHA - THROAT

ANAHATA - HEART

MANIPURA - SOLAR PLEXUS

SVADHISHTHANA - SACRAL

MULADHARA - ROOT

First Chakra
Muladhara
Root Chakra

The root chakra... located at the base of the spine... the untapped dormant Kundalini Shakti is also located here... The primal energy of survival of fight or flight...

Second Chakra
Svadhishthana
Sacral Chakra

The sacral chakra... located just below the navel... Sexuality, pleasure, reproduction, creativity, sensory perception is associated with this chakra...

Third Chakra
Manipura
Solar Plexus Chakra

The solar plexus chakra... located three fingers approximately above the navel... Personality, ego, identity, will power, purpose, motivation, choice, and self confidence is associated with this chakra...

Fourth Chakra
Anahata
Heart Chakra

The heart chakra... located at the center of the chest on the sternum... Love, devotion, compassion, kindness, empathy, and soul feelings are associated with this chakra...

Fifth Chakra
Vishuddha
Throat Chakra

The throat chakra... located between the collar bone and larynx in the neck...
The ability to express, communicate, and honesty are associated with this chakra...

Sixth Chakra
Ajna
Third Eye Chakra

The third eye chakra... located between the eyebrows... The sixth chakra...six sense... spiritual awakening, true seeing and enlightening experiences are associated with this chakra...this chakra not only unveils the maya realm but sees right through what is, when it is, where it is, and how it is...

Maya Leela

Seventh Chakra
Sahasrara
Crown Chakra

The crown chakra... located on top of the head... Enlightenment itself, connection to Divinity, pathway cord to higher realms beyond the immediate perceived world is directly associated with this chakra... this Divine chakra is the portal access to super consciousness database... upon activation... the soul being itself will be shockingly astonished by what is now known and that infinite access to know...

Power Unknown...

"You've witnessed...
  My intoxication...
  Yet unaware...
  Of the realization...
  Serpent contains...
  Venomous poison...
  Poisonous venom for all fatal...
  Yet venom empowers the serpent...
  Power awaits you to own...
  Yet your power remains...
  To you unknown..."

Hugh Shergill

Kundalini Shakti...

"Sitting locked up...
  In your energy body...
  Unlocking key...
  Resides in your soul body...
  Shakti blesses Kundalini's acquire...
  Igniting burning energy...
  Refinery fire...
  Burn opening to...
  The hidden treasure...
  Scattering jewels...
  Of Divinity pleasure..."

Hugh Shergill

Kundalini Shakti…

Kundalini Shakti…Divinity's spark of very powerful potent energy that sits reserved in the energy aura body…awaiting for activation through the soul body's karmic awareness… Kundalini is the Sanskrit word meaning 'the coiled power' in reference to the 'sleeping serpent Shakti' sitting in the root chakra at the base of the spine… Upon awakening activation…the process begins of one's Shakti sparked energy processing and proceeding towards the eternal higher super consciousness Shiva…infinite union of Shiva and Shakti…Divine's spark with Divinity… Invisible power yet invincible power…the Divine energy itself…

Those showered with the bless will refrain to confess…Kundalini Shakti energy goes beyond words to describe…each experiencial blessing is soul unique…each power unique… If the soul is the traveler traveling on the Divine routes of energy…Kundalini Shakti is its powerful vehicle…

Now the soul is driving a very powerful force…discovering and threading paths that were once unthreaded…unlocking paths…making ways…for the soul driver's liberation destination of Moksha… whilst being in Nirvana bliss…a journey so fine…beyond any confine…

One's Soul holds the key to unlocking the Kundalini Shakti… Soul body is the key to Kundalini awakening not the energy aura body…yes deep chakra stimulations is totally possible for the soul being's energy aura body through various practices including tantra and yogic practices such as specific tantra, yantra, mantra, yoga, meditation…yet it is the infinite soul energy that will determine when and how its soul key will unlock the dormant Kundalini Shakti that exists resting in the energy aura body…this unlocking process is determined by Divinity within the soul itself through the soul's karmic journey to that point…which could be immediately instant or take many multiple soul's physical realm lifetimes…

Warning:

The Kundalini awakening process should never be attempted by force…nor is it technically possible to force…Karmic processes can not be held nor rushed…this is a precisely Divinely timed soul journey… Never be fooled by someone offering 'Kundalini Awakening' services…as at the very best they are perhaps able to very highly arouse and stimulate your energy chakras through tantric, yoga and or other practices…which oneself can practice oneself through deep meditation, specific mantra chanting, yoga, veda knowledge and karmic practices at your own Divine pace and process… never rushed… There is no quick fix for Kundalini Shakti fully awakened state… Dormant Kundalini stimulation to an active fluctuations and vibrations is totally possible for a soul being… Yet true Kundalini awakening to a fully Kundalini awakened state is a very highly rare occurrence… awakening process perhaps for many however fully awakened are not many…not as false information tries to popularize the awakened state…

The Kundalini awakening process to fully awakened state is a soul journey of multiple life times…as in this energy aura body itself…the Kundalini Shakti not only has to travel to, cleanse, bless, fully activate each primary 7 chakras…but also all 114 chakras…and then even further purify multi thousands (approximately 100,000 nadi channels) in any given moment… this process is a double edge sword…

On one edge, it is the most blissful experience one may possibly feel...Divinity Love making with you in your energy aura body...a Nirvana experience in the tri soul bodies...much more pleasurable than any sexual orgasmic experience to any indulged intoxication... Revelations of revelating reveals... higher consciousness activation...resulting in also vast expansive brain activation...

Yet on the other side... Kundalini energy stimulation awakening process can have very intense repercussions... especially for those that have unresolved pending Karmic debts accumulated from lifetimes of the soul's journey...the purification purging process is not for the faint hearted...as the fully awakened state requires every of the tri bodies to be crystal clear purified...purification is essentially necessary...that is the reason forced Kundalini stimulation via particular methods and or consumptions have left a lot of individuals mentally and physically unstable...as without purification, this powerful energy can not be handled... During the purification purging process, first event that will immediately occur is Maya Leela illusion awareness paradox...aware of Maya without yet aware of what are you becoming aware of...during the lifting the Maya realm veil... it is highly possible that everything in your life will flip 180 degrees intensely and even possibly horrifically...sudden life changing events...losing people close around you...Maya being family and friends gaslighting and gang stalking...accute emotional pain and hurt...physical and emotional abuse...mysterious health issues like symptoms will suddenly occur with no physical diagnosis available as the energy aura body has no doctor than Divine itself...physical pains, abnormal pains, sanity shattering energetic vibrations must be faced...false diagnosis and treatments will be absolute hindrances in this...as this is a fearless required journey...as those with even the slightest fear may easily become a confined victim to mental institutions and hospitals... Purging and purification is a must process...unavoidable... bringing to the surface of what now serves...what now doesn't serve you...with multiple past life soul memory karma residual that has to be faced, fought, conquered...face it fearlessly...fearlessly surrender...before the awakened warrior of Shakti is able to fearlessly walk in bliss with this energy... where Divinity's supernatural powers become your new natural...

One should just hold trust in one's own soul journey... Divine timing...continue on your righteous Karmic path, follow your particular spiritual practices, seeking more, exploring more...creating a soul platform for infinite possibilities...where all will be revealed to whom, when, and how it should be destined to be...

Divine Rave...

"Those who face the pain...
 Whilst remaining sane...
 Shifting from the conform trodden...
 Daring to walk into the untrodden...
 Privileged are those who remain brave...
 Are those who get to enjoy this Divine rave..."

Hugh Shergill

Asura Chakra…
Asura Dominant Energy…
Asura Diabolical Energy…

Maya being's energy aura body consists entirely of only one universal collective diabolical asuric energy…the 'Asura Chakra' is extremely negative… antagonist diabolical asuric energy possession sphere that covers the whole entire Maya being's energy aura body like a dark cloud that blocks access to Divine sunshine forever…

As there is no soul in a maya being, therefore there is no soul body… their diabolical asuric energy aura is programmed to hinder the soul being's positive chakra activity…dimming their soul light is their priority…by extracting and consuming their soul prana Shakti energy… All processing, execution, and experiences for a Maya being is strictly biological and asuric… There is no chakra activity energy for Maya beings…as there is no possibility of any positive chakra activity due to their entire energy aura is one whole soul less diabolical asuric energy field of the asura chakra sphere…therefore Kundalini Shakti existence and activation is entirely out of the question…

Instead of the multiple Prana Shakti energy chakras…the Maya Being itself is dominated and operated by one single mega asuric energy chakra sphere that surrounds their entire body… As described earlier…the 'Asura Chakra' is a large spherical negative energy ball three times the physical height radius of that particular maya being…in which the asuric chakra is spinning clockwise direction when it desires to give out their negative energy…spinning counterclockwise when it craves the soul being's Prana Shakti to fuel their ever depleting Asura Maya asuric energy…as for Asuric energy requires absolutely soul prana Shakti energy to exist in this Maya Leela play realm…soul energy is the extremely diabolical asuric energy's primary fuel…

We all have, at some point crossed our life play paths with certain individuals that whom we outright refer to being very 'Cold Hearted' or 'Heartless'…this 'Heart' we are referring to is not the physical body organ pumping blood…it is referring to that this particular individual is devoid of having a heart chakra of the energy aura body…that innately embodies Love, compassion, kindness, empathy for soul beings…this is a fact…indeed for these diabolical soul less entities there is no heart chakra…they indeed are energetically heartless…and commonly referred to as narcissists…

Also, the spherical diabolical asura chakra aura is so negatively vibrating…that is is the reason why when we come across certain individuals, we feel immediately that they carry such a 'Low Vibration' 'Toxic Energy' 'Negative Energy' 'D spirit' this discribal feeling is not merely coincidental nor just a quick judging assumption…even when you happen to just pass by them in close proximity for a second or two…your soul feels that asuric shiver…you are able to experience their particular aura immediately…a dim light never shines bright…energy aura of Maya beings is extremely low…this is absolutely the truth…truth that is always felt…especially resonating for the soul being's inner voice corresponding to their specific chakras, such as…

"Gut Feeling" - Solar Plexus Chakra
"Heart Felt" - Heart Chakra
"I See Through You" - Third Eye Chakra

For the Maya being, there is no energetic vibrating aura, no chakra activity energy, no nadi active energy, no Kundalini energy (both dormant and active), and especially no soul energy...all these powerful complex energies are forever devoid...that is a major factor why sensitivity towards others, kindness, empathy lacks significantly...and on the flip side, one mega asuric chakra that permeates all throughout their energy aura body...covering them completely...giving them an heightened illusionary ego and narcissistic personality...they tend to feel mega important spinningly rotating in this Asura Chakra...riding away like a bike rider entrapped in a cage ball circus...speeding and making rumbling acceleration exhaustion noises...in continuation circles yet going nowhere... Maya being is just a low vibration diabolical asuric soul less entity...energetically very fragile...almost like a walking demised presence...yet screaming out exuberance of importance...when in reality they are continuously desperately begging for soul energy fuel supply...ironically pathetic indeed... As an energetic fragility example, if every soul being shunned access to their energetic treasures to fragile energetic maya beings...the maya beings would eventually perish and decompose from the Maya realm itself...as that is how desperately reliant they are to soul energy for fuel...

Pure meditation, spiritual practices, Shakti awakening, authentic yogic practices, tantra, mantra, yantra will absolutely not be possible for the maya being...a pure non distraction higher conscious energetic aura state is impossible for them...yes they may be showing off attempts, yet they will never go beyond the physical body confines due to their asuric energy dominance...as harsh as it sounds, avoidance, and leaving them in their eternal soul less asuric energy...while absolutely denying them their craving for your soul energetic aura is the best approach for a soul being...

"Examine their energetic aura emission in your presence...they will tell you exactly who they are... examine their energetic aura emission...not your idea of whom you had possibly hoped them to be... Energy is not defined by relationships...relationships are defined by their energy..."

**"Beauty is way beyond skin deep...
Ugly goes through to the bone...
Before proximity seep...
Aura speaks alone...
Hesitation to take that leap...
Must have experienced their zone..."**

Hugh Shergill

The Demon Particle...
The Glimpse of Diabolical Asura Chakra...

Interestingly, way back in 1956, theoretical physicist David Pines predicted that electrons in a solid could do something very horrifyingly strange... Traditionally, electrons have both mass and charge... But Pines asserted that combinations of electrons in a solid could form a composite particle that is massless, has no charge and does not even interact with light... He called this a 'demon' particle...a diabolical particle that is not a particle in the traditional sense like a proton or electron...

This 'demon' particle existence is the low vibrational diabolical asuric energetic particle...that is devoid of charge and interacting with light...this is the scientific discovery glimpse of the diabolical asura chakra...describing essentially all the characteristics of the asuric energy asura chakra...that it is the devoid charge and direct interaction with light is which drives the asuric energy to attach to soul energy field and extract energy for its survival...as soul energetic field is extremely high vibrational... high potency charge and direct Divine light interacting...

This theory interestingly was apparently kept very low key by the obvious certain asuric threatened... yet truth always prevails...as the demon particle existence was recently proven and published by a group of researchers in the University of Illinois, Urbana-Champaign...first time ever where science discovering a slight glimpse component of the diabolical asuric energy field...fascinatingly, something that the Rig Veda presented in scriptures fifteen thousand plus years ago...

"A Particle...
  Is also a Wave...
  Both are Energy...
  A Demon Particle...
  Is Diabolical Energy..."

As mentioned earlier...the quantum physics 'Wave Particle Duality Paradox' phenomenon...where quantum entities exhibit both wave and particle existence simultaneously...and each is available to be witnessed in each form with the particular circumstances...therefore the scientific discovery of the existence of the 'Demon Particle' also directly indicates that there is also a 'Demon Wave' that simultaneously exists...both the 'Demon Wave' and the 'Demon Particle' is essentially at its quantum existence simply energy...'Diabolical Energy'...in other words 'Asuric Energy'...which is the dominant energetic field of the Maya Being... As the common reactive statement we often hear in reference to some individual committing a horrendous act that "this individual is clearly under the influence of some Demonic Energy" ...Indeed I agree...they certainly are...absolutely are...

Soul Being's Driving Force...
Is its own Soul Energy Source...

Take water...there is water in a glass...and there is also water in the ocean...confined water in the glass is limited to certain energies...yet the water in the ocean holds vast energies...from supporting vast eco-systems...climates...to destructions...and regeneratives...the vast flow factor determines the capacity...similarly, a soul being in an unlightened awareness...has encapsulated its potential energy possibilities...yet upon enlightening awareness...those potential energies are capable to flow to unlimited possibilities... The key is becoming aware...aware of your soul energy source...and that key will open unlimited locked realms...from physical body...to energy aura body...to soul body...further... where Divinity is completely embodied...

Maya Leela

Soul Currency

"Importantly just…
  One's Soul Currency…
  Managing is a must…
  Its expenditure frequency…
  Priority as soul's lust…
  Honouring its excellency…"

Hugh Shergill

The Duality Paradox of Beings…

"They require energetic fuel from you…
  There is no existence without you…
  Without them is an ascension for you…
  They need you…
  You do not need them…
  Without you…
  Energy devoid experienced…
  Where they would be left dead instead…
  While you would flourish instead…
  They are triggered by your aware…
  Your success lies by being beware…"

Hugh Shergill

Asuric Energy requires Soul Energy…
Soul Energy has no place for Asuric Energy…

Low vibrational soul less diabolical asuric maya being entities absolutely necessarily require, crave, hunt for high vibrational soul energy for survival… Without soul energy…asuric energy can not survive… Asuric energy is the duality consequence of the Maya Leela realm…it is the shadow energy of soul energy…without the existence of soul being there is no shadow being…

For example, think of Divinity as the projecting play of sunlight, soul being as the primary physical body, and maya being as the shadow of the soul being's body…
Without the soul being's body…there is no possibility of the sun's creation of a shadow of the soul being…and ultimately if there is no sunlight…there is absolute darkness… Soul being without the Maya Leela play sunlight would blissfully entangle and merge into the Divine darkness state of Turiya…where all infinite possibility of existence exists… However Maya being without the light shining soul being…

222

would vanish immediately…as if there is no body…there is no possibility of a shadow…a shadow is merely a by-product effect of the shining light… Thus, a soul less asuric maya being absolutely requires a soul being for its existence…however a soul being does not require maya being for its existence… there is no need for a shadow…further without the maya being, the soul being would ascend into the Moksha Nirvana state of Divinity…fully merged and liberated in the bliss euphoric tranquility state of the Divine realm… Your existence keeps maya being existence…no maya being existence…is your direct Divine ascension… You soul being are a need for them…they are not a need for you…

Action…
Reaction…
Interaction…

"Your action, reaction, and interaction are the three triggers for potential extraction of your soul energy by the diabolical asuric maya being…"

Be aware of all your actions, reactions, and interactions with the soul less maya beings…use the power of your soul's intuitive discernment powers to maneuver your own soul energetic frequency on a higher ascension level where you do not give any potential access to the soul less asuric maya beings of your Divine spark of soul energy…

"As I observe hearing the surrounding words…
  It became evident to pay attention to all worlds…
  What is often said…
  Has often been first read…
  Time to shake…
  The perceived establishment…
  By first deviating from…
  The initial development…"

Hugh Shergill

"Observe them…
  Not absorb them…
  Protect your energy…
  Perhaps even talk to them…
  Just don't let your energy…
  Walk away with them…"

Hugh Shergill

All prolonged eye contact, communication, interaction, reaction with a soul less maya being is a potential energetic extracting opportunity for the maya being...and a potential energetic depletion session for the soul being... We shall go more into depths in regards to communication in the upcoming chapters...however it is important to note that in terms of energy, communication and interaction with maya beings must be approached with highest soul cautious discretion...as frivolous talk, debates, discussions, arguments with them may be an attempt by you to get your valuable truth point through...for them it holds no importance of the potency of your words or pure intentions...it is all about your soul energy potency extraction opportunity...it is the asuric soul less maya being that is deep within joyous to have this opportunity to extract energy from you for its survival...not your valuable truth nor its approval... Thus, no debate nor discussion...they see as they soul less perceive... you see through your soul as what they actually are...

Soul senses energies... even before it is aware of its abilities to sense energies... just as a person that has the ability to see... yet has been born in an environment of complete darkness...it still senses the ability to have vision of the environment... yet has not seen anything due to the darkness... until the light enters its environment... suddenly to actually experience the already existing ability to see... comes into access...that forever seeing...finally experiences its sees...

Exploring Into The Eyes...

"Exploring into the eyes..
Revealing where the body lies...
Looking at your immediate health...
Glancing into your energetic wealth...
Seeing your unseen soul's Divinity...
Romancing your eyes in tranquility..."

Hugh Shergill

The eyes hold a unique distinct deliverance of each of the three bodies at a particular given moment... with the dominant body influences showing up more profoundly...

The physical body shows one's biological processes through the eyes... This is why one's health condition and biological processes are revealed through the eyes... For example, ancient ayurvedic doctors were precisely able to detect one's health condition just by looking at one's eyes and heart pulse detection only...

The energy aura body shows one's energy aura with its corresponding emotions through the eyes... from lust, greed, guilt, fear, aggression, envy, jealousy, anger, hurt, sorrow...to Love, romance, seduction, excitement, joy, happiness...shows up correspondingly through the eyes... interestingly the energy aura body eyes also are powerful energy exchangers that upon eye contact energy aura exchange is highly possible...making eye contact with a maya being either makes one's energy aura cringe due to their asuric low vibration energy...or your high vibration soul being energetic aura makes their diabolical asuric energy rattle in discomforting irritated disturbance due to their innate incapacity to handle your soul spark Divine energy…

The soul body shows one's infinite spark of Divinity through the eyes…the tranquility state of infinite peace, calmness, euphoria, fearless bliss, meditative soul intoxicated nirvana…lights up the eyes and its immediate environment surroundings…when one makes contact with a soul being in its dominant soul body state…Divinity kisses your soul through their eyes…

Using strict caution when, whom, and how long you maintain prolonged eye contact with…as this is both an immediate energy aura preserver and depleter… Constantly seeking attention and making intentional unnecessary direct eye contact with random passing strangers throughout the day is such a powerful soul energy depleter that one doesn't even realize its energy depleting consequences… masking its effects with false justification for oneself as just experiencing 'a hectic tiring day'… One aesthetic convenience that helps is wearing sunglasses in highly populated environments…wear them unapologetically confidently even in certain indoor settings…as there it may appear no need to protect from sunlight…yet more important is to often protect one's own light…as your play performance is forever Soulabrity bright… You are the Soulabrity…Superstar of Divinity…

"Untied irrelevences…
 Freed revelences…
 Disrupted tendences…
 Revealed true faces…
 Provoking senses…
 Evoked confidences…"

Hugh Shergill

Soul Viruses Thoughts…

All negativity source stems from soul energy depletion…
Force yourself to not even allow thoughts of specific maya beings to consume you…
Even their mere thought is parasitic…
Intruding into your soul energy as a soul virus…
Feeding off and depleting your Divine soul energy…
Indeed it is difficult…as their presence and actions manifests into many emotions…
Yet this must be consistently practiced… afterall it is your soul at stake…

Energy Conductors are Powerful Exchanges…

Everything in existence holds energy… metals and water absorb and retain energies very potently… further, metals and water are very powerful conductors to transfer energy… therefore it is highly ideal to avoid these potential energy depleting and energy burdening exchanges through metals and water very strictly… No metal exchanges…such as coins, jewelry, watches, furniture, technology equipment etc… Even more importantly, never share water spaces with these diabolical asuric soul less maya beings…

ever…wherever possible… Water is not only a conductor of electricity…it also both releases and absorbs energetic aura energies very powerfully… In physical ground presence, one is able to avoid direct energetic aura exchanges with someone by one's physical height distance multiplied by three…this radius distance surrounding circle around you is your immediate physical energy aura environment…yet in the presence of common water exchange, such as a public swimming pool… one easily exchanges and absorbs foreign energetic aura of others even if they are a mile apart… Therefore, sharing public swimming pools and water spots with others is the most effective way of potentially consuming their negative aura energies…avoid strictly for your Divine soul self energetic preservation…

Sinergy…

Energy shared with repelling energy is an energy sin…Sinergy…be very cautious about whom you share your energy with… The highest sin upon oneself is to sabotage your Divinity's spark of soul energy within… Your soul energy is your most precious priceless gift from Divine…honour it…cherish it…and most importantly…protect it…

"May perhaps unclothe the physical…
  Never dare to uncloak…
  My soul…
  May experience the touch of physical…
  Never dare to touch…
  My aura awoke…"

Hugh Shergill

Intimacy Exchange…
Most Powerful Energy Intrusion…

Intimacy in its Divine form between two pure souls is Divinely euphoric ascension…yet intimacy without extreme strict discretion is a very dangerous and most powerful intrusion of one's entire energetic existence…from biological, mental, energetic aura, to spiritual…

"Not to take intimacy…
  Ever lightly…
  More intimately involved…
  Than intimacy itself…
  Beneath skin surface…
  Energy consequences to face…"

Hugh Shergill

Have you noticed in majority of people...two individuals who are in an intimate relationship... regardless of their pre-relationship physical attractiveness levels...upon being intimately energetically involved and gradually with recorded time... Two profound possibilities come to existence:

They either become an even more energetically attractive vibrant couple together...which is a rare occurrence exception of an ascended soul being couple...

Or more often than not... the regularly intimately involved couple will gradually either begin to resemble each other more physically...or one partner becomes more physically attractive, while the other loses their pre-relationship physical attractiveness to a significant degree...yes the couple's similar diet fitness lifestyle choices will be an important factor of this...yet not the only one...as there is something even more energetically unawaringly occurring...as the biological intimate energy exchange is so profound that the biological aging rate and physical attributes become entangled with each respected partner...from body weight fluctuations...skin, nails, and hair quality changes... ear size growth... nose shape change and abnormal growth...body fluid retention etc...either one partner being more impacted or both beginning to look more similar than their pre-relationship physical attributes... as mentioned, this goes way beyond health diet fitness lifestyle...this is direct energy exchange ramifications clearly being witnessed on display... To a point when one often sees an elderly couple that have been together for many decades...their physical attributes, health, posture and even walking style is so similar that one could easily mistake them as siblings or even in some cases twins...

Intimate energy exchange is absolutely never to be taken lightly or casually...it is the most direct powerful exposure and possible attack to your physical, mental, health, and most importantly to your soul aura energies...be very extremely responsible, highly discretional with complete soul discernment in regards to whom you select as your intimate partner...yes exterior maya illusion realm impression, accolades, and accomplishments may be illusionary attractive in a partner...yet it will not modify the particular individual's innate permanent energetic frequency...soul energy can never be purchased as it is absolutely priceless and unattainable... Intimacy is a beautiful aspect of one's soul journey... choose your intimate partner with complete soul discernment... As for the soul being...the most impactful asuric diabolical curse for a soul being is...when a soul being is intimately involved with an asuric maya being...very cursing detrimental and energetically descending...an extremely very powerful maya jaal entrapment...one must advise that be halted and rejected immediately...may Divinity help you my soul...

Certain physical encounters...regardless of how immensely attractive beautiful the partner was and how pleasurable it may have been...post the intimate encounter...it leaves such a negative dull asuric cloud on your energetic aura...a very discomforting deploring burden...confusing at first as physically it may not make any immediate sense due to being hidden behind the pleasurable experience...but energetically it certainly leaves its undeniable burdening presence...

"You can wash your skin...
 Not your biological kin...
 Hidden behind romancing...
 Biologically left burdening...
 What was mistaken as intimacy...
 Was all actuality interferency...
 Those moments of Love making...
 Was actually soul energy depleting..."

Hugh Shergill

Microchimerism...
Kama Antaraya...
Phenomenon of Intimacy Interference...

It is commonly understood that saliva exchange is not only bacterial exchange (over 80 million plus distinct bacteria) but further saliva exposes one to viruses, hormonal and foreign DNA exchange... that is why one should strictly not saliva exchange irresponsibly...and not share their or share others consumed food and beverages irresponsibly...

Saliva alone is such a powerful transmission of bacteria, viruses, foreign hormonal and DNA exposure... What is even shockingly further and even more powerful is the biological phenomenon of microchimerism...the vedic Sanskrit word named 'Kama Antaraya'...phenomenon of intimacy interference...where the female body absorbs and retains genetic DNA in their brain from every male they have ever been intimately involved with...a biological foreign DNA stored bank that permanently lingers in the female brain...this not only intrudes and interferes with one's own natural biological and energetic existence (mental, physical, and spiritual disruptions) but is even more powerfully capable of being intruding to your biological future children and potential future generations...

Astonishingly, as majority are unaware of this...for the respective Divine life providing biological female body...certain physical genetic traits of previous intimate partners (from certain to various bodily fluid exchanges...sexual and intimate exchanges) can be potentially passed on to her future children and potential multiple generations...to whom ashtoningly, ironically, and biologically have no genetic direct connection to their mother's previous male partners...yet they are potentially biologically connected to not only their obvious biological father's DNA genetic profile, but additionally potentially susceptible genetically to their biological mother's previous intimate partners DNA genetically through the biological pathways of microchimerism biological influences... This intimate male partner's genetic profile and DNA is permanently stored lingering in their biological mother's brain... Just imagine taking a very potentially dangerous vaccine out of ignorance...and experiencing its lingering side effects for one's remaining biological existence...this is just how powerful microchimerism is...

This phenomenon of 'Kama Antaraya' intimacy interference...is not confined to just the biological female body...as this biologically connects to all of us regardless of being a biological male body or a female body...as we all are forever biologically connected to the female womb that gave us our physical birth...

Additionally…microchimerism is a major contribution factor for those who are highly active intimately with multiple partners…tend to often suffer more from very extreme deep depression, suicidal thoughts, and various mental health issues as they age….as there is a powerful overwhelming burdening interference of foreign biological influences on to their brain's processing functionality… Energetically this is even more intensely detrimental and extremely dangerous if it is a soul being that is experiencing an intruded stay of diabolical asuric soul less biological influences upon their body…

Microchimerism…
Kama Antaraya…

"I can't get you out of my mind…"

This common Love quote…Literally…

Ancient vedic cultures of ayurveda health were very aware of this genetic microchimerism phenomenon named 'Kama Antaraya'… Before the women suppression confines imposed by strict religion and cultural institution structure… In the Vedic era, the pre-religion era…the majority of females were Divinely respected and protected for their Divine Shakti energy representation…not out of unjust control, suppression, or domination…instead out of purity of Divinity Love, protection, and preservation…both for the particular individual and their future generations… As absolutely the Divinity's Divine feminine Shakti energy is all…gives all…and also undeniably absorbs all…respect this blessing…cherish this gift…otherwise succumbing to its ignorance…is only your loss…

Microchimerism…this biological intrusion trigger phenomenon has been known to ancient vedic cultures 15000 years plus ago… yet it is only until very recently modern science discovered of this… researched discovery of this intimate genetic phenomenon should be very concerning for those who are intimately irresponsible…potentially for example, a lingering genetic illness trigger of a mother's previous intimate partner is responsible for causing the same genetic illness in the mother's future children…this is just how powerful Kama Antaraya…intimacy interference…microchimerism is… sexually transmitted that results in spiritual transmitted dis-ease…as just the thought of potentially having a maya being's diabolical asuric DNA genetic biological profile forever Intruding and lingering in one's physical body permanently is the most horrific thought in itself… Be aware…Beware… I encourage those who are further interested to research this phenomenon of intimacy interference…

Intimacy abstinence in ancient vedic cultures was not intended to portray intimacy as being something disgracefully perceived…as soul being intimacy is forever Divinely respected and celebrated for both genders equally…yet abstinence is such a powerful energy aura preserver that under certain specific conditions and perceived time frame…it can build up your energetic aura significantly…especially during one's Maya threat trying moments in life… There is no gender favouritism nor exception… yes indeed there is no denying that on a biological level, there are distinct separate differences on the effects and processes of intimacy specifics for both the female and male biological body… The intricacies of intimacy effects differ specific for the female body and the male body…however there is no exception…as the male body is equally affected in a particular way both physically and energetically through intimacy exchange…thus the male equally practiced abstinence…as there is no gender of your soul energetic aura body…the Divine union of both feminine and masculine of Shiva Shakti is undeniably present equally in your soul energy…Shiva Shakti…consciousness and creation...the Divine fusion essence of all existence of every realm... Further, intimacy abstinence was also Divinely practiced during certain Tantra, Yantra, Mantra, and meditative practices to protect and preserve the purity of one's energetic and biological aura from unnecessary foreign intrusion during those certain specific practices, especially protecting one from asuric energy intrusion through intimacy...the most powerful form of Maya jaal entrapment...

Those who use over indulgence in intimacy and multiple partners as an excuse of certain particular Tantric practices are unfortunately very unknowledgeable, misinformed, and ignorant... Majority do not even have slight the knowledge of authentic Tantra...let alone being Tantra advocates and experts... In all actuality...majority that lust excuse their intimacy over indulgence as a Tantra practice...are just diabolical asuric soul less entities that desperately crave soul energy...scavenging and desperately hunting for their uncontrollable soul less asuric lust... Interestingly, those who actively participate in these mere Tantra excused lust over indulgences...simply view their physical face...it will surely be visible...a very apparent dull energy drained and rapidly aged face... Well so much for being 'experts' on mere 'excerpts'...

"Intimacy is a beautiful aspect of one's soul
   journey...choose your intimate partner with
   complete soul discernment responsibly..."

Be Aware...
Of your Awareness...

Be careful of where your attention flows...as wherever your attention goes...energy flows...and with prolonged attention...quantum zeno effect takes over...as attentive energy refuses to fade away...

The most beautiful and powerful state is becoming one with the Divine through your innate soul's quantum entangled connection through the meditative state of higher consciousness...then prolong sustain that energetic power through quantum zeno effect attention...experiencing immediate liberating euphoric nirvana state even before complete liberated moksha state...

Treat yourself as a walking valuable corporation entity...that at all times is aware of its soul energy, energy aura exchanges... interactions... security... growth... as one company evolves...more one must be aware to continue to grow...

Aware...

"Aware...
Who is who...

Aware...
Recognizing who...

Aware...
The stage set...

Aware...
My value...

Aware...
My performance...

Dear illusion...
I am now Aware..."

Hugh Shergill

"As more you become Aware...
The more there is to Beware..."

CHAPTER 12.

MAYA
THREAT

Staged War...Soul Target...

"Once the Soul being awakes...
An immediate target overtakes...
Upon lifting the veil experience...
Target is on you with extreme vengeance...
They can not stand that you now know...
Disrupting their entire illusion show..."

Hugh Shergill

Maya Threat…

What just has been revealed so far in these writings…is very powerful reality shifting information…from spiritual revelations…corresponding scientific explanations…to the core of the very ancient scriptures references…these revelation reveals hold ramifications within that will shift the entire trajectory of the rest of your soul energy journey to eternity…a mere paradigm shift would be a understatement…as this information is entire life shifting… With what you have just read to this point in this publication… even though much more in depth details of these soul less entities will be revealed in the preceding chapters… Yet knowing now what you know at this point…nothing will ever appear the same…from your closest associations to casual connections…to this point in your life…you were living among a majority of soul less diabolical asuric entities that all along and currently are your direct antagonist nemesis… purposely deliberately placed in the illusion play of your perceived life…

"Whole reality…
 Only soul reality…
 Just as what your soul…
 Has just now discovered…
 Nothing will ever appear as before…
 Those whose real reality is discovered…
 Will also never treat you ever as before…"

Hugh Shergill

When you touch a beehive…to extract the honey nectar…one must expect and anticipate an intense mass bees attack… Similarly, when you unveiling touch the Maya realm…to reveal the true reality… expect an intense mass soul less entities diabolical attack…

A human being with a soul is an interesting person…that immediately becomes the person of interest upon being enlightened by the truth…by those who are forever devoid of the truth… Truth devoid deplore those whose truth is impossible to deny…resulting in immediately a hostile threatening scenario…that puts the soul on target… and sets the soul less inevitable destruction…

You have figured them out…they also now energetically know that you have them figured out…they will now never support you…they will now never be truly there for you…they are on a separate and opposite spectrum…that was forever established yet just now fully exposed…now their hidden horns will begin to show…as they all are your oppositions…they all are your opponents…they all are your soul's primary and potentially most dangerous nemeses…

"For we are not fighting against
flesh and blood enemies,
but against evil rulers and authorities
of the unseen world,
against mighty powers
in this dark world,
and against evil spirits"

Holy Bible (Ephesians 6:12, NLT)

"People don't realize how a man's
whole life can be changed
by one book"

Malcolm X
(Renowned Human Rights Activist)

"There has been a piercing occurrence...
Of the illusion reality veil...
Higher Divine's realms juice nectar...
Have began flowing in through...
Overflowing nectar is going to flood...
Purification of this illusionary realm...
Where all impurities will rise to the surface...
Which now are required to be removed..."

Hugh Sherglll

Highly advised to continue living your normal life...yet I assure you...immediately after knowing what you now know so far into this revelating read...you will now effortlessly detect individuals around you immediately shift their energetic demeanor towards you...as their diabolical asuric energy has been intensely rattled triggered by the revealing of the reveal to you...this will occur strangely, miraculously, and instantaneously without you even sharing this information with them or anyone else...which is definitely not recommended to do so... What you will now witness and that shall begin to notice is how the lifting of the illusionary veil of perceived reality...majority will begin to give you ice cold stares towards you more often than usual...there will be those specific soul less being's family members and friends that without any apparent reason show more deplore and repel towards your soul aware energetic aura...this should be Divinely be appreciated as a blessing...congratulations...rattling of the illusion validates its existence...you have now began lifting the veil of this play...looking at the play stage from behind...resulting in these soul less maya being entities no longer Loving and supporting you from behind...thus now there is no looking back and nor ever turning back...

Yet also pleasantly and relativity…you will immediately begin to receive the gift of attracting those very few Divinely energetic soul beings around you…those that resonate and reciprocate your angelic soul aura presence…that will immediately find your soul energetic aura much more attractive than ever before…as you have accomplished the ultimate feat of Maya existence by unveiling the Maya existence… This will paradigm shift your reality of existence towards self Love and much more appreciation of the Divine spark that you forever carry within…this will begin your undeniable glow up going forward…congratulations…energetically flow into your new Soul glow…

"Not you verses them…
 It is us verses them…
 What is your real world…
 Exists out of this world…
 This battle is not just yours…
 It is a multi-realm star wars…"

Hugh Shergill

"The higher we soar the smaller we appear to those who cannot fly."

Friedrich Nietzsche
(Renowned Philosopher / Poet)

"As above…
 So below…
 As within…
 So without…
 Control over perception…
 Customizes the deception…
 Enjoy the play Soul rider…
 Submit to your Divine provider…"

Hugh Shergill

Once you have unveiled the illusion Maya realm and discovered the existence of maya beings… immediately you will be on their target radar…this occurs energy innately while the soul less maya beings remain completely unaware of it on a physical processing state…yet on a subconscious level…they are absolutely rattled, irritated, triggered, and threatened…resulting in them immediately targeting you and directly attacking you…through prolonged strange peculiar staring, gossiping, resentment, ostracization, persecution, humiliation, insults, and in some cases direct physical and emotional hurting abuse… unfortunately this is the unfortunate new reality for the aware souls… With true protection only now exists with complete elimination of yourself from them…as once you discover the theatrics of the play and its actors...there is immediate realization that this is nothing but merely a theatrical illusion play...which no matter how good and entertaining the theatrics are...they are just mere theatrics...which confines the actor...to just their appointed role...taking away their authentic identity value beyond the role...their authentic self identity...which causes a sense of intrusion and devalue of their real self...which manifests as a counter threat to those who are soul aware…

"O Ghalib…
  Their comfort luxuries…
  I envy…
  Those in possession...
  Of an unaware mind..."

Mirza Ghalib (Renowned Poet / Writer)
Poetic Translation by Hugh Shergill

"Not at all…
  Am i annoyed…
  By you…
  O life…
  Instead…
  Indeed very astonished…
  By you…
  O life..."

Gulzar (Renowned Poet / Lyricist)
Poetic Translation by Hugh Shergill

Awakened...Are Never Celebrated...

"Awakened...
  Are never celebrated...

  Isolated...
  Ostracized...
  Persecuted...
  Or at best...
  Tolerated...

  Yet the Awakened...
  Are never celebrated..."

Hugh Shergill

Soul Target Stage Drama...

Ostracism...Persecution...Isolation...
Gang Stalking...Gaslighting...Gossiping...and even further unfortunately acute Physical and Emotional Abuse...are all possible potential actions that may be executed by your fellow stage sharing actors... that have you now as their primary focused number one target...due to the threat of your soul energy performing credentials...leading you to first initially feeling stage fright and hurt...until you become aware of the deeper Maya Jaal entrapping script operating ways...with this soul knowingly... the main star of the Maya Leela play now is none other than you...now immediately you transform yourself into being the prime protagonist of the play...the innate soul confidence emerges...shifting the entire script and co-players performance dynamics...all re-shifting to accommodate your rising performance...this leaves all others on stage threatened by the shifting dynamics of the play...

"You will continue to go through it...
  Until you grow through it..."
  Destiny...Created for you...
  For you Co-Creating...For You...
  You have been provided the canvas...
  Your creativity now creates the art..."

Hugh Shergill

"Confidentiality is enlightening...
 Pretentious is pretending...
 Vulnerabilities become villains...
 Frailties become flaws...
 The reality for every rose...
 There are many more thorns
 Blessed with volatile enmities...
 Blessed with blessed immensities...
 Embrace these nemesis more...
 They are empowering your core..."

Hugh Shergill

"The heat of the midnight tears...
 Will bring you to God..."

Meera
(Renowned Mystique Poet / Divine Devotee)

Maya Weighing Scale...

Maya weighing scale...on one side sits your soul energetic aura...the other the collective asuric diabolic energetic aura represented by those appointed soul less maya beings in your particular Maya Leela play script...

Upon comparison energy weighing...your singular protagonist soul energy spark weight is lower in comparison to the high volume collective antagonist asuric soul less energetic weight...which appears heavier with more quantity dense volume...yet lighter goes higher...heavy is descending...light is ascending... The Divine karmic balance prevails in your favour as the lighter protagonist balance side rises in ascension while the heavier protagonist side sits lower to its descension...this ascension rise of the Maya Leela play star creates immense envy and hate from its surrounding maya beings...very often resulting in retaliatory acts to target you and your performance...to the intended point of possible complete removal of you from the maya stage...this potentially presents a very dangerous and volatile sequences of scenarios and occurrences...where your physical realm existence is threatened by those who are now extremely threatened...

"All proximate presumed to participate...
 Will not be truly equipped to resonate...
 Left threatened they shall ostracize...
 Respond fully with your will to survive...
 Never place the soul less in the hunter seat...
 Allowing them to feast on your soul meat..."

Hugh Shergill

Just as the best performing actor becomes the target of envy and jealousy from its contemporary co-actors...similarly, the spiritual rising soul being becomes the vicious target of spiritual attacks from its surrounding and associated maya beings...the mediocre actor feels frustration and intense envy and jealousy for the superior performing actor...as it is aware that the superior performer has tremendous potential that will excel them much beyond this particular stage and play...while due to their innate lacking capabilities and limitations, the challenged actor will most likely remain confined limited to this stage play only, due to their own mediocrity...

Similarly, the maya being on a subconscious level is fully aware of the soul being's tremendous potential of energetic soul power that will excel them from this illusionary realm stage to the highest stage, the Divine realm of Moksha experiencing Nirvana...while they will be merely dissolve collectively into the asuric cloud...becoming completely non existence yet forever karmically responsible suffer...right after exit from this maya stage...this intense envy for the privileged soul being transforms into an intense unrelenting hatred that is capable of breaking all limits of destruction in order to eliminate the soul being...if your soul succumbs, any means of your destruction is possible... With extreme unfortunate possible attacks...from false accusing mental disorder labels... confinement... suicide...murder...both "upon" or "on"... However, fighting through all these spiritual attacks...assures maya stage victory...with immense infinite possibilities of soul ascension to higher Divine realms...

"Commonly found are tangibles popular...
 Diamonds form in occurrences miracular...
 Your existence's masterpiece...
 Protecting it is your peace...
 Karmic revenge occurs itself...
 Rotten fruit simply falls itself..."

Hugh Shergill

Law of sedimentation

"Purity rises…
 Impurities settle below…
 Pure clean water rises…
 To the top surface of the river…
 While the impure debris…
 Settles at the bottom of the river…
 Soul beings rise above the Maya realm…
 Maya beings forever settle below…"

Hugh Shergill

"Fear is optional…
 Danger is real…"

Curtis James Jackson III (50 Cent)
(Renowned Artist / Rapper / Actor)

Maya Threat…Deadly Game of Roulette…

"Maya threat…
 Deadly game of roulette…

 Risk increase with each removed bullet…
 Survival dependent on status of the chamber…
 Soul game is reoognizing the maya member…
 Game over with the final shot trigger…
 illusion over when refusing its representor…

 Maya threat…
 Deadly game of roulette…"

Hugh Shergill

"Being aware you are the target…
 Is your first step towards protection…
 They thought they wrote you off…
 Yet you never write back…
 Instead save that paper…
 Make a plane…
 Flying it above…
 All their access…"

Hugh Shergill

No Fear…Danger is Real…

"Fear is merely an illusionary moment…
 Movement surpasses danger involvement…
 River flows cautiously meandering…
 Without restrictive fear wondering…
 Existence is not a fearful moment…
 Existence is whilst in danger movement…"

Hugh Shergill

"Disappointment arrives without an appointment…
 Often revealed on stage of non contentment…
 That seed of resentment…
 Was destined commandment…
 For the unique soul assignment…
 All remains forever in alignment…"

Hugh Shergill

As desperation creeps in for the diabolical soul less maya beings…so does their soul target attacks increase… Victory inevitably shall be yours…as long as you move forth with your soul energy and awareness…move forward and battle with righteous duty of karma…along with the soul purpose of dharma…

"Absolute end of their season…
 Searching for a saving reason…
 Cowardingly recruiting liaison…
 Dying flame attempts to save on…
 By increasing its own flame…
 Before its inevitable demise…"

Hugh Shergill

"Never worry about the pawn…
 Victory is established before dawn…
 It is not who is against you…
 It is what that is always with you…
 You will absolutely rise…
 Witnessing all their demise…"

Hugh Shergill

"There are no coincidences…
 Only Divinely timed incidences…"
 Your current mess…
 Involves a soul less…
 Knowing is your wisdom message…
 Doing is your Karmic passage…
 illusion set is how you process it…
 illusion left is how you dealt with it…"

Hugh Shergill

"Keep showing…
  Keep silencing…

  Eliminate their desire for you to stop…
  Your credentials shall take you to top…
  Divinity has you backing…
  Revealing you their hacking…
  To stop your rise is not in their capacity…
  You are way beyond their confined territory…
  Embrace your own Divinity vibe…
  You Love are valued by your soul tribe…

  Keep showing…
  Keep silencing…"

Hugh Shergill

Spiritual Warfare…

"Spiritual Warfare…

  Lower dimensional beings…
  Versus Higher dimensional beings…
  Lower vibrational beings…
  Versus Higher vibrational beings…
  Every interaction between them…
  Is spiritual warfare…
  Every close interactive proximity…
  Is a spiritual war battle ground…

  Spiritual Warfare…"

Hugh Shergill

"Maya being's intimidating…
  Often their soul envy intimidating…
  The illusionary fright…
  Often all bark with no bite…
  Counter with a Soul aware fight…
  Witness their entertaining self destruct…
  Right in front of your sight…"

Hugh Shergill

It is on…
On me…

"Dear bartender…
  Darling what was this?…
  Strangely during indulgence felt…
  A slight suttle illusion apprehension…
  Tonight while leaving the bar…
  Seems like all of the outer world…
  Is out against me for war…
  Yet the Divine spark…
  Burns confidently within…
  Fueling my undeniable urge to confront…
  From the fearless Lion within…
  Faced many…
  Extinguished many…
  Please bartender…
  I request…
  This next last round…
  For the many remaining nemesis…
  It is on me…
  Fill their glasses to the very top…
  Before their inevitable demising cut…
  It is all…
  All on me…
  Dear bartender…
  War on…
  Spiritual warfare…
  It is on…
  On me…"

Hugh Shergill

Maya Leela

Divine Intervention…
Divine Protection…

"No weapon that is formed
against thee shall prosper,
and every tongue that shall rise against thee
in judgment thou shalt condemn.
This is the heritage of the servants of the Lord,
and their righteousness is of me, saith the Lord."

Holy Bible (Isaiah 54:17 King James Version)

"Iron cuts iron…
Poison kills poison…
Pain extinguishes pain…
Not ever someone's game mere pawn…
Script shall be revealed amongst explain…
You are the purpose till the destined dawn…"

Hugh Shergill

"Unapologetic intolerant of the tolerant…
One's existence is attacked eyes on…
Blind viewing only in their peripheral…
Insinuating its objectification…
Soul's non obsequious satisfaction…
Creativity held on pedestal…
Performativty consequential…
Victorious adulation…"

Hugh Shergill

An ancient eastern legend…

An old bad hunchback priest indulged into deep meditation on the river bed…suddenly is attacked… gets violently kicked from behind into the river by an ill acting man as an entertaining joke…when the priest manages to somehow get out of the water…miraculously…something the priest always prayed for…occurs…his back is now fully normal, erect, and healed…standing and walking straight now…he approaches the man with joyous gratitude…thanking him for healing him…

No matter how much effort and weapons are targeted towards you… Divinity always has miraculous script improvisations in store for you…always having everything in occurrence for your higher soul good… What immediately may seem as a disadvantage…is in all actuality your utmost advantage…it is all meant to unfold for your higher ascension… Preservation, determination, with Divine intervention shall overcome all as your Karmic play script proceeds forward…never give in nor give up…keep performing aligned with Divinity…all shall work for you effortlessly…

"Only a few roses…
  Among the many thorns…
  Interferences through causes…
  From their diabolical horns…
  Treat it as mere pauses…
  Failure make falls…
  As rose petal morns…"

Hugh Shergill

Maya Elevation Distractions…

Be very aware…whenever you are indulging into living from your authentic soul realm…perhaps it is meditation…yoga…spiritual karma…spiritual dharma…or any spiritual practice that you intentionally attempt…whomever interrupts or distract you from those precious moments…is innately creeping towards you…forcing you to descend back into the trap of maya jaal entrapment…these moments and particular individuals should be on your spiritual radar highly…to strictly disregard their disruption… and with only very certain rare occasions discretion…should be otherwise immediately be on your top ranking of Maya Beings…whomever disrupts your ascending acts…is a clear soul less agent of this Maya tricks…Matrix…Maya realm…

Weapon of Knowing…
Is Victory Carving…

The most powerful weapon in your spiritual warfare battles is to be aware that you are the Soul Being… Pain hurts when it is simply pain…yet pain felt with its knowing cause…becomes wisdom…pain hurts… wisdom heals…

Even only one individual Soul Being holds immense triumphant capabilities over many multiple Maya Beings…unlocking the key to these capabilities is becoming knowingly aware of the Maya Leela play and its participants…

"Where there is knowledge…
There is no pain…
What pain is understood…
Is now wisdom…
Embrace the known…
Never raw pain…
Pain hurts…
Wisdom heals…"

Hugh Shergill

"Till it is Divine's will…
Oceans shall never be still…
Instead friction with it and fade…
One must ride it to defeat the wave…
Becoming those sturdy sail travelers…
Remaining calm even among chaotic waters…"

Hugh Shergill

Refrain from Worrying…

Should one allow Divinity to look out for oneself… Or does one disrupt the frequency of blessings for one's higher self with worrying?

Every moment one spends in worry…a reason to worry manifests…that reason seed has been created in the infinite quantum field…which shall now be on its way to you… It is very important to counter the urge of indulging into worrying at the very moment it creeps into your thoughts…by interception…deviation from the worrying and shifting your thoughts towards something pleasant, pleasure, appreciation, gratefulness…shifting focus to feel better…this breaks the worrying manifestation cycle…indeed you may not be in the desired state…yet by deviating your thoughts from worrying…the perpetual worrying manifesting reasons for those worries is broken and deactivated…

Happiness is reality minus expectation…regardless of how high our expectations may be…becoming aware of an even higher reality shall immediately result in a more happy blissful state effortlessly…

"You are already your tomorrow…
 The tomorrow that you worried about…
 Is now your survived day without doubt…
 Happiness is reality minus expectation…
 Separating reality from this illusion…
 It is because I know of this…
 I now happen to be in this bliss…"

Hugh Shergill

"No resistance in existence…
 Understand the illusion essence…
 Stress is a misuse of imagination…
 Worrying manifests its worry…
 What is being experienced…
 Is already past existence…
 Become to the illusion…
 Become not the illusion…"

Hugh Shergill

"If there is a target…
 There must be an arrow…
 Arrow of solution…
 Shot from the…
 Bow of knowledge…
 Targeted now targets…
 Unleash that warrior…
 Never a worrier…"

Hugh Shergill

"For every attack…
 Lies the opportunity…
 For a more vicious counter attack…"

CHAPTER 13.

MAYA
UPAYA
SOLUTIONS

"Maya is the illusionary realm...

Maya Jaal is entrapment...

Of the illusionary realm...

Upaya is the means to solution...

Solution through performance...

Performance that counters...

The entrapment...

Soul performer performance...

In the play of Maya...

Maya Leela..."

Hugh Shergill

'Upaya' is the Sanskrit word that is defined as 'means to solution'... Maya and its forever entrapping illusion attempts...requires a dynamic systematic calculative counter performance...to not only defend oneself from the entrapping tendencies but offensively defeat them completely by overcoming...rising further ahead in one's Divinity led soul performance...

"Love all,
 trust a few,
 Do wrong to none:
 be able for thine enemy
 Rather in power than use,
 and keep thy friend
 Under thy own life's key:
 be cheque'd for silence,
 But never tax'd for speech."

William Shakespeare
(Renowned Poet / Playwright)

In the beautiful combative sport of boxing...more so than the aggressive offensive fighter...the most dangerous fighter is the active counter puncher...allowing its opponent to throw its blows...anticipate the attacks...defend oneself...upon the opponent's offensive attack...discover its opening state...the fragility glimpse moment between offense and defense...lies a gifted opening...this is the moment to counter attack...even a single precisely timed counter hook is capable to leave the opponent totally shook... Use your opponent's offense against them...let them attack...your intense counter attack will leave them flat on their back...

"Maya Upaya...
 The Upper Maya...
 Means to solution...
 Existing and performing...
 From one's super conscious field...
 Absolute victory setting to yield..."

Hugh Shergill

Deceive the Deceiver…

"When not affected by the illusion…
 You begin to affect the illusion…
 Such satisfying pleasure…
 Deceiving the deceiver…
 The nemising energy giver…
 Now the succumbing receiver…
 Improvising your role scripting…
 Rewriting the play unfolding…"

Hugh Shergill

"And no matter what game they play
 We got something they can never take away"

Bob Marley
(Renowned Artist / Musician / Poet)

All in your illusionary realm existence experience so far…moment after moment…you have been entrappingly attacked by your particular karmically assigned diabolical asuric soul less entities… Hurt, pain, betrayal, insults, anger, abuse, unjust frustration…to even near death experiences…has been suffering felt to the core…shaking your physical, mental, energetic states to question 'Why?' 'Why Me?'…

Well…why not you? It is the precious soul within you for why you were selected…you are the chosen Divine soul spark…a limited rare commodity among these diabolical soul less community…you are the reason for all this perceived existence…you have always been aware of this in your elevated realms… Congratulations and celebrations to your soul…you have now began to understand your special chosen existence in this physically perceived realm as well…additionally knowing now and becoming aware of your surrounding stage soul less maya being entities…this is indeed an immense blessing to discover the key that unlocks the hidden truth of existence…lifting the veil of illusion…of the Maya Leela play… Moment has arrived to now deviate from past hurt and suffering…moment is now for soul elevating…

The stage play's main star actor does not complain or become depressed by having the most prominent role of the play…on the contrary…the star actor celebrates with gratitude for being in such a valuable position of being the star performer…appreciating the beautiful opportunity regardless of how much effort and preparation is involved in performing the role… Embrace your soul celebrity superposition… You are the Soulabrity…Superstar of Divinity…

Maya Leela

Soulabrity…Superstar of Divinity…

"Daily I feel celebrity famous…
  Soul force around the soul less…
  Without any effort grabbing attention…
  Knowing is their threatened intimidation…
  Reality of being a soul celebrity…
  Existing amongst soul less fragility…
  The Soulabrity…
  Superstar of Divinity…"

Hugh Shergill

"When you find yourself in a room
  surrounded by your enemies
  you should tell yourself
  'I am not locked in here with you,
  you are locked in here with me.'

  This is the kind of mindset
  you should have
  if you want to succeed in life.
  Get rid of that victim mentality."

Bruce Lee
(Renowned Martial Artist / Actor / Revolutionist)

"To perform on stage,
  you have to run through your paces
  till you are perfect.
  Despite the script and director,
  the actor makes or breaks the play."

Zeenat Aman (Renowned Actor / Model)

Maya Leela

"Maya the illusion say…
  Leela is its staged play…
  Soul beings temporary stay…
  Among where maya beings play…
  As I change my reincarnated clay…
  I continue to view this karmic play…"

Hugh Shergill

"As much there are stars in the galaxy…
As much equivalent flowers earthly…
What you perceive as complete…
Are just an illusionary meet…
What is the paranorma…
Is the unveiling aroma…"

Hugh Shergill

"De Ja Vu…the wow factor…of Soul…
Vu Ja De…the wowing factor…of Awakening…"

Revisiting now…the phenomenon of 'De Ja Vu'…seeing new instances that resonate and recall in a very familiar way…appreciate and enjoy this sub conscious preview trailer glimpse of the upcoming Maya play…as the wow factor… Often one's soul path and co performing soul beings will be part of your preview Maya play trailer recall phenomenon of De Ja Vu…

Further…upon awakening and unveillance of the illusion…the shocking realization that the majority living entities around us that we had always perceived as family, friends, or Loved ones…are actually in fact Maya jaal entrapping diabolical entities…soul less asuric low vibrational maya beings…this shift from your previous perceived reality to the real unveiled reality will often result in regularly experiencing 'Vu Ja De' the duality opposite of 'De Ja Vu'…where instead of experiencing new instances in a very familiar way…now one will see familiar instances in an entirely new way…

The key is to embrace the phenomenon of 'Vu Ja De'…where one is seeing those very familiar instances in an entirely new way…embracing the familiar in an entirely new vision is what makes one wow…this is Vu Ja De…it is the evolution of the soul from illusion to reality… Those triggered experiences from the past…should now only be triggers from the past…dissolving away all the preconceived perceptions of the past…shifting to an entire new perspective that shall last for eternity…those previous associations, relationships, Loved ones are now revelatingly revealed in their authentic actuality… this is the ever wowing factor of Vu Ja De…your unveiling discovery of reality…

"Each moment…
One touch of the river…
Is a new moment…
New water in the river…
You new touches as meant…
Impossible to repeat replicate…
Forever an ungraspable state…"

Hugh Shergill

"You can't win,
 If you're not right within"

Lauryn Hill
(Renowned Singer / Song Writer)

Mastering Soul Performance...

"Only reality is the truth...
 Treat all illusion as an illusion...

 Thoughts are illusionary processes...
 Of Maya existence...
 Emotions are illusionary reactions...
 To Maya thoughts...
 Perform in the illusion play...
 Do not let the illusion play you...

 Only reality is the truth...
 Treat all illusion as an illusion..."

Hugh Shergill

Thoughts...Emotions...Feelings...

"Thoughts are illusionary processes of Maya existence...
Emotions are illusionary reactions to thoughts..."

All emotions are illusionary reactions to thought triggers...confined to exist only on an illusionary physical realm...only existing on the three dimensional Maya level...physical biological perceived existence thought processing...is the only method to process emotions... Elevated evolved conscious level existences are devoid of emotional triggers, process, and responds...as all of these require physical processing existing...

An unhealthy state of physical existence that has abnormal, inefficient, deficient processing mechanism is possible to be completely emotionless... In all actuality, it is not devoid of emotions but devoid of the processing of thoughts...therefore devoid of reactions to the thoughts...

"Emotions are the enemy of facts"

Emotions are simply reactions to thoughts...emotions are never facts... Like the theatre actor deeply indulged in its method acting performance...exuberating reactions to the play script processes by acting out what is processed and understood...all within the strict confines of the play script... The actor holds no control over the play script, which is the sole factual element of play... The actor does however have the ability and liberty to how it processes and understands the script…this is in the actor's full control…which ultimately results in how it actually reacts to the processing and understanding of the play script…this is its acting…the actor's performance…reactions to processing of facts…not reactions of the actuality of the facts…

Having mastery control over one's thoughts…results in having mastery control over one's emotions… Control the trigger processes…gives control over the trigger reactions…ultimately and inevitably…

"No one can take your energy…
 You only give your energy…
 Only those spiritual…
 Actually have a spirit…
 Souls are never truly lost…
 Just surrounded by the forever lost…
 The only personality disorder…
 Is soul's surroundings not in order…
 Every successful trap must enclose you…
 Every emotional relationship encloses you…
 Never react…
 Instead respond…
 Sacrifice of class must be avoided…
 When dealing with those devoided…"

Hugh Shergill

Soul Aura Access…

Giving attention to them connects your soul to their low vibration frequency…and vice versa even worse giving them access to connect to your Divinely blessed high frequency…a very low vibrational energetic entanglement…potentially allowing them to access, attack, hinder, deplete your soul aura energy…

"No fishing is possible…
 Without access to water…
 What was once feasible…
 Now one just knows better…
 Take your intentions where invisible…
 The soul has risen tougher…"

Hugh Shergill

**"You will continue to suffer
if you have an emotional reaction
to everything that is said to you.
True power is sitting back
and observing everything
with logic."**

**Bruce Lee
(Renowned Martial Artist / Actor / Revolutionist)**

**"For those who have conquered the mind,
it is their friend.
For those who have failed to do so,
the mind works like an enemy."**

Bhagavad Geeta

**"Deserving emotion unnecessity...
For the particular entity...
Respond intellectually...
A non emotional react...
Disrupting immediately...
Their active soul less act..."**

Hugh Shergill

Emotional Intelligence...

"Observe your emotions...
Utilize discreet discretion of its absorption..."

Emotions are an integral component of one's personality essence...emotions should not be seen in a negative light...it's how one interprets it...utilizes it...and ultimately experiences it...in the illusionary play of Maya Leela... Emotional intelligence is the key to blissful play experience indulgence...

Feelings...

"Feelings are felt...beyond processing and reactions... Feelings are much above and beyond all thoughts and emotions..."

Feelings are something that goes beyond emotions...feelings are consciousness felt...beyond Maya... and the only authentic feeling in conscious existence is Love...existing in certain modified existence dependent on each individual's conscious state capabilities...as either one is feeling Love or lack of...

ever existing beyond all processing and reactions...with indeed the possibility to be then processed as thoughts and reactions as emotions on the illusionary maya conscious state...but are never confined to, as feelings are not defined nor dependent to the confines of processing and reacting...

An individual in your presence can non reactively make you feel immense Love or immensely revolting lack of Love without any perceived demonstration of what they truly feel for you...going way beyond words and actions...however that intense felt feelings still exist and so ever felt by those in tune with their higher consciousness states... feelings are felt far beyond thoughts and emotions...even more so powerfully in higher conscious states...such as sub-conscious state...and even further for some... soul beings in super soul conscious state...the direct Divinity existence...felt deep within...beyond all thoughts and emotions...

As an individual in an extremely unhealthy state of being...such as being in coma... where they may be completely thoughtless and emotionless however yet still feel...and feel deeply...sometimes even breaking the barrier of unhealthy physical state and actually triggering overwhelming feelings of Love not thoughts...by gesturing a smile...or shedding a tear...while still in a thought deprived coma state... This is the power of felt...the feeling of Love...processed higher consciousness...ever existing way beyond all thoughts and emotions...

"Whenever you happen to cry...
  Wipe away your own tears...
  If someone else wipes them...
  There shall be a demanding cost...
  For they shall absolutely demand...
  For wiping your tears..."

Salim Khan
(Renowned Writer / Script Writer / Philosopher)
Translation by Hugh Shergill

Emotions should be acknowledged and respected...but further more and more importantly... understood...that all emotions are mere illusions...illusion reactions to illusionary thought processes of perceived perception... Therefore it is highly important to understand one's emotions that are reactions to thoughts...and why those thoughts... For this, one must go beyond the emotions and understand the thought triggers of the emotions processed...

Being emotionless is impossible on a perceived physical existing realm...as even hiding particular emotions are also particular emotions... A soul burdening state... Emotions should therefore be understood as physical processing mechanisms...acknowledged, respected, understood, and processed accordingly with soul conscious discernment felt filtration...

"Your world is in control...
Entire world is in your control...
Having emotional control...
Having life in control...
Your world is in control...
Entire world is in your control..."

Hugh Shergill

Power of Patience...

When one is going through a volatile storm...it is impossible to calm the storm...instead the key is to practice patience...calming oneself...The storm shall pass...what will be left is your state of being...if that remains intact...you have won over the storm... This is the power of patience...as all shall pass... embrace the triumphant victory...while letting go of what required your very trying patience...

"Divine timing...
Beyond planning...
Neither fast...
Neither last...
Destined prime...
Arrives on time..."

Hugh Shergill

"Pain will leave you...
Once it has finished teaching you"

Bruce Lee
(Renowned Martial Artist / Actor / Revolutionist)

"Unable to please...
Unable to be at ease...
Just breathe...
It is just a certain day...
Not an entire life per say...
Days of disruptive mood order...
Is not some mental disorder..."

Hugh Shergill

Escape is your healing closure...

Escape is your healing closure...Their diabolical asuric attacks on to your soul is your closure...their disrespect...their ostracizing of you...their persecution of you...their contempt...their gaslighting... their ghosting...their insults...them speaking ill will on to you...their repeated unrelenting cruel abuse is your closure...their disgusting asuric ego driven unapologetic behaviour is your closure...their unremorseful fake apologies without any changed behaviour is also your closure...their fake self pity playing the righteous victim and perceiving you actually as the script villain is your closure...take all these as closures that shall be sparks of your healing eventually...your immense blessings only arrive only after these diabolical soul less entities are fully exposed and escaped from...therefore one must first diligently completely break away from their diabolical venomous fangs...take your escape healing closure and head towards your ascension...your beautiful soul treasures await to embrace you Love....

Foggy path is destination closer...

"Your foggy path is destination closer...
 Over destinations appearing clearer...
 Mighty mountains above appear clear from far...
 Valley destined treasures hidden much closer...
 Hidden in fog from your eyes sight...
 Yet felt very close to the heart...
 Evolve over every challenging might...
 Till your shadow becomes your shining light...
 Your foggy path is destination closer...
 Over destinations appearing clearer..."

Hugh Shergill

Hurt History...

"Entrapped in hurt history...
 Is entrapped hostility...
 Letting go is a must...
 Whatever that was...
 Whatever filth held on...
 Only discomfort results...
 Moment to turn to the next script page...
 To the next chapter of the play stage..."

Hugh Shergill

Even their asuric passing thoughts attach to your soul heavily…do not entertain their diabolical thoughts…indeed it is very difficult to do as the innate emphatic Loving soul energy that you carry is very sensitive…however one must strive to maneuver one's soul energy for its utmost high version possible…when their thoughts haunt in…distract yourself with positive Loving thoughts…deviate and remove them from entertaining your thoughts…

"I use memories…
  I don't allow memories to use me…"

Lord Shiva (Shiva Sutra)

Let it go…
You are walking in snow…

"Let it go…
  You are walking in snow…

  Take a complete footstep…
  You are walking on snow…
  When walking in deep snow…
  One must lift each footstep…
  Completely out of the snow…
  To proceed to the next step…
  Any residual dragging footstep…
  Shall accumulate the snow…
  Eventually leaving you stuck…
  Still in the snow…

  Let it go…
  You are walking in snow…"

Hugh Shergill

Each moment of the theatrics of the Maya realm experience must experienced and then completely step out and let go in order to proceed to the next experience…any residual holding experiencing… shall counter advancement…resist the temptation to accumulate psychological baggage by continually revisiting and re-experiencing a past situation again and again…embrace that experienced journey instead…as without it, there would not be this you…yet revisiting each experienced step of the previous journey makes you re-experience it…Which is compromising your deserving new experience moments… embrace it and then let it go…you are walking in snow…you have to completely take your foot out of the snow before you move towards your next step…take a complete footstep from the snow…you are walking on snow…Be wild…be free…free from self pity…

"**Never regret any of your past version…**
  It was an imperative learning season…
  That is no longer you…
  Yet made way for this you…
  Embrace that path you have tread…
  Without it your this would be dead…"

Hugh Shergill

"**Re-Visiting…**
  Re-Experiencing…
  Re-Energizing…

  Peeling away your old scabs…
  Will only lead to bleed…
  Reopening those old pending tabs…
  Will hinder upcoming leads…
  What was is now forever set in stone…
  Only now for soul witness alone…
  Holding on to other's ill towards you…
  Is ill energy that does not belong to you…

  Re-Visiting…
  Re-Experiencing…
  Re-Energizing…"

Hugh Shergill

Let it end…
Let it hurt…
Let it heal…
Let it go…

Instead of revisiting and torturing yourself by the past events and those traumatic multiple attacks from these soul less maya beings…appreciate your space away from them now…this is your true blessing…your gift…a peace of mind away from them…do not let your Divine protection gift of being away from them and yet still be hindered by them by revisiting thoughts of those same diabolical soul less beings… Embrace and appreciate your new acquired peace of mind…

Maya Leela

Let it end...
Let it hurt...
Let it heal...
Let it go...

"No scent infused into the sewage...
  No spectator tour within the wreckage...
  What is left with the savage...
  Was the final point of associative vantage...
  You have excelled beyond any advantage...
  Now your flight is your gift of courage...
  Rising winds is your soul's fragrance..."

Hugh Shergill

"I never saw a wild thing feel sorry for itself"

David Herbert Lawrence
(Renowned Poet / Writer)

Soul Unself Pity

"Be wild...
  Be free...
  Free from self pity...
  Never pity...
  Or feel sorry for yourself...
  Externalization of blame...
  Externalizes your power..."

Hugh Shergill

"In the wild world of existence...
  Self pity is absolute non-existence...
  Destined those as your resistance...
  Frivolous to expect any assistance...
  Stage of Maya is set in an illusion trance...
  Where one must perform its Leela dance..."

Hugh Shergill

"What is already there...
You can not wear...
Everyone has problems...
No need to wear your problems...
What is uncomfortable to wear...
Deserves an undressing tear..."

Hugh Shergill

"Reaction Perfection...
Responsive Reaction...

Perfecting acting...
Is perfecting reacting...
It is in reaction that lies all power...
Conscious reaction that's higher...
The art of reaction exchange...
Holds the key to all change...
Reaction or lack of...
Devoids the perceived power of...
All interactions...
All situations...
Perfect your acting...
By perfecting reacting...

Reaction Perfection...
Responsive Reaction..."

Hugh Shergill

Contemplation is required to understand emotions before acting and reacting on them...by indulging deep within higher conscious realms... The more one contemplates within...the more understanding of emotions one receives...with repetitive contemplating...it becomes highly instinctive...highly fast...not even requiring more than a few neurons firing zeptoseconds at most of conscious feeling understanding...giving and gaining control over emotionally triggered actions and reactions...

"How people treat you...
 Is their karma...
 How you respond...
 Is yours...
 Let them accumulate karmic debt...
 Distance yourself and best left...
 From entities incapable of being you...
 Your higher existence is only for you..."

Hugh Shergill

On an even higher level of contemplation... Meditative state through meditation...one is able to first understand and then further modify feelings by getting answers of why one feels what it feels...this conscious indulgence makes one the master of one's emotions...which brings mastery over one's actions and reactions...resulting in karma modification...by mastering one's karmic performance... ultimately mastering one's destiny...the Maya Leela play performance and script...to one's soul preference...

"World is so frivolous...
 Truth becomes intimidating...
 Too much knowledge...
 Too much grief...
 Reality is more than collective agreement...
 Give your intuition unconditional commitment...
 Tackle every obstacle as an opportunity...
 To expand one's soul creativity..."

Hugh Shergill

Tear Crystals...

"Save your tears...
 Crystalize your tears...
 Likely no one is truly with you...
 Yet be assured of your undeniable value...
 Cherish your painful soul blisters...
 Shall manifest into priceless crystals..."

Hugh Shergill

Release for Peace…

The over emphasis on fellow Maya stage performers takes away one from the performing wealth abundance of the staged totality…as one should merge as a reflection expression of the beauty of the traveled destination…not a deliberately attached response to the fellow travelers…

Therefore, one should practice to eliminate focused regard on just one element of nature…human beings…by giving more focus regard through Love and concentration to nature in whole totality… that blesses us with unconditional care and Love…earth itself…plants, trees, air, water, sun rays, cool moonlight, stars, galaxies…the blessed beautiful illusionary stage of Maya…staged for our soul indulgence experience… This shifting focus from just one element of nature to nature in totality… enhances one's capacity to receive and reciprocate abundance of Love beyond the mere existence of one or more fellow beings…that shall continue to exist with or without you…and vice versa… Simply continue performing and enjoying the play instead of performing for the enjoyment of the other performers…

"Be entertained by the play…
  Not entertaining the play…

  Become your ascendant master…
  Mastering one's consciousness…
  Masters the performance…
  Mastering the play…
  Masters a breakthrough performance…

  Be entertained by the play…
  Not entertaining the play…"

Hugh Shergill

Lifting of the veil and the opening of the third eye corresponds more often than not…as awareness of the truth behind the staged stage appears…the more Divinity communication appears… synchronicity… synchronous situations…synchronous individuals…specific words noticed…specific number sequences…powering intuitive thoughts…all communicating with you…from one moment to another…revealing step by step to you…for you…

Maya Leela

"One knows a little...
 When little is revealed...
 illusion occurrence innocence...
 When Maya makes no sense...
 Once the curtains are lifted...
 Core reality has forever shifted...
 Now one happens to look back...
 Sees the illusion trajectory track..."

Hugh Shergill

"When people are determined
 they can overcome anything"

Nelson Mandela
(Renowned Revolutionary Leader / Philanthropist)

"Instead of strict positivity...
 Embrace multi-realm reality...
 Life without purpose...
 Is merely a curse...
 There are no coincidences...
 Only precisely planned incidences...
 Every consequence...
 Divine occurrence..."

Hugh Shergill

"Acceptance of inability to change...
 Change the inability of acceptance...
 Embrace darkness as all light...
 All light is created from darkness...
 One must travel to the deepest darkness...
 To fully illuminate one's lightness..."

Hugh Shergill

Soul saving is Soul Living…

Protect your true power…your soul…your authentic beyond illusionary Maya existence…Soul saving is soul living…action of daily practice…repeatedly till one is in tune in totality of soul living existence…

Knowledge is Power…
Awareness is True Knowledge…

The essence power of the performance is knowledge… Awareness is true knowledge… The more you know…the more control you have over your emotions…less disappointed you become…less hurt you experience…as you know more…performing in the play with wisdom…

The way the Maya stage interprets it…is that if you did not appreciate a particular scene or act…you would not be feeding it with your attentive soul energy…therefore resulting in a more perpetual defining experiences of that particular scene and acts will dominate your consciousness… Be mindful of where your soul energy is going at all times…do not let your primary energy become dormant through diabolical distractions…

Awareness is true power…a serpent never warns one before biting…that it is going to bite you or how venomous the implications of its bite shall be…the serpent is simply following the confined innate route of its existence and behaviour… Very similarly, maya being's confined route is maya jaal entrapment and feeding itself through soul being's soul energy existence in the Maya realm… undoubtedly the maya being forever shall do whatever it takes to accomplish this…as this is nothing personal against the soul being but it is survival mechanism for the maya being… Likewise it is also important for the soul being to be aware of this and take all necessary precautions to preserve their soul energy and stay on route for their highest purpose…which is beyond the illusionary Maya realm…

"Rebel Soul…

  Heart bleeds…
  Act provokes…
  Soul bleeds…
  Truth evokes…
  Rebel seeds…
  illusion revokes…

  Rebel Soul…"

Hugh Shergill

Maya Leela

Be the Rebel Soul...

Rebelliousness is often rooted in soul memory...
Notice how the most enlightened beings in some point of their life rebelled in some form or another...
an interesting example is teenage years...rebellious teens rebelling within are an example of this...
as after growing and processing their early years...now as their intellect broadens...some are
subconsciously tapping into their previous soul journey experiences that compels them to question
more than the imposed conventional norms placed upon them...as most norms keep one confide to
a particular agenda based realm...not to say rules and regulations should not be followed however
without questioning and understanding...it is confided slavery... To truly see what is and why it is...
one must question...one must soul investigate...

The rebel soul is often alone...as it even rebels and questions those in its previous close circles...
particularly their acts...their motivations behind their actions...their blindness to actual reality... These
deep examinations of the maya being's soul less diabolical characteristics both threaten the maya
being and forever disgust the soul being...resulting in the inevitable forever separate paths of their
distinct existences...

"Performing advantage of the play...
 Is in the script strategy of the play...
 Reveal of reality...
 Truth of humanity...
 Rebel without hesitate...
 As performance is on stake...
 For illusionary advantage structured...
 Revelating revealed have rebelled...
 Ignorant to disregard...
 As power requires regard...
 Those in aerial view of existence...
 Do not fear death existence...
 Rebel soul are always sole...
 Infinite living totality of whole...
 Where threat become threatened...
 As reveal rises from the once complied..."

Hugh Shergill

"What road?...
Only my road...
Refusing to be lead...
By the spiritually dead...
Not running on the hamster wheel...
Opening the entire cage for real..."

Hugh Shergill

Greater the Power...
Greater the Responsibility...

With great power comes great responsibility...just take care of your responsibilities and never compromise your soul consciousness performance...and all true successes shall follow you...

"During all time throws...
All the highs and extreme lows...
Either predetermined to earn...
Or submittingly determined to learn...
Mastering your evolution...
Becomes revolution..."

Hugh Shergill

Success and Efforts...

"Your success will...
Continuously walk...
Your efforts are ridiculed...
With insultive talk...
In efforts there only will be...
A few some...
In success there will be...
Many to come...
Discipline will keep you...
Afloat remember...
Succumb to sinking...
Shall vanish you forever..."

Hugh Shergill

"The True Rules of Success...

  Always keep your eyes...
  Low in humility...

  Never argue with anyone...
  By revealing one's soul intent...

  Keep your character behaviour...
  At its most highest standard...
  Morally and ethically...

  True Success Shall Be Inevitable..."

Mohammed Rafi (Renowned Singer / Artist)
Translation by Hugh Shergill

"The night should never celebrate sunsets...
  As the sunrise is inevitable...
  A particular game ends then resets...
  The next winning awaits with the shuffle...
  Dropping the ladder upon reaching tops...
  Only makes way for a violent fall..."

Hugh Shergill

Self Preservation...

"Do not let anyone...
  Take your power away...
  Never ever...
  Do not dance to someone else's moves...
  Playing out their particular tune...
  Find your own music...
  Play your music...
  Dance to your music in the dark night...
  Whilst illuminating your soul light..."

Hugh Shergill

First law of nature is self preservation...honour it...accept it...be confident... Use true sense...notch higher than common sense...using one's higher soul intelligence...for every situation, circumstance, individual...always use your own soul conscious validation...as if deep within...someone or something...if it is not perceived as being right...and does not resonate as being right...it is not right... never doubt that...as doubting that will ultimately lead to immense hurt through maya jaal entrapment punishment...

Star Maya Performer vs Maya Puppet...

**"You are the Star Maya Performer...
Not the Maya Puppeteer's Puppet..."**

Be that star Maya stage soul performer...not a mere Maya stage string puppet...that is entrapped and fully under control at the mercy and amusement of the puppeteer...the Maya jaal agents... Perform the Maya leela play as the star protagonist soul performer always...never as the antagonist puppeteer's maya string puppet... Be no one else's puppeteer's string reactive Maya Leela performer... by delivering a Maya jaal entrapped performance...an entrapped performance as a puppet, at the mercy of the puppeteer...by letting other co-performers extract the performance they desire from you by pulling on to their strings of entrapment at their desired will...that is their Maya jaal entrapment power...and your soul depletion underperformance...devoiding you of your soul power essence and soul ascension...which ultimately shall be Maya jaal entrapment victory for the puppeteer...never for their controlled puppet...

**"Be the Maya Leela matador...
That is not a Maya slave...
Instead a Maya successor...
Divert the Maya bull's momentum...
This shall be an attack back at it...
Let them fall on their own attack...
Be the Maya Leela matador..."**

Hugh Shergill

"Only reality is the truth...
Treat all illusion as illusion...

You know your true self ...
Be true to yourself...
Most important relationship is true self...
The one in truth with oneself...
Your true self...

Only reality is the truth...
Treat all illusion as illusion..."

Hugh Shergill

Be the soul observer of your physical existence...at all times...as being and staying ready will not require getting ready... Observe all your energetic interactions...all actions...all emotions...all thoughts...this is your highest level of observational intelligence that guides you through the guiding voice within...questioning all...is this action...correct or wrong?...legal or illegal?...morally and ethically correct?...harming someone in some way or form?...creating positive karma or negative karma?... The sensibility of your soul intelligence discernment will always guide your physical existence to follow in the harmony of the Divine...which is always Love...Love for one and all Love...

Be Aware of the Unaware...

You can not change anyone else's consciousness...and or elevate someone's perception beyond Maya...trying to do so, only results in wasting your valuable time and soul energy...a cactus plant shall never blossom roses...however a rose seed holds the potential to blossom beautiful roses...a maya being is incapable of soul awakening...and an unawake dormant soul being shall eventually be an awake soul being...whether it is the very next moment or many further maya leela performances and play acts lifetimes away...

Peace of mind is the highest form of maya stage bliss...

"Your power...
Not my tower...

To take someone's power...
Expect nothing ever...
Exclude their entrapping power...
Include your unexpecting forever...

Your power...
Not my tower..."

Hugh Shergill

Life is a blessing that should be enjoyed every moment...don't waste time energy soul by attentive care and regard for the antagonist...let them be free to play their dedicated low vibrational performance...while you enjoy your performance...hold on to no expectations...resulting in no disappointments...peace of mind is a state of bliss...

Law and Human Rights Filter...

Use law and human rights filters when dealing with others. Fortunately, collectively, globally...human beings have to a certain degree...some nations more or less...evolved from the primitive savage "law of the jungle" to "law of civilization".

Every nation has certain laws, regulations, and particular human rights scope...which each civilian is mandated to rightfully comply by, honour and respect...anything beyond is higher humanity moral grounds and spiritual expectation conduct...which one always indeed hopes for...for the higher karmic good for one and all... this is however an expectation bound to disappoint ...as not everyone is capable of doing so...especially these diabolical asuric soul less entities...that unfortunately primarily both govern and destroy on a vast level...

Human beings collectively and individually are absolutely responsible for certain behavioural living conduct based on particular laws, regulations, morals, and ethics... These are imposed and required. Anything beyond that brings the element of spiritual being, behaviour and development is not your responsibility, however you are responsible for how to deal with others while on your performance journey...

Karma is responsible for Karma...

"Karma is...
  Responsible for Karma...
  Karma...
  Ultimate governing law...
  Of all existence...
  Beyond crime...
  By governing sin...
  Karma on every act...
  Shall react..."

Hugh Shergill

Crime vs Sin...

Seldom, there is often the possibility of distinct dichotomy between crime and sin...crime is particular societal based laws and regulations ...subjective to some dominant approval, conformity, or lack of...fluctuates its leniency or stricting based on the discretion of the few selected...as a crime may very well be morally justified...whereas, a sin is always a sin...that makes one's soul shiver in revolt thinking of the action and consequence...that vibrates the vulnerability of the core of soul existence...

morality, humanity, ethically...all feel the threat of the Maya sin invade...crime may go undetected and unpunished...however, a sin is always detected...karmically...and dealt inevitably karmically...even if it goes perhaps undetected societally...however it shall be justly served karmically...always has...always is...always will...

"One may escape crime...
One can never escape sin...
Sin is inescapable...
Karmically covered completely...
On the radar of someone something...
Much more beyond you...
No need nor require to stress over...
Divinity is watching...
Watching all...
Trusting existence...
Trusting Divinity...
All is dealt karmically..."

Hugh Shergill

Maya being's lack of spiritual conduct is also a part of nature... Maya beings lack of spiritual conduct must be perceived the same...as long the absolute required human being ethical conduct and complying to societal rules and regulations are honoured...which was not always such a dominant case as history unfortunately reveals...however fortunately, at least for now, generally globally there are at least some laws in effect to ensure this...and any deviation is globally condemned and actions must absolutely be taken...beyond the human being level personal responsibility of following laws, not participating in criminal acts, and ensuring a human being conduct expectation...expecting any higher spiritual morality expression from another human being...is absolutely pointless...and actually ridiculous if the human being interaction experience is from a maya being...as that is utter ignorance on the part of the soul being...ignorance that eventually develops into hurt and pain...therefore it is a must to perform and respond from the higher soul conscious awareness of the soul being...when in interaction with others, specifically a maya being...as a fellow soul being will already through their performance acts reveal higher soul conscious awareness...through Love and humanity...

"There are no coincidences...
All synchronized incidences...
Simply listen to the universe...
As the Divine radio sends...
Its Divinity signals...
Both for your entertainment...
And your intuitive discernment..."

Hugh Shergill

**"I believe there's an inner power
that makes winners or losers.
And the winners are
the ones who really listen to
the truth of their hearts."**

**Sylvester Stallone
(Renowned Actor / Writer / Filmmaker)**

Escapologist is the ultimate strategist…

No need to overly focus on remaining positive…just eliminate the negative…if a maya being is doing something certainly soul offensive to you…instead of reacting "why are they like that?" and further overly stressing to remain calm and positive…shift the focus to your inner soul power knowing… knowing exactly that you do know why this maya being is demonstrating and forcing maya jaal energy towards you…remain calm…eliminate any possibility of taking in their maya jaal attack…countering it with your shield of knowing…your arsenal of awareness…

Concentrate on your soul performance… Your responsibility is to your soul only, not anyone else… as no one else will ever be responsible for your soul… As anything beyond your soul is meaningless illusion… Concentrate your focus on the 'mean' and eliminate the 'less'…

While with the loving attempt to feed and care for an abandoned dog… The dog reciprocates with furiously aggressively barking at you…does not require you or make it appropriate for you to confront the dog with why that was highly inappropriate and the aggressive tone of voice bark is unappreciated…or a thorn stinging you while you reach out to smell the aroma fragrance of the beautiful rose growing in your garden…or while on a exotic tropical vacation…you are lying on the white sandy beach enjoying the sun and a cloud suddenly blocks the sun…you would not get up and initiate an argument with the cloud that this is your last day of the vacation and your sun blocking is being an hindrance to your beautiful vacation experience…even the most ridicule mind would find these examples highly ridiculous… As we innately understand the nature behaviour of nature and its organisms…from the gentle single flower blossoming to the extremities of natural disasters…all is understood and accepted…the same understanding applies to the soul less asuric diabolical maya beings… It is like watching reruns of the same horror movie…there is no exciting edge of the seat thrills…as one already knows what next shall occur… Similarly…we know these diabolical soul less asuric entities…and all their potential horrors…understand and exit from their horror play…

"You can not set yourself on fire
  To keep others warm...
  Protect your soul conscious...
  Light the candle of awareness...
  Shining light to oneself...
  While illuminating the entire ambience..."

Hugh Shergill

Often soul beings specifically become targeted...whether it is experiencing bullying, physical abuse, emotional abuse as a child...discrimination...casted out at institutions, work, family, friends etc. This is no coincidence but subconscious synchronicity of spiritual warfare playing out on the Maya Leela stage... As you perform by just being...they outcast you...detest you...ironically unknowingly knowing the truth...they base their dislike targeting on illusionary frivolous judgments...as they are unaware of the truth on a lower conscious level...but their maya subconscious is aware of the soul being...the soul Divine aura is undeniably detected...as them being maya beings...are extremely threatened by your existence...the immense power you hold...as their existence is because you exist...

"The rejection...
  That's my encouragement...
  It's a challenge...
  Are you going to accept...
  Their evaluation of you?...
  Or are you going to...
  Evaluate yourself?..."

Sylvester Stallone
(Renowned Actor / Writer / Filmmaker)

The simple awareness shift...from the soul burdening stressful question of "why is this individual acting this way?" shifting to the understanding statement of "i am aware of why this individual acts this way"...opens up new profound performance and evolution possibilities for the soul being... releasing them from the most common forms of maya jaal entrapments...through dispowering maya pawn maya beings Maya Leela performance power...by simply being aware...this simple shift immediately eliminates a lot of those reprogramming and counseling sessions many undergo due to figuring out why others treat them the way they do...instead what is important is who is it that really is performing those actions...once the source being energy is revealed through awareness...there is no longer the need to be the "why?" victim...

Simply put...they just don't know better...not only that...they are absolutely incapable of knowing any better... When you realize this fact...then all attachments and expectations vanish from your consciousness...there is no longer any internal hurt and disappointments...as you just know better...a two way opposite roads must travel separately...any mergence...shall result in head on collision...stay in your soul being lane...there is no fitting in...any attempt is a conscious conflicting energy that shall never meet...just live and let live...let them just be...their negative karma soul less self... Divinity is witnessing all...karmically being notified...so it is absolutely necessary to just surrender and enjoy the process...as you continue on your Maya Leela life performance and enjoy this temporary maya realm illusionary platform...never letting some annoying party attendees to spoil your party experience...cut the cord and cleanse...disassociate and enjoy this return ticket Maya Leela play party...

"One that explodes...
  Mere scattered fountain...
  One that implodes...
  Remains potent within...
  Power exudes...
  When able to maintain..."

Hugh Shergill

No issues in illusions...

"No issues in illusions...
  All issues are illusions...
  Perceived existence is illusion...
  Unveiling awareness truth...
  Vanishes all issues...
  No issues in illusions..."

Hugh Shergill

Indeed the weight of Maya realm illusionary existence undoubtedly entraps one and consumes their consciousness soul energy...by creating fear of every perceived threat of every perceived issue... however in all reality...the harsh reality truth is that your perceived worldly existence shall expire with your physical death and every issue being experienced shall also expire with it... Whatever is inevitably going to expire and cease to exist...dwelling on that and focusing one's entire energies upon it...in all reality is truly a waste of perceived time... This is a difficult process to accept due to the Maya realm illusionary Maya jaal entrapments...that constantly consumes one with bombarded reminders of all perceived issues...unfortunately leading many to extremely depressive states of existence... this Maya jaal entrapment victim acknowledgement must be battled...and the first step of the process is to acknowledge the issues...of what are they...and everything conclusive answer to every issue is an absolute illusion...harsh to accept and unveil...however once one is soul evolved to face the truth...the bliss of the truth blesses...the Maya Leela soul performer is able to face each and every play script act state and situation...by performing in an aware performance conscious state...to face each issue head on...with all capability capacities...especially with the highest weapon available...the absolute truth...treating every issue as it actually is...nothing but a mere illusion...

Intuitively Correct...Always...

"Your intuition is always correct...
 Yet interpretation may falsely percept...
 Indulge deep within the intuition energy...
 Witness all perfection with its synergy...
 What is real will be filtered left...
 Through dissolving the untrue swept..."

Hugh Shergill

Trust your intuition always...your soul knows much more than what physically portrays...the branch of the tree may fluctuate here and there...yet the birth of the seed shall never disguise you...trust the seed within...and trust and observe its trunk and branch...the growth will overwhelm you...the fruits of the branches shall overturn you...the fruits of truth shall be presented...accepted or rejected...yet it shall never take your undeniable fruit bearing magic away...your soul seed creates all...is all...

Self Love Kills the Enemy...

Love yourself unapologetically...as when there is infinite Love within...there is no place for the Maya antagonistic influences...which means there is no enemy within...no enemy within...no effective enemy in the out...

Tri-Shastra...
Tri Protective Weapon...

Shastra Weapon 1.

Cut contact and proximity access to all your personally identified maya beings that are in your life play... Although it may not be an easy task to execute, it is absolutely necessary for your highest ascension...

Shastra Weapon 2.

Shield yourself with your very powerful soul energetic aura from these diabolical soul less asuric energy maya beings who only are placed for entrapping you through their thoughts and energy attacks. Elimination of the descend...only helps your ascend...

Shastra Weapon 3.

Choose your Maya stage drama battles wisely… Not everything requires your soul energy to be attentive and reactive to… Learn when to often walk away… If it is not putting your soul energy at ease then it is not worth it for you to ever tolerate it…

Moment has arrived to take your Divine power back…you my soul star performer Love…you are the primary protagonist of this play…improvise the Maya Leela play script…you are more than equipped…

Fakeer…the Mystical One…

**"Alive are those that embrace the demise reality…
Dead are those that fear this reality…
Today it is someone else…
Tomorrow it will be myself…
Remember these words of a fakeer my child…
As in joy when experiencing happiness…
Be even more joyous in hurtness…
Happiness comes to the surface in moments…
Hurt underlies in all moments…
Happiness is that encapsulating courtesan…
Only available for mere moments…
Hurt is that one forever loyal friend…
Always eternally available till the end…
Both mere temporary living illusions…
Embrace it all joyously…
Your perception of existence shall shift…
Entire worldly existence will be under you…
As you shall inevitably rise above all…
Now wipe away your tears my child…"**

**Kader Khan
(Renowned Poet / Writer / Scholar / Actor)**

**Fakeer Baba Scene Dialogue
Movie: Muqaddar Ka Sikandar
Poetic Translation by Hugh Shergill**

The Maya Institution..

"Maya is the platform institution...
 Leela is its play education...
 Maya beings are your testing exams...
 Moksha is your placement ranks...
 Nirvana is your graduation celebration...
 Welcome to the Maya Leela play illusion..."

Hugh Shergill

"Enrollment in any institution...
 Is an act of solely introduction..."

CHAPTER 14.

SOULITUDE

Never Leave Lonely…

"Embrace loneliness…
  It is the Divine romance…
  Eternity Divinity Love presence…
  One's most beautiful intimate romance…
  Never leave being lonely…
  Ever lonely…"

Hugh Shergill

More evolved...more isolated life...as more karmic lessons have been more achieved... In this play of Maya Leela...the soul's play journey is primarily to truly understand oneself...not to be understood...

"We're born alone,
 We live alone,
 We die alone.
 Only through our Love and friendship
 Can we create the illusion
 For the moment that
 We're not alone."

Lenny Kravitz (Renowned Artist / Singer)

Anything empty desires to be filled...soul seeker seeks the truth for fulfillment...as anything other than the truth, is empty for the soul seeker...untruth is empty...untruth living is empty...untruth lives are empty... therefore there is an innate deviation from others... Also, when the soul seeker experiences fulfillment... it is no longer empty...therefore again innate deviation from others... Ultimately all the journey of the soul is solitude...soul attitude...fulfilled is never lost nor lonely...fulfilled never seeks unfulfilled...unfulfilled is the illusion...as the soul seeker is seeking its truth within...where it has no desire of others to be in... Soulitude Sanctuary...

"It's beautiful to be alone.
 To be alone
 does not mean to be lonely.
 It means the mind is not
 influenced and contaminated
 by society"

Jiddu Krishnamurti
(Renowned Philosopher / Writer)

"Understand me.
 I'm not like an ordinary world.
 I have my madness,
 I live in another dimension
 and I do not have time for things
 that have no soul."

Charles Bukowski
(Renowned Poet / Writer)

"To be one...
 With oneself...
 Is the most...
 Powerful company...
 Weak are those most...
 Dependent on an external entity...
 One is to understand...
 Not to be understood..."

Hugh Shergill

"What felt remained were some...
 illusion cover of reality alone...
 Then there was always that one...
 Realizing actually there was none...
 Soul path traveled upon...
 Other's Love was forever gone..."

Hugh Shergill

"And then there was just one...
 All the rest fell one by one...
 Memories remain of some...
 Remaining journey among none...
 Now illusion identifies lone...
 Journey was all along alone...
 And then there was just one...
 All the rest fell one by one..."

Hugh Shergill

"Not nice…
 Good…

 Not liked…
 Respected…

 Not commanded…
 Commended…

 Not approved…
 Proved…"

Hugh Shergill

"You don't have to take in everything that comes towards you…set your vibrational boundaries high… where only those who are elevated…actually get access…"

Au Revoir…Nice…

"Unapologetic for the strict refrain…
 Unshy to overstep my previous pain…
 Complacently remaining that nice corpse…
 Headed towards its demise worse…
 Indeed I am no longer your nice…
 Instead I firmly choose good…
 I do good…
 I live good…
 I am now good…
 Not sure how to further emphasize…
 Shall part with this statement size…
 A farewell with a sword cut slice…
 Au revoir forever to your nice…"

Hugh Shergill

"Life changed...
 World changed...
 A conscious gift...
 Uniquely equipt...
 Today discovered...
 One's new uncovered...
 Found myself reaching where...
 Divinity is not far from there...
 May no one hinder my present journey...
 Anyone from the previous journey..."

Shakeel Badayuni (Renowned Poet / Lyricist)
Poetic Translation by Hugh Shergill

Diamond Lies Alone...

"Amongst all alone...
 Diamond lies alone...

 Hidden within coals...
 Extracting accomplished...
 Precisioning cut polished..
 Existence expression...
 Exceptional presence...
 Shining among...
 Striving above...

 Amongst all alone...
 Diamond lies alone..."

Hugh Shergill

"Utmost powerful true romance...
 Between loneliness and silence...
 Loneliness is Love ...
 Silence is the Love...
 Indulgence of the lone affair...
 Most deepest romance flair..."

Hugh Shergill

Maya Leela

"No inclusion in existence...
 All exclusion is existence...
 Beyond soul connection...
 All illusionary perception...
 Hidden amongst crowd...
 Soul shines aloud..."

Hugh Shergill

"illusionary influence of lie...
 Frustratingly you ask why...
 From your highest high...
 To your most hurting cry...
 Destined transformation to fly...
 From the caterpillar...
 To the butterfly..."

Hugh Shergill

"The voyage is not to bare...
 Upon cease no one will care...
 Of your soul's wear...
 As one who is aware...
 Shall never share...
 Life is a journey of just a brief flare...
 So continue one without a glare..."

Hugh Shergill

Sole Solace Traveller...

Traveling alone has a certain level of natural peace...as you hold the least expectation of your surrounding fellow travelers...minding one's business is a natural response when traveling alone... resulting in a solace peaceful state... Similarly the soul's journey through this life is exclusively solo on a primary level...thus having the least expectation of your surrounding beings...results in a solace peaceful state of being...untampered by deploring diabolical soul less entities...

"I hate who steals my solitude
  without in exchange,
   offering me true company."

Friedrich Nietzsche
(Renowned Philosopher)

"The butterfly does not…
  Attend caterpillar parties…
  Eagle does not take lessons…
  From a hen's flying essence…
  If you don't want to be possessed…
  Stop hanging around cemetery graves…"

Hugh Shergill

"They laugh at me
  because I'm different;
  I laugh at them
  because they're all the same."

Kurt Cobain
(Renowned Singer / Musician / Writer for rock band 'Nirvana')

"I'm not at all anti-social…
  I'm just socially selective…
  Distancing myself from others…
  Is not for teaching them a lesson…
  Nor concern of the remificating bothers..
  One's next move…
  Should be the best move…
  Associations remain that are Divinely meant…
  I'm just simply applying the lessons learnt…"

Hugh Shergill

Alone Amongst Many…

"Alone amongst many…
  From far…
  One among many…
  From close…
  Eliminates every…
  Amongst many hear the crowd…
  Yet alone noises aloud…
  Concentrate perceives population…
  Concentrated reveals isolation…
  Alone amongst many…"

Hugh Shergill

"You are fighting for your soul…
  In a spiritual warfare battle…"

Whatever one fights for…fights by one…the Maya realm of existence…is a constant spiritual battle of Maya entrapment versus Maya escapism…the wrongly prisoned prisoner does not become genuine best friends with the prison guard…they both are on strict opposite lines of the battle…interaction perhaps in certain moments is required…yet overly interacting is an absolute hindrance…they will never be fond of you…thus never truly for you…and what is not for you…will never truly be of any help to you…the quicker you accept this…the quicker you shall excel from this…

"Some people
  will never like you
  because your spirit
  irritates their demons."

Denzel Washington (Renowned Actor)

At the most authentic core intrinsic level…only energies interact…without even saying a word…a soul being and a maya being are always in conflicting energetic existence…each one is the opposite of the other…yet the most disadvantage position is by far for the soul being…as not only the soul can not at all stand the diabolical asuric soul less energy of the maya being…it is further in a potentially very vulnerable state as the maya being requires and feeds off the soul being's high vibrational energy… entrapping their aura…sabotaging their energies…feeding off their energies…could be even termed legal energetic cannibalism…never allow this volunteeringly…ever…your soul energy is your power of performance…to preserve it you must practice soul solitude solace… Soulitude…

"Life is too short
 o spend time with people
 who suck the happiness out of you."

Lenny Kravitz (Renowned Artist / Singer)

"If a man knows more than others,
 he becomes lonely."

Carl Jung (Renowned Psychiatrist)

"A man can be himself only so long as he is alone;
 and if he does not Love solitude,
 he will not Love freedom;
 for it is only when he is alone
 that he is really free."

Arthur Schopenhauer (Renowned Philosopher)

No matter how expansive the performing stage is…how many multiple performers are on stage… how much interactive script and dialogues are exchanged between the performers…or how many mass audiences are in attendance…ultimately you as the performing actor are only performing your performance only…a strict sole performance…that regardless of the surrounding theatrics…your conscious delivers a performance only from your within…a sole delivered performance…thus embrace that sole driving force…not the hindering theatrical distractions…

Soulitude…
The Awakened New You…

Anything and everything may appear to fall apart from your pre-awakened unveiled perceived Maya time line…this is an absolute must to reset and create space for your soul desired life fruition…destruction process proceeds creation process…first implodes…then explodes…leading to a creation infinitely expansive…

"Enlightened path…
 Double edged sword…
 One edge cuts the illusion…
 Other cuts all relation delusion…
 One will forever appear alone…
 One yet will never be alone…"

Hugh Shergill

Maya Leela

Treat Others...As 'Others'....

For the soul spark of the Divine... There is no over the top fascination of other people... including even those who one may be extremely physically attracted towards...or very emotionally connected towards... or even on the surface certain celebrities admired... Other people...remain other people...shall always remain other people...always external...and anything external is not your energy...nor one desires to externalize and potentially jeopardize one's energetic power into the hands of someone else... For the ascended soul being... one remains in an euphoria experiencing state within one's own energetic aura... Treating others with formal respect and energetic distance... indulging into only those interactions that are soul vibing... never soul depriving...

There is an over emphasis on human interaction relationship to the perceived world experience... indeed somewhat important but it is not what defines one's world experience... explore.. travel... connect with nature... indulge in arts and entertainment... music, poetry, and literature... These artistic interactions are as if not more important than fellow human interactions... further for an experience that transcends to multiple realms of entire experience... indulge yourself into the tranquility depths of meditation...unveiling realms of worlds that are both foreign and yet brilliant...from any world ever experienced before...

"Solitude is not isolation...
 It is Divinity connection...
 Those who strive continuation...
 Do not imbibe every interruption...
 Surrounded by dichotomization...
 Become enlightened by its realization..."

Hugh Shergill

So miraculous occurrences are occurring in this very moment in your perceived Universe... Creations and eliminations...from biological life forms...to infinite multi-verses, galaxies, and planets... yet one remains trapped in ignorance when immediate present life experiences seems isolated stalled... even then the heart reminds us of Divinity movement as it ticks on continuing beating forward...you are not isolated...nor stalled...you are moving...just soulitude preserving...once you tap into this protective energetic frequency...the allure of soulitude... becomes very precious and extremely addictive...

"In a crowded line...
 All shadows disappear...
 When one stands alone...
 Soul core truth appears...
 Fortunate that it unveiled...
 Moment to celebrate the revealed.."

Hugh Shergill

Kindness Absence...

"Born with empathy...
  Dealt with apathy...
  Innately feel for others...
  Their selfishness bothers...
  Often those who give...
  The most kindness...
  Are the ones who felt deeply...
  Its absence..."

Hugh Shergill

As you have a soul my Love...you are forever connected to all infinite realms beyond the physical... where others may perhaps witness occurrences of others at best... Yet your soul energy feels the occurrences of others extremely deep within...even when you have felt this deep sense of empathy is innately within your loving soul...cherish this blessing of Love...never disregard it as a curse...your kind loving soul is empathy essence...continue to feel it...yet use your soul discretion whenever you feel that someone who is not really feeling but manipulating...seeking advantages from your soul loving essence... You are Love...deserving to touch Love...give to Love...yet honour your Love...by not putting it in the hands of those who are forever soul devoid of feeling your Love...

Soulitude...
Soul Rider...

You are exactly where and what your soul experiences...in the illusionary canvas blanket of space time... Your soul is the observatory rider of your infinite parallel physical existences...switching...branching... tapping into a particular precise universe form that aligns with your karmic soul experiential existence... derived from your soul karmic actions...

Every person comes with a built in disappointment...quit thinking highly of others...which will result in quit from the disappointment... View everything in terms of energies... Disregarding the distracting physicality based synergies...

"One's personality...
  Is their personal reality...
  Scripturally unfolding...
  In entirety...
  Rich is...
  What enriches...
  Your soul experiences...
  Blesses...
  While it teaches..."

Hugh Shergill

Maya Leela

Refrain from External Validity...

"Ego chases validity...
  Spirit embodies clarity...
  Never expect validity...
  From those lacking clarity...
  Those who were played by destiny...
  Refrain to play others for eternity..."

Hugh Shergill

External Approval Deviation...

We are Maya jaal entrappingly programmed to deny ourselves in order to gain approval...What we deny often holds more soul value than what we seek to gain...The only thing that maintains is what one maintains...true authentic soul value must be prioritized beyond any distraction deviation of external approval...

Sages lived isolated secluded lives as it effortlessly helped immensely towards liberation...enriching one's potent soul energy towards powerful ascension... Crowds are distractingly draining... Soul beings must have the highest discretion in terms of whom they interact with...which environments they spend their presence... As ironically...in more 'socially dominant' societies, soul beings suffer more soul suffering as their soul energy is highly exploited and depleted... Majority may recall...those densely populated social gatherings... what supposed to be a fulfilling event for one...more often ended up as another energy draining session...

"Many incompatible...
  With the one...
  One incompatible...
  With the many...
  Refrain from...
  Outer world pleasin'...
  Outer world is outer...
  For a reason...
  Not everyone...
  Is for everyone...
  Simply enjoy...
  The life ride vessel toy...
  Imbued within...
  The Divine energy joy..."

Hugh Shergill

"Simply observe…
 Resisting to absorb…
 Simply aware…
 Of what to care…
 Resisting affected wear…
 Realizing you are rare…"

Hugh Shergill

Tantra…Yantra…Mantra…

Tantra - Technique
Yantra - Tool
Mantra - Performance

"Tantra…Yantra…Mantra…

Yantra ..

The Soul Physicality…Yantra…
Yantra is your physical body tool…

Tantra…

The Soul Technicality… Tantra…
Tantra is your soul knowledge technique…

Mantra…

The Soul Performativity…Mantra…
Mantra is your soul sound performance…

Tantra…Yantra…Mantra…"

Hugh Shergill

Take complete care of yourself by yourself…be yourself the very best…each and everyday…as every blessing day of this physical existence should be a celebration of gratitude…

Maya Leela

As a specific diet is required for one's body...also a specific diet is required for one's brain... It is no coincidence that the human brain and the human intestines look physically very similar...metaphorically the brain is also one's digestion...where its mouth is its ears and eyes...feeding the brain what they consume... Be very careful of the particular diet that you feed your brain...as the stomach digestion eventually digests...yet the brain digestion forever accumulates...

Perform multiple roles for taking complete care of yourself...be your own disciplinary coach...follow a daily routine that benefits yourself...be your own knowledge life coach...by learning and reading more that interests you and is in tune with your forever powerful intuition...Pamper yourself by indulging into your hobbies and interests daily...enjoy things you truly like to do that are not harmful in any way to yourself and others...books, music, movies, entertainment, hobbies, arts, crafts, sports, play, creativity etc...you deserve to enjoy as your absolutely deserving... be your own personal chef... learning, preparing and cooking foods that are both nutritious and indulging...be your own personal trainer... motivating and guiding yourself to consistent and progressive physical exercise routine...be your own beauty hygiene coach...by keeping yourself optimally cleansed and beauty pampered daily...be your own style fashion coach...look your very best daily by styling yourself to what you desire to look and feel... find your own style as you are the absolute unique main protagonist performer in your Maya Leela play... enjoy my soul...

You are the Soulabrity...
Superstar of Divinity...

You are the Soulabrity...honour yourself...as you have the Divine gift of soul... A mere celebrity is the resulting work of many others which all contribute towards their perceived celebrity status... Yet you my soul are the one and only unique authentic celebrity...the Soulabrity...direct sparkling superstar of the Divine...
You are the Soulabrity...
Superstar of Divinity...

Honour, cherish, and respect your Divinity gifted Soulabrity superstar status... Your Soulabrity status is your true soul mate... Your true soul mate is being your soul's mate... Every day is a date...enjoy...treat yourself to your soul date...enjoy a dinner feast...play your favourite song... dance with Divinity...you and the entire infinite universes are interactively romancing with you at this very moment...like that unknown romantic crush...open explore its possibilities...indulge deep into Divinity soul romance...enjoy your soul date...

"The world is full of…
 Much more…
 Spectators…
 Than performers…
 Be truly yourself…
 And perform…
 At bare minimum…
 You will be…
 Highly unique…
 At best…
 A trendsetting mystique…"

Hugh Shergill

Keep Spiritual Distance…

Spiritual Distancing…
Stick and Stay in your Lane…

The highway of Maya Leela is very unique…running as a two way opposing direction multiple lane highway…yet strictly scripted one way on each direction…an absolute one way street…with no u turn option whatsoever…nor any option to change direction…each is dedicated on to their own path road… one leads to Maya existence for the maya being…the other to Maya escapism for the soul being… traveling on the journey dependent on their own particular karmic evolution speed…option to accelerate, decelerate, or just remain dormant at one's own karmic will…however any attempt to change direction shall be a severe wrong turn into a no entry zone…enviatabally leading to a disastrous collision… therefore the key is to stay in your own lane and let others travel simultaneously in their respective directed lanes…knowing your path and acceptance of the paths of others…which is either running parallel to yours…or opposite to yours…but never precisely identical to yours…

"It is no measure of health
 to be well adjusted to a
 profoundly sick society."

Jiddu Krishnamurti
(Renowned Philosopher / Writer)

Similarly… As one drives on a road, there will be moments of discovering neon orange cones placed on the road that assist you to stay in your correct lane…soul less maya beings are those cones… being aware of them and continuing on to your correct path is the key to your nirvana destination… pausing and colliding with the cones shall take you off your valuable path…cones are not mobile…as there is no travel for them… no destination to reach for them…they either assist you to your correct path if the traveler is wisely aware or create obstacle resistance through path deterrence if one collides…you can either crash or surpass... performance choice is yours... Detecting these Maya being cones and steering away by continuing swiftly to your correct path is the priceless maneuvering art to soul bliss...

As there are cones on the road...there is also the duality and relativity effect in place that manifests into road signs... these are synchronicity signs...that take the form of fellow soul beings...giving directions and assisting the soul traveler to their particular destination... This is the magic of Leela...for each locked blocked door...there is also a key in existence that unlocks...just requiring aware synchronization seeking to search discover and uncover... Fellow soul beings shall spontaneously appear at the correct destined moment that not only shall provide direction but motivation to remain on your correct path... the path that steers away from the cones...assisting one to remain and continue traveling to the soul's desired destination...this is the power of Divine synchronization...

Be the Rebel Soul Traveller...

When one is traveling in a train...seated facing the rear side of the train...upon taking a peek outside the window...all of a sudden, it seems everything is moving ahead passed you rapidly...leaving you behind...yet in reality it is your rapid travel that is moving you forward...this is the illusion of the path of true success of one's soul journey...when one refuses to conform to the majority norms of how to move ahead in life...and remain with rebellious conviction to their own unique soul journey...initially the illusion may make you perceive that everyone is moving ahead in life and leaving you behind...when in reality...it is your sheer determination of remaining on your soul's Divine journey that is moving you ahead rapidly... leaving all the rest behind...

"Nothing lost for the soul...
 Either is...
 Or non soul...
 A rock lying bottom of the sea...
 Remains entrapped...
 Yet perceives free...
 Floating ice berg shall become...
 Sea upon melt...
 When the surrounding...
 Sea's resonance is felt..."

Hugh Shergill

"The body is the vessel of the illusion...
The perception of bodies is the illusion...
Body creation as pottery of clay...
Displayed on the Maya stage...
In the Leela play...
Empty pottery...
Mere perceived existence...
Devoid of soul potion...
Of true existence...
Your authentic existence...
Is fully soul...
Your resistance...
Is the empty non soul...
Separating the empty from full...
Is the key...
To your performance victory...
Of becoming soul free..."

Hugh Shergill

illusionary frivolous dwell...
Of others from your past...

"illusionary frivolous dwell...
Of others from your past...
Just as one's past...
illusionary lurking to last...
Embrace the acts of others...
As the act of galactic stars...
Long gone of actual existence...
Mere remains of residual presence..."

Hugh Shergill

Do Not Preach...Just Lead...

"You can not change...
The people around you...
Yet you can change...
The people around you...
Rejoice embrace the change...
The truth just found you..."

Hugh Shergill

Maya Leela

Deep subconsciously they also know who you are and are core threatened by that...preaching soul consciousness will only result in conflict...those that are unaware through being incapable of being aware...they are innately incapable of processing your preaching...and on the other hand, those that are already aware or still dormantly aware...are already deep down aware of your particular preaching and or shall eventually become fully aware to their particular self true discovery... Therefore all preaching is either useless or unnecessary... Instead, value your gift of awareness and practice your preaching through your own Maya Leela performance...performance of your unique creativity...those that resonate with your performance shall absolutely inevitably shall so...so concentrate on your soul performance with the greater intent of serving others...not forcefully convincing others...

"Undeserving must be put to pause...
 Uncompromising one's respect...
 Choosing the higher cause...
 Never the illusionary effect...
 Honour your stage space...
 Let others remain set...
 By honouring your presence...
 Your Divinity existence..."

Hugh Shergill

"Understand through innerstand...
 Just release your illusions and rise...
 To rise above Maya...
 One must be above...
 Through understanding Maya...
 Understand by rising above...
 Which results in the Maya realm being...
 'Under' understood...
 Which happens through...
 'Inner' innerstood...
 Going 'inner' to rise above...
 Lay the Maya realm 'under'...
 By being aware...
 Of those unaware..."

Hugh Shergill

"Where the heart doesn't give any emission...
That is where there's no Divine permission...
Whenever the soul is not at agreeable ease...
The blessings of the Divine cease..."

Dharmendra (Renowned Actor)
Poetic Translation by Hugh Shergill

Instincts vs Intuition

Instincts is biological...survival in essence...on a physical realm... Intuition is consciousness...survival in essence...on the infinite realm... Instincts are confined to one's physical limitations...nothing beyond... Intuition is infinite...beyond all...knowing all...the Divinity of existing expressing... The Divine is beyond conceivable and unconceivable...knowing and unknowing...as it is all...therefore when you connect with the very depths of your soul consciousness...you truly know all...as you are all... Respect your instincts... for physical survival...honour your intuition without ever deviating...for your remaining eternity...

"What you reveal...
From your intuitions...
Are often leaked...
Through your communications...
Having control over your words...
Empowers your worlds...
Words grant you...
Invincibilities...
Words also expose your...
Vulnerabilities..."

Hugh Shergill

"Your words grant you invincibilities...
Your words also expose your vulnerabilities..."

CHAPTER 15.

DIALOGUES OF MAYA LEELA

"Actor's dialogues hold the power…
Accolades of the stage performer…
Having control over your words…
Empowers your worlds…
Knowing what and when to reveal…
Is the artist's attractive appeal…
What the lips slip becomes history…
What the lips hold blesses mystery…
First in your mind do weigh…
Before putting speech on play…"

Hugh Shergill

Maya Leela

Words are felt as sacred...each word is a vibrational mantra essentially...respectively in each and every language...as it is one's consciousness association to the words that associatingly sparks the vibrational magic consciousness through those words...which can be either magic of positivity...or black magic of negativity... Even such as the sacred word "Love" can be further uplifting vibration for someone who is currently intensely in Love ...and yet the same word could trigger further vibrational hurt for someone who just experienced Love betrayal... It is all in the vibrational magic of one's consciousness association and the interpretation of words... Words hold potential force to grant and reward one the highest accolades...taking them to dazzling heights...and yet words can also take one to such unimaginable lows... Therefore, the depth and delicacies of words must be powerfully respected, honoured, cherished...and most importantly chosen wisely with one's highest discretion and discernment...

"Snakes and humans...
  Both poisonous specimens...
  Fangs and tongues...
  Both venomously hazardous...
  Humans lack fangs of poisonous venom...
  Tongue words are their poisonous venom..."

Hugh Shergill

"ill words sent...
  Towards ill aware...

  One shall never feel ill...
  When words spoken...
  Against you are ill...
  ill words are spoken...
  By those who are ill...
  ill indeed they are...
  Loving Soul is rare...
  You are ill aware...

  ill words sent...
  Towards ill aware..."

Hugh Shergill

"Your word is pure magic,
  Misuse of your word is black magic."

Miguel Ángel Ruiz Macías
(Renowned Writer / Spiritual Philosopher)

Cursing is the Curse...

"Bland foods require use of spice...
  To add some exquisite taste...
  Shallow words require use of curse...
  To add some linguistic weight...
  Cursed speech extemporary...
  Limited amateur vocabulary...
  Cursive swearing...
  Is tongue make up...
  For poor inefficient...
  Vocabulary cover up..."

Hugh Shergill

Cursing is 'Lack of Vocabulary' Make Up...

It is commonly observed that geographically regions that suffer from the most extreme poverty and economic deprivation, tend to incorporate and understandingly so...much more use of hot spices for adding taste in their cooking to compensate on the bland basic economic foods available... Similarly, individuals that lack vocabulary and depth of words in their communication, often compensate by generously including curse words in their speech...to create additional illusionary communication power to their highly apparent lack and devoid of appropriate vocabulary and depth of words... Thus, cursing is a 'Lack of Vocabulary' syndrome make up...

"Do not just talk...
  Just to say words...
  Of what is said...
  Becomes loosely light...
  Of what is not said...
  Remains heavily intact..."

Hugh Shergill

Maya Leela

Word intentions…

All communication is devoid of true peace…as when in true peace…there is no urge to communicate when one is truly content…
Just speaking the same language does not result in that you are able to actually communicate…
Listening is more powerful than speaking…as what observes…absorbs…becoming potently saturated…
Speaking releases…emptying…that potent energy within…

"Clouds that often agitate...
  Only seldom precipitate...
  Clouds that roar...
  Often never pour…
  What was initially calm…
  Becomes finally a storm…
  Loudness is mere expression...
  Quietness commences into action…"

Hugh Shergill

"Raise your words,
  not voice.
  It is rain that grows flowers,
  not thunder."

Rumi (Renowned Sufi Poet)

"To express oneself…
  As an expression of the Divine...
  One must be a replica of the Divine...
  Silent...
  Suttle...
  Yet extremely impactful...
  Revealing all…
  Without saying all..."

Hugh Shergill

Silent words are a powerful force...

"Silent words...
  Are a powerful force...

  What the lips kept...
  Was what they really felt...
  Most impactful words said...
  Were those left unsaid...

  Silent words...
  Are a powerful force..."

Hugh Shergill

Maya Words...

Silence is never a pause...it is forever speaking..it is a perennial flow of language...interruptly paused by the use of words...whatever is felt at a particular moment in free flow of silence...becomes catered to what one says or hears at that particular moment...

Each time we speak...consciously we are obliging to the other to a certain degree...our approach, mannerism, and efforts...modifies according to whom we talk to...from a particular gender to a particular age...there is a certain variation effort that is involved to modify one's speech and words accordingly... save that effort...save that soul energy...for where it is absolutely required...or even more importantly when it is soul desired...as small talk is not soul talk... Going into deep long conversations with soul less maya beings is a very powerful energy depleter...as besides being drained from the conversation... nothing else will occur...they are not in tune with your higher consciousness frequencies...they will never understand you nor relate to you... Value your words...don't waste your potent words for the soul deprived ears...

Whenever it is a must...one is required to communicate with them... Whisper talk in a lower pitch as possible when talking to them...as a Soul being...even the sound of your Divine's spark of soul voice feeds and energizes maya being's diabolical asuric aura...preserve your speech sound for those truly soul deserving...

"Verbal talk is never completely free...
  Modified effort to a certain degree...
  Frivolous small talk...
  Is never soul talk...
  Save the effort...
  For the soul deservant..."

Hugh Shergill

"A fool is known by his speech,
  and a wise man by silence."

Pythagoras
(Renowned Philosopher)

"Wise men speak
  because they have something to say;
  Fools speak
  because they have to say something"

Plato (Renowned Greek Philosopher)

"Those who know do not speak.
  Those who speak do not know."

Lao Tzu (Renowned Philosopher)

"I talk less...
  So I don't end up to know...
  Myself less..."

Vedic Proverb

"A superior man is modest in his speech,
  but exceeds in his actions."

Confucius (Renowned Philosopher)

"Speak when you are angry
  and you will make the best speech
  you will ever regret."

Ambrose Bierce (Renowned Poet)

Your Words…
Your Swords…

"Your words…
 Are your swords…
 Verbally war forwards…
 Oftenly regrets afterwards…
 Use discretional cords…
 Before slicing conversational boards…"

Hugh Shergill

"Open your lips…
 As petals of a…
 Rose blossoming…
 Speak such…
 As the aroma of a…
 Rose fragrancing…"

Gulzar (Renowned Poet)
Translation by Hugh Shergill

"You talk
 when you cease to be at peace
 with your thoughts"

Khalil Gibran
(Renowned Poet / Writer / Philosopher)

"Larger the personality…
 Smaller its verbality…
 What we speak…
 Is our soul leak…
 Less words said…
 Less problems to dread…"

Hugh Shergill

Maya Leela

Your Aura…
Speaks For Itself…

Most impactful image of oneself is the one that is portrayed without uttering a single word… your powerful energetic aura speaks for itself…whether it is your physical appearance…the way you carry yourself…or your personality demeanor mannerisms…these are much more authentic impactful perceptions amongst others that your own frivolous self selling bragging words can never reach… Your aura speaks for itself…

When the soul's appropriate moments present themselves…talking is the need of the hour… Soul being's speak completely confident…precise…resonance… Speaking words that shall age well… Your voice is your unique instrument…honour it…by respecting it… Do not dishonour and disrespect your gift of voice…through egorance…ego, ignorance, arrogance…by letting one's voice be merely a verbally noise making sound hazard… Instead utmost honour and respect it as that powerful beautifully resonating unique instrument it absolutely is…where even a single string guitar note…goes to unparalleled depths of emote…

"The note of the guitar string…
 Was heard by the crowd…
 Yet who was it?
 That heard the pain…
 Of the string aloud?
 The guitar chord…
 Everyone heard…
 The Pulse chord…
 Which heart heard?"

Sahir Ludhianvi
(Renowned Poet / Lyricist)
Translation by Hugh Shergill

"Did you know that the human voice
 is the only pure instrument?
 That it has notes
 no other instrument has?
 It's like being between
 the keys of a piano.
 The notes are there,
 you can sing them,
 but they can't be found
 on any instrument."

Nina Simone (Renowned Singer/ Artist)

"The voice lives on…
  Beyond the body gone…

  Honour your words…
  Respect your words…
  My word is my contract…
  My soul is the assurant…

  The voice lives on…
  Beyond the body gone…"

Hugh Shergill

"Non-interested in their initiated talk…
  Non-interested in their dedicated walk…
  Instead following my destined outlined chaulk…
  While the respondents accumulate talk…
  I simply listen to my soul that spoke…
  Whilst walking realm depths awoke…"

Hugh Shergill

Spell casting words…

Words consist of letters…letters 'Spell' words…this is spelling…Interestingly in Vedic traditions define the word 'Ling' referring to Lingam, which defines and symbolizes generative power to create…'Spell' 'Ling' of letters creates words…choose your spells wisely…spells casting through words resonate to one's core energetic aura field of creation and manifests into one's reality…be wary of the words you utter both internally and externally…they are powerfully influencing and creating your perceived reality… constantly…

"The loudest one in the room…
  Is the weakest one in the room…"

Frank Lucas
(Character Dialogue from the movie
"American Gangster" 2007)
Writer: Steven Zaillian

Maya Leela

**"Have more than you show,
Speak less than you know."**

**William Shakespeare
(Renowned Poet / Playwright)**

**"Wordful spineless…
Has a lot of words…
Yet shuns from said words…
Coward runs from what was said…
As self empty words forever dead…
Fragile ego keeps its corpse on the run…
Upon confronted remains horrified numb…
Wordful spineless…"**

Hugh Shergill

Your Sound…
Your Vision…
Your Power…

To unlock and tap into the wealth of the visual form of the universe…where all the knowledge of discovery of the unseen is seen…one must first unlock that through the sound form of the universe… sound is not just confined to audio frequency…sound is vibration…sound is conscious thought of vibration…non hearing do vibrate…sound is mantra…sound is affirmations…sound is uttered thoughts… sound is inner dialogue…sound is felt thoughts…therefore unlock the universe through your vibrations… your particular sound shall tap into and manifest your specified vision…your sound becomes your vision…your sound is your sacred power…

Sound…
Cymatics…
Mantras…

Cymatics…the science of visualizing physical form of sounds…where waves become matter using a specific instrument called tonoscope …a fascinating experiment was done by renowned Cymatics scientist Dr. Hans using the tonoscope where the mantra "Om" (pronounced A U M) …when the mantra word "AUM" was recited…surprisingly, scattered fragmented matter all of a sudden took on precise complex geometric pattern…discovering further…this pattern was a precise replica of an ancient sacred yantra pattern referred as the "Shree Yantra"…a powerful visual pattern that attracts Divine aura…and resonates Divine aura… One can imagine just how profoundly this mantra affects the complex biological, conscious, and energetic aura realms of an individual within when uttering this particular mantra…indeed very powerful…

"AUM is the bow,
 The arrow is the Soul,
 Brahman the mark,
 By the undistracted man
 Is it to be penetrated,
 One should come to be in it,
 As the arrow becomes one with the mark."

Mundaka Upanishad

AUM...
Is a word...Mantra...
A symbol...Yantra...
A sound...Shakti...

AUM is the sound of the entire infinite universes...all existence of the Maya realm gave birth from this vibration... When you chant the mantra AUM, the vibrations of these three sound word correlates with the sound of all three conscious realms... from consciousness...sub consciousness...to super consciousness...

Sound 'A' - Consciousness state
(three dimensional realm)

Sound 'U' - Sub Consciousness state
(fourth dimensional realm)

Sound 'M' - Super Consciousness state
(fifth dimensional Divine connect realm)

Mantra is a Very Powerful Potent Portal...

Mantra is not merely words...it is your soul voice of thoughts...even those devoid of speaking and hearing...do hold an internal voice of thoughts...when that inner soul voice utters particular fully felt thoughts words...those words become very powerfully potent...holding the power shift one's reality from one realm to another realm...from Maya to higher...one universe to infinite multi-verses...

Duality speaking...there is the contrast opposite effect of Mantras as well...the soul's internal voice of thoughts Mantras also can become a very powerful potent curse...if one is irresponsible of what they utter with their soul voice...again very capable of power shifting one's reality from one realm to another realm...from Maya to lower...

Disregard their tongue walk...

"Talk is merely tongue walk...
  Let others continue their tongue walk...
  People are and will say...
  Often less of more...
  And more of less...
  The walking feet of others don't bother...
  Nor should their waggling tongue walks...
  It is all illusionary movement...
  With havoc intent for the soul advancement..."

Hugh Shergill

There should be absolutely no need to regard or give value to what others say...human beings are linguistic beings...often much more indulged in verbal expression than physical expression... They said what they said...it perhaps came from a hurt space and resonates in to a hurt form...giving it any further value in terms of attention and response enhances what was initially said...much beyond what was said...and those words that were uttered become much more powerful and giving even more powerful illusion existence presence to the one that uttered those words... Save your soul...save your moments...let loose lips sink their ships... Instead indulge into something that satisfies your soul...and enjoy...you are not here forever so make the most of every moment...this is precious...whilst ignoring the malicious...

"People will say...
  People are supposed to say...
  Deviate from all this frivolous...
  Moments passing by...
  Are precious..."

Anand Bakshi
(Renowned Poet / Lyric Writer)
Poetic translation by Hugh Shergill

"The truth is like a lion;
  you don't have to defend it.
  Let it loose;
  it will defend itself."

St Augustine (Renowned Philosopher)

Truth requires release...
Never to please...

Truth never requires to be defended...release the revelating revealing truth...and simply observe...all reactive ramifications shall begin to occur...in precise degrees occurrences of what truth was revealed... thus there is absolute no requirement of any defense of the truth...there is nothing to debate or argue... Truth requires independent release...never dependent to please...

"Never argue with someone...
 Whose TV is bigger than their bookshelf"

Emilia Clarke (Renowned Actor)

Nothing to Debate...
With the Unrelate...

Most people think they are arguing over factual debating... When in reality they really are just arguing about feelings... Feelings...how does one feel the unfelt...your soul energy is your authentic feel... which remains forever the soul less unfelt... If one decides to engage in a debating conversation with an extremely mentally ill patient...it will now appear that it is you who is actually mentally ill enough to engage in a debate with the other mentally ill individual...as your mental capacity remains for the mentally ill unfelt... Same scenario exists when one decides to engage in depth conversation, debate, or argument with a soul less maya being entity...it is you that will be soul questioned within as are you actually a soul being or just another typical soul less maya being...? Where there is absolutely no hope... there is no need for effort... For a soul being...a soul less maya being is forever obtuse...there is just no hope...thus no need to exert even your slightest soul energy effort... Instead of wasting valuable performing time trying to save and convince the forever unsaved...focus should be on oneself to save oneself from their unsaving diabolical core existence... Debates and discussions require a certain minimum mutual level...when there is no hope or any possibility of being on the same level...debating is ineffective and hindering on every level... Attempting to get someone who's not on your higher soul energetic frequency to understand...is parallel to sending a message where there is absolutely no reception...therefore simply completely disregard them...au revoir...

"Maya beings regard soul beings to exist...
 Soul beings require...
 To disregard maya beings to exist..."

Your Disagreement...My Agreement...

"Absolutely no relate...
 Pointless to debate...
 If I'd agreed with you...
 I'd be wrong with you...
 Your disagreement...
 Validates my agreement..."

Hugh Shergill

"Politely refuse to debate...
 With those who unrelate...
 Soul devoid debated...
 Soul energy depleted...
 Escapist agree...
 Makes both wrong...
 Confidently disagree...
 And be long gone..."

Hugh Shergill

The Arguing illusion...

Never debate or argue with anyone...especially with a diabolical asuric soul less entity...as you will never be "talk to"...but will be instead "talked at"...expecting you to say only what they want to hear...nothing else...ever...if you do...conflict shall arise...as separation of conscious level shall eternity remain...the frequency is completely incompatible...dualism will always exist...therefore communicating is absolutely ineffective...only serves conflict levels to rise...where they gain the edge feeding off your soul energy and depleting your soul energy via maya jaal entrapment of your soul reaction... Keep your detection confidential and give them a parting gift of silence...

Deep Sea Explorer...

"Those exploring deep sea waters...
 Exclude diving into shallow waters...
 Wasted drops is not your power...
 What imbibes is your shower...
 Being aware of what is at play...
 Like the river finding its way..."

Hugh Shergill

"I am not Anti Social...
 I am just very Socially Selective..."

Once you grasp this revelating information and apply it to your daily lives...you will begin to become highly aware of the Maya jaal entrapment scenarios and of the Maya jaal soul less pawns i.e maya beings. This information of detecting maya beings should remain confidential within, not used to call out maya beings as the soul less diabolical entities that they are or any other similar implies...as that defeats the purpose of true spiritual living...as calling out others gives false sense of righteousness importance impression of oneself, which is an elevated ego state...no better than anyone else experiencing and expressing such egoism...

Instead, treat the apparent distinction awareness similarly to other distinct perceived awareness that you come across daily...such as how you behave, conduct, respond around a child or elderly person differentiates sub consciously without one even realizing the distinction perception experience... this distinct awareness should continue when one comes across another person that seems to have an unappreciated aura, negative energy state, extremely low vibrational with highly elevated egorance (ego, ignorance, arrogance) state of being, Maya entrapment behavioural traits...within one recognizes all these tendencies and can immediately realize their state of human being experience...which is highly soul less diabolical asuric based...now hold your power of being aware of this and conduct your maneuvering responsive behaviour accordingly and appropriately...

This is your direction of your performance... you are not required to become anti social...however being very socially selective is an absolute must...socializing with a soul being is a soul enriching Divinely experience...to detect these beautiful connections, one must be selective and aware to whom you open yourself to...those souls out there that have personally shared those deep soul tantalizing conversations perhaps would resonatingly agree...

The power of being aware and responding through your behaviour accordingly by soul conscious being state which is genuinely loving oneself through positive karmic performance and expressing respectful but aware conduct when sharing stage with a maya being...this is your victory...this is your power...your awareness...in confidentiality...expressing awareness within...

"Dealing with one...
Or all is the same...
Play stage theatre...
Is a chess game...
Weak square spaces...
Pawn surely races...
Entrapping not to the move of pawn...
Putting forth the advantageous queen...
Playing from the highest state...
Inevitably victorious doctorate...
Uponed the pawn is queened...
Destined checkmate indeed..."

Hugh Shergill

Maya Jaal entrapment is not going to create a web of resistance for you...that is coming from complete strangers...that would be somewhat expected and leaves one much more emotionally unaffected... indifferent...further innately prepared...as experiences from complete separate strangers is a deviation merit in itself... A spider can not attack you from a far distance... For the spider to lure you into its entrapping web...close proximity to its web is a must...thus those who are your soul less entrapping nemesis entities in your life play must come from your closest emotional proximities...not strangers... and there is nothing closer to an individual than its Love, Loved ones, family members, and perceived best friends...

Maya Leela

As each soul unveils the illusion through diving deeper within… discovering of the higher truth…the soul light within…while simultaneously integrating the new energetic pool of existence experience…you will definitely rise in frequency…very high vibrational energetic frequency…which will lead you to becoming less and less affected by what transpired in the previous illusionary three dimensional Maya stage…and all the drama from your karmically dedicated co-actor performers sharing your Maya Leela play stage… friends…family…Love…Loved ones…or any other antagonist nemesis…all will be unveiled along with the Maya Leela play stage… Shifting viewing perspective from physical entities to energy entities…all your relationships and interactions will become extremely crystal clear… You will now see them all for who they actually are…not what you thought or desired they were…

"Soul expose of the once skeptical…
   Now exposing the truth spectacle…"

CHAPTER 16.

FRIENDS

"What often is…

Will not often be…

All serve a purpose…

Within an expiration…

Beyond the expiration…

Purpose dissolves into poison…"

Hugh Shergill

"Words are easy, like the wind;
  Faithful friends are hard to find"

William Shakespeare
(Renowned Poet / Playwright)

"Every relationship comes
  With an expiration date..."

Salim Khan
(Renowned Writer / Script Writer / Philosopher)

"There is some self-interest
  behind every friendship.
  There is no friendship
  without self-interests.
  This is a bitter truth."

Chanakya
(Renowned Philosopher / Revolutioner)

"Perceived true friend?...
  That illusion shall end...
  What loyalty they send...
  Mere a timely lend...
  Seeming like a forever ascend...
  Shall be tested upon descend..."

Hugh Shergill

"That late night home intruder...
  Finds entry in thorough silence...
  Most dangerous enemy often...
  Finds entry into your life...
  With complete ease silence...
  Either as a perceived friend...
  Or even disguised as Love..."

Hugh Shergill

The Maya illusion of perceiving a friend as Love…yes true soul Love friendship is possible yet extremely rare…at best, one may deeply Love someone forever without the intent of any further proximity and association…however a true friend that holds you into their heart without any self interest motive is very extremely rare…if not completely impossible…as companionship and association itself is a motive of friendship…
A true authentic friend shall Love you authentically even when the association ends…

Often soul beings will be much more exposed to potential friendship possibilities with maya beings exclusively…this is the most popular convenient Maya jaal entrapment scheme of the Leela play script… discreetly scheming…as the most efficient manner of influence upon one comes disguised in the form of a friendship… Associating…informing…convincing…influencing… to the sustained fixated entrapment to the Maya realm…

"Friendship exists…
  Until it serves a certain purpose…
  All friends are beings…
  All beings are nothing…
  But an active state of energy…
  Constantly in motion…
  Changing preference purpose…
  Changing always as a person…
  Challenging the changed friendship…
  Every friendship is forever changing…"

Hugh Shergill

Maya Leela

My best friend's name is Truth…

"My best friend's name is Truth…

   The only true friend is the truth…
   It is one's most loyal friend…
   Accompanying beyond the end…
   Truthfully serving conscious…
   Infinitely eternal bliss…
   The only friendship…
   Truth partnership…
   That has no expiration date…
   Only an assured liberating date…

   My best friend's name is truth…"

Hugh Shergill

"In this life…
   You only have…
   Two true friends…
   One is…
   Success…
   The other…
   Failure…"

Guru Dutt
(Renowned Movie Director / Actor / Writer)
Translation by Hugh Shergill

Success and failure…your two shadow friends that continuously walk with you throughout life… Everyone else is in it to win it… They are all disguised competitive performers… Some genuine and others…well others…but both deep down on deeper depths of core existence…they couldn't care less for your higher purpose journey…all friendships are just mere illusions…

"Not on stage...
 To make friends...
 This illusion platform stage...
 Serves its performing purpose...
 Undesire seeking popularity...
 In bliss executing objectivity...
 Not on stage to make friends...
 On stage for my performing purpose..."

Hugh Shergill

Our imaginary friend that we create within our maya level consciousness...we continue to force that illusionary image on to others...which shall never be lived up to as that is your illusionary creation not another being creation...

"Show me an individual...
 With lots of friends...
 You are showing me...
 A core weak individual within...
 A friend of all...
 Is its own enemy within..."

Hugh Shergill

Friendships are a very popular form of Maya attachments...perhaps due to the fact that it is a relationship we perceive to have established ourselves...unlike immediate family where we do not have any choice of what particular individuals are your biological family...

"With lots of friends...
 Your enemies keep away...
 Not your enemy's intimidation...
 This is your enemy's realization...
 They are very aware...
 Not even enemy compare...
 To those who are close to you...
 Of what they are capable of...
 Doing to you..."

Hugh Shergill

Maya Leela

Frenemy…the Maya Jaal Friend…

Maya entrapping maya being…silently…creeping into your soul with their sweet venom…

"Dangerous than your enemy...
 Is your dearest frenemy...
 Disguised as your closest friend...
 Yet your enemy till the end...
 True ill intents always kept hidden...
 Capable enough to backstab you bed ridden...
 Your counter power lies in becoming aware...
 Complete detachment yet forever beware..."

Hugh Shergill

"They associate with you...
 With a reason...
 For a particular season...
 Not all perceived in conflict...
 Are necessarily foes...
 Not all perceived in conciliation...
 Are necessarily friends...
 Some exist for a season...
 Some exist for a reason..."

Hugh Shergill

"Your evolution pace...
 Not dependent on...
 Your friend's evolution pace...
 Appreciate the past connection...
 Love from a far away distance...
 Appreciate those past moments...
 Whilst moving to the next chapters..."

Hugh Shergill

"It is not daily increase
 but daily decrease,
 hack away the unessential.
 The closer to the source,
 the less wastage there is."

Bruce Lee
(Renowned Martial Artist / Philosopher / Actor / Director / Revolutionist)

"Become intuitive within wary...
 Of what has reached expiry...
 Each separation...
 Is a graduation...
 Destinations are set to be met...
 Destinations are not met in set...
 Lessons unlearned is a repeat revolve...
 Once learned is the escape evolve...
 Moving power is the soul award...
 To manifest your destiny reward...
 Where progress begins prevailing...
 Where opportunities begin revealing..."

Hugh Shergill

Friendship...

"Hold friendship on a priceless standard...
 Hurt with the reciprocation abandoned ..
 When it was not met...
 I simply decided and left...
 An emotional entrapping send...
 A word that includes both 'fried' & 'end'...
 As a previous friend...
 Often emotions are enduringly fried...
 Before the realization...
 Friendship had already end..."

Hugh Shergill

Those...All...

"Those decisions...
  Those repercussions...
  Those destructions...
  All had one common...
  All involved a pen...
  All had your sign..."

Hugh Shergill

Lost When Crossed...

"That hurting moment is long gone...
  Time to move soul as one...
  Do not explain yourself...
  Instead embrace yourself...
  They forever lost you...
  When they crossed you..."

Hugh Shergill

Associations are not your Friends...
Just Associated Strangers...

Colleagues...business partners...co-workers... customers...associates...are strictly considered mere business associated strangers...not necessarily friends...as friendship forms only when one opens up to the particular potential connection that may be either soul felt or quite often on the opposite, an entrapping Maya illusion... Associated strangers serve a working professional purpose...they are only connected to you due to your particular current dharma pursuits...in other words...your current career profession and work pursuit...

Indeed...yes they are also potentially very powerful Maya jaal entrapment influences at play at your work...that desire to lure you in...entrap you...extract your Divine soul energy...they desire more to feed off your soul energy than their actual consumed food... However, being already aware of the minimum personal emotional connect you have with them...makes it much more easier to remain on guard and professionally indifferent to their entrapping influences...the 'strictly business' and 'strictly professional' approach keeps one's thought process much more disciplined with clarity...much less distracted and influenced in regards to them...if that is not currently the case already...then one should surely begin to think in those terms regarding them...use your soul intuition and discernment before pursuing more potentially deep friendships with these professionally associated strangers...do not force unnecessary friendships...nor get forced into friendships...this is not only imperative for more conscious peace but also for your soul energy protection...as more often than not...it is such a blissful soul energy protection experience by remaining strictly formal...politely and respectfully refraining from excessive soul energy draining talking and at even worse the soul poisoning gossiping...remain professional... indifferent... spiritually distance protection...

treat work for what it is...strictly just business...work professional purpose...instead of becoming an energetic soul prey by their potential soul less diabolical asuric influence...

Karmically, the Maya Leela play is extremely complex as it already is...make the effort from your current performance to keep your Leela play script simple and peaceful as possible...cut out the unnecessary Leela drama...treat work as work...not a forced un-destined energy draining frivolous friendship ground...

As you Grow...
You will Outgrow...

Reality is as one awakes from the illusionary Maya Leela play...a lot of friends will be out grown...both due to the distinct differences of evolving...or when the soul becomes aware that those particular friends are actually soul less maya beings with dominant diabolical asuric energy...who have been forever placed staged distractions to entrap by hindering your evolving, awakening, enlightening potentiality... the larger the friend circle group...the more heavy dense are the entrapments...the more emotionally invested friendship...the more acute the entrapping betrayal influences...

"Experienced this friendship society...
  Separately left in pity...
  Loyalty in friends long gone...
  Lost each one...
  One by one...
  One by one..."

Kaifi Azmi (Renowned Poet / Lyricist)
Translation by Hugh Shergill

Your Soul Vibe...
Will Attract Your Soul Tribe...
Yet Always Prioritize Your Primary Vibe...

Along with Maya unveiling threat ramifications... Pleasantly due to duality...your soul vibe will also now attract your soul tribe... As an act of moving away from those past friends...the duality of the Maya Leela play will attract individuals who are now on your enlightening alignment frequency...these perhaps will not be considered as becoming close friends...yet they will be a part of your 'Soul being tribe' that have and are going through similar awakening experiences...they are your fellow soul beings...primary protagonist performers in the play of Maya Leela...please feel free to connect with them...yet don't become overly attached dependent on to them...as evolving and ascending further is a continuous Soul's sole priority purpose...your 'Primary Vibe'...

Appreciate and have Divine gratitude to be blessed with your 'Soul Tribe' yet never let it be a compromising hindrance towards your 'Primary Vibe'... your 'Soul Vibe'...as each individual member of the 'Soul Tribe' is continuously actively experiencing their particular karmic Maya Jaal entrapping attacks, energy exchanges, and Maya threat circumstances and vulnerabilities… Appreciate them… interact with them…yet remain protectively differentiated from them…as there is absolutely no compromise towards Divinity euphoric ascension…as your Maya threat homeless nights will also include your 'soul friend' less nights…

"Patience, righteousness, discretion, literature, courage, vow of truth and faith are friends in adversity"

Goswami Tulsidas (Renowned Spiritual Poet)

Karmic Friends…
Your 'Karma Action' Friends…
Your True 7 Karmic Friends…

In the Time of Need…
In the most toughest times…
You have assured seven friends…
To help you cope and overcome…

Patience
Duties
Common sense
Art and literature
Courage
Truthfulness
Faith

Friend 1: Patience

Look at the overall picture…often doing nothing patiently supports you more than doing something impatiently…patience more easily endures even the most testing times…

Friend 2: Righteousness

To follow the righteous Karma path of being karmically conscious of not doing unto others that one does not desire upon themselves…proceeding every step with righteous justice…making this your friend as your highest necessary form of life path…your Karma Dharma…

Friend 3: Discretion

Using a high level of discretion to filter the positive from the negative of every circumstance, situation, environment, and individuals…using your intuitive intelligence and discerning wisdom to know what is the actual good from what is not…this filtering friend is required for soul purifying and potency…

Friend 4: Arts/Literature/Information

The powerful friend of learning and gaining informative knowledge from others…this can be multi various forms of literature, arts, information…books, biographies, quotes, poetry, music, movies, arts are some examples of this friend…a friend that inspires, helps, motivates and encourages you by revealing knowledge through its artistic means…nothing is new under the Maya Leela spotlight sun…whatever you are going through…although never completely exact as each every soul being is on its own particular karmic journey that is playing out in the play of Maya Leela…yet there are profound similarities that someone somewhere else has also similarly experienced that Maya Leela stage script…this is an arsenal of knowledge…a friend guiding you from personal experience for your healing to reviving success…

Friend 5: Courage

Being consistently firely courageous by keeping on pushing forward attitude without being discouraged…facing everything bravely…as this friend is capable of moving mountains for you as you soul perform…

Friend 6: Truthfulness

Staying genuinely truthful no matter what…when we remain truthful…then the Divine helps us truthfully as well…truthfulness is not just confined to one's words…as standing by the truth in terms of your actions is even more important…unhindered purity of one's path…makes this soul journey to rise unhindered…

Friend 7: Faith

Having faith in Divine…all infinite multi-verses are working with you…for you…everything happening is not to you…as everything is happening for you…trusting having full faith in this friend…will absolutely deliver…making all the perceived impossible…possible…

Embrace thy Soul Friend…
Existence Within…

Indeed, as one deviates upon realization of a Maya being friend…the law of duality consequential shall eventually introduce you to your true soul friends in this realm or another…those that are enlightened… those who are aware of the unveillance of the illusion…those who are empathic towards others… understanding the values of authentic soul friendships…and the harsh consequences of hurting betrayals… These rare few soul friends are beautiful exceptions… Embrace them if one is fortunate enough to have cross paths with them on this Maya Leela stage…

If not…regardless of whom is present on the Maya Leela stage accompanying you…always embrace that soul friend within…your soul is your best friend…the one that accompanies you beyond the perceived very end…nurture it…embrace it…listen to it…as it shall never betray you…always have nothing but infinite Love for you…

Maya Leela

Maya friends and associates come and go throughout one's play journey on the Maya stage…as the relationship is self selected…therefore there is much more ease to shift from the 'self selected' than the 'unselected'… Now what about your 'unselected' destined family?…

"Does the illusion stop…
At the betrayal of a friend…
Or continue where even…
One's family is the causing end…
Wishful thinking…
For blindly family linking…
If betrayal of friends hurt…
Wait till you witness…
Your family's true worth…"

CHAPTER 17.

FAMILY

"Hair that grew out...

Hair that growed out…

Once deviated…

Forever separated…

Merging back to reattach...

Growing back into its batch…

To rejoin complete…

Is an impossible feat…

Once the strands split...

No possibility of regrowth…

What was on you...

Is no longer for you...

What was through you...

Was never of you...

Our child is through us…

Yet not of us…

We are through our parents…

Yet certainly not us..."

Hugh Shergill

The soul is not inter-dependent to be created by another soul...as the soul's source is directly and absolutely the Divine itself...nothing else...therefore the prerequisite of the soul's forming and existence is only the Divine... As for the prerequisite of the human being illusionary existence experience is dependent on its biological and Maya realms... So one or even both parents who are soul less maya beings are potentially capable of producing a biological soul being...and vice versa...soul beings are fully potentially capable of having soul less maya being biological offsprings...as the soul's container realm here is the three dimensional human being physical vessel...but the soul is always Divine's direct source itself...just like the soma nectar beverage...that exists not dependent on all the factory supply of drink glasses...it only selects the privileged few to be the tool of the soma nectar consumption...

It is a beautiful rare commodity to find a family that are entirely consisting of all soul beings...this is highly rare or almost non existing...if deep down your soul is in complete ease vibration with every family member of yours...congratulations...be extremely grateful as this is an extremely rare fantasy occurrence and highly contradicting and conflicting for the Maya Leela play script existence...as conflict drama is necessary for the play...and real resistance is absolute reality...thus each family has those at least one or few maya being individuals that are the testing and antagonistic resistance forces for the soul being's evolution...whether it is one or both parents... guardians...siblings...grandparents... immediate relatives...extended family...dominant portion naturally will lead to Maya jaal dominance...as if one reflects back...if one leads a completely confirming life according to the ideal standards scenario of one's family...the soul's potential evolution and real growth is highly compromised or even at worse left completely entrapped...

"An awakened being...
 Never for family satisfaction...
 Shun being the suggested being...
 Soul being is a sole being...
 Your expectations are met by only a few...
 Why should all their expectations be you...
 Those appreciated by all...
 Are inevitably trapped to fall..."

Hugh Shergill

Family is one's close belonging...yet one's understanding remains longing... From immediate family to extended family...no one truly understands you beyond yourself...not even your perceived nearest Loved ones...including your own family...spouse, children, parents, guardians, siblings, relatives etc. Family concept also includes one's extended family...where one is closely associated to certain groups, organizations, cultural and institutional communities...as the illusion of belonging to a certain family lineage, cultures, communities, groups, organizations, institutions, and relationship ties...creates the illusion of one's close certain belongings...which is nothing more than the hidden illusion of Maya jaal entrapping influences... These are all mere three dimensional biological existence relations and associations primarily...with perhaps a few karmical privilege exceptions of beautiful soul connects... who are beyond your physical existence family and are actually a part of your soul tribe... while most

338

commonly all the rest are selfishly on their own asuric soul less maya journey...and ultimately interested in only influencing you...entrapping you...keeping you in regression...and feeding off your soul energy... never in authentic agreement nor support of your true ascension evolution...this is the bitter truth... unfortunately very often difficult to swallow...

"We swallow greedily any lie that flatters us,
  but we sip only little by little
  at a truth we find bitter."

Denis Diderot (Renowned Writer / Philosopher)

"Family...

  F...
  Am...
  I...
  Ly...

  Fail to see?...

  For I...
  A Lie..."

Hugh Shergill

"A person's enemies will be
  those of its own household."

Holy Bible (Psalm 41:9)

"Knife requires to be close...
  In order to cut you...
  Relation requires to be close...
  In order to betray you...
  Invasive cut makes you bleed...
  Betrayal makes your solitude lead..."

Hugh Shergill

**"Over-attachment
for one's close relatives
is simply born of ignorance.**

**Every creature in the world
is born alone
and dies alone.**

**The belief that
one person is the relation of another
is nothing more than an illusion."**

Lord Krishna, Bhagavad Geeta

All your perceived true Loved ones… Love…family…friends…groups…all may state and portray their unconditional Love for you and are always and will be there for you…however this is a frivolous attachment illusion of the Maya realm…no one will be physically there for you beyond the confines of this temporary physical being experience…some will depart earlier or later than your dedicated soul performance duration…never as you or with you…no one is responsible for your soul karmic actions beyond yourself…and beyond this perceived life…the soul existence of yourself and your soul Loved ones are simply and ultimately the Divine expressing itself…what therefore remains is only Divine and the Divine's infinite Love…no one else…ever…therefore your soul journey is your secluded karmic performance manifesting expression of the Divine…

Once you identify with your core essence importance…your soul energy…all physical associations begin to hold less importance… instead of being illusionary attached…practice detachment, have compassion, and let go… Your multidimension energetic soul associations…embracingly await you with unconditional infinite immense Love…your true family…

**"The truth shall set you free…
Yet will first pull roots apart…
Of your immediate existence tree…
You were never all…
Forever remained…
For them just a part…
In reality always apart…
Overachieving outgrew branch…
Intentionally confined by surroundings…
Till the wind of awareness…
Blew it free…"**

Hugh Shergill

"Identifiable biological existence...
 Energetically a far away distance...
 Knowing of this from the initial day...
 Yet forced to camouflage without a say...
 All came crystal clear with the unveil...
 No looking back after revelating reveal..."

Hugh Shergill

Entrapping Maya Jaal...
Entrapping Web of Blood...
Much More Empowering...

"Never let anyone be your unease flight...
 Commiting the ultimate robbery heist...
 Robbing you of truth yourself...
 Be who you really are for oneself...
 Not what others want you to be...
 They are forever entrapped not you...
 You soul never were...
 Your soul never shall be...
 Those who travel blind treaded way...
 Audacity to actually interfere in your way...
 Do not follow their instructional path way...
 Of those who are eternally lost in their way..."

Hugh Shergill

The Elder's Gift of Memory...

Parents/elders have the additional memory/legacy responsibility...one hopes that parents with Divine's blessings should never have to experience the loss of a child...as that is not something anyone should experience...yet unfortunately it does happen... In general, children lose their parents first in the natural biological chronological order...therefore it is the child that is handed over the memory weight of their parents/elders memories/associations...as the elder, one must strive to make that weight a plethora of pleasant loving soul enriching memories...that is your last karmic deed on this realms particular physical existence...do not destroy this deliberately and or ignorantly...you owe that responsibility to your offspring...

Do not allow...
Frauds to provide you advice...
Never Blindly follow their Advice...

In order for a fraudster to fraud you...it has to communicate with you...it has to provide false advice... to lure you in... convince you... to eventually entrap you...by fraud...and ultimately frauding you... Be very careful of who you allow yourself to receive advice from...as a soul... you are surrounded by these diabolical asuric soul less frauds...regardless of how close the relationship may perceived to be on a physical three dimensional illusion...

Blindly listening to your particular family, siblings, and especially parents indiscriminately...is the most common convenient Maya Jaal entrapment...as those who are incapable to find their true way...do not blindly follow...those who are perhaps most often than not...forever completely lost in their way...thus using your soul discernment firmly is a must...for your soul ascension and Divine purpose...

Whole heartedly...ask yourself this question...whomever is giving you advice...would you switch places with them in whole totality?...would you desire their Spirituality ascension or lack of? Mentality? Intelligence? Physicality? Health? Looks? If any (or most likely all) are strict crosses for you...I would encourage you to put a big cross stamp on to their advice...the forever lost offer no direction to those who are suffering eternity lost...

Others are not your Maya Leela performance director...which is offensive to Divinity itself even as a thought...therefore, treat all co-stage performers as performers only...never the director... Would you rather listen to the play director or a co-performer? Is it more important to have the audience's direct feedback...or the feedback of co-performers? Which one are the true judges of your performance?... as no co-performer truly cares about your excelling performance more than their very own...but the audience puts your excelling performance as utmost accolade driven priority...as the better your performance...the more outstanding experience of the Maya Leela theatrical play for all...

"Finest stage performer is the director's actor...
  Theatrical accolades gifting the artist's actor...
  Untapped exploration of all its potentiality...
  Artist's magician expressing play artistically...
  Surrendering all in the hands of Divinity...
  Remembering all is in the hands of Divinity..."

Hugh Shergill

"True utmost failure is...
 The individual that lived...
 A life of full lacking...
 With no spiritual backing...
 Unsatisfactory tears ripping tears...
 Especially within their final years...
 Dwelled horrifically further drenched...
 With their cowardly fear of death...
 Instead fear requires redirecting...
 To the inevitable consequences awaiting..."

Hugh Shergill

"A man who views the world
 the same at 50
 as he did at 20
 has wasted 30 years of his life"

Muhammad Ali
(Renowned Boxer / Revolutionist / Philanthropist)

"Maturity is Ageless...
 What is older...
 Not necessarily elder...
 Age manifests older...
 Evolve manifests elder...
 Your age leads as the outnumber...
 Your immaturity has one wonder...
 Maturity remains always ageless..."

Hugh Shergill

Being older is associated with someone who is aged...however being elder is associated with someone maturely evolved... One has come across many immature old individuals and one has also fortunately come across many mature yet very young individuals... Reality is that there are many six year olds that hold more evolved mature wisdom than many sixty years olds...

"Evolution is the art of process...
  Evolve manifests into excellence...
  Fermented grapes mature into wine finely...
  Merely aging grapes rotten completely...
  Finest wines are forever cherished...
  Rotten grapes have already decomposed..."

Hugh Shergill

As Varuni...the Goddess of Wine... found her Divinity through experiencing mergence with the Divine... Individuals that evolve by seeking their higher consciousness potential...marinate maturely like the finest wine that ages into excellence... Otherwise simply aging without evolving results similarly to grapes left exposed unfermented that inevitably shall simply rott away as they continue to age...

"It is in true maturity...
  To not acknowledge immaturity...
  Those who can not self understand...
  Deserve not your presence stand...
  Toxic blood leads to self rot...
  Fatal fate as a blood clot..."

Hugh Shergill

Maturity reciprocates respect...

Age and a perceived longer life span of existing are not and should not be default reciprocates of commanding respect... Just because someone has been existing in a particular human body form longer than oneself does not mean that they are more mature than you... Nothing can be further from the truth... Age is an illusion of time accumulation...however maturity is saturation of knowledge accumulation experience... Maturity is ageless...maturity does not come with age...nor is anyway dependent upon age... Maturity accumulates with experience and more importantly...the process of knowledge processing those experiences and evolving through the experience process...this process is intellect...therefore the more saturated the intellect, results in more maturity...

One can effortlessly come across commonly ignorant immature low intellect elderly individuals...and fortunately one can also impressively come across very young children with profound insightful intellect and mature wisdom... Being aware of this...as this saves one's soul from unnecessary soul tampering influences of perceived elders that we generally as a society have been programmed to honour and respect every word that they express... this is a very common form of maya jaal entrapment influence... Be very aware of this...Love, care and respect everyone regardless of perceived physical and emotional constructs...however honouring every word other's state is an evolutionary hindrance and a very potent Maya jaal entrapment that must be absolutely filtered through one's soul intuition highest discretion discernment...

Respect Children…

They say respect your elders… which is absolutely important to a certain degree humanely… but what is far more important…is to also respect your youngsters…as energy wise…for a certain some… their energetic soul existence is often much more ancient lifetimes than yourself…

Respect a soul child's wisdom…as you are not aware of all their previous wisdom filled soul journeys… even in all actuality of perceived time reality…the child is younger than you…therefore the child's previous soul journey is more recently completed than you…in terms of this perceived timeline…as you are still on this particular soul journey…yet within your current particular timeframe soul journey… the soul child is already completed one soul journey and is now on to this one…bringing with them a soul memory of wisdom experiences more often broader than you yourself…thus their intuition and soul discernment should not be outright disrespected and disregarded…listen to them respectfully… acknowledge their say…by letting them have their say…it may potentially provide soul insightful wisdom or a synchronicity hint for you…or at the very least do your karmic duty of guiding the child correctly by Lovingly acknowledging their still developing processing progression all respectfully…never rejectly…

"Absorb what is useful.
 Reject what is useless.
 Add what is essentially your own."

Bruce Lee
(Renowned Martial Artist / Philosopher / Actor / Director / Revolutionist)

It is highly important to honour your soul intuition…as there is no entity nor thought beyond… that Is worthy of replacing your soul intuition discernment…any deviation may temporarily seem as the right thing to do in forced emotional trapped moment…however you are simply following an illusionary path…a path that is a dead end for your soul's performance journey… With that said, it is understandable that the confines of physical and emotional exuberance attachments…that exclusively attach on a Maya realm is natural…one perhaps feels inclined and obligated to follow the ideological map path of their dear perceived Loved ones and attachments…this urge should not be harshly resisted but instead filtered through your own soul intuition discernment…acknowledging what resonates within and excluding all the rest… Every being has at least one quality of worthy enough to absorb and acknowledge…this should be perceived from a synchronizing perspective…essentially accepting what resonates within one's soul consciousness and rejecting all the rest…This is your soul performance power…that one can continue to physically exist acknowledging perceived dear and Loved ones…and yet live your life on your highest terms…soul intuition performance living… Love your dear ones whole heartedly but never compromise your true living performance… Master your family…never let yourself be mastered by your family…

"It is those that you heartedly provided…
  Only those that leave your heart divided…
  It is those that are close to you…
  Only those that wound you…
  It is those that are your own blood…
  Only those that make your heart bleed…"

Hugh Shergill

"Blood is thicker than water…
  Salt in blood is the wound irritator…
  Blood is thicker than water…
  Is thicker actually gentler?…
  Fabricatory confined…
  illusionary of mind…
  Water gives moments for survival…
  Quick sand entraps upon arrival…
  Surface trauma is merely water…
  Blood wounds run much deeper…"

Hugh Shergill

"Respect all…
  By being aware of all…
  If they don't think right…
  They will never treat you right…
  Save your loyalty…
  For those in tune ability…
  Master your family…
  Never be mastered by family…"

Hugh Shergill

Family... Beautifully Fabricated...

"Family is the beautiful curtain...
  Covering the beautiful window view...
  While viewing just the curtain...
  Everything seems at its peak beauty...
  Luxury comfort view within its surroundings...
  Until the curtains are open...
  Revealing the paradise surrounding existence...
  That was hidden by the beautifully fabricated..."

Hugh Shergill

Anonymous Love Protection...

"Moment you were conceived...
  Hidden forever never revealed...
  Those involved in your creation...
  Were yet unaware of your existence...
  Yet you remained protected anonymously...
  Only taken care of by Divinity..."

Hugh Shergill

There are absolute fact moments of your physical existence of when you were physically conceived...
yet both of your biological parents were not yet then aware..in those moments...Divinity revealed as your
infinite protective parent... forever did... forever will...
Divinity is your true parent...and always will be there for you...beyond all physical family association...

"Biological vessel...
  Existential soil...
  Soil gives growth to the seed...
  Which emerges as a tree...
  Now it is the tree...
  Shining its capabilities...
  Bearing its fruitivities...
  Throughout all survival...
  Before its destined soil revival..."

Hugh Shergill

Family and Loved one's approval... the ultimate Maya jaal entrapment...true authentic soul value must be prioritized beyond any distraction deviation of external approval...regardless of whomever the Loved one or biological family members it may be...

"A large perceived joint family unity...
 Is primarily dominated by...
 Soul less maya being community...
 What seems as Loving unity...
 Is actually a soul energy feeding factory..."

Large perceived joint family unity may appear as a blessing supporting beautiful family structure... yet exploring deep within...it will come to your realization that certain ancestral curses and Maya jaal entrapment structures were intentionally placed for you...to permanently feed off your Divine soul energy supply...to distract and cause hindering traps...jeopardizing your potential for soul ascension... For example, a multi generational family structure that advocates wealth gain at any cost and encourages unrelenting urge of selfish greed...is aligned for the diabolical asuric soul less entities of the family... where the relationship between wealth and oneself is extremely sickening unhealthy...a timophilia sick obsession...however this is a direct entrapment suppression of the soul being family member...who if complies not only will accumulate negative karma but also be an entrapped soul by the Maya jaal web of entrapment... Become aware and beware of these types of multiple generational imposed certain structured ideologies that are not soul aligned for you... As no family rule is ever above your Divine soul rule...

Early age trauma...
Was the seed for entrapping...
The soul performer..."

Specific childhood traumatic events and experiences were not accidental but intentional...they were all placed in your play script specifically...serving two play script alternatives... for you to either remain in descension or trigger ascension...to either forever Maya jaal entrap you from your this very biological beginning preventing your true growth...or ultimately trigger you towards a lifelong path of soul awareness, enlightenment, ascension, reform, and growth...

What you went through by these soul less diabolical asuric entities...was to keep you traumatized, suppressed, depressed, descend, deeply into the Maya realm to the point of killing your internal soul hope and drive to strive... What they did to you was not just their mere behaviour or actions...where in all actuality...there always was and is a deeper intentional workings going on...all serving one main objective...to keep you forever Maya jaal confined and entrapped in their soul less dominant realm... being their permanent soul energy feed supply hostage...

Upon awareness and enlightening... the realization of the immediate what is going on...to the actual what is going on...one will face the harsh reality of those who you really cared and Loved...were always the ones that couldn't care less and forever truly never Loved you... All one can do after this heartbreaking epiphany is to self Love...prioritize oneself...protect oneself...detach...distance oneself... eliminate their influence...deactivate their soul energy feed supply...cut cords and cleanse oneself from these illusionary fake family members...that were never for you...as they were never of you...

"If you don't fight for what you want,
 Don't cry for what you lost?"

Lord Krishna, Bhagavad Geeta

Spiritual Warfare…
A Common Family Affair…

Spiritual Warfare…A Common Family Affair…Often ignites from those most perceived close to you…upon your awakened ascend…you will become the soul target of your family and immediate social circle…Unfortunate as it may seem…it is necessary and permanent…there is no going back…what is seen can never be unseen…
Only options are to give in submission…or fight ahead your spiritual battle towards inevitable ascension…

War On…

"War drums are signalling…
  Entire army is approaching…
  Krishna tells O Arjuna awake…
  Spiritual battle is at stake…
  They're not your real friends and family…
  Portray no Love for the deceiving enemy…

  War on…
  War on…
  War on…"

Anand Bakshi (Lyrics)
Yudh (Movie Soundtrack)
Reference (Mahabharata - Bhagavad Geeta)
Poetic Translation by Hugh Shergill

"What is one…
 Protects one…
 One's own immune system…
 Has to rescue…
 Foreign intruding virus…
 On its bio escrow…
 When one's own blood is under the soul less…
 One must attack one's own to be virus less…"

Hugh Shergill

True Blood

"True blood that one can count on…
 Is the one that ticks your heart…
 When this bleeds away…
 Life passes on…
 All other blood remains separate…
 True blood is only your own one…
 The rest remains a distraction state…"

Hugh Shergill

Burn all bridges…this is the test…compromising with them…is just submitting your soul to them…very sinful…

"Those that travel high, travel light"

Cut all ties and attain bliss…Giving them attention…is imposing upon one self tension…

"Do not break bread together…
 With your unloyals forever…
 Sharing your table is a deserving feast…
 For those who's truth never retreat…
 The rest deserve your strict partition…
 Never dare to offend this realization…"

Hugh Shergill

"Certain occasions...
 Particular situations...
 There are additions...
 Through subtractions...
 Face those losses...
 For those wins...
 Endure pain...
 For the gain...
 Nothing changes...
 Without changes..."

Hugh Shergill

Ancestral Connection...

Rest in peace... do not disturb their peace...
Ancestors serve as a physical existence contribution stepping stone not an emotional trap...

Remembrance is one's own occurrence...

Life's purpose is one's legacy performance...

Remembrance is dependent on one's own performance...whether it is an art, performance, creativity, particular deeds or an establishment that remains after the physical demise is totally the responsibility of the individual itself...any forced remembrance by others is frivolous if their particular performance was devoid of impact beyond their physical existence duration performance...

Forcing a legacy of the demised that lack the performance content created by themselves...this only either disturbs the continued soul's journey that is currently in some other form or if it was a maya being...or it just creates collective negative Maya jaal energy increase with those that are some way energy connected to the demised individual...

Soul purpose performances that are worthy... live on...as that purpose of performing was achieved... This is why certain art, artists, athletes, performers are eternal as their legacy continues to live on...not imposed on...

Fitting Not...

"Not fitting in...
  The puzzle of life...
  Pressures attacking sharp...
  Like a knife...
  True freedom lies only...
  In higher conscious flight...
  Elevating oneself to...
  A perfect crystal clear sight...
  Where the unfitting escape...
  The puzzle trap...
  Shedding all confines of...
  The entrapment wrap..."

Hugh Shergill

Fitting in...is actually being Locked in... Why don't you fit in? Find your true place...
When you don't fit in...figure out the puzzle...as you complete the puzzle...you will either find your missing spot...which reveals your entrapped locked position within the puzzle...or better...realize that you don't fit in the puzzle at all...as you were never meant to be in the entrapped puzzle...therefore elevate your conscious to your true home...the Divine conscious realm...rise above and find refuge in your true true home conscious realm...and view the complete finish puzzle that answers exactly why you didn't fit in...

Cutting off...
Is a must...
Upon the Unveil...

Just as in certain unfortunate cases, an acute severe infection may require amputation to save the individual's physical being...similarly an unfortunate toxic family relationship requires to be completely cut off for one's well being...regardless of how close that relationship is...never compromise your well being for anyone...your ascension soul journey is an experience not a suppressed compromise...

Never be concerned of those family, friends, Loved ones that the Divine dynamically removed from your life upon your awakening from the illusion...they always have had ill intentions for you that were yet undiscovered...yet Divine witnessed it all...It has heard conversations that remained hidden from you... it saw actions against you that remained hidden from you...all these acts are forever foreign to your soul performance... you would never do what they have done...ever... Divine Leela is play witness and dynamically directing scene after scene...act after act... this Divine play is for your Soul...these diabolical asuric soul less Maya beings are only co-performers providing resistance for you...resistance that is a dynamic fluctuation and recycling...thus some of them completely fall off and replaced by other co performing extras... Just continue in your soul shining performance without any regrets or regards for those stage jumpers...Believe and always trust the Divine script written for you...it will never mislead you...nor misplace you...

"Certain co-actors face stage fright...
 Jump off stage taking the dark flight...
 Director observed their inadequance...
 Your act froze them to complete silence...
 Your performance is par excellency...
 Undeserving stage share with inadequacy...
 What is not on your level...
 Shall never remain on your level..."

Hugh Shergill

All illusion is temporary…
Sharing of stage is temporary…

All illusion is temporary… Sharing of stage is temporary… Every co performer on the shared stage is also temporary… Including the existence of all family members…all remains in Divine balance…they will be replaced…you will be replaced…the loss inevitably hurts…attached to the loss…is the Maya Jaal entrapment… Appreciate what was…Appreciate what is…

"Mother passed away...
 Father passed away...
 Brother passed away...

 Those three left me...
 These three came to me...

 Wife came into my life...
 Daughter came into my life...
 Son came into my life...

 Soon I will also leave...
 Soon someone else will replace...

 Life remains in Divine balance...
 Indeed what is lost...hurts...
 Yet one can not carry that along...
 One must appreciate...
 Those who are left among..."

Jackie Shroff (Renowned Actor)
Poetic translation by Hugh Shergill

Divine Family...
Divine Parents...

Maya Leela

Eternally…

Identify with your true creator… your Divine parent… surrender yourself to Divinity… This will create an entangled identity with your infinite Divine parent… making your immediate physically identifiable parents… just a relationship experience… however beautifully pleasant or unfortunately unpleasant…that is inevitably destined towards expiration…all mere temporary…all mere illusion…

Deep down…when everything falls apart…you yearn for your parents…realizing either they are not there… or impossible for them to be truly there…yet digging deeper…you will realize…you will feel within the spark of your soul…that within you exists your mother…as you are the Divine spark of Shakti…within you also exists your father…as you are the Divine spark of Shiva…cherish that fusional Divine Shiva Shakti energy forever within you eternity…and you will forever be blessed with the infinite Love of your eternal Divine parents…your true eternal Loving family…Shiva Shakti…always was there…always will be there… for you my Loving Soul…

**"Friends…
Most attractive entrapped illusion…**

**Family…
Most encapsulated entrapped illusion…**

**Love…
Most Soul deep entrapped illusion…**

**Select your illusion…
Or it selects your illusion…"**

Hugh Shergill

"Friends…family…indeed impact…yet it is Love…Maya Leela's greatest stage impact…in its Soul purity…it is the Divine Love union of Shiva Shakti itself…however in its deceptive diabolical asuric impurity…there is no harsher entrapping than those matters of the heart…"

CHAPTER 18.

LOVE

"Love is the stage play scenes...

Remaining beautifully...

Memorable betweens...

Love is both...

The epitome of reality...

And the spark of illusion...

Depth enough where...

The deepest ocean lie...

Dizzying heights that go...

Beyond the sky..."

Hugh Shergill

"To Love without condition,
 To talk without intention,
 To give without reason,
 Care without expectation,
 That's the spirit of true Love."

Lord Krishna, Bhagavad Geeta

This perhaps is the most profound and beautiful description of the spirit of true Love…from the respective Divine words of Lord Krishna from the Bhagavad Geeta…

"The intrinsic authentic…
 Pure essential energy of Love…

 Is without condition…
 Unconditional Love…

 Exists without intention…
 Pure Love…

 Gives without reason…
 Generous Love…

 Cares without expectation…
 Compassionate Love…"

Hugh Shergill

Love…what else does one say about Love…the more one may say…shall never be enough…Love is the seed of all existence…it is the epitome of all existential experience…Love is all…all the rest remains forever…nothing at all…

"Don't forget Love…
 It will bring all the madness you need…
 To unfurl yourself..
 Across the universe…"

Meera
(Renowned Mystique Poet / Divine Devotee)

Love is imbibing oneself with another that it becomes one…Love is complete…Love is whole…Love is never a fall…Love is all…the Divine union of Shiva and Shakti…marriage of consciousness and creation itself…expressing itself both within Maya and beyond Maya…

"Love is essence...
 Of Soul...

 Opulence...
 Of existence...

 Unrequired...
 To mention...

 Devoid of...
 Logical sense...

 Yet undeniable is...
 Its presence...

 Surpassing beyond...
 Every realm...

 Love is never a fall...
 Love is all..."

Hugh Shergill

"Love is not Love
 Which alters when it alteration finds,
 Or bends with the remover to remove:
 O no! it is an ever fixed mark
 That looks on tempests
 and Is never shaken."

**William Shakespeare
(Renowned Poet / Playwright)
Sonnet 116**

Be in Love with Love...

Love is often associated with romance...the romantic Love one is blessed to experience...however Love is not confined to romance...Love is the most powerful entangled force of soul expression that Divinely lights all that its expressionism touches... children... family...associations...nature...passion... interests...fondness...and above all with Divinity itself...

All souls are forever in Love...falling in Love...being in Love... yet in an individual's soul journey particular dynamics... Perhaps devoid or not confined to romance Love...yet remains forever in Love... the simple act of involuntary breathing itself is Lovemaking existential of life air...each breath taken...each heart beat is the proof of Love existential experience...

Maya Leela

Soul Love and Maya Love…

This chapter will focus on the romantic Love aspect…however the Maya Leela conflict of Soul Love vs Maya Love transcends to every other dynamic manifestation possibilities of Love…which one can easily shift to and relate to…whether it is the Love of one's Love partner, child, family member, friend, passion, drive, interest etc…each one will hold the same eternal conflict of Soul Love vs Maya Love…

"My bounty is
 as boundless
 as the sea,
 My Love as deep.
 The more I give to thee,
 The more I have,
 for both are infinite."

William Shakespeare
(Renowned Poet / Playwright)
Romeo and Juliet, Act 2, scene 2, lines 140 – 142

Let the Romance begin…

Soul Love…

Infatuation…Love…Connection…

Infatuation defined as Love intensifies and then down regulates in 14 days homeostasis adaptation in the physical realm…what is authentic Love arises from one's subconscious state…and in even further powerful state, true Love requires soul connect within…Love arising from the Divine soul conscious state…which merges one with Divinity itself…shining soul resonance from one soul to the one that is Loved…this is Love's most purest Divine form…the rest are just Maya attachment entrapment states…

"The infatuation of Love…
 Similar to the longevity of a rose…
 Sharing parallel existence…
 Of apparent limitation…
 Without the depth of soul…
 Or soil cultivation…
 Both shall fade to extinction…
 Within their dedicated play existence…"

Hugh Shergill

No Doubt in True Love…

Anything that we doubt or question, is not authentic…true Love goes towards Love… Sunlight, air, food, water, environment nature is absolutely blessing us with unconditional Love and care towards us… that intent resonates from the purest form of Love expression…all true Love should be this…reality is Love…standing next to a tree, one is assured with any doubt that the tree will bless the Loving gift of oxygen upon us…regardless of what our intent and actions for that tree are…that unconditional Love is ever present exuberance…communicating to us through authentic Love intent expression…that Love is reality…if we question Love…then it is not Love…true Love speaks for itself…vibrantly breathing on non communication…only Love expression from being Love…in its authentic selfless state…that is true Love…

"Love goes toward Love "

William Shakespeare
(Renowned Poet / Playwright)

Love at First Sight…

"Love at first sight…
 Very possible…
 Was it really the first sight…
 That immediate ease…
 Holds much more…
 Than what it actually sees…
 Love realm connection…
 Beyond any immediate explanation…"

Hugh Shergill

Love at first sight…
Possible beyond the illusion…
Impossible for the illusion…

Love at first sight absolutely exists… Now here is the catch… Love at first sight…on a physical three dimensional level is impossible… however Love at first sight…on a fifth dimensional consciousness level is totally possible…

Three dimensional physical level immediate connection consists of attraction, association, and infatuation…yet not immediate Love…as conscious energetic aura connection is absolutely required for true Love connection… This is the reason why the majority incorrectly assume a three dimensional physical connection as Love…and when the physical level becomes dominant by homeostasis down regulation adaptiveness…then further incorrectly, the parties involved incorrectly assume that they have fallen out of Love… This perpetual cycle continues to repeat…partner after partner…yielding the similar outcome…one explores to attain true Love…where it never ever even exists… Two soul less maya beings in a presumed Love relationship will forever repeat this illusionary ineffective perpetual cycle… continuously seeking what is not there…as true Love requires soul energy…an energy that the soul less are forever devoid of…

On the other hand… Love at first sight on a higher frequency of fifth dimensional consciousness experience absolutely exists…exclusively for the Divine spark soul energetic beings… Surprising and perhaps vulnerable state as it sounds…or even a far fetched fantasy movie reel theatrical experience… for two destined soul beings to cross paths, Love at first sight on a soul level is very powerfully possible…pre-written stage script already has dedicated the particular soul Lovers and the depth of their loving romance before the actors even step on to the stage and come physically face to face… Similarly, holding your own child upon its birth…goes beyond the biological connection…it is the most powerful Love at first sight…as pure Divine Love is way beyond the immediate illusionary Maya stage realm…when they see each other…they immediately are aware of each other…in their higher realm soul existence…immediately in connection…as they were and will always be in connection…

Moment…Sequence…

"Moment is powerful…
 Rest is a sequence…
 Love decides…
 In just a few moments…
 Where there is Love…
 Leaves no other scope…
 For its immediate decision…
 Forever devoid of forced decision…
 Instead one freely flows in its resonance…"

Hugh Shergill

As for pursuing fifth dimensional driven Love at first sight…holds its illusion entrapping risks also… Questioning…vulnerabilities…insecurities…strict cautiousness…filtration…are all indeed and absolutely required…especially in today's society…where illusion and its illusion beings are dominant…creating Maya jaal entrapments at every given opportunity…thus going in within deep one's soul intuitive powers and discernment is absolutely necessary…patience is a necessity…taking one's deserving prolonged process moments generously and getting to thoroughly understand that flame of immediate soul connection is a beautiful Loving romance in itself…as what is meant shall…as there is a Divine destiny realm working…ensuring to keep the connection flame burning…

That Someone...

"Seeing someone...
 I recalled...
 That someone...
 Not sure who...
 Yet I immediately felt...
 That someone...
 Perhaps it is...
 That someone...
 Infinite fragrances of scent...
 Divinity destined reminiscent...
 A drop of the ocean...
 Of those waters I've imbibed...
 Inevitably left...
 Perishly swept...
 Yet the same water drop re-emergence...
 Creating a soul ripple of mergence...
 Reintroduction of the previous character...
 Yet now completely in a new avatar..."

Hugh Shergill

On the other hand, for a soul being to fully fall in Love with a maya being shall take much initial apprehension, confusion, longer duration and prolonged apprehensive moments...as one's soul energy will feel immense apprehension and unease due to the intense rapid Maya jaal entrapment lure coming from the maya being...something just does not feel in tune with one's soul energy...as one's soul discernment will initially resist at its best abilities to deviate until the entrapping illusion takes over and overwhelms them...Illusion of impression...through attraction, status, and other accessory external impressive factors...all illusionary presented for your soul hunt... The soul less are the authors of delusion... What one often excuses as 'getting to know' phase...becomes your soul's 'being lured entrapped hunted' phase... Physical knowing is mere three dimensional...energetic aura knowing touches even fifth dimensional...

Soul Being's Love...
Natural Born Soul Saviours...

Soul beings are natural illusion destroyers...they show up as saviours in people's lives...especially in Love relationships...at the very precise moment before that particular soul...yet still unawakened...is about to or has become Maya jaal entrapped by a soul less diabolical asuric maya being...as the unawakened soul is not aware of what is actually going on at that moment...thus resulting in either acceptance or more commonly often rejection of the saviour soul being...yet rest assured:...upon spiritual awakening of the unawakened soul...it shall eventually realize... either with satisfaction gratitude of being timely saved or unfortunately more often with immense regret for volunteering and allowing themselves to be readily available as the diabolical soul less maya being's entrapping captive prey hostage... Indeed, there is more to one's Love rejection than the immediate illusion perception...

Love is felt...not understood...

This is very apparent and resonates within one...as one may not be able to explain why it is so...but soul conscious energy receiving Love feels it and reciprocates the Love through some form of conscious Love... Compassion...empathy...philanthropy...kindness...regard...care...passion...
Love for all...and Love for the one...both aware...and unaware...

Love is the most powerful energy source...the direct Divine energy source...cannot be created nor destroyed...only changes its form expression...from the expressor expressing to the expressed and ultimately to the expressor...True Love intention is always reciprocated...if not from what is Loved...then from the Divine energy source itself...playing out karmically...in the infinite realms of Divinity...on stage... off stage...beyond stage...

World Word...

"I was no part of your world...
 Yet remained within your world...
 Separated due devoid of word...
 Reconnected due use of word...
 Uncovered more my authentic world...
 Separated remains the inevitable word..."

Hugh Shergill

Presumed successful and unsuccessful Love...is not actually Love...as Love is an eternal infinite sacred expression...not confined to a particular achieved destinational point...if one perceives a finish line for Love...then that perceived so called Love is also finished with that line...

"Love induced...
 Journey...
 Destinations...
 Experiences...
 Embedded always remain...
 They do not vanish...
 With the steps of...
 The Love traveler..."

Hugh Shergill

**"The irony is quintessential…
Of Divine Love essential…
It leaves…
Yet retrieves…
All moments after destiny parted you…
Remained forever spent with you…"**

Hugh Shergill

Falling in and out of Soul Love…is the illusion…

You are incapable of falling in or out of Soul Love…that is Love in its truest form…purely eternally infinite from the Soul…not what we perceive Love through other forms of attachments… Previous true Love and fading of a previous true Love is just an illusion as everything simultaneously exists beyond all the confines of Maya time and space…previous true soul Love still exists…current true soul Love exists… future true soul Loves also exists…all in this very moment…only being categorized and separated by illusionary perceptual experience of time and space…a particular universe realm…one of infinite multi-verses realms…one particular lifetime's experience…each play script chapter is collectively existing in the entire Maya Leela play script in totality…never individually…this book contains all chapters together simultaneously…just because one is reading one particular chapter does not make the other chapters vanish…as all is co-existing…always…one play script chapter does not represent the entire play script… therefore one must honour and embrace each chapter and yet be aware of the unfolding of each chapter…and acknowledge this by being aware of the co-existing chapters…past chapters and future chapters…all are actively present in your play book of Maya Leela…

Love requires no approval…seeking what is not required…offensive to core ever non approval…

**"Love is beyond allowed…
Love never requests…
Love is where the heart bowed…
Love requests none to persist…
Love is what Love felt…
Love is not…
What you or not…
Perhaps felt…"**

Hugh Shergill

"The illusionary realm illuminates...
 With the truth of Love...
 Love manifests life into Love...
 Scarcity and challenges hold bliss...
 When one is blessed to experience Love...
 All associated experiences enhance...
 When associated with Love...
 The anticipation of Love reciprocates...
 As the anticipated Love...
 The illusionary realm illuminates...
 With the truth of Love..."

Hugh Shergill

One may recall, those moments of being in the intensity of Love...the glimpse of a more enhanced conscious state of euphoric bliss...regardless of all your and outer world perceived challenges and issues were...those moments of being in Love remains within you as perhaps one of the most blissful moments of one's particular life memory... Associated parallel life experiences from that time regardless of how challenging tend to be recalled from a loving blissful appreciative state...due to the enhanced Love experience that one experienced and was experiencing...

Beyond youth and youth environ...hormones and biological urge to reproduce...other majority factor why being in romantic Love is highly likely to occur for youthful beings is the alignment of high Love receptive vibration frequency with high Love anticipation energy frequency...which no doubt allows Love to be more easily flow and freely able to be attracted into one's life as a vibrant anticipation...reciprocated as Love anticipated...desire Love...open to Love...attracts Love...

"Love never leave us..."

Bob Marley
(Renowned Singer / Poet / Writer / Musician)

"Let the heart be broken...
 Let the heart be open...
 Let the heart be awaken...
 You were Love...
 You are Love...
 You will only be...
 Love..."

Hugh Shergill

All Love is Fulfilled…
Unfulfilled Love is just an illusion…

"Unfulfilled Love…
  Forever fulfilled Love…
  The moment of acceptance…
  Is illusionary acceptance…
  Be grateful for the illusionary blessings…
  While being conscious of the true occurrings…
  Acceptance in impermanence…
  Is just a temporary reoccurrence…
  Embrace what remained unfulfilled…
  Which shall remain forever lived…"

Hugh Shergill

Unfulfilled Love is an illusion…every experience is completely fulfilling as it is a complete experience within existence…fulfilling and unfulfilling are just illusionary perceptions…experience of the illusion…is complete in itself…as it is experienced within existence itself…

The only separating factor between attained and unattained Love…is an illusion…the illusion of the physical existence proximity presence…therefore Love in its purity essence is beyond any illusion of perceived existence and proximity…beyond all illusionary perceived time and space…Love is always complete…attained…successful…ever existing…beyond any physical perceived existence, distance, time and all the confined human processing limitations…

Perceived unattained Love…is Love   forever…eternally complete…never tainted with further emotional and status interferences…
There is nothing as unfulfilled Love…just an illusion…both perceived attained Love and unattained Love are parallel identical illusions…
No failed Love…Love is eternal and always just Love… much beyond the illusion of time and space…

"Untouched is the illusion…
  Every Love is in touch…
  Unattained is the illusion…
  All Love is complete…
  Reciprocation is the choice…
  Not your Love's refuge…"

Hugh Shergill

Maya Leela

Love Purity…

Love is pure...the Love is so magnanimous that is beyond any confined perceived biological existence...
so it is beyond being perceived attained nor unattained...it in its pure form of non selfish state of selfless
Love...it shall and is being reciprocated...if not in this realm of perceived world...then in another realm
world...Love afterall is the highest source of Divine...a desire may not be answered immediately through
the Maya time and space confines...but Love reciprocates immediately...as pure Love expression is
never devoid of pure Love reciprocation...Love is never unattained nor attained…nor lost or gained…
on the illusionary stage of Maya existence...a physical expiry date pending existence can not possibly
encapsulate all of Love...it is forever active attained...always... If you Love purely...and I mean absolutely
purely to Love someone...your Love shall feel it and shall absolutely reciprocate it equally...even if
it is perceived many lifetimes away… Therefore as a soul being… Love purely… unintentionally…
unconditionally… that soul Love is vibrating in reciprocation...if not immediately detected perceived in
the illusionary perceived confines of Maya time and space...then eventually it shall detect and reveal...
absolutely surely...

Love requires no action, gesture, words...Love is simply Love beyond all... Sometimes...privileged and
destined...you are in the position of Love experiencial existence always...as that is essentially all of its
existence itself...but the power of the illusion Maya Leela play prevents that experience through the
illusionary perception…

Love Potent Purity...

"Love is singular...
 Never plural...
 Always one...
 Always complete...
 Love potent purity...

 Love never has...
 Additional addition...
 Additional interference...
 Additional hindrance...

 Love is only Love...
 Always one...
 Always complete...
 Love potent purity..."

Hugh Shergill

Maya Leela

Intricacies of Love...

"The intricacies of Love...
  Beyond the calm surface water...
  Where the swan floats upon...
  Undercurrent intensities...
  Always remain hidden...
  Love appearance...
  Is its clearance...
  Love is always...
  Remains forever one sided...
  Two way is either...
  A compromise...
  Or a commitment..."

Hugh Shergill

Love Possession...

Love possession...is Love oppression...leading to Love destruction... The beautiful rose exuberates Love that also reciprocates Love from those privileged to be in its presence... Hindrance in its Love environ... destructs the Loved one... A rose cut off from its rooted stem to be possessed...its longevity is forever destroyed...no matter how many pure watered crystal vases offered to preserve its destined destruct fate...the rose days are now severely numbered...True essence of Love is in its unhindered state of exuberating Love...upon possession...it is no different from a mere lifeless worn glove...may provide illusionary Loving covering of warmth...yet forever devoid of its skin felt essence of Love... Have Love emerge as a life force tree...let it remain forever free...let Love be...let Love free...

Let Love...Love Be...

"I let Love...
  Love be...
  Forever have...
  Set it free...
  Confining is conditional...
  Freedom is exceptional...
  Honouring its impeccable...
  Love is forever...
  Beyond you or I...
  I let Love...
  Love be...
  Forever have...
  Set it free..."

Hugh Shergill

Maya Leela

"Love forever remains...
  One sided...
  Both sided...
  Manifests into either...
  An agreement...
  Or a relationship..."

Rajesh Khanna (Renowned Actor)
Poetic Translation by Hugh Shergill

Relationships are Conditional...
Love is Unconditional...
Relationship requires Rules...
Love is beyond any Relationship...

Every relationship is conditional...Love is forever unconditional... Love is beyond any relationship...these two distinct dichotomies should not be confused as one... Indeed, Love often relates immediately and immensely...yet as we enter into a 'Love relationship'...an undeniable infused structure forms... which has both its respective loving beauty... and in duality, also a particular structure...from which manifests expectations... any deviation from the perceived expectations...then frustrations, disappointments, and even perhaps hurt shall also occur...this is the dynamics of Love infused relationships... A 'Love relationship' often has a set of unsaid rules of how each should behave towards each other... wherever there are rules...there is a certain loss of authentic core freedom of one... regardless of how loving, morally, ethically imperative those rules are... This is the duality of all Love relationships... which has both its own respective beauty and conformity... one must take on both for the relationship to flourish...as anything that involves more than your own soul comes with certain conditions and responsibilities... Yet true freedom is beyond conditions... Love with conditions is conditional Love... true authentic essence of pure Love is always unconditional... Love is so powerfully pure that it is even beyond the confines of perceived time and space... True Love seeks nothing...demands nothing...expects nothing...just releasing the exquisite fragrance of Love...to the privileged and fortunate to experience that essence of true Love... like experiencing the close proximity of the rose...imbibing oneself with its loving fragrance experience...so powerful that even when no longer in the physical presence of that rose...the rose loving essence continues even without your no longer proximity exchange...by never shunning its fragrance... where the aromatic romancing perfume is forever experienced even with a glimpse into consciousness of that pure entangling Love... Understand the Love infused relationship conditions...honour Love without conditions... Embrace relationships as conditions as that at its very core they are... never confuse and offend your soul essence of unconditional Love with them...respect both...however separately...

Quantum Entanglement Love...

Quantum entanglement reflected profoundly with ultimate Divinity expression...Love... Where Love is expressed it is absolutely received...regardless of one being aware or unaware...Love is energy...just feeling selfless Love for someone entangles them to that selfless Love...that Love energy within felt from an unselfish selfless state taps into Divinity Shakti itself that Love entangles both the one expresses to the expressed...knowingly or unknowingly...but inevitably received and felt...the highest Divine form of

370

Love making...making Love through feeling Love...therefore without any apprehension...send Love to the one you Love...that Divine energy reciprocates by dynamically being entangled and Love creates... Love is loving back...beyond the illusionary confines of time and space...

Desperation for Love Reciprocation...

"Desperation for reciprocation...
  Is Love desperation...
  Forcing illusionary...
  To become reality...
  Only possible through mere act...
  Always remains far from the fact..."

Hugh Shergill

Dissolve to Evolve...
Love is not Attachment...

"Your body failed to recognize...
  What your soul is able to recognize...
  The soul is correct...
  The body is clearly not...
  Detaching as i commence to fly...
  Pleasure to present my final bye..."

Hugh Shergill

Beauty of the 'Let Love Go'...

Love is beyond attachments... If the play of Maya Leela takes one to go separate ways...one must honour that with Love...The beauty of cherishing and letting go...even if there is no closure...regardless of how profound reality shifting desire one holds to reveal...one must let Love go...as letting go and releasing...dissolves the karmic entangled debt...Love is beyond distant and separation...attachment is the illusionary Maya jaal of entrapment...attachment to others including your Loved ones is simply attachment...not the true essence of Love...every one is confined to their own capacity of evolution... as only you can only be responsible for your soul performance in the play of Maya Leela...and if there is perhaps a karmic entanglement that the Divine director of Maya Leela desires...then the Divine director will stage that in your play inevitably...in this or another world...

"That tale devoid…
 Of any conclusion…
 Is best left beautifully…
 In transition…"

Sahir Ludhianvi (Renowned Poet / Lyricist)
Poetic Translation by Hugh Shergill

"If you're brave enough to say goodbye,
 Life will reward you with a new hello."

Paulo Coelho (Renowned Writer / Lyricist)

Love desires giving…its illusion is craving…

"Love desires giving…
 Its illusion is craving…
 illusionary desire of Love…
 Crave held above than give…
 Instead desiring being for you…
 It desires merely of you…"

Hugh Shergill

"Love is the soul romance…
 Beyond Maya…
 True perception…

 If it is indeed Love…

 The rest is mere…
 Play of Maya…
 Entrapping deception…"

Hugh Shergill

illusionary Icing...

"illusionary icing...
  Covered the cake...
  Upon its slicing...
  Revealed the make...
  Web of distasteful entrapping...
  All for your soul energy sake..."

Hugh Shergill

Soul conscious connect is Divine and eternal...
Infatuation lasts two weeks before biological homeostasis downgrade... What follows is either commitment, attachment, attraction, or further ascension of soul conscious connection... Love is the absolute conscious state not an emotion nor dependent on any emotion...Thus be aware of the illusion of emotions and ultimately the Maya Leela play illusion...

"Even audaciously...
  Dare to go ahead...
  Demolish...
  Any religious structure...
  That you may desire...
  Destroy every might...
  Destroy everything in sight...
  Yet never dare...
  To break that...
  Love filled...
  Divine heart...
  Truly Loves you...
  Resides..."

Bulleh Shah (Renowned Sufi Poet)
Poetic Translation by Hugh Shergill

Maya Love...

illusionary Love Entrapping Artists...

Soul less diabolical asuric entities are innate illusionary entrapping artists...mirroring your preferences of the particulars for association...to lure you in and entrapping you deeply into their Maya Jaal web...the association motivation is and only is to feed off your soul energy in any way possible... It is their survival need...they are soul energy predators...you are the hunt...you are the desire hunted...by any means possible...by any illusion possible...

Maya Leela

This entrapment is often commonly associated with perceived Love relationships yet it is not restricted to that as maya being associates, friends, and particular family members also illusionary Love mirror entrap you for your soul energy with the desire to keep you close to them and long term soul energy feed…

"The most hurtful experience…
Is to fall in Love…
With a soul less maya being…"

In perceived Love relationships…the Maya being creates a deep entrapping web…Maya Love… manipulating your biological desires along with emotional desires to create an illusionary mirroring desire for them…they create an illusion persona that mirrors your preferences before they hunt you down…this is the Love illusion entrapment…this entrapping is much more beyond the physical body…as there is always an option to feed off an even more desirable physical body through other means and mediums… actually it is your Soul existence that is extremely craved by them not just your body…it is and always will be them desiring of entrapping your soul energy feed for their diabolical asuric soul less energy… whether it is for a short term quick energy feed…or a long term constant feed…your potent soul energy is their desired fuel top priority…by any means necessary…

Upon your soul being's energy hunt…once hunted…that is the moment of the first hint of the illusionary Love entrapment reveal…this reveal only strengthens further as you continuingly get fed off and fed up… All the emotional and physical manipulating dishonest driven illusions come to surface…either abruptly immediately as a feast diet meal…or time release gradually as a long term daily diet… This harsh reality of heartache, betrayal, sense being used, manipulation comes to one's soul senses…which is a very difficult phase that follows…as one comes to the full realization that you are nothing more than their diabolical asuric soul less energy feed…

**"Betrayal's gateway…
Is your door…
Outdoor betrayal doesn't last…
Indoor betrayal destroys most…
Toughest battle exists not…
One stepping outdoors…
It exists within indoors…"**

Hugh Shergill

Beware…By Being Aware…

True Love will undoubtedly enhance one's performance in the play of Maya Leela…even if it is experienced for a very short duration glimpse of one's perceived Maya time line…otherwise it shall be an intense entrapping distraction that creates a perpetual trajectory course of maya jaal entrapment…both discoursing and disruptively descending one's potential soul rise…

"Truly in Love with the maya world...
Definitely a double edged sword...
Piercing always an opposite attack...
Emotionally agreed reasons attached...
Sugar coated cake sweetly iced...
Upon the sweet icing is ingested...
Distasteful cake shall be tasted..."

Hugh Shergill

Love...
Maya...
And the Maya Being...

Love and maya beings are distinct dichotomous paths that only illusionary cross...the soul less diabolical asuric...the maya being is truly incapable of truly genuinely loving someone...and a soul being will never truly experience Love from a soul less maya being...only an illusion entrapment that is incorrectly labeled as Love...repeated upon realized reasons reaching...time after time...simply an illusion entrapment that is labeled Love incorrectly...repeated upon realizing reaching...perceived time after time...viscously repeating...scene after scene...act after act...

What instead is real is reasons... attraction...infatuation...emotional...attachment... commitment...agreement... all catered reasons offered metaphorically as a Love cake... all sweetly coated and presented in the illusion icing of Love... once the sweet icing is ingested...the extremely distasteful reason cake must also be unfortunately tasted...

'I Love you...'
Coming from a soul less...
Is a heartache oxymoron...

Maya Being is the Narcissistic Love Partner...
Maya Being's Incapable of True Love...

Maya being Love partner is a narcissistic Love partner...someone who possesses all the conventional established psychological diagnostic narcissistic traits and much more... including having an inflated false sense of their own importance...a deep need of admiration...sense of entitlement or superiority... non empathic...manipulative and controlling behaviour... strictly focused on one's own needs...ignoring the needs of others... aggressive...non tolerance for personal criticism... and above all... possessing soul less asuric low vibration energy...a soul less maya being entity... antagonist resistance for those who possess Divine spark of soul energy...strategically karmically entrappingly placed into the play of your life...the play of Maya Leela...

"Initially heart let...
 illusionary Love felt...
 Envitabally was a regret...
 Entrapment labeled Love incorrectly...
 Repeated upon realizing reaching...
 Time after time viscously repeating..."

Hugh Shergill

Soul Ghosting...

A maya being is incapable of loving anybody besides themselves...a hardcore narcissistic is their personality core... The rare connection that they feel for a soul being is motivated by a particular attractive attributes they possess...whether it is physical, financial, or a particular status motivation... However, once they come close to the soul being...their diabolical asuric energy begins to rattle with the threat of the Divine energy spark of the soul being either awakened or becoming awakened... The extremely threatening moment when the lifting of the illusionary veil begins...the ending of the relationship begins...This immediate reaction leads to the relationship between them to head towards the end... Interestingly this scenario yields two distinct reactions...

One...gang stalking...resulting in further torturous gang stalking attacks on to the soul being to punish them for awakening...and further suppress their awareness of their new reality discovery...if successful...the Maya jaal entrapment suppression of the soul being is sustained and long term hostile suffering relationship continues on the soul being unfortunately...

Or two...soul ghosting...further upon fully exposure discovery of the soul being discovering the maya being and their Maya illusionary Love...the maya being feels fully exposed threatened and ups their soul energy depletion attacks through their diabolical asuric energy attacks and then eventually flees...

Soul ghosting is persecution and ostracization of the soul energy being...targeting them and then isolating them as a punishment for discovering the Maya being's true soul less diabolical asuric identity...

Soul ghosting interestingly develops as where initially without any perceived on surface issues...the soul less maya being immediately shuns away from the soul being without any explanation...this rude behaviour is much more deep than it appears...indeed the maya being is capable of being very rude and disrespectful innately...however this particular act of immediate cut off is a desperate attempt for the maya being to eliminate any possible threat of Divine energetic energies revealing and identifying them to who they actually are...the soul less diabolical asuric entities that they are...this unveiling extremely irritates their soul less asuric low vibration energy...bringing out their sympathetic fight or flight reaction abruptly...often unfortunately abusively and violently...

Just like gang stalking can possibly come from any maya being regardless of the relationship or association...Soul ghosting is not confined to come from Maya being Lovers only...as any perceived Loved one...whether romantic Love, Loved one, family, friends, associates...all are capable to soul ghost you upon your unveiling discovery of the actual them...

As a soul being who may have experienced this ill treatment...please do not be offended or hurt...please treat this as the Divine blessing it actually is...as you were saved further from a particular relationship that would have extremely depleted your soul energy further...therefore rejoice and celebrate...just never repeat...as all lessons are repeated on the Maya Leela play stage if not learned...

**"I came for the sake of Love devotion...
  Seeing the world...
  I wept..."**

**Meera
(Renowned Mystique Poet / Divine Devotee)**

Save your Soul...
Give your Love to only a Soul...
True Love is Soul Love...

Only a soul being is truly capable of Love...as Love is the soul's core...a maya being is only capable of providing an Illusion of Love...as illusion is its core... maya Love provides an illusion of Love... hiding their true intent of transaction in the perceived Love...

Soul Love is beyond all illusionary confines... time and space are irrelevant finites... for the infinite realm of Love... Love has no proximity or distance...nor a start nor an end...an era or season... Love is beyond all these illusionary confines... irrelevant finites...

**"Soul being loving...
  A soul being...
  Is the most beautiful...
  Fulfilling soul journey...
  Soul being loving...
  A maya being...
  Is unfortunately just a...
  Soul's tragedy..."**

Hugh Shergill

Maya Leela

Soul Love Story... Never Ending...

"Play of Love ...
  Is never ending...
  Only characters come...
  Destiny forever sending...
  Only characters are gone...
  Love story forever remaining..."

Hugh Shergill

The epic soul Love story of Laila Majnu...is almost parallel identical to the epic Love story of Heer Ranjha...different times...different locales...yet the soul Love resonating essence of their Love stories is one... Lovers leave...yet their Love stories are complete...again and again...repeat after repeat... same Maya stage...same script...different scenes...different actors...repeat after repeat...even further inspiring famous tragic Love story play scripts such as...Romeo and Juliet...West Side Story... This is not a mere coincidence...it is a destiny repeated incidence...

Laila My Heer...

"Soul Love spear...
  Laila my Heer...

  Unequivocal beauty beyond all shades...
  Laila blesses the eye with exquisite glimpse...
  Struck Majnu froze ice cold in the hot desert...
  Physically depart from Ranjha yet never apart...
  Heer beautifully shed her final tear...
  Giving all to whom not be her's here...

  Soul Love spear...
  Laila my Heer..."

Hugh Shergill

"Love shades…
  Legend aides…

  Shirin your dramatics in the name of Love…
  Sassi your subconscious lost your Love…
  Laila your empathy brought hurting essence…
  Sahiba your betrayal with such innocence…
  Sohni your determination beyond ocean depth…
  Heer your tears still remain forever felt…

  Love shades…
  Legend aides…"

Hugh Shergill

"Before you die,
  experience the Love
  of a writer, poet or painter.
  If you're lucky enough
  to be an artist's muse,
  they will immortalize you."

Soledad Francis
(Renowned Author / Artist / Professor)

Actually Love You…

"How much do I…
  Actually Love you…
  Not immediately aware…
  Beyond imaginable measure…
  Yet I cannot exist…
  Actually without you…"

Majrooh Sultanpuri (Renowned Poet / Lyricist)
Poetic Translation by Hugh Shergill

Maya Leela

Love Tribute…

Following, is a tribute to this Divine blessing of Love…from the highest form of Divine Love…to Soul Love…and also certain intricate dynamics of Maya Love…whilst exploring their Loving depths with poetic words…

Meera…My Love…

"Meera…
  My Love…

  I feel you intimately…
  Devoting Divinity…
  To feel…
  That feel…
  Beyond the deepest reveal…
  Deserving of the lip's seal…
  To forever Love is continuation…
  True Love is beyond apprehension…
  Tranquil of that Love sacrifice…
  Acceptance of every heart bled slice…

  Meera…
  My Love…

  From…your Rebel Soul…"

Hugh Shergill

We Are Not…And Yet…

"We are not…
  And yet…

  We are not in Love…
  We before today…
  Have not even met…
  Yet there is something…
  That I see in your eyes…
  A connection that ignites…
  Beyond many lifetimes…"

  We are not…
  And yet…"

Hugh Shergill

Foreplay of Eye Play…

"The potency of that first kiss…
  Was extremely imbibing bliss…
  Questioning further one's query…
  Why such intense immediate flurry…
  Discovering undeniable fueled foreplay…
  Of those previous eye contact play…"

Hugh Shergill

Attractive Moments…

"Attraction confined to youth…
 Regret emerges when without…
 Moments strike at the mercy of the subjective…
 Time overwhelms what was once attractive…
 Separation of moments…
 Brings regret with pain…
 Continuation illusion shall now…
 Forever remain…"

Hugh Shergill

Long Gone…

"What is gone…
 Frivolous to long…
 What has left…
 Remains hiddenly slept…
 All is the play of infinite energy…
 You the participatory synergy… "

Hugh Shergill

Moments…

"Each moment in your presence…
  Was Divinity's blessed essence…
  Connected paths were Divinely kept…
  Separating paths were Divinely left…
  Appreciate the moments we spent…
  Appreciate the moments we couldn't…"

Hugh Shergill

Admirer Irony…

"The irony of the admirer…
  All Is until the inevitable fader…
  When remains shining in demand…
  Holds many others at command…
  Once struck by the abandoned wand…
  Shockingly loses even oneself at hand…"

Hugh Shergill

Occurrence…

"Like is a particular preference…
Love is an authentic occurrence…
Being liked and being Loved…
Are polarizing different…
One is based on a particular preference…
The other is an unforced occurrence…"

Hugh Shergill

Exiting Cheating…

"Being with a person cheating…
Hard actuality it's you that's cheating…
Being a victim of recycled energy repeating…
Third party unwanted energy accumulating…
Hear your soul's torture hurt refuting…
Wisdom lies within your exiting…"

Hugh Shergill

Flower of Loyalty…

"Indiscriminately exuding fragrance…
  All experiencing beauty exuberance…
  Joyously celebrating when sent…
  Mourning loss with those who went…
  Never an unloyal moment of fragility…
  Become that flower of loyalty…"

Hugh Shergill

Secret My Love…

"I know you know…
  You know I know…
  Revealing the known…
  It will become unknown…
  True enlightening reveal…
  Shall be open for others to steal…
  Please don't ask about the one I Love…
  That shall eternally remain a secret my Love…"

Hugh Shergill

Every Rejection...Divine Protection...

"Every rejection...
  Divine protection...

  Rejection is not a hurt prescription...
  Often rejected is the unaffordable option...
  What is not in destined conception...
  Shall be removed from your perception...
  The attraction was a disguised descension...
  Rejected making way for your ascension...

  Every rejection...
  Divine protection..."

Hugh Shergill

Conditions for the Unconditional...

"In the realm of betrayal...
  Of perceived Love unconditional...
  The confines of conditions...
  Often unfortunately overwhelms...
  One casts the spell of illusion...
  The other imposed the illusion..."

Hugh Shergill

Unequivocal Eyes of Champagne

"Unequivocal eyes of champagne...
Unveiling paradises where reign...
Expressing in unintentional vain...
Experiencing in widrawal of sane...
Undeniable bliss when in remain...
Unrelenting departure left in pain..."

Hugh Shergill

Intent Shift of Desire...

"Head on with intent to acquire...
Realized it was all to inspire...
Shed all importance of prior...
Emerged to surface the require...
Moment was when heart had desire...
Moment is where heart is the desire..."

Hugh Shergill

Separating Stairs... Separate Realms...

"Last conversation taking place...
 In the middle of a staircase...
 Leaving without the revelating reveal...
 Perhaps one incapable for the unveil...
 Never one shall ever await...
 Forever be enclosed separate...
 Dissolving forever that karmic debt...
 Embracing forever the unknown fate...
 Duality realms on a platform feat...
 Where steps separating souls meet...
 While one headed towards stairs descend...
 The other headed towards the stairs ascend..."

Hugh Shergill

That Kite...

"I was attracted and desired that kite...
 That roamed unapologetically in flight...
 I cherished the space below of its discovery...
 Seeking the source of its ancestry...
 Yet it landed at a point...
 Of self destructing attire...
 Dissolving its identity...
 While shunning all its desire..."

Hugh Shergill

I Let Glow…

"I let go…
I let glow…

I had fully unrelated let go of her…
Yet she still remained somewhere…
Let go of being in drunk illusionary fixation…
Yet I remained in her glowing intoxication…
All her dreams were revoked eliminated…
Yet I remained disturbed by her insomniated…

I let go…
I let glow…"

Hugh Shergill

I Do Not Remember You…

"I do not remember you…
As I never forgot you…
What is gone is gone…
Honouring life by moving on…
Yet what has been in my journey…
Shall always be cherished in my story…"

Hugh Shergill

Let go of Love…

"One non reciprocity in a situation…
 One non remained in that situation…
 Attractive flame of your eye…
 Lit the pathway to fly…
 I exist within you…
 Within each dark blink…
 I exit from you…
 With each eye open think…"

Hugh Shergill

"Solitude Love…
 Has no Intrude…

 Love in solitude…
 Love has no intrude…
 Felt from loneliness…
 Possession of onlyness…
 Kept in one's dreams…
 Existence forever realms…

 Solitude Love…
 Has no Intrude…"

Hugh Shergill

Destined Play...

"Last page of one chapter...
  Leads you to the next chapter...
  From where we left...
  Was where destiny sent...
  All now makes sense...
  The destined play essence..."

Hugh Shergill

True Intimacy...

"True intimacy key...
  Confinely free...
  Being into me...
  Not on me...
  Deeply felt...
  Truly kept...
  True intimacy key...
  Confinely free..."

Hugh Shergill

Soul Erotica…

"Soul erotica…
  Foreplay of soul aura…
  Intimacy beyond the clothes…
  Desire uncloaking what is soul's…
  Climaxing revealing provokes…
  Potent secrets the soul emotes…
  Soul erotica…
  Foreplay of soul aura…"

Hugh Shergill

Love Attract…

"Confession is not a lie…
  Immediately felt…
  You were my…
  Never met anyone like you…
  Feel no one quite like I…
  That momentarily the kiss of eye…
  Left alluringly seeking that tie…
  Confession is not a lie…
  Immediately felt…
  You were my…"

Hugh Shergill

Is You...

"My eternal dear is always you...
  Moments experience have experienced...
  My most closest witness is you...
  What no one else saw you have perceived...
  My most deadliest enemy is you...
  Unbeated heartbeat rejected from end..."

Hugh Shergill

Met... Reconnect...

"First time we met...
  Yet felt as a reconnect...
  What was a pre-destined incidence...
  Was illusionary perceived coincidence...
  Happen to leave...
  Is the delusion...
  Happen to keep...
  Is the illusion..."

Hugh Shergill

Moment…

"Moment…
   More meant…

   Sacrificing moment…
   After a moment…
   Desiring that moment…
   Surprising moment…
   Arriving at that moment…
   Departing from the moment…
   Lost in the previous desired moment…
   Stole away this very moment…

   Moment…
   More meant…"

Hugh Shergill

Remaining Recall…

"Removing you from my memory reel…
   Is the most appropriate ideal …
   Yet no dream you are…
   Existence realm aware…
   Rising Love or merely a fall…
   That is the remaining recall…"

Hugh Shergill

Love Recall...

"The eyes met romantically merge...
  Love horizon commenced verge...
  Physically there was nothing...
  Spiritually was forever something...
  I Love recalling it all...
  Moments that never happened at all..."

Hugh Shergill

You Are My Muse...

"You are my muse...
  One that we never choose...
  Meeting an unknown cause...
  Activated occurrence upon loss...
  The artist's art source...
  You are my muse..."

Hugh Shergill

Unsaid...

"Some things left unsaid...
  Some messages unread...
  What was destined stayed...
  What was not betrayed...
  Never let the illusion dread...
  Forever it remains dead..."

Hugh Shergill

Holding Ice...

"Holding ice...
  A melting price...
  Destined to leave...
  Impossible to retrieve...
  Wisdom lies to let it go...
  What was always meant to go..."

Hugh Shergill

Power of Attraction...

"Never waste their time...
 That is a waste of time...
 Weakening is attention...
 Power lies in attraction...
 Embrace your soul space...
 Let the chemistry chase..."

Hugh Shergill

The Candle Flame...

"The Candle flame flawlessly shines...
 Under protection of wall confines...
 Upon exposed to the naked winds...
 The life of the flame rapidly ends...
 Among societal gazes...
 All the magic erases...
 Love expressed in private contact...
 Remains enduringly intact..."

Hugh Shergill

Maya Leela

Arose Rose...

"The loving fragrance...
  Of the rose...
  Rose...
  The hurting smoke...
  Of the burning rose...
  Rose...
  Intertwined romancing mist...
  Awoke the rose...
  Arose Rose..."

Hugh Shergill

Real eyes...Realize...Their lies...

"Real eyes...
  Realize...
  Their lies...

  The lips hid everything...
  The eyes revealed everything...
  One's eyes are the real lips...
  Revealing truth without slips...
  Looking requires just two eyes...
  Seeing is where the third eye lies...
  Besides intuitive gaze into their eyes...
  All other physicalities are mere lies...

  Real eyes...
  Realize...
  Their lies..."

Hugh Shergill

Separation…

"Separation manifests from apart…
Yet a difference in every depart…
Attained emotions are felt…
Remained memories are kept…
Some heartfelt individuals leave…
Some heartache individuals relieve…"

Hugh Shergill

I See…

"You are not just you for me…
Whenever in your presence…
I see purity…
You are that Love evoke for me…
Whenever in your presence…
I see poetry…"

Hugh Shergill

Your Are…

"You are my Goddess…
Would never think of less…
Overwhelmed by your energy…
Soul choked by the synchronicity…
Forever yearned for you…
After experiencing a glimpse of you…"

Hugh Shergill

Maya Leela

See…Sees…

"Divinity showering drops…
  Through your eyes resonance…
  The purity is so spiritually enticing…
  I reciprocate through its indulgence…
  Imbibing one with each every drop…
  What your eyes see…
  See…
  Yet what my soul sees…
  Sees…"

Hugh Shergill

Measure of Love…

"Intensity of Love…
  A depth so foreign…
  Measure of my Love…
  Beyond all measure…
  Love you beyond all relate…
  Where even space time fade…"

Hugh Shergill

Soul's Romance…

"Deprived to be your first Lover…
  Inspired to be your last Lover…
  Moments cherishing well..
  Forever etched in this realm…
  Eternal Love euphoric affair…
  Together beyond this realm…
  Devoid of Soul Love Romance…
  Yet never of your Soul's Romance…"

Hugh Shergill

The Emphatic Heart…

"The emphatic heart feels your weeps…
  Your tears make me wipe my cheeks…
  I desire to transform your fear…
  Creating a fearless strike spear…
  Where nemesis fall furious…
  Only Love reigning victorious…"

Hugh Shergill

"Not all receive that Love…
  In this particular life…
  Privileged are those…
  Who experienced that blossom…
  In this particular life…"

Indeevar (Renowned Poet / Lyricist)
Movie: Janbaaz
Translation by Hugh Shergill

Not every soul is presented with the stage soul romance it desires immediately…karmic sequences and karmic debts open up to the scenes of soul Love romance sequentially…romance exists in that destined scene…just requires your karmic mean…current soul performance on this Maya realm stage is unique for each and every soul…each dedicated a Maya script that it shall play and perform its particular soul calling…the artist's art romance requires its instrument…the warrior of the play requires a sword not a rose…the spiritual healer holds meditative beads and Divine scriptures…yet it does not indicate that the upcoming scenes will not present the destined bouquet of roses…each phase…each victory…each evolution…will reveal the next series of scenes in continuation…

Desire Acquire…

"Desired them to be in my world…
 Yet it did not happen…
 Instead experienced the entire world…
 Result of that did not happen…
 That what was the one desire…
 Was destined route of all acquire…"

Hugh Shergill

Self Love Trance…

"When the drink is…
 Devoid of the mix…
 One must indulge it neat…
 When no loving soul…
 Is in destined sight…
 Love your own soul…
 In celebrated might…
 Soul's greatest romance…
 Is the self Love trance…"

Hugh Shergill

Your true Soul Mate…
Is being your Soul's Mate…

Soul loving is the highest form of worshiping one's Divine spark of soul energy…authentic pure soul loving with the blessings of Divinity… Loving one's own soul is the essence of Divinity…nothing else… nothing more…the most romantic Love story romances exists in the deep depths of soul within…

occupied indulging into the greatest Love romance of all…Loving one's own soul…your soul is whole on your own…being within whole…experiencing one whole…soul whole among all…

Love yourself freely… completely… unapologetically… you are absolutely complete…as your Divine spark is all that could ever exist… enjoy…indulge…celebrate…with one's soul oneself…you are complete…celebrate Love…you are the Love…you are whole…you are all…you are Soul…Love…

The potent drink remains potent as is…not dependent on the mix…neat is absolutely complete… the essence of potency remains complete…any addition…is dilution…potent drink honours the shot glasses neat…mixing further would dilute it complete… Your soul energy is completely potent as is… any energetic intrusion is potential dilution…enhancing potency with other souls perhaps a possibility… yet potential dilution also simultaneously exists… Keep your soul energy potent…you are complete as remaining neat…

Karmic Connections…

"Breath is to existence…
  Love is its Soul fragrance…
  Karmic connections…
  Soul ascensions…
  Or illusionary descends…
  Unveiling what the stage sends…"

Hugh Sherglll

"The traveling wanderer…
  On the streets of beauty…
  Coincidently meeting many…
  Some effortlessly forgotten…
  Some remembered forever…"

Anand Bakshi
(Renowned Poet / Lyric Writer)
Poetic Translation by Hugh Shergill

Maya Leela

Soul Connections…

"When there is a connect…
  That is a connection…
  When there is not a connect…
  That also is a connection…
  Amongst its variables…
  Exists its constants…"

Hugh Shergill

Soul Mates and Karmic Entangled Crossings…

There are two components to karmic connections…both hold capacity for one soul to excel…soul karmic connect…and maya karmic connect…

It is a misconception that one only comes across other soul beings as a karma connection…when one also comes across many more maya being karma connections…

Soul being karma connection resolves soul collective karma and ultimately help each other to enhance further towards ascension to ultimately liberation…Moksha… and eternal bliss…Nirvana…

Maya being karma connection are maya representatives that serve us lessons…usually harsh…hurtful… but definitely a blessing in disguise…actually more potent as they exist entirely for the soul being…as the karmic maya host…that serves opportunities to evolve within our soul…and learn the karmic lesson… once learned and overcome…it takes the soul on a much enhanced path…

Both serve you karmically…one enhances through association…the other enhances through evolving…

"There is no soul mate…only soul mates…"

The soul mate concept…one's twin flame…no matter how fantasizing attractive this seems or how much one yearns to experience this…this is a mere Maya illusion… There is no other individual being beyond the soul being itself that can honourary hold the illusionary tag of being their singular soul mate…the only one true soul mate of the soul being is its own core existence energy source…the Divine itself… that was all…is all…shall remain all…simultaneously all…beyond all space time duality relativity confines of the Maya realm…your only primary soul mate is your soul source…the Divine…the souls that are also indulged into the Divinity pool of Love…are your soul mates…

Your soul is an unique expression of the Divine itself…that can not be compared to anyone else… so beyond the Divine itself…there is no singular parallel identical soul expression to you… Yes, due to duality of maya platform of illusionary existence…there is certainly a direct opposing energy being to you…your most prominent opposing nemesis…the primary antagonist in your maya leela play…your primary maya being opponent…deep down as one reflects in retrospect in their life journey…one can easily distinctly extract out and recognize that one individual that provided the most resistance in one's performance existence...that was either the trigger to all the rise and achievements by overcoming and defeating it...or contrastingly being the submissive downfall by being overwhelmed and defeated... This power or lack of...is the choice of one's play performance...in the Divine's Love expressed through the Maya Leela play...therefore, one should not fall in Love...but rise in Love...

"Your soul is unique...like no other...however your soul source is the Divine itself, which is also the identical source of all your fellow soul beings...your soul mates..."

Deep Soul Connections...

Indeed some connections run deep... very deep...beyond any explanation...acting just as the sympathetic strings of the instrument sitar...that vibrate and play automatically without even a touch... simply from the primary sitar strings interacting vibration...close proximity...a deep felt thought...parallel vibration resonates without any explanation...

With that said, the Divine spark of soul that exists in one also exists in other manifests of soul...your soul mates...the Divine spark of soul that exists in one and also in all manifests of soul...

Soul mates...are individual soul beings that are binded by the destined karmic play of Maya Leela... they emerge on the Maya Leela stage at the most appropriate scenes...providing revelating insights, synchronicity triggering effects, support, encouragement, and undefined unprocessed Love ...all that empowers the soul being to potentially excel ascend further through their karmic performance in the Maya Leela play...

One never has to make an effort to recognize these soul mates...as soul conscious intuition sparks the energy within...sometimes immediately...which is a fruitful blessing providing opportunity to reciprocate the soul connect gesture with Love expression...immediately and blissfully... but sometimes one recognizes these soul mates with delayed processing...often after the karmic crossing of the two souls took place...creating time delayed awareness of what those soul mates meant for karmically soul crossing with one...this delayed realization creates a wondrous appreciation long after the soul crossing...and this is a powerful Love state within for these soul mates...creating immense gratefulness and appreciation...knowing that one would not be where they are in the acts and performance scope of Maya Leela without them...each and everyone of them...

Hold and value each of these soul mates in the remainder performance acts within the illusionary particular existence scenes...cherish their contribution, insightful revelating information they provided, and the soul unprocessed Love they showered towards the particular one... All those valuable contributions from the soul mates hold hidden clues to the ultimate ascension liberation...which regardless coming from the soul mates...but those soul mates themselves may perhaps be unaware of this...as processing information and providing information...is separated through one being soul consciously aware or soul conscious dormant state...

Maya Leela

"Blessed with Love and Loved ones...
Then celebrate conscious within...
That resonates to infinite universes...
Keep those Love blessings discreetly within...
Don't offend Divinity's blessings of Love...
By frivolous worldly attention exposures..."

Hugh Shergill

"During the actor's stage performance...the character's thorough preparation, stage props, and accessories...truly bring out the impeccable performance...acts of self Love enhancing your soul performance...by being your core essence...the Soulabrity...Superstar of Divinity..."

CHAPTER 19.

SOULABRITY
SELF
LOVE

"The self loving actor…

Is the prepared actor…

Its stage props…

Is its preparedness…

Fully aware of the script…

Dialogues thoroughly rehearsed…

Efforts exerted towards being performing fit…

Physically, mentally, and spiritually…

To give the performance of their life…

On the stage of Maya Leela…

Superstar of Divinity…

Here enters the Soulabrity…

Lights…

Camera…

Action!…

You are the Soul Attraction…"

Hugh Shergill

**"A great man is hard on himself;
A small man is hard on others."**

Lao Tzu (Renowned Philosopher)

Soulabrity Secrets...
Performer's Preparedness...
The Soul Spark of Discipline...

Prioritize unapologetically your soul performing preparation...If it is not visible when you face the mirror...it should fall in line behind to what is obvious and immediately present in the mirror...your health, fitness and wellness...that energizes not only your physicality but your Divine soul energy...

Discipline is the igniting spark of your soul...be persistent...be consistent...take full advantage of this return ticket vacation play experience...by honouring your unique physical vessel existence with immense self Love discipline...from welcoming witnessing prepared for each sunrise to the satisfying sunset indulgence...do all with the soul spark of discipline...discipline of self Love...

An ancient tale of an aging Prince...

Legend has it...there was a young Prince that due to his excessive indulgences and particular lifestyle...he was aging very rapidly and becoming ill... Out of concern...he consulted with his kingdom associated priest... The priest told him that it has the magic formula of youthfulness and health...

The priest instructed, for the next 30 days...just before sunrise, the prince has to run from the palace to its near located highest hill peak...where it shall find a cloth bag... Now the prince has to simply touch the bag but not open it until the last 30th day... From where the prince has to run back to the palace before the sunrise takes place...

The prince complies...and follows the instructions precisely for the next 30 days...and on the 30th day...the prince opens the bag and discovers a note saying:

"Now go back to the palace and look at yourself in the mirror...you shall be granted your youthful appearance back"

The prince enthusiastically rushes and runs back to the palace and looks into the mirror... Astonishingly, the prince is taken by surprise by its renewed youthful and fit appearance... The priest's magic formula had done its magic...

As the task had to be completed before sunrise...the prince had to wake up very early in the morning before sunrise...which resulted in sleeping earlier at night...as also running was involved...fitness was acquired...which resulted in a diet plan consisting of light yet more nutritious food and hydration for the optimum energy requirements...the 30 days straight process resulted in consistency... The prince now discovered that the secret magic formula was not in the cloth bag...but in the process of self Love disciplinary consistency...

**"When there is harmony between
the mind, heart, and resolution,
then nothing is impossible."**

**Rig Veda
(the first humankind known written scriptures)**

**"Some doors open...
Only from the inside...
Necessity to unlocking...
One must go within...
Meditation is the key...
Eternally opening to the Divine..."**

Hugh Shergill

Meditation...

Meditation is the act of clearing the mind...
Meditation is training the mind to rest in a particular focus that leads to a connection to the source of consciousness itself... Meditators can focus upon specific spiritual concepts, visions, mantra chanting, breathing, yoga, deep precise one focus thought while disregarding all distractions of hindrances...ultimately attain unbounded consciousness...

**"Meditation is being in a pure
quantum entanglement state
with the Divine..."**

During meditation...the meditators contemplate upon specific spiritual concepts and ultimately attain unbounded consciousness...creating direct quantum entangled communication with Divinity itself... the more one indulges into meditation...remaining in the meditative realm for prolonged period...the more powerful the Divine entanglement becomes...so powerful that with consistent practice, one is able to soul shift from immediate three dimensional realm to unbounded fifth dimensional realm...in less than a blink of the eye...However, it can take anywhere from days of practice to entire lifetimes or beyond to attain the perfected results... It depends on the spiritual evolution of the practitioner's soul's evolution... One cannot predict the evolution achievement...however one can highly encourage a soul to surely discipline themselves to be consistent and concentrated with their meditative practices...as what shall be attained is priceless and unattainable in this three dimensional Maya reality...

Maya Leela

**"When I would meditate,
 I realized I could master my mind."**

**Vinod Khanna
(Renowned Actor / Spiritual Seeker)**

**"Your meditative worship...
 Is your higher realm ship...
 Invoking you to astral travel...
 Inviting you to that hidden level...
 What is not only powerfully inviting...
 Is even more powerfully elevating..."**

Hugh Shergill

Practice...Consistent...Patience...

Patience shall remove all the distractions...in your meditation journey...key is not to reject or fight your distracting thoughts...instead acknowledge them and let them pass by as the clouds in the sky...do not focus on the clouds...instead keep your focus on the revealing beautiful blue clear sky...

Enjoy and appreciate the progressive joy of meditative concentration...that joy of concentration reciprocally starts working more towards increasing that focused joy state...by facilitating more focus... The more you learn to relax, surrender, open up and enjoy your meditation...the less reasons there are for the mind to get restless distracted thinking of other thoughts...

Buddhist Tale...

Once Buddha was walking from one town to another town with a few of his followers... While they were traveling, they passed by a lake. They decided to stopped there to rest...and Buddha told one of his disciples:

"I am thirsty. Please do get me some water from that lake there."

The disciple walked up to the lake... When he reached, he noticed that right at that moment, a bull cart started crossing through the lake. As a result, the water became very muddy, very turbid. The disciple thought: "How can I give this muddy water to Buddha to drink!" So he came back and told Buddha:

"The water in there is very muddy. I don't think it is fit to drink."

After about half an hour, again Buddha asked the same disciple to go back to the lake and get him some water to drink. The disciple obediently went back to the lake. This time too he found that the lake was muddy. He returned and informed Buddha about the same.

412

After some more time passes by…again Buddha asked the same disciple to go back. The disciple reached the lake to find the lake absolutely clean and clear with pure water in it. The mud had settled down and the water above it looked clear clean. So he collected some water in a pot and brought it to Buddha. Buddha looked at the water, and then he looked up at the disciple and said:

"See what you did to make the water clean… You let it be…and the mud settled down on its own… and now you got clear water. Your mind is also just like that… When it is disturbed, just let it be. Give it a little time. It will settle down on its own. You don't have to put in any effort to calm it down. It will happen. It is effortless. Having 'Peace of Mind' is not a strenuous job…it is an effortless patience process."

Kundalini Shakti…

Just like an ape is only a small fraction dna difference from a human being…yet worlds, capacities, abilities apart…a fully Kundalini awakened state human body experience is only small fraction awakened enhanced version…yet extremely worlds, processing capacities, abilities apart…a super human state…with super soul powers…

As mentioned earlier in the 'Energy Treasures' chapter… Kundalini Shakti awakened state is the enhanced version state of the soul like no other…there is no comparative example…no euphoric equivalent… With a blink of the eye…one awakened soul is capable of traveling to higher realms back and forth…taking soul discernment and wisdom to dizzying heights where one is guided not just a few steps ahead but many lifetime journeys ahead…super human powers…super intelligence…super intellect…super memory…super creativity…impeccable brain processing abilities and intellectual capabilities that were previously were dormant untapped…energetically proficient capable enough to connect with the higher realms above…revelating revelations…formally hidden informations… Even further, for a certain few highly advanced…there is even an expansion of one's vision spectrum field scope…where now particular energetic auras become visible to the naked eye itself…abilities to see visually energetic auras of oneself and very shockingly of others…

Undistracted deep meditation is the key to unlocking the locked Kundalini…the rotation twisting of the key to unlocking is the power of Tantra…where Divinity Mantra chanting through this physical body form Yantra…connects separate realms together through the act of Tantra…

"Whatever purifies you, is the correct road."

Rumi (Renowned Sufi Poet)

Mantra…

Mantra chanting during deep meditative state is extremely powerful Divinely entangling…

As for specific soul mantras...I am compelled to mention...as it is very disheartening to witness specific sacred mantras just ignorantly universally shared and encouraged for everyone to chant... whether an individual with a following or a certain institution...this is extremely incorrect and very misleading... For those who can see beyond the illusionary Maya realm...this type of open ignorantly mantra sharing, mantra chanting, even further large group mantra chantings aloud is just deceiving Maya jaal entrapment practices...majority of these are hosted, operated, and largely participated by asuric soul less maya beings...directly performing Maya tricks...Maya trix...Matrix...by keeping the uninformed ignorant vulnerable soul beings trapped on the surface Maya three dimensional level... preventing true soul ascension...which is their most horrific threat... Aloud mantra chanting reduces its potency significantly as the mantra energy is now dispersed and faded throughout the environment... even the very fact of indiscretion use of Divine specific mantras to be chanted universally by all is highly ignorant and irresponsible... These factors result in a less effective outcome for the soul being... by weakening its effect on your soul's Divine connect as it is no longer potent within... A large brightly lit stadium may illusionary appear more bright lighting powerful...yet no comparison to a single sharp precisely focused laser beam...that is powerful enough to burn through the same stadium walls... Meditation and mantras are practices above and beyond this physical realm...extremely unique, precisely intimate, secretive, and at its most potent form...completely silent...thus any physical and immediate environmental influences are only hindering distractions...ignorance sugar coated with spiritually labeled social practices...

Just as one's food is another's poison... similarly one's positive mantra is another's negative... the reason for this is simple... every specific soul is unique...on its unique soul journey...with multiple Divine energetic influences...including specific Divine Deity influences (that the soul is most often unaware throughout their whole physical lifetime)...cosmic vibrational and energetic influences... specific astrological influences...Karma influences (both past and present)... physical influences... genetics... ancestral curses/blessings influences... and particular daily lifestyle influences... All these influences will interact with any mantra ignorantly chanted... which is most often negative by creating repellent imbalances in one's authentic soul energy aura... imbalanced energies equals imbalanced soul performance...
Therefore, all these multiple influences must be extremely meticulously dissected with complete detailed analysis before a specific Soul mantra is revealed to the soul being...

Divinely potent mantras are secretive treasures... often discovered and given in discreet secrecy...in ancient times, the sages would whisper them into the ear of that certain soul being that was destined to receive it... mantras are not for the expressional realm... upon discovery or receiving...the mantra should not be shared with anyone...it is your potent power that is not of this worldly realm... therefore has no place to openly share on this realm...

"Your Mantra...
 Is your Tantra...
 Your secrecy...
 Is your potency...
 Magician presents magic...
 Yet never reveals the tactic..."

Hugh Shergill

Rest assured...if destined...your specific personal soul mantra will find you...what you perceive as your research...is actually in your search...it will not necessarily be rooted from perhaps that certain religion or culture you were born into... nor a common institution or an individual that you to a certain degree follow... Divine authenticity will shine bright amongst all...whenever your soul is prepared and determined to embrace and imbibe it within...or even reject a particular mantra due to its soul burdening effect due to certain unpleasant repercussions within and your immediate environment... Divinity will correctly guide you through your own soul discernment...it is all an evolving process just like Kundalini Shakti awakening that should not be imposed nor forced...only witnessing upon experiencing...

As for Tantra and corresponding Tantric practices are not advised generally...and even its mention is kept to the bare minimum...not due the lacking information...but the volatile ramifications of when ignorantly and incorrectly attempted...as it is not for the faint hearted...nor the narrow minded...and definitely not for the ill intended...

Yoga...

Yoga..so vast and potent...just like unveiling the play of Maya...or indulging into the very hidden deep depths of Tantra...Similarly, to talk about Yoga in depth would also require one to specifically write a complete book on it itself...as all existence and experience itself in all three consciousness realms is essentially Yoga...

There are three paths of yoga...

Karma Yoga...
Bhakti Yoga...
Jnana Yoga...

Karma Yoga is the path of Action...
Bhakti Yoga is the path of Devotion...
Jnana Yoga is the path of Knowledge...

Everything in perceived existence experience is rooted in yoga... For example, writing of this book is rooted in the path of Bhakti yoga (devotion)...this book itself is rooted in the path of Jnana yoga (knowledge)...reading of this book is rooted in the path of Karma yoga (action)... even further ultimately, the whole entire Maya Leela stage play itself is Divinity's Karma yoga...

As we focus on the physical advantages one should act upon…for now, the focus will remain on 'Hatha Yoga' the physical activity of Yoga…it is the root path of Karma yoga…action… specifically Hatha yoga… the physical body exercises consisting primarily of postures and breathing…

**"Yoga and Breathing exercises
  are as if not more vital and necessary
  as your heart beat…"**

Every soul being should absolutely incorporate some form of Hatha yoga in their daily exercises… yes daily…I find it very strange how the majority do not stretch and do some form of exercise daily… Pandiculation is the physical body nervous system's natural way of waking up our sensorimotor system and preparing us for movement…that is why the majority of humans and animals often involuntarily stretch out upon waking up… Every day experience is physical movement…then why not enhance that experience to its optimum level by doing hatha yoga daily… from physical health to mental health…from posture to fitness… every aspect of the physical body benefits from daily hatha yoga…further a complete Ashtanga Vinyasa Yoga routine alongside a few bodyweight exercises is intense enough to provide all your daily fitness requirements…

Breathing…

Along with hatha yoga daily practice…a daily practice of deep breathing exercises is a must… There are many breathing practices found in hatha yoga…each respectively focusing on a specific component of breathing…both during yoga exercises and or stand alone practice…breathing as an exercise is absolutely essential…whether deep inhalation and deep exhalation…inhalation hold control…exhalation hold control…

An advance breathing technique called 'Kapala Bhati' meaning 'Skull Shine' referring to detoxification…I take it further and refer to it as the 'Asuric Detoxifyer'…this breathing technique consists of rapid breathing with emphasized exhalation repetitive reps…this is very reinvigorating for one's energetic aura… cleansing away both physical and surrounding energetic toxins…immediate dopamine producing mood enhancing effects…especially when one has been around mass diabolical asuric maya being energies for a prolonged period…as wave energy accumulates within the physical body due to constant air interaction…thus the mere presence of high populated asuric maya being zones and or close proximity to them creates heavy diabolical asuric wave energy buildup within the the soul being's physical body…which requires more exhalation breathing techniques to remove that suttle regular breathing just doesn't tap into…this is one of reasons why a heavy breathing cardiovascular work out feels so refreshing and rejuvenating…Kapala Bhati specifically targets elimination of residual unwanted asuric interaction energy buildup…this breathing technique is worth researching and implementing in one's daily hatha yoga practice…highly recommended…

Diet…

Following a particular diet plan for the soul being is an absolute…where eating your food as medicine, prevents eating medicine as your food… A diet that is focused towards preserving one's high vibrational energy is a must…unlike low vibrational diabolical asuric soul less maya beings…who are already vibrating on such low level frequency that they can eat whatever they crave…as those who are already on the lowest vibrational frequency can not go anymore low…thus only remain there…

Indeed one's food is another's poison... taking it further...maya being's desired fuel is certainly soul being's poison... The Divine light spark of soul energy...deserves an illuminating diet...

Sattvic Diet...
The Soulabrity Diet...

Sattvic is a Sanskrit word meaning 'Light of Purity'...any act, activity, consumption that brings the light of purity to the body, mind, and soul is referred to as being 'Sattvic'... On the opposite, any act, activity, or consumption that brings impurity and disruptions to the body, mind, and soul is referred to as being 'Tamasic'...impurity...

The sattvic diet provides not only nutrition but purification of one's body, mind, and soul... One should aim to consume 80% or more sattvic foods in their daily diet...to both feel and perform in high vibrational energy throughout the day...

Particular sattvic diet selection... Essentially, the Sattvic diet...is pure authentic ingredients... unprocessed foods... Pure clean unprocessed foods in their natural state are the best options for diet consumption...beans, rice, fruits, and most vegetables are examples of sattvic diet options...long list of sattvic food options and preferences are easily accessible upon research...the more clean pure one's diet with optimum hydration...the more clarity in one's aura energetic state...

Further, what is very important and specific...each soul to their own...one's food is another's poison... use intuition, discretion, discernment, intelligence, and complete personal body reaction detection feel to the particular diet and your particular lifestyle...making specific modifications to one's diet and lifestyle accordingly...as primary body dosha, genetics, cosmic planetary influences, mindfulness, lifestyle, activity levels, also all play major roles of how one should select particular foods in their daily diet...as simply eating sattvic foods without specific deep research into one's own body would be highly ignorant...

Art of Eating...

"Treat your food as art...
  As you shall be its masterpiece..."

Sattvic diet is the art of eating not only for the physical body but also for soul energy... Fresh clean simple high nutrition food is primarily consumed with no more than two full meals per day, along with light optional snacks...

Further how to eat is also very important, regardless if one is sitting on the floor during eating such as done in certain cultures...or one is sitting on a seat...the upper body posture and spine should be upright erect straight...to allow for proper chakra energetic flow alignment to consume the nutrients and energies optimally... Art of eating also plays a major role, ancient ayurvedic traditions have emphasized how food should be consumed with Love, gratitude towards Divinity for providing the meal, less or no distractions, allowing the meal to be a spiritually imbibing feast in itself... Eating should be at a slower pace while thoroughly chewing the food... Ancient ayurveda suggests the '32 Chewing Bites' rule to allow for maximum absorption of the nutrients per bite of the meal...and complete digestion… This rule is perhaps subjective to the particular food…as chewing on a bite of watermelon 32 times would completely dissolve in the mouth by then, however the focus should be to thoroughly chew and enjoy each bite of the meal…

Instead of stationary hand mudras (more on this later)…one should welcome generously… the moments whenever one gets the opportunity to eat with their hands… this is a powerful nutritional enhancing method…as each vibrational element touches the food that creates a dynamic synergistic effect of the fingers and the fiery representative of the thumb that energizes the food further and stimulates metabolic activity for digestion…as an additional bonus, the energized food increases its taste bud capabilities, making the food further tastefully satisfying… Observe cultures that dominantly eat with their hands…are more in their ideal fit weight…this is the thumb fire element interaction with the fingers that readily head starts the stimulation of the metabolic and digestive system optimally…

Water…

Water/beverages is consumed prior to the meal, and at most during the meals, however not after, as that causes digestive disruptions by reducing fire agni pitta elements required for optimal digestion… drinking water/beverages after the meal washes away gastric juices within causing indigestion, bloating, weight gain, lethargy…

"Drinking water before eating is a Yogi…
Drinking water while eating is a Bhogi…
Drinking water after eating is a Rogi…"

(Yogi: Yoga lifestyle)
(Bhogi: Indulging lifestyle)
(Rogi: Diseased lifestyle)

Drinking water before eating creates an additional full stomach hack that lets you enjoy the food in smaller quantities than a total empty stomach… Drinking water is an indulgence that works with food for digestion… with only small suttle sips…as if one is indulging in fine dining with some fine wine…this stimulates the digestive system for further enhancing metabolism of the nutrients… Yet… drinking water after a meal is a total destruction of one's digestive process…not only it washes away the crucial digestive gastric juices within the stomach that assist in optimal digestion…but also pours water on the fire element of digestion… extinguishes all the potential metabolic fire available…which is ultimately less fire available for digestion and metabolism… which results in inadequate digestion and more lethargic energy and fat storage…

Animal Warning…

Those that ignorantly disregard the predatory food chain cycle…are deeply entrapped into the illusion's delusion…perhaps having their mouth open in front of a mirror and detecting perhaps their own existing carnivore teeth may help break their delusion…nature must be faced and accepted as it is Divinely set…and we humans are physically are part of this Maya stage…acknowledgement and acceptance is authentic soul living...now the next step before indulgence is using our higher soul discernment and discretion...where awareness intelligence prevails over animalistic instincts...the Soul performer is way beyond...to just merely animalistically bite and chew on anything in site...

Animal sources of food if must be consumed (if even so) with extremely very strict discretion...as there is a karmic residual build up in the aura of the particular animal prior to providing its flesh source... which when consumed is extremely burdening on one's energetic soul aura...it is the asuric Maya jaal entrapment in its food form...highly tamasic...highly impure...this is why it is very important to be aware of why is it necessary to whether even consume?... If so, what particular animal is it?... Is this animal associated with any possible Divinity representations in any worldly culture throughout history? Just as a collective respective place of worship has Divine's presence...also collectively given Love and respect to corresponding animals associated with the Divine itself holds a very powerful undeniable energy associative aura...which must be energetically respected... On the other side, is the animal generally more inclined to filthy behaviours such as consuming its own excretions? That filthy residual will also burden your energetic aura absolutely... What was the animal's particular precise diet?...Natural or genetically modified? Organic or pesticides induced? Antibiotics? Hormones? Medications? What was the particular environment of the raised animal? And most importantly, what was the treatment of the animal before it was slaughtered or sourced...what was the duration of the slaughtering process...as immediate sudden slaughter (such as the ancient Vedic tradition of Bali Jatra) will hold much less animal trauma than to mentally torture the animal with long draining duration death... As there are unfortunately and heartbreakingly, some establishments that currently severely electrocute the animals to death on a mass level in large pools of water, just so they don't have to deal with the excessive drainage of blood by instead frying their blood...which is also extremely torturous in itself...as every prolonged dying moment of the animal's thoughts and experiences will leave a haunting residual... All and any of these possibilities series of animal tortures and treatments will leave a very powerful torture discomfort residual in the animal's flesh and sources... This will absolutely extremely burden you both your energetic aura and physical aura...especially if you are an aware enlightened soul being...as your energetic sensitivity and perception is on another Divinely blessed level...please pay attention to it and respect it... If collectively all individuals used very strict discretion before consuming animals and their sources...majority of the psychological madness and mental health issues would be immediately eliminated...as those who act/react like an animal...should refrain to consume an animal...

If one opts for non vegetarian options for high protein source...natural fish from uncontaminated natural waters and organic free range eggs that are not fed soy and animal by-products are much better options energetically than animal meats... For example, fish curry made with primarily sattvic ingredients along with basmati rice/green peas is a high protein highly nutritional primarily sattvic meal example...

Third Day Feeling/Looking Rule...

The power of diet is undeniably powerful as it is besides air/water...the direct external consumption into one's physicality...which imbibes and interacts both with your each and every biological cell and your energetical aura... Just by analyzing one's previous two days diet (completely break down) and how we are truly authentically feeling today on this third day...and even for most, how we look like in front of the mirror before our shower/bath answers all our questions for itself...your energy, aura, and physicality are extremely honest towards you...and will present exactly what is as it is...all answers will be provided to what and what not to be consumed...live with this rule...vibe by this rule...

Ayurvedic Dosha Diet...

Ayurvedic dosha structured diet holds immense benefits...realization and modifications of one's body dosha temperament state is a highly intelligent approach to how to structure and select one's diet plan... Unbalanced doshas is unease of the body...unease is dis ease...disease...

Just like there are three primary body types...there are three primary body dosha temperament states...

Ectomorph:
Lean and slender and tends to have less body fat and muscle...

Endomorph:
More stored fat, medium muscle, and gains weight easily...

Mesomorph:
Naturally muscular, low fat, athletic, strong...

Three primary body temperament doshas...

Kapha:
Water/fat dominant Endomorph

Vata:
Air/dry dominant Ectomorph

Pitta:
Fire/heat dominant Mesomorph

Researching one's particular Ayurvedic body dosha temperament and then designing a diet structure that puts less emphasis on your dominant dosha is ideal... Key word is 'less' emphasis on the dominant dosha...but not entirely pacifying it...as dominant dosha should still prevail slightly as it is one's natural body energetic state... for example an Endomorph Kapha body type would benefit to avoid Kapha dominant foods and lifestyle (less sweets, fats, low calorie diet along with much more emphasis on a non lazy active lifestyle) this will up their vata and pitta doshas...creating more balance in their three dosha make up and help them overcome their dominant dosha issues...rather than to just follow one common diet exercise routine issued for all... For example an individual suffering from dry skin and bone pain issues should avoid vata dominant foods/lifestyle...or let's say a individual who is very pitta dominant and is suffering from acne prone skin...it would ridiculous to have them consume further a pitta heat forming dominant diet that will aggravate their issues...regardless of how so called healthy and effective that particular complex diet plan may be...

Interestingly, your vedic astrology lagna first house will reveal your physicality structure, looks, and metabolism...your second house will reveal your diet preferences and what you should or should not eat according to your cosmic make up...worth the research indeed...

Physical Exercise...

"The more you put your body to work...
The more it shall work for you...
The more pain you go through with it...
The less pain it shall give you..."

Same rules of the three primary body types and three primary body dosha temperaments apply to exercise as well...it is important to be aware of your physical make up and influences...and then design a workout routine that works for you effectively... For example, a Vata dominant Ectomorph individual...who is naturally lean with little muscle mass and prone to bone related weakness issues...it would not be ideal to have them do primarily daily long distance running... Similarly, a Kapha dominant Endomorph individual...who is naturally prone to be more overweight with a lethargic energy demeanor...having them focus primarily on low intensity brisk walking as exercise is going to yield little or no results...as the body is very smart...it adapts with every move to perform with least effort exertion...so a high rate high intensity exercises that makes initially their mind shiver in intimidation is what will be transforming... The key is to fight your dosha temperament body type tendencies and adjust the intensity accordingly...nothing in the realm of Maya is without facing resistance...

Also, investing in your own personal fitness equipment is an energetic investment...as all physical objects attract, accumulate, preserve, release certain energetic energies...sharing fitness equipment with many other individuals, especially unknown asuric strangers...is a heavy energetic intrusion burden that goes way beyond the weight of the actual physical weights and equipment...

Drugs...Steroids...Hormones...Pharmaceuticals...

"If it is not in you...
It will never be in you...
The Lion reigns wild...
Not a coward in hide...
Fight with what you have...
That is bravery...
Seeking assistance...
Is slavery..."

Hugh Shergill

This is the Maya Jaal entrapment of your physicality...the diabolical asuric soul less organizations out there are extremely determined to completely destroy you...entrapping you...confusing you...confining you...enslaving you...making your body extremely low vibrational dependent on external factors beyond your natural diet, exercise, genetics, discipline, cosmic vibrations...

Imagine what if you were stranded on an untraceable tropical island?...without no access to the outer world or technology for the rest of your physical existence... How would you be physically? Powerful or weak?... A real authentic being regardless of how much their physical age will adapt and transform into a more healthy fit super muscular wild version of themselves...even while using the limited diet sources and still shining in natural authentic brilliance...Where as a fake voluntary pharmaceutically assisted being will resemble a deflated balloon shriveled weak both physically and mentally with no hope waiting for its demise...I pity those who live such a weak cowardly illusion based existence... this is no soul warrior...the lion hunts its prey with hunger...not drugs...stay hungry...stay driven...not a weak beggar given... Be the brave healthy owner of your body....not a weak temporarily renting your body...

Never indulge in a path that does not have your destination...Never externalize your power... Maya realm's victory lies for the soul being to be in its authentic truth...and there is nothing more honest in this Maya world than your own physical being...what and how you treat it...will be reciprocated with complete full honesty...

Addictions...
Maya Jaal Entrapping Favourite...
Your Addictions are not Accidental...

Every addiction is an illusionary protective escapist protection... where the soul finds illusionary solace refuge in... through both dosage and frequency... Yet behind the illusion...it is a very powerful Maya jaal entrapment mechanism...often embedded into your soul journey for multiple past soul life journeys... further more often than not...this particular soul life journey takes birth in a biological ancestral family that for multiple previous generations have been generationally cursed by similar addictions and destructions...creating not only biological genetic entrapping cravings and specific vulnerabilities but for even your soul also... Your addictions have a much deeper meaning than what meets the eye...once you unveil the illusion entrapments... Nothing is accidental nor coincidental... all is part of your dedicated Maya Leela life play script...your powerful soul was specifically selected to first face the soul traumatic experiences...indulge in the addictions...explore the addictions very deeply... become confined and entrapped into the addiction for your soul to authentically experience its entrapping destructive forces... Now only then it is your soul's decision to either ascend or descend...by breaking these generational curses and soul entrapping karmic influences that shall continue to repeat infinitely until learned... Never externalize your soul power to deceptive entrapping illusions...break the cursing chain of addiction...shift your perception from it being an addiction...to being merely an indulgent...that your power soul's discernment shall decide to even ever or when to indulge or not...not allowing the addictive indulgence to consume your soul... Flame provides heat to cook your food...flame provides heat to keep you warm...yet the same flame is capable of completely burning you alive into your grave...Your soul holds all the power required to break any entrapping addictions that you awakened desire... you are a soul warrior...fight for your soul wholeheartedly...

act upon it with full commitment and consistency...and you shall ascend...no doubt about it... Bonus advantage... Interestingly, when you zero down on the hidden culprit enemy that is creating the addictions...the addiction cravings also begin to cease...

"Fight your asuric demons...
  Your addictions will...
  Automatically cease..."

Additional Indulgence...

"Initial indulgence...
  A poetic romance...
  Additional indulgence...
  Introduces its vicious jealous past...
  Determined to spoil and not let it last...
  Dare to ignorantly indulge it...
  Surely you shall regret it...
  Where the enemy without...
  Becomes enemy within..."

Hugh Shergill

Maya Leela

I Drink It Oh My…

"Experiencing euphoria already…
 Yet still sipping in such a hurry…
 Lured I crave that additional drink…
 Being controlled by the enemy's blink…
 What I feel one desires to do…
 Is what it desires one to do…
 Lifting of the illusion veil…
 Realized the connecting trail…
 Giving in is inevitable demise…
 Standing firm I continue to rise…
 Abstinence is mere running fear…
 Control is the empowering spear…
 Indulgence yet refraining…
 True conqueror crowning…
 That entrapping one blinking…
 I am eye on confronting…
 Where the poor previous retreated…
 I fearlessly dance with it fully heated…
 What remains destined is to be indulged…
 Sipping sweetheart in your very presence…
 Whilst remaining in soul essence…
 I drink it oh my…
 Not it drink I…"

Hugh Shergill

Health in our Hands…

Indeed health is primarily essentially one's karma blessings and ill health is a ramification of a particular karmic debt…all these perfectly precisely placed in the physical body with the destined outcome contributing by genetics, cosmic vibrations, and particular lifestyle tendencies… Now, immediate lifestyle holds the power of 'Agami Karma' which is the power to create immediate karma to influence upcoming karma…this is where healthy lifestyle actions taken can if not completely heal but definitely improve the health conditions for the particular ailments of the disease drastically… Along with righteous living/good karma actions, meditation, prayer, diet, yoga, exercise, ayurveda… Marma Chikitsa (Vedic Acupressure) and Hasta Mudras (Hand Gestures) are ancient 5000 plus years of vedic practices that non medically and non invasively promote specific health promoting energetic flow within the body to both heal, balance, and energize…

Every disease is dis ease…disruption of energy that results in unease…unease due to being devoid of its natural energy flow…flow of energy happens through its multi thousands of energy centers known as 'Nadis'… optimal energetic flow of each Nadi with blood flow energizes, strengthens, and if required...heal that particular energy nadi... Depending on the individual, there on average 72,000 to over 100,000 plus energy nadis within the physical body...the quantity is dependent on one's energetic evolution through soul energy, certain meditative techniques, and Kundalini stimulation... These energy nadis have corresponding acupressure points in the body...approximately 1000 acupressure energy points depending on the individual... With Marma Chikitsa (Vedic Acupressure) techniques... when a certain specific pressure is applied on to a particular energy point...this releases energy blockage, promoting optimal energetic flow that heals and increases energy in the previously disrupted energy nadi zone... Researching this healing technique is advisable for those it may interest...

Further, with the ancient vedic technique of Hasta Mudras (Hand Gestures) the physical body is dissected and defined by the five elements...fire, air, ether, earth and water... Healthy state is ideally a balance of these elements within the body... and an unhealthy state would be a disruptive imbalance in the body...

These five elements are represented in the hand by its four fingers and thumb...where each represents a particular energetic element flow...thumb is Fire (Agni) , index finger is Air (Vayu), middle finger is Ether (Akasha), index finger is Earth (Bhumi), and the little finger is Water (Jala)...

Mudra is a Sanskrit word for a particular gesture, symbol, or expression...hand mudras manipulate these five elements of energetic flow for a specific purpose by locking energetic flow for a specific purpose...channeling energetic flow from mind, body, and soul... There are approximately 500 specific types of mudras...each specific mudra holds a specific purpose, from balancing of the five elements of the body...to stimulation of a particular element in the body... For example, someone suffering from high fever would find relief by performing the 'Varun Mudra' the touch of the tip of the little finger with the tip of the thumb...high fever is elevated fire heat element in the body...the little finger represents water...it takes water to put out the fire...thus the touch the tip of the thumb with tip of the little finger...in this Mudra, the water element will increase in the body and bring down the fire element in the body, resulting in high fever reduction... However, in a normal healthy state, this particular mudra would cause excessive bloating and water retention in the body due to causing imbalances between water and fire elements...by increasing the water element in the body and reduction of the fire element in the body...

I am mentioning this in detail to bring attention that hand mudras are double edge swords...very powerful effective when specifically required...however also extremely detrimental in terms of causing energy imbalances when performed ignorantly...no one requires to daily imbalance their particular innate energetic flow...many individuals sit daily in a meditative state holding a mudra for prolonged period...this is absolutely counterproductive...regardless of how concentrated the particular mudra is...no one should be performing daily mudras or prolonged mudras ignorantly...as the mudra is increasing a particular element and decreasing another element...which is essentially an acute imbalance...

The particular Natya Shastra of Indian classical dance forms...especially Kathak and Bharatnatyam dancing styles...are primary examples of how hasta hand mudras are aesthetically correctly included within the dance performance perfectly...the beautiful sequential flow from one mudra to another is in constant movement...evoking energetic Divinely experience yet with continuous movement and modifications of the mudras are kept flowing that create both dynamic and yet balancing effect... this is the correct ancient art form of hand mudras...not prolonged idol energetic imbalancing form...

A healthy mind and body requires balance not imbalance...use strict discretion when or if performing hand mudras...afterall your health is in your hands...

Energy extensions...nails and hair...

Your body protein physical extensions are your nails and hair...keeping longer hair (especially scalp hair) immediately provides high vibrational energy...this is why from ancient vedic culture to more recent Rastafarian culture...the power of longer hair was encouraged and emphasized...

Yes particular cultures, society, aesthetics can be both influencing and restricting...however simply avoiding shaving/hair cutting on Tuesdays and avoid nail cutting on Saturdays will keep one's mars and saturn energetic influences positively aligned in one's physical energy extensions...aligning discipline with action...action without discipline is destruction...discipline without action is a mere idol exhibition...unleash powerful energy and vibration by this rule alone...also, half the chaos of the world could be avoided by this collective rule alone...

Do not externalize your power...

No matter what lucky jewelry, object, gem, stones etc. If it exists beyond you physically...it is external power...it can be taken...it can be lost...it can be destroyed...it can fade...then what? That threatening scenario immediately depowers you... If you prefer jewelry...great...just do not energize it being an energetic extension of you...treat it just like how you wear your clothes...put on...take off...casually with no attachment just like clothes...you have your particular preferences and style... beautiful...yet it is not your is all for existence...treat all accessories casually...

Also...wearing any kind of jewelry, metals, gems, crystals influences and alters your own unique energetic aura flow...which can possibly be either enhancing or even very disruptive...especially rings on finger...as mentioned earlier in regards to Hasta Mudras (Hand Gestures)...each finger and thumb represents a particular energetic element flow...thumb is Fire (Agni), index finger is Air (Vayu), middle finger is Ether (Akasha), index finger is Earth (Bhumi), and the little finger is Water (Jala)...wearing rings alters and disrupts their natural energetic flow...potentially causing disruption and imbalances in energetic flow...

Imagine placing a metal rod on a live exposed electric wire...immediately it will short circuit...the goal of a soul being is to preserve and increase one's energetic soul vibration...be an open circuit...tuned and entangled with higher realms...jewelry keeps your energetic aura very grounded...which is fine for the common majority...as indeed certain specific individuals will benefit to align their aura to a more grounded experience...this is where vedic astrology and specific consultancy examination would be required... For example, the Kundalini awakening process will be much more powerful precise when there is no disruption in energy flow...therefore no jewelry/metals on the body is advised... In general, if one is feeling energetically drained or low...remove all your jewelry...immediately you will feel an uplifting energetic vibration burst in your entire physical realm aura...your authentic soul energy will vibrate without any disruption… Observe children…majority don't wear jewelry…their vibrancy and energy is further enhanced… Observe the less privileged…with all the sufferings for their majority… who cannot even afford complete clothes, let alone jewelry…their vibrant smiles and energies remain high amongst all their perceived struggles…

"Your true lucky priceless jewel is your Divine energetic soul…preciously placed in the jewelry box of your physicality…"

Speaking of physicality…what I am about to mention may not digest well for some…yet one can not refrain from presenting the truth…as seeking external approval validation is non desired… Need to talk about tattoos…especially in popular culture as tattoos are very popular both in popular culture and spiritual communities…yet a very powerful potentially dangerous double edged sword…

Just as one cannot overemphasize on the power of words…as each word uttered and written is a Mantra…the entire Maya realm existence is sound based interaction Shakti… Similarly…Each pattern…symbol…image…written text…is a powerful yantra… Yantra attracts cosmic vibration…Yantra attracts, controls, binds, influences the immediate environment both external and internal…these influences can be both positivity attracting and unfortunately also negativity attracting…dependent on each precise environment…further as each Yantra attracts from all the way from cosmic attraction to one's immediate environment…any shift of environment…even a slight centimeter of a movement…resets…rearranges the Yantra vibration… Temples Shrines Worshiping collective locales are Divine examples of Yantras…carefully selected located in particular locations that at the most part are environmentally fixed…incubation accumulation of positive vibrational energies… Even a fine art piece has its dedicated fixed spot for a certain duration… Now imagine placing a Yantra on your external physical body that is constantly in movement…shifting in environment…movement after movement…act after act…deed after deed…and having that Yantra interact along with you every movement…regardless of how positively you may perceive it to be…even if it is a symbol of Divine… you must remember that we are also surrounded by diabolical asuric forces that are antagonist forces creating resistance for us at all times…which will only increase resistance with furthering its targeted attacks…as it is constant interaction vibrational energy that is fluctuating and influencing both your internal energy and your environment…both positive and also negative… It is impossible for someone to chant mantras aloud 24/7 to wherever they go…then why carry around a Yantra on your body 24/7 that is constantly in interaction with its surrounding environment…the Soul being is too powerful and evolved to be using its physical skin as its expressive billboard exhibition…this is absolute spiritual warfare…never allow the enemy glimpse of access to your particular energetic arsenal…

Like an actor performing on stage that is already perfectly lit…yet the actor is performing while holding swinging a flashlight around…distracting counter productive of optimal performance… Enjoy the theatrics of the circus…just don't become the circus…

Some environments will be in tune with your particular tattoo…yet some environments shall not be aligned with the Yantra vibration of the tattoo…positive and negative…good occurrences and bad occurrences…wrong place at the wrong time…will also be your responsibility…your call…caution is advised…

Maya Leela

Personally, to take it even further, one refrains from tattoos as it externalizes my power...it reveals my thoughts...it reveals what is my interests...what I feel for...what is precious to me...well...who makes these surrounding unfiltered beings immediately worthy of peeking into my intimate aura?...absolutely not...secrecy is my potency...nor am I so weak to seek or reveal external validation triggers...all my tattoos are carved within my soul...kept within only me to know...let my external persona aura reveal glimpses to those that it may resonate...leaving the rest to forever guess hesitate...

"There is no ink...
That tattoos my heart...

What resonates within...
Will not be exposed at will...
No ink tattoos the heart...
This is what sets it apart...
External validation...
Is internal deprivation...
Whether it is jewelry, tattoos or piercings...
It is a naked exhibition of one's feelings...
The king of the jungle roams wild free...
No crowns nor ornaments for one can see...
True power remains powerfully enclosed...
True confidence is that is unimposed...
The soul triumphant above their interrupts...
Yet be assured the illusion world disrupts...

There is no ink...
That tattoos my heart..."

Hugh Shergill

Cleanliness and Hygiene...

This is obviously necessary for everyone in terms of healthy living...and can not be emphasized enough...as some sort of complete physical cleansing and hygienic ritual routine should be strictly followed every day...including physical senses cleaning such as oral, nasal, vision, hearing etc...every aspect of the body requires respective attention in terms of healthy care, cleaning, and hygiene... This not only cleanses and purifies one's complete physicality but also cleanses away one's energetic aura disruptions that have occurred throughout the daily interaction between one's environment and complete physicality... A clean pure physical body enhances the foundation of physical existence by being free from impurities...thus allowing a clean free flow environment for your energetic aura to connect with the forever pure realms of higher consciousness much more powerfully...

Additionally, the same rule applies to one's immediate environment... One's daily surrounding environment and home should also be efficiently clean and clutter free from potential impurities regularly...that not only cause impurity for your physicality but act as very negative yantra energetic disruptions for your immediate surrounding environment...which ultimately influences your energetic aura field...

Clothing...

There are various deep lineage ancient vedic traditions that have throughout eras placed high emphasis on the importance of a pure sattvic clothing selectional routine and its energetic interactions...as clothing is the cloak to one's soul... Ideally and efficiently effective...one should change their clothes three times per day minimum...there is one's night wear...out wear...and home wear...ideally none of those set of same clothing should never be repeated again and worn without washing...deserving to be welcomed by your laundry basket, not again your body...especially those clothes that are more direct contact clothes that touch your body skin close...compared to a casual once in awhile worn jacket...use your intellectual discretion of priority importance and consistency... yes this may be an additional inconvenience yet with direct efforts not impossible...as budgeted simple multiple clothing and persistent discipline cleaning regimen routine will address easily... Being lazy, filthy, and disregarding what is self loving soul essence is an asuric diabolical trait of the soul less maya being...not for the soul being...

As for clothing fabric...one should attempt to primarily wear natural fabrics for clothing such as 100% cotton, 100% Linen, Bamboo, Denim etc. As synthetically produced fabrics such as polyester, nylon, spandex, rayon etc. disrupts the natural energetic flow of one's energetic aura...especially with the new technological techniques that add metallic wiring in the clothing produced...this is very energetically disruptive...often causing premature fatigue, lethargy, and irritability...Use your discretion when selecting clothes and bedding, especially undergarments and underwear that directly touches your skin...as synthetic fabric jacket is going to have minimum effects on your energetic aura than a synthetic fabric underwear... Also, hygienically synthetic fabrics often trap heat and moisture abnormally...even synthetic mesh net fabric is strangely abnormally heating...perhaps that is the illusion...whereas natural fabrics work with your body temperature to allow both warming and cooling as required... Fortunately in this era, wearing Denim jeans with a pure cotton t-shirt is not only timeless fashionable but energetically viable...

Wearing real leather and any other actual animal skin...is highly energetically burdening...as each animal holds energetic residual prior to its unfortunate slaughtering and torture...which imbibes into each of their cells including their physical skin cells...therefore wearing their skin on to your body... burdens your energetic aura significantly... Again fortunately there are synthetic leather options such as faux leather...a much better option if one desires to wear a leather style jacket, belt, bags, and other accessories...

As for specific colours...in general each colour represents a particular chakra and planetary influences...such red shades for Mars and Sun...white and ivory for Moon...yellow for Jupiter...green for Mercury...dark grey for North node of Moon...brown for South node...dark blue, purple, indigo, and also black for saturn...light sky blue and white for Venus...dark red for Pluto...green blue infused shades for Uranus...dark blue for Neptune...

In general the colour white repels and protects one from external energies… White is purity… protection from surrounding impurity energies… For example, That is why in Vedic traditions, everyone wore complete white when attending a funeral to prevent the absorption of the demised rituals and its surrounding energies…this is especially crucial when one is attending a maya being's funeral as there is no soul ascension process for the soul less, resulting in very asuric diabolical energy in the surrounding funeral environment that is highly active…be aware…beware…

The colour black absorbs external energies… The colour black will miraculously absorb both external positive energies and negative energies…yet there is a positive protective catch of wearing black… those who are energetically evolved soul beings…are able to repel the negative energies, therefore being aware of the negative external energies in all actuality works as a protective mechanism…as often awareness in itself is maneuvering preparedness…

Clothing is a significant component of your physicality…use your soul discernment along with your fashion preferences…to choose your clothes…

Note: As the colour repellent white example used previously…which strangely and spontaneously came to thought while writing…regarding to funerals…I was not planning to mention however I shall now as some information is destined to be shared… Please use strict discretion upon attending funerals as an enlightened soul being…your presence in itself opens that higher consciousness realms where Tantra and Tantric occultism entrapments are very accessible…both positive and negative… especially asuric entrapping energetic influences… Hurt, sorrow, loss, and condolences that are genuine from the heart do not require the stamp of one being a witness… From ancient Vedic era, passing of Loved ones was a very simple, respective, private small gathering…unlike unfortunately the mass ingenuine theatrical spectacles of today…which is deliberately executed by the soul less asuric collective energy that desires only Maya jaal entrapping descension of souls… Your physical birth was a private affair…so should be your physical death… Please use your soul discernment discretion strictly as I will leave at that…as going in any further will be deviating from Maya to Tantra exclusively…

"Now that we have gone in depth with various influencing factors and self Love practices of one's mind, body, and soul… We shall now look into that X factor of cosmic energies that are often ignorantly disregarded despite being extremely influential and undeniable…Maya Astrology…"

CHAPTER 20.

MAYA
ASTROLOGY

"When you enter the play theatre…

There is often the theatre programme…

Beside your seat…

Holding all the sequential…

Insight details of the performing play…

Providing further insightful…

Information of the play…

That goes beyond the performing play…"

Hugh Shergill

Maya Leela

Maya Astrology…
Your Soul's Maya Stage Map…
The Maya Leela Play Programme…

Your physical birth was no coincidence…
it is a precise cosmic expression incidence…
We are cosmic…our bodies are celestial…any element in our body that is heavier than iron has travelled through at least one super nova…we are a part of this cosmic creation…never apart…astrology is as if not more valid as astronomy…astronomy is the study of the universe…not its influence upon us… astrology is the study of the universe's complex energetic influences upon us…if one accepts the concept of night and day and acts upon its influences accordingly daily…or even acknowledges seasons and their influences…is actually also a believer in astrology…

We all acknowledge the influence of the Sun and Moon in our earth's existence…yet we ignorantly disregard the other surrounding planets and star constellations… One cannot just select one home in their neighbourhood as their neighbour…and totally disregard all the other surrounding homes in your neighbourhood… Your home is absolutely under the influences of its design, building, construction, surroundings, area, neighbourhood, and further its particular city, state, country…which all are major awareness contributing factors that determine your home's influencing factors, potential, and value…

For one to be aware of the astrological influences…allows one to work with the tide instead of being carried under by the current…We all deal with the influences however the key is working with them which is for ourselves…or against them which is against ourselves…

"Awareness of the vessel…
 Driving soul's essential…
 Enhancing the voyage…
 Not determine the voyage…
 The destination reveal…
 Exists within one in vessel…"

Hugh Shergill

Astrology take is also much more agreeable than not…biological processes beyond genetics (as two biological siblings can be totally structured opposite)… even two biological identical twins can possibly carry entirely different energetic cosmic makeup as even a slight zeptosecond difference between birth time is its unique degrees of cosmic map of influence in its own entirely…this X factor is influenced by astrology…as the bio make up of an individual exists physically on the three dimensional realm… conscious and super-conscious states hold power to evade such influences… with that said, it is beneficial to study one's vedic ascendant sign, nakshatra, and even more precise, the particular pada of the nakshatra…this makes you aware of your biological capabilities and potential…just like one may decide and be very consciously determined to drive up to the mountain peak top…however the vehicle your driving shall determine the driving dynamics of the ride and its success…eg. 4 wheel drive jeep vs sports car will completely be a different outcome experience of that drive... while the steering wheel remains in your driving control...

Life is a game of performance...just like we select a particular vehicle in a racing game...where we become aware in advance before the race commence of what is the particular potential capabilities of our selected vehicle...similarly it is an absolute advantage to be aware of our physicality capabilities for one's most potential optimal performance in the game play of life...

Master your vehicle's knowledge...in order to have further control in your driving performance...your biological vessel is your body...knowing its further depths...gives you further conscious control of mastering it...

"The actor's performance is enhanced...
 When it realizes its unique capabilities...
 Conscious awareness overpowers...
 Mental emotional tendencies...
 Physical awareness overpowers...
 Physical pitfalls...
 As you must become aware...
 Of the fall prey...
 To truly rise..."

Hugh Shergill

Maya Escape Artist...
Is the Astrology Escape Artist...

All planets, galaxies, universes are confined to the realms of illusionary Maya...as higher consciousness awareness is true Maya escapism...which is beyond Maya...it is therefore consciously beyond Maya... beyond all influences...which includes all astrological influences... The soul performer is a soul performer...having or striving access to the Maya escapism realm...which is beyond and above all planetary, galaxies, universes influences on one's conscious state...

"Soul is beyond all Maya realms including the perceived universe itself...however one's physical existence is a part of the universe...not apart...existing...co-existing...cooperating..."

Soul consciousness is beyond any confines of the realms of Maya... With that said, one cannot deny the soul vessel of perceived existence...the physical body one resides in and all the profound influencing factors of the physical body...such as genetics, biological, lifestyle, personal, societal, educational, and also importantly, environmental...environment does not have a closure wall as the entire universe and infinitely multiple parallel multi-verses are beyond your environment...including the specific dedicated unique planetary, galactic, universe influences that are a specified influences determined karmically and exposed upon the time of this particular birth...as nothing is never coincidental...never...everything occurs with Divine precision...

Astrology is a double edge sword...as majority interpreting and practicing are unknowledgeable and ignorantly uninformed with questionable motives...which understandably creates caution for one... however the astrological influences do not cease to exist even if one ceases to acknowledge its impactful influences... We all unknowingly are practicing and influenced by astrological influences... as even a single complete day of life is confined to living according to the sun's rise and set...night and day...and most importantly life existence would not be without the sun's rays...as one who does not believe in planetary influences...does not believe that sun light influences their life existence...

Therefore the key is to move away from Maya jaal entrapment of ignorance and simply accept and understand the vast cosmic influences upon oneself...understanding it on the most fundamental practical level as possible...

Interestingly...the first to outright reject astrology are the diabolical asuric soul less entities...as deep down energetically...they are fully aware of what actually over influences them fully and what is their diabolical tasks to execute...

Cosmic Influences...
Positive Primarily for Souls...
More Negative for Non Souls...

Indeed maya beings are also influenced by cosmic vibrations however much lesser degree positively due to their diabolical asuric energy dominance... that asuric energetic sphere that surrounds them...which shields and repels any positive cosmic energetic rays that are creation sparks of Divine itself...instead attracting more negative aspects of the cosmic energy vibrations much more... Yes...each cosmic vibration is a part of the universe...not apart...therefore also confined to the universe rules of duality and relativity...for every positive vibration...there is also an opposite negative vibration...which is the asuric energetic field that dominantly attracts and influences the soul less being...

For example, a soul less being cosmically dominant with the beauty associated planet Venus energetic influences... certainly will be blessed with very attractive physical beauty...however how they use their blessed beauty will be negatively influenced by using it for manipulating means that serves their primary purpose...which is entrapping souls and feeding off their soul energy...

Therefore maya beings are also astrologically influenced but much less positively as there is that asuric negative energy dominance sphere over them...also there is no influencing effects of south Moon Ketu shadow effects...as they have no past life existence nor will they ever be individually reincarnated...or even further...will never be on the liberation ascension journey as the Soul being that strives for Moksha and Nirvana...

Treat Astrology as Sacred Knowledge...

For the Divine soul...acknowledge astrology as an imperative influencing sacred knowledge...not the life prediction knowledge route...even though there is very potent knowledge that I shall mention for informative purposes that is powerfully accurate in terms of life predictions...yet treat Astrology similar to Ayurveda...one is physical health influence science and the other is planetary physical influence science...nothing more...nothing less...as the key is to uncover the sacred knowledge...understand discover your physical energetic influences...while unleashing your power to create the rest...

Vedic Astrology...
Jyotisha...
Sidereal Astrology...

What has been profoundly impacting in the discovery of astrological sciences is the ancient vedic system... Jyotisha is derived from the Sanskrit word of 'Jyoti' which means light...and the study and influence of these astral lights covering our perceived immediate universe is jyotisha...the study of astral lights...first mentioned in the Rig Veda... Jyotisha is Vedic astrology...which is sidereal astrology not tropical astrology...sidereal astrology is much more precise technically as it maintains precision between astrology signs and constellations via an ancient miraculous vedic technique between relativity of component and movement known in Sanskrit as 'Ayanamsas'...whereas tropical astrology is universally seasonal based on seasonal cycles of the northern hemisphere...which is much more general than precise...that is why it is more popular in the west due to its mass generalized more entertaining media approach than actual precision report... Vedic Astrology, precisely based on ancient vedic systems of sidereal astrology and ayanamsas dynamic fusion...creating a whole universe of astrological sciences to discover and explore... This is not the commercially easily available tropical 12 zodiac sun sign predictions predicted daily for the entire human race population...

Remarkably, Vedic astrological influences are also in direct correlation with one's Maya Leela play script foundation and obtaining this information is knowledge asset that acts as a study guide for the environmental universe influences on one's physical existence experience and innate capabilities...

Vedic Rising Sun Sign (Lagna Rashi)

Your physical realm attributes...upon discovering that information...helps to understand what innate attributes are available for you to optimize your Maya Leela play performance...in your karmically determined Maya Leela play script...

Astrology is visible on one's body itself. Astrological influences are indicated on the physical body itself...the body's built, metabolism, ayurveda dosha, body type, palm lines, palm mounts, finger thumb prints, forehead, eyes, feet, facial features and structure etc. are some examples of astrological physical influences...

Every attribute of a sign, is dual... If it's a vulnerability, it will be your strength after shadow self work... Every negative thing that is said about a sign, has a gift that can be unlocked from the other side of that same polarity...

To simplify, and yet touch upon these factors...from a vedic astrological perspective...the key is to be open to awareness of the first house ascendant influences...this is your specific eastern rising sun sign at the precise time of physical birth and all the possibilities of stars and planets aspecting both directly and indirectly the ascendant...

The key to this knowledge for the soul performer is to separate, focus, and regard the first house ascendant and its direct effect influences primarily ...indeed analysis of the other 11 houses influencing knowledge is very valuable...as the opposite 7th house source of energy is one's Shakti energy influences that is seed of energy source...and other direct indirect aspects of the other 11 houses influence can be very useful...however knowing one's vedic ascendent and nakshatra is sufficient enough...as any more indulgence in the rest of the astrological factors begin to take some maya realm components in regard...which all are susceptible to potential maya jaal entrapments... Further, beyond knowing the scientific based eastern rising sun sign, star constellation and any possible planet inclusions...the rest is delicately put on someone else's interpretation... As mentioned earlier, even ancient vedic authentic knowledge has continuously been doctored with and incorrect vedic astrological life predictions are direct proof of the maya jaal entrapment influences...

Why then should one even regard the first house vedic ascendant astrological influences? This particular knowledge is the physical aspect of one's perceived existence...which just like genetics, is fixed physically...one's physical energy influence presence has a profound impact on one's personality and approach to processing and performing in the play of Maya Leela... Being aware of this astrological influencing factor knowledge...even though not necessary as one knows one's own personality from within...however the influence factors of how the universe influences your particular physical existence cannot be ignorantly denied...it is valuable knowledge tool as your physical soul vessel was not accidental and was chosen for the soul being for you by your previous karmic journey like existences... and also for the maya being dedicated by the Divinity scheme of the Maya Leela play... Simply, astrological science knowledge reveals what exists and is influencing collectively...knowledge is power and being open to knowledge by bypassing ignorance is one's true power...

The more knowledge one accumulates about oneself the better... Therefore becoming aware of the knowledge of the innate strengths and weaknesses of one's physical astrological factors helps realize one's body more in depth...which is ultimately the vessel that the soul traveler steers... Knowing of the positive influencing impacts and also the negative bombarding influences upon one...and then through conscious determination enhancing, overcoming, and excelling is true power performance...

The ascendant planetary influences are easily recognized and can be validated immediately by simply looking at oneself's physicality traits beyond genetics... As even two genetically identical twins shall fractionally be distinct in perceived physical attributes, as one is slightly perceived more physically attractive even though their DNA is precisely identical...as each zeptosecond planetary combination influence birth time is entirely distinctly unique in itself...exhibiting a particular distinct physical effect ... as each being is unique in itself... One highly influenced by saturn energy influenced being shall be taller even though all of their rest of their gene family members are shorter... One sibling is more fit muscular stronger naturally through mars and sun influence than other siblings even though they had other almost identical diet lifestyle upbringing...

Therefore acknowledge astrological influences correctly on the perceived physical existence within the maya realm only...never of incorrect illusionary entire life script predictions...as what is predicted tends to occur...not due to the predictions itself...but the belief in the predictions shall manifest... and they do...as our perception is our creation... Indeed the precise trajectories of cosmic influences can be precisely predicted for one's entire play script...especially particular soul's corresponding constellation script...yet it is subjective and thus subjective to error...such powerful potent play script knowledge requires very sufficient competent interpretation...whereas in today's world there are much more pretenders than actual contenders... Therefore it is best to treat astrology as distinct physical influence factor knowledge only...nothing less and nothing more...even though there is much much more...yet one must be responsible and cautious...knowing that there are constant influences upon you is your knowledge power...the power of immediate agami karma holds the key for a breakthrough performance...by becoming aware, rectifying, and channeling one's physical energy pool for optimum higher soul purpose performance...

"Karma dedicates your physicality...
 Physicality influences personality...
 Personality influences one's thoughts...
 Thoughts influences performance...
 Performance determines your Karma..."

Hugh Shergill

As an example, if one physically is highly influenced by mars's martian energy...one must channelize the extreme intense physical energy with determined focused self discipline...and life performance and quality shall inevitably enhance...indeed even personally...being a particular martian energy influenced vedic Scorpio ascendent, this completely resonates with one's energy channelization trajectory lifestyle... On the contrary, some particular planetary influences tend to influence lower energy, lethargy and indiscipline tendencies that one must make much extra conscious effort to overcome to ensure one's performance is not compromised as a result... An individual highly under the influences of the fluctuating moon will be overly emotional, mind fluctuating, and extremely sensitive that shall require one to use those energetic influences to focus much more on developing emotional intelligence than to fall prey to emotional outbursts... Further, if one is aspected by sensuality attraction beauty of venus... one must deviate from physical overindulgence tendencies and channelize that sensuality energy to transforming energy through creativity...from physical creativity through self Love, fashion, care, and fitness...to various arts such as performing and visual arts, entertainment, music, poetry, literature etc... revealing true beauty of one through one's manifesting creativity...

Nakshatra..Stars and Constellations...

Amongst billions of stars and constellations...there are immediate 28 close proximity influencing star constellations influencing each soul...these star constellations are called Nakshatras...the beauty of knowing and researching about your particular nakshatra is not only going to give deep understanding of your personality and physicality...in addition with each set of precise degrees called 'Pada'... Interestingly, this information will reveal an ancient Maya Leela play script legend for that particular nakshatra that will run again once more in your life... These few words of legendary verses...when deeply understood will reveal extreme shocking similarities of your particular Maya Leela play life script...your character...your parallel provided script...your conflict...your performance...your triumph... your soul learning...all already written in your influencing star mapping...which is fascinatingly informing...

"Traveller's travel is their own...
    Destination is one that is desired...
    Being more in tune...
    With the means of traveling...
    Unlocks the knowledge...
    Of the innate capabilities...
    Revealing how one travels...
    Bringing in tune...
    Blissful traveling experience..."

Hugh Shergill

Again it is important to emphasize...please be aware of the maya jaal influences of self proclaimed astrological experts that lure and mislead through their particular self interests... Fortunately there are technology routes that lets one put in their particular precise birth information and it shall reveal your particular ascendant sign or as in Sanskrit 'lagna'...and find out what particular planets (if any) are directly in and or aspecting the ascendant lagna... From there one can personally research the physical and personality influencing traits themselves... As any self research is self discovery...

Nadi Astrology...
The Most Ancient, Advanced, and Exclusive... Predictive Astrology...

As mentioned earlier...the sacred Nadi Granthas...the First Concept of Library Source...the Nadi leafs... where scriptures were first written and stored on specific palm leafs...
One fascinating aspect of these sacred leaf written texts is the 'Nadi Astrology'...where certain souls have their entire soul journey predicted with extremely precise accuracy written by ancient sages on these leafs many multiple centuries ago...even before the first concept of books...revealing their past, present, future in extreme shocking accuracy...to the point of when in the perceived timeline...that this particular individual will arrive at this specific leaf and its location...from what earth direction will they come...what will be their first and last name sound initials...what are their prominent Maya Leela play co performers, asura maya being nemesis, and why so...what is their true life purpose...what is their particular specific life situations and conditions...to what has happened in previous lifetimes...and what is going to happen in the future lifetimes... Please note, not everyone's leaf exists nor was ever destined to be written...only a certain specific souls remain that are fortunately privileged to receive these soul journey revelations... Please beware of fraudulent services that promise to deliver your unique Nadi astrology leaf and it's readings...as authentic unique leafs that currently exist is extremely very limited... anyone providing one a unique leaf reading service that is potentially available for the entire population of the world is highly absurd... Interestingly, one does not forcingly required to seek the leaf...as if it is destined for your soul...the already existing destined leaf shall seek you and ultimately without any doubt...shall surely find you...

"All that is left to do now is celebrate...
Knowledge is now your power...
Self Love sources is your tower...
You have survived the Maya jaal entrapments...
Escaping all that were sent to destroy you...
Congratulations...
Your elevation...
Is your elation...
Sabrage...
Soulabrate...
Yet Secretly...
Your Soul smile took a while...
Cherish it with secrecy..."

CHAPTER 21.

SOULABRATE SECRETLY

Enclosed is Priceless…

"Enclosed is priceless…
  Enclosed holds…
  Exposed unfolds…
  Closed remains priceless...
  Open rains worthless…
  Valuable is the hand enclosed…
  Open palm reveals its all…"

Hugh Shergill

"Travel and tell no one,
  Live a true Love story and tell no one,
  Live happily and tell no one,
  People ruin beautiful things."

Kahlil Gibran (Renowned Poet / Writer / Artist)

Soul Survivour…

"Each heartbeat…
  Celebration beat…
  Successful revival…
  Of Soul survival…
  Success existence…
  Your existence…
  Pure elevation…
  Your elation…
  World is now a Maya illusion villa…
  illusionary staged play of Leela…
  Primary stage performer...
  Divinity's Soul like no other…
  You are…
  Soul Survivour…"

Hugh Shergill

The Maya realm of Maya Leela…conflict embedded within the script…which for the soul is the duality consequence of facing intense unrelenting unforgiving resistance constantly…from Maya jaal entrapments delivered through its dedicated diabolical soul less asuric agents…the maya being…

Knowing the illusion…
Through knowledge infusion…

"Pain is no longer pain…
  Pain protection through wisdom…"

Pain is no longer pain…once it experiences the infusion of knowledge…then the pain transforms into wisdom of awareness…knowing what the pain is and why it is…this previous pain is now your power… power of knowing…power of knowledge awareness…knowing the illusion…through knowledge infusion…

"Intense storming river crossed...
By the one who fell in deep...
Ironically drowning the one...
Who had safely stood...
At the river bank..."

Majrooh Sultanpuri (Renowned Poet / Lyricist)
Translation by Hugh Shergill

Soulabrate...
Live Truly...
Live Fully...
Live Discreetly...

Congratulations Love soul...you survived to this point...without giving up and into the harsh Maya jaal entrapments...by the fact you have survived as a soul and able to actually read this book...is a celebration achievement in itself... Your Maya nemesis desired for your drowning demise a very long time ago...yet it was the Divine depth of the river current that became your victory passing...taking you to a realm undiscovered...while your nemesis drowned only a step slip from what was thought as its safety zone refuge covered...

This is your absolute victory...yes will the entrapping attacks from other and more maya beings stop? Unfortunately not...as long as one is existing on this realm of Maya Leela...the play will continue with its conflicting duality plot...however now the dynamics of the entrapping attacks have shifted through our awareness of knowing...knowledge of the unveillance of the illusion of this realm...knowing the illusion... through knowledge infusion...
Now the illusion spell of Maya tricks has been broken...we are now protected from pain by wisdom... this is our powerful protection...being two steps ahead and many realms ahead of these diabolical asuric soul less maya beings and their Maya jaal entrapping webs...

Now your existence is an eternal infinite soul existence...now your knowledge of the truth is your greatest power...you are so protected...you are so Loved...you are that Love soul...

"Get High...on your own Soul Supply..."

You are Divinity's spark of soul energy...have gratitude for your Divine soul spark existence...Love your priceless soul energy...embrace your soul energy...go ahead...indulge deep into your soul energy unrelentingly and passionately...go ahead...indulge...get high...on your own soul supply...

Moment has arrived to celebrate...or as I say 'Soulabrate'... embrace your Divine soul energy...enjoy this Divine play of Maya Leela...for what it is...an entertaining play of existence consequence...enjoy thoroughly through self Love and Divinity gratitude...embrace the blessings of having now the knowing of the illusion unveil...while remaining fully aware of your surrounding entrapments and their dedicated agents…therefore do celebrate…yet secretly…by keeping the knowledge of knowing to yourself…this not only protects you from further excessive entrapment attacks but also keeps your blessings away from their negative soul less diabolical asuric energetic eyes and ways…

"Revealing your cards…
 Is folding your cards…
 Premature exposing their defeat…
 Is gearing towards your forfeit…
 Secrecy is a winning trajectory …
 Staying strong is inevitable victory…"

Hugh Shergill

There is no failure…
In an illusionary existence…

"There is no failure…
 In an illusionary existence…
 What does not exist…
 Is forever extinct…

 Live by your soul desires…
 Not what the other admires…
 Fully follow your dreams…
 You have access to higher realms…
 Embrace the play…
 Shape it as your clay…
 Soul consciousness connects above…
 Soul's essence is self selfless Love…

 There is no failure…
 In an illusionary existence…
 What does not exist…
 Is forever extinct…"

Hugh Shergill

There are no goals, accomplishments, dreams, or desires on the Maya stage that are a failure…as the three dimensional existence is confined to the illusionary realm…therefore all perceived failures of one are also illusionary… Strive with your all for what you desire to accomplish… you may or may not reach in the immediate desired moment…yet you will never fail…

The only failure is of one's higher soul existence...that is beyond the three dimensional realm of Maya... where one's soul performance is at stake... where not learning from each karmic lesson...shall inevitably be repeated until learned...act after act...scene after scene...birth after birth...

Fully follow your dreams...you have access to higher realms...there is no failure...in an illusionary existence...what does not exist...is forever extinct...embrace this play...shape it as your clay...and perform your performances with your own vision, dreams, and soul desires of selfless Love...true success inevitably exists in your true existence...there is no failure...in an illusionary existence...

Follow your true higher conscious dreams and aspirations...as there is no failure...you can not fail within an illusion realm...as the Maya realm itself fails to to authentically exist in reality...therefore give your highest and most soul desire performance by striving towards your highest purpose...whilst remaining confidential of your purpose...which is Divinely set and shall reveal as much required...when and where it is Divine moment required...

"Water fuels streams...
Hope fuels dreams...
Without hopeful visions...
No dream ever envisions...
Keep the flame of hope ignited...
Indulge into your dreams enlightened..."

Hugh Shergill

"Having a sense of humour
in one's life
acts as shock absorbers
for the trying times"

Javed Akhtar
(Renowned Poet / Lyricist / Writer)

Keep the film rolling...always forward... perceived life is just like a movie...relax and enjoy...do not take it too seriously...continue putting things in real reality perspective...keeping in mind at all times that this three dimensional realm is the Maya Leela play of illusion...as there is a much higher more profound soul reality...unveiling all the confines of the immediate illusion... Apply your enlightened awakened wisdom with a touch of innate silent sense of humour...this will keep the proceedings and processes of the Maya Leela play slightly more deservingly secretly light and entertaining...

Secrecy... Strict Soul Confidentiality...

"Secrecy...
 Strict Soul Confidentiality

 Share your joys...
 Their envy deploys...
 Share your hurts...
 Their smile starts...
 Keep all within enclose...
 Open only for a few those...

 Secrecy...
 Strict Soul Confidentiality"

Hugh Shergill

What is a secret...

"What is a secret...
 That is forcibly imposed...
 What is a secret...
 That is not capable to explode...
 What is a secret...
 That does not implode...
 What is a secret...
 That could be exposed..."

Hugh Shergill

Ever notice? A premature reveal to others of an anticipated pleasant pleasure experience... actually curses it? The joyous anticipated event unfolds much less desirable and fulfilling...if at all... Sharing your anticipated joys and goals...especially to innate ill intent diabolical soul less maya beings influences a hindrance of pleasure and joy for the soul being... please strictly refrain and protect yourself by practicing secrecy and strict soul confidentiality... what you hold...is your power...any reveal...you lose power...

"Mystery Protects…
Your History…

Those with an exterior appearing calm…
Are born from an interior chaotic storm…
What is personal remains potent…
Portrayed results in potency inference…

Mystery Protects…
Your History…"

Hugh Shergill

"What remains…
Becomes germaine…
Extremely spiritually unhygienic…
Revealing others your soul organic…
Saliva when in mouth is healthy nectar…
Upon excretion is merely a spit spectre…"

Hugh Shergill

The Power of Privacy…

Divine enlightening awareness… Kundalini awakening experiences… multi realms experiential information… abilities of viewing energetic auras…the Maya Leela play realization… the particular play characters…all this must be strictly confidential within oneself… Unnecessary reveal should be avoided… regardless of how close you may perceive your dearest Loved ones…as once revealed… especially to a soul less maya being…it will surely create extreme havoc in your immediate personal life and directly threaten your well being… you are the extremely threatening glitch of this maya tricks matrix…that is now capable to disrupt and eliminate the confines of this maya play itself… this power is very potently powerful…and even more powerful is your soul target threat… only those who have survived the severities of that may witnessing agree…as that targeted soul threat is capable of threatening your entire immediate three dimensional Maya realm existence…if you don't practice extreme discretion of revealing this information indiscreetly… especially to your antagonist diabolical soul less maya beings…

Your enlightening awareness is yours and for yours only… you are the soul being protagonist of this play… your soul duty is to play this play aware… not to unnecessarily share…which threatens your power by putting a target on you… remain confident and confidential in your truth…at the very most only referring to oneself as a soul…as the majority inaccurately also refer to themselves with the cliche oxymoron that 'We are all Souls'…nothing could be further from the truth…

Maya Leela

Secrecy...

"The precious priceless reveal...
  Must protect it from steal...
  Not slept all night...
  Trapping fear of a dream...
  Revealing my secret...
  With a member of my team...
  Will not fall for it...
  By non indulgence with it..."

Hugh Shergill

Only karmic exception of revealing of the unveiling...is helping someone who intuitively for you is a suffering soul being... someone who is entrapped and suffering from every angle of existence as the Maya threat target... from perceived misfortune to mistreatment to mislead...for these suffering soul beings... the power of true perception will undoubtedly shift how they view this illusionary play and their particular co-performing actors... this information holds potential of being their most powerful weapon that ups their Maya Leela performance to unforeseen ascension heights...

With that said, I must emphasize on sharing information for those in absolute need... not a self proclaimed awakened status boosting practice... which just means you are just another 'self proclaimed awakened' egoistic Maya bot being that is more interested in self interest than to prioritize others interest...

"Soul awareness is a double edged sword...
  Used correctly...
  Capable of slicing through the illusion veil...
  Used incorrectly...
  It is also capable of eliminating...
  Your existence without a coffin nail..."

Hugh Shergill

450

Deceive the deceiver…

"Deceive the deceiver…

  Act simply proper…
  Around the prop…
  Just another from the…
  Antagonist crop…
  Mirror their unaware…
  With your illusion unaware…
  Appearing unaware…
  In reality fully aware…

  Deceive the deceiver…"

Hugh Shergill

Refrain Destruct…

"Loud is destruction…
  Growth happens in silence…
  Do not appear to win…
  Place importance to win…
  What is hidden…
  Holds Importance…
  Seed of the tree grows in silence…
  Destruct of the tree creates noise…
  Refrain destruct through your voice…"

Hugh Shergill

Power Fist...

"Fist is power...
  Fist is protector...
  Where destiny aligns...
  Contraction of palm lines...
  Priceless is fist enclosed...
  Open the fist reveals its all..."

Hugh Shergill

Self Telling...

"Loud sirens deliver the alert...
  Silent satellites manifest the alert...
  Self talk is a worthless deal...
  Be careful of what you reveal...
  Telling of one self...
  Is telling on your self..."

Hugh Shergill

Remain Low Key...
Working Overtimely...

"I may seem to remain quiet...
  Indulged within internal riot...
  Refusing to cover up with a lie...
  Where revealing truth does not fly...
  Instead of accepting to explode...
  I chose the challenging implode...
  Calm as a swan on the water surface...
  Internally moving waters vigorous..."

Hugh Shergill

The Divinity Guide…

The soul performer is a soul performer…not a sole performer…one is never alone as Divinity is your guidance…that manifests through your soul higher consciousness as deep soul intuition…providing you pure intuitive discernment… When one is aware that Divinely walks besides you at all times…throughout all the journey of your Maya Leela play experience…all of one's fear and doubts disappear…as one experiences Divine guidance every step of their soul journey…regardless of what circumstances and situations…the Divinity is with you at all times…

Synchronicity…
Your Divinity Dancing Partner…

Synchronicity is your dancing Divine partner…listen to the Divine guide and you shall never be lost… Be aware of your thoughts and surrounding signals…seeing particular angelic numbers reoccurring…a word…a slogan…spontaneous song being heard during a traveling thought…a book being read that answers your concerns…a movie being watched that suddenly a particular scene takes over your attention that is parallel aligned with your that moment thoughts…or even someone saying or doing something at the very moment when a corresponding thought occupies your mind… These are some examples of synchronous signals that inform you to or against a certain decision trigger… Listen carefully and do not casually ignorantly disregard them…your perceived life's script guide book exists within your higher consciousness…written with the Divinity pen…read it from a pure undistracted state and act accordingly…you shall never be misguided…

With that said…continue your celebrations…soulabrate soulabrity…what you knew…what you know…is a Divine trance dance of ascension…most deserving of its Divinity music…

"No celebration is complete…
  Without its music scene…
  Vedas…
  Puranas…
  Verses…
  Prose…
  Stanza…
  Poetry…
  Would be incomplete without…
  Indulging into the…
  Divine musical depths of Maya Leela…"

CHAPTER 22.

MUSIC
OF
MAYA
LEELA

"Meditation is direct sympathetic Divine connect...
Music is suttle parasympathetic Divine connect...
When the stage dialogues fail to resonate...
Enjoy the background sounds to elevate...
Refrain energy wasting from the soul deprive...
Indulge into music that uplifts your soul vibe..."

Hugh Shergill

Shabd Brahman...
Sound Form of the Universe...

"The universe holds two distinct form...
  One is the sound universe...
  The other is the visual universe...
  Only the one that knows...
  The sound form of the universe...
  Shall be the one to know..
  The visual form of the universe..."

Maitrayani Upanishad (Sacred Scriptures)

Interestingly, as written in the sacred Maitrayani Upanishad scriptures...it clearly states that each universe holds two distinct forms...one is the sound universe form called 'Shabd Brahman'...the other is the visual universe form called 'Prakash Brahman'...further, it states that 'only the one that knows the sound form of the universe...shall be the one to know the visual form of the universe...'

The universe is never is or was ever silent...it is actually sounding alive with vibrating energy... Shakti energy...vibrating from the deepest cosmic realms to the vibration of our biological ear drums... anything that is vibrating...is exhibiting a particular sound... The entire perceived infinite universes of multi-verses carry a symphony of particular vibrations... The play of Maya Leela is a musical play that even in its most pin drop silence is an eternal vibrating musical...

Even the unfortunate hearing devoid deaf can feel the vibrations produced by the music being played and are easily able to imbibe those vibrations throughout their physical body... The humming sound produced by picking of string based instruments or the vibration of drums can be felt very easily by them... Every baby in the Divine womb of their biological mother...regardless of being capable of hearing or not...yet feels the musical vibrational interaction fusion between their heartbeat and the heartbeat of their mother... Remarkably, this symphony experience of music begins even before one's stage debut in the play of Maya Leela... Interesting it is...a poetic metaphor...when the rhythm of one's heartbeat music expires...so does one's physical existence...

Thus, music is the Divine celestial sound...the Shakti of sound energy is much greater than any other power in this Maya realm world... invite music into your aura...listen... imbibe...become one with Divinity...even out of the four primary ancient Vedas...one entire Veda...the respective Sama Veda... is the particular Veda dedicated exclusively to music melodies and chants...connecting one to Divinity through music Divinely...

"Music fills the infinite between two souls"

Rabindranath Tagore
(Renowned Artist / Poet / Writer / Philosopher)

"Music…
 Loves…
 Feels…
 Soothes…
 Embraces…
 Connects…
 Empathizes…
 Inspires…
 Nurtures…
 One's soul…
 Capable of bringing a tear…
 Giving goosebumps…
 Within a single musical note…
 Essentially all that happens…
 Happens in the presence of sound…"

Hugh Shergill

"Music of Divinity…
 Spiritual Musicality…
 Raaga Raagini…
 Romancing Kundalini…
 Meditative with Divinity…
 Musical date with Divinity…"

Hugh Shergill

Raaga...Divine Music Sound...

"Raaga Divine music sound...
   Powerfully unmatched unbound...
   Privileged are those hearing Tansen singing...
   Witnessed even one's surroundings burning...
   Whilst singing the Deepak raga...
   Fiery lighting lamps lit like lava..."

Hugh Shergill

Legend has it that the great classical musician and vocalist Tansen used to sparkly heat its surrounding environment so much, with his powerful raaga singing vibrations that even things around him started burning... the power of those particular vocal chords, music notes, rhythm ignited powerful sympathetic resonance in its surrounding environment... that these musical forces of vibration interacted with the strands of the candle wick... resonating and vibrating to the perfect frequency friction which lead to igniting sparks and the candle's wick were lit...

This is the power of sound and in particular music... Sound energy resonates deeply into one's soul energy...including in one's physical, psychological, and surrounding environment as well...

"A musician is a medium through
 which the raaga manifests"

Ravi Shankar
(Renowned Musician / Sitarist)

There are main seven notes:

"Sa Re Ga Ma Pa Dha Ni"

These seven notes arranged in a particular set fashion creates a 'Raaga'... These seven mystical notes arranged in a particular sequence from ascent to descent, descent to ascent, and every other possible combination composition creates a Raaga...

These raagas is music not just for the ears, also and more importantly, for one's soul energy vibration... holding powerful Shakti capabilities that has a profound vibrational influence on oneself's soul aura and immediate surroundings...

The seven notes are associated with the seven primary chakras of a soul being that just by hearing these seven notes music raagas vibrate, influence, evoke the previously rested Kundalini Shakti energy within... Also raagas have even been associated with supernatural effects such as bringing rain or causing fire... Ancient royals treated raagas especially when played on the classic instrument Sitar as a supreme luxury royalty...not to solely make a statement but the magical aura that this powerful music resonates and is associated with...

The six main Raagas, from which all multi thousands other Ragas emanate, and each one emotes a certain specific energetic vibration that undoubtedly resonates within the soul...

Raaga Bhairavi (dawn)
Raaga Hindol (morning)
Raaga Megh (midday)
Raaga Shri (dusk)
Raaga Deepak (evening)
Raaga Malkauns (night)

All raagas can be played and listened to the flexibility to one's particular preference... however listening to them exclusively on instrumental mode and especially on the sitar instrument works on your soul energy chakras... Upon experimenting and exploring listening to a vast variety of ragas...there will be that one particular one discovered that resonates very powerfully within...this is subjective to each individual depending on their particular soul aura... Raaga Bhairavi from personal experience is a very powerful uplifting music that blesses Love, power, protection to your soul straight from the Divine Shakti...highly recommended to energize oneself and surrounding environment...especially on those days when one has to deal with a little extra challenges of the Maya realm and its diabolical soul less...

Sitar...The Mystical Musical Instrument...

The instrument Sitar holds a mystical sound aura...along with its primary melody strings...there is a series of sympathetic strings beneath...upon particular raaga sequence notes played on the primary melody strings...the Shakti sound vibration influences the sympathetic strings to involuntarily play also without the actual touch of the musician...this is the epitome of Divine power of music on display... resonating within the soul upon its play... Goddess Saraswati is associated with knowledge, wisdom, arts, literature, speech...it is noted from the earliest images associated, she holds playing the sitar instrument prominently... whenever the sitar plays, her associated energies are highly activated...additionally affirmations and visualizations made during the play of the sitar create a very powerful boost towards their manifestation fruitification...

"Each time you touch play on that song...
  You are touching Divinity singing along...
  Indulgence into the musical vibe...
  Company amongst your angelic tribe...
  Sounding of Soul tantalizing...
  Discovering depths without realizing..."

Hugh Shergill

Maya Leela

All Real Music is Beneficial…

Listening to music in general is beneficial, especially real music/singing recordings to one's preference… real music refers to authentic non tampered music hertz frequency and the non auto tuned…which fortunately was the norm prior to the digital tampering of music…

With that said, please do use discretion when listening to the highly doctored modified music hertz frequency…those auto tuned bot music which has an opposite effect on your soul energy… dimming its vibration to lower levels… this is the reason why due to technology, one has the luxury to indulge into music more now yet more individuals remain on a lower vibration… nothing presents itself without a reason… This low vibration music is a powerful Maya Jaal entrapment tool that collectively the soul less use…

"Sound is all…
You and I…
Divinity vibration itself…
To all the realms of existence…
Reaching even beyond…
The illusion of time and space…"

TWO ADVANCED
LEVEL BONUS
CHAPTERS

Time and Space...

Two Advanced Bonus Chapters... 'Advanced' due to its immense complexities for many to even conceptualize... This immediate three dimensional illusion perceived reality is so powerfully intertwined and confined in the realm of time and space...that even imagining a reality beyond time and space is a very difficult task from a human conscious processing level...

Indeed the book of Maya Leela is to one's preferred informatively complete...
yet the Maya Leela Play reveal would be still incomplete without exploring the Maya illusion realm of time and space...

Two Chapters...
Dedicated to Time and Space...
Advance Chapters...
For the Advanced Maya Escape Artist...

Maya Time...Maya Kaal...

Maya Space...Maya Verse...Maya Multi-Verse...

Before the concept of time was established... Before any perceived space existed... What was that... that actually existed?... Was there no actual time?... Was there no actual space?... Whatever that was... actually is...and shall forever remain...
That is the core reality...

"Maya Leela play stage's...
 Veil curtains...
 Consist of material fabric...
 The particulars of each universe...
 Are enclosed in...
 Space and time fabric...
 While lifting the veil of life truth...
 Those illusion entrapping curtains...
 On stage of the Maya Leela theatre...
 Curtains that are fabricated...
 Intertwined illusion of time and space...
 Upon fabric curtains lifted...
 So does time and space..."

Hugh Shergill

CHAPTER 23.

MAYA
KAAL
TIME

"What is a Play…
Without its Play Timing…"

Time for an illusion…

"Time for an illusion…
Time is just an illusion…
Just moments put into collection…
Each individual frame of reel…
Is a moment projected feel…
Combined frames series of projection…
Time only then manifests into conception…
Time for an illusion…"

Hugh Shergill

"The experience of
the past, present and future
is nothing more than a
stubbornly persistent illusion."

Albert Einstein (Renowned Theoretical Physicist)

"Time is nothing more
than backdrop,
outside of life."

Isaac Newton (Renowned Scientist)

"Maya kaal…
Maya is illusion…
Kaal is time…
Time is…
Maya's illusion…
Maya kaal…
Kaal time…
Maya's illusion…"

Hugh Shergill

Everyone has personally experienced this…perceived time after time…when one is in some painful discomfort suffering…time simply doesn't pass by…yet when one is experiencing joyous filled true happiness…time flies by so quick…similarly a soul connect conversation could be an hour yet seems like time just flew within a few minutes…with on the other hand an unpleasant interaction with someone that lasted for only a few minutes seems like hours long… Another example is sleep…while one sleeps… there is no conscious connection nor recollection of time…upon waking there is no conscious feeling that one has been asleep for even perhaps multiple hours straight…yet the same hours spent insomnia awake seems like time simply didn't pass by…

Time therefore is nothing more than one's conscious experience of momental reference points that collectively society agrees on, measures and keeps track of… Time is Maya's illusion…

Time is Maya's illusion…measurement of each slight moving moment of energy…all that is perceived…is time bound …what is beyond perception…is time less… Time is never linear…
Always just a collection of each and every conscious moments… As time is not linear… everything exists in its happening all at once… the past… the present…the future…all is in its actuality occurring simultaneously…

The Maya realm is continuously in movement...as Shakti energy is forever omnipresent and forever actively moving...even each slight micro movement or fluctuation of energy in the most lowest possible perceived measurement is a single frame of perception...like those classic cinema scope movie film reels...take that one single frame...that is a single perception of maya...now take more than one frame... then a series is created...that perception series of the frame reels is what we perceive as time...each frame is a single unit of the time measurement...no frame of perception...is beyond Maya...beyond time...

Time bound is the Maya realm of illusion...
Turiya is the Dark Divinity spaceless...timeless...eternal...once the illusionary veil is lifted...the Divine realm Turiya is all and is...never was or will ever be confined to the time bound Maya realm...

What we from pure conscious intent desire, wish, pray for is absolutely granted in Divine timing... whether immediate, in a perceived lifetime, or after multiple lifetimes...however it is not granted in the Maya realm's timing...as there is no time existence in the realm of Divinity...only moments manifests according to Divine's precise will... This is the reason why the majority feel frustrated with impatience when what they desire manifestations do not arrive within the Maya timing...as Divinity is never operating from Maya's illusionary timing...all Divine's moments will manifest in its manifestation moment...never a moment before...nor after...

Even one's physical body is not confined by time measurement...aging is not a number of years measurement but biological, genetical, diet, activity, lifestyle, astrological, and environmental influences that is being processed of one's physicality evolving...that is why two precise aged individuals will have complete different biological aging processes that are dependent on these factors not sharing years of similar title age...

Every moment of time is ungraspable...whatever moment in time you desire to grasp...react to... respond to...it is already many precise moments away...gone...the trigger frame and reaction frame are always forever separate...

Moments...

All moments are events and dates...a date is a particular moment that inevitably shall pass by...cherish the moments...yet be aware they are and always be just passing moments...

Incidental Experience

"Incidence is never the experience…
   Conclusion one determines the incidence…
   This determines the incidence…
   Experience is an innate preference…
   Recipient one determines the incidence…
   This determines the experience…"

Hugh Shergill

True Time

"True traveling is…
   Not in distance…
   But in realms…
   True time is not linear…
   But moments…
   There is no perceived assistance…
   Where time space is non existent…"

Hugh Shergill

Time is a restricted realm…
Consciousness is realm less…

Just as every perceived universal law is confined to a particular realm…so is time…time is a conscious awareness processing tool established to put immediate familiar consciousness perspective in some organized measured recorded form… Time is Divinity's blessing to prevent everything coming to one's perceived consciousness and happening on the three dimensional Maya realm all at once…

"Time is the processing structure that…
   Keeps the Maya stage together…
   Play timing is dependent…
   On the scene specifics of the play script…
   As the scene shifts…
   Time exists…"

Hugh Shergill

Everything in existence...
Is cyclical and nonlinear...

Observe this particular universe...every creation in the universe follows a particular curve round shape as every process is cyclical and nonlinear...time and space both are bending and flowing...there is no square creation...there is no rigid linear lines...these are a human being's categorization and organization perception...thus this is the same approach that it takes to perceive time...

Time

**"Some openly wear Time on their wrist...
Some keep Time in one's pocket...
For some...
Time is all that is...
For some...
See Time as is...
All shall bow to Time demanding respect...
Or pay consequences for Time neglect...
When an artist is hostage of Time wasted...
Time presents it a canvas already painted..."**

Hugh Shergill

"Time is not the absolute consciousness existence...it is a conscious processing structure for existence..."

The theatrical play requires an organized structure and sequence for projection of the play...each scene act must unfold according to the primary script...further, each scene requires only a particular dedicated scene script and casting...performers precisely particularly dedicated for that particular precise scene... otherwise it is inconceivable to even imagine to have all scenes, acts, performers playing out the entire play script all at once on stage... Therefore time must be respected for its utmost importance in the realm of maya...and one absolutely respects time...as an organizational tool of existing perceived consciousness experience...as one acknowledges and respects its undeniable consciousness perspective contribution... Therefore, it is of utmost importance of conserving and utilizing time effectively within their perceived existence...as one who does not value time is utmost undervaluing their existence... However, it is also important to be aware that time is not the absolute consciousness existence...it is a conscious processing structure for existence...

Time awareness ceases...Consciousness never ceases...even in the most unconscious state...there is a conscious state...it is one's receptive capabilities that determine the processing capacity of the realms as the consciousness realm is infinite...

The theatrical sequence of play unfolds with each scene...entering and exiting of each sub scene and its cast...but the observing audience remains seated...awaiting for the next scene...with the play eventually concluding...ending...ceases to exist further...however the audience still exists...

The boat representing the perceived one's physical existence may exit the river or no longer exist...with that, so does its duration... however the flowing river of time continues in existence...but just as a recycling component...that within the confined earthly realm...a mere component of the infinite existence...

Time awareness stalls for a coma patient...as immediate conscious awareness stalls... However consciousness never stalls...as deep rooted sub consciousness continues...and for some...further discovery of realms of the infinite consciousness continues...which is infinite beyond all time and space constraints... On the contrary, time is confined to immediate Maya realm conscious awareness... anything that is confined...has an end point...a restricted realm... As there is the absolute reality beyond time where everything is existing and actually happens all at once...the entire play script exists...but for the processing of immediate consciousness...plays out only scene by scene in precision... Higher realms of consciousness are infinitely beyond the concept of time...on infinite ever existing realms...in infinite universes... which is in all immediate consciousness inconceivable to perceive... Therefore to perceive further...one must seek further...and it shall inevitably reveal further...

"For the consciousness reveal...
 Through consciousness unveil...
 Submersible conscious vessel...
 One seeks further...
 Where infinite consciousness...
 Leaks further..."

Hugh Shergill

Maya Kaal...

"Maya Time illusion...
 Time Kaal...
 Time is the ultimate Maya illusion...
 Very stubborn to conceptually deviate from...
 Appearing precisely linear...
 Yet existing nowhere near...
 Just as time feels real...
 Yet remains an illusion...
 The participation in the play...
 Of Maya Leela feels very real...
 Yet also remains a mere illusion..."

Hugh Shergill

The time controversy...It feels real...always there...in constant movement...flowing like a river...forever...directing...advancing...in a particular order...moment after moment...a measured duration...the period between events...with a magical presence of the perceived present moment of real...making only now that real...now this real is able to conceptualize and arrange all other moments in a particular order of sequences and durations...a reflection of the perceived change...constructing a sense of time as if it were flowing...fitting together moments to make time seem linear...making it 'feel real' is the illusion...that at any particular moment of present...the past already happened and the future has not yet unfolded...the thought within creates an illusion to fit in all the moments linear to experience one's particular past, present, and future...

Time is the stage where moments distinctly appear...the separating distinction of moments is change...succession of perceived distinct changes...changing continuously...thus time is only a reflection of the change...creating a sense of time as if it were flowing...

Time is always a subjective experience...what one feels as duration between two moments of change from their attentive experience...this is very subjective as for one individual a particular moment that is perceived by collectively agreed time as being long in duration may just be experienced as just in flash glimpse of a moment...and vice versa...what collectively agreed time may be a mere few seconds...could be experienced as long as one's lifeline...

Collective objective illusionary time was necessary to put everyone's moment experience in some form of collective linear agreement...first collective time agreement was observed in natural nature environment...then further developed into perceived time sequence...the most basic form of collective time is the experience of sequences of the environment...interacting with sequences of the sky...sunlight and movement of sun...night and day...light and darkness...similarly an actor on stage takes cues from the stage lights above...giving indication of what scene act shall be presented next...just as the stage and lighting setting...all perceived in one's physical reality...is all Maya...including all experience of night and day...therefore time is nothing more than Maya's illusion...

Conventional time is a micro dissection of fragments of moments...given a collectively agreed number sequence to document...Time is the ultimate Maya illusion...appearing linear...yet existing nowhere near...

CHAPTER 24.

MAYA
VERSE
MULTI-VERSE

"What is a Play…
Without knowing the particular theatre…"

"Infinite stages of play…
All at once at play…
Actor switches…
From one stage…
To another stage…
Each enact scene reel…
On a unique timeline reel…
All infinite plays…
At play…
At once always…"

Hugh Shergill

Maya Leela

Maya Verse…
Maya Multi-Verse…

Infinite multi-verses… Maya is Divine's duality projection mirror…everything within the mirror is also confined to duality…the mirror within contains two mirrors that dualistically face each other…when two mirrors in precision face each other…multiple reflections of additional mirrors appear…further in precision multiple mirrors facing each other…more mirrors appear…further in precision facing…infinite mirrors appear… extending into the infinite…each additional reflection is progressively darker…fading into invisibility of Divine darkness of Turiya…the ultimate reality source of all existence…

Each universe mirrors itself…with further karmic active reactive fluctuations of the mirrors facing each other…forms additional infinite universes…parallely co-existing facing each other…this is multiple universes…infinite multiple universes…multi-verses…this is Maya Verse… Maya Brahmand Ananta… Maya Multi-Verse…Maya Verse…

Maya Brahmand Ananta…
Maya Multi-Verse…

"This particular universe…
 Is an illusionary bubble…
 Floating among…
 Infinite parallel illusionary bubbles…
 In the infinite Divine darkness of Turiya…
 Accessing that space is Moksha…
 Existing in that space is Nirvana…"

Hugh Shergill

Infiniverse…
The infinite parallel universes…
The ultimate key to shift your destiny…
By shifting your universe…

As Shakespeare said:

"The world is a stage"…

I would like to add to that in all actuality:

"The world is an infinite pool of multi stages…"

Maya Verse…

Your Personal Unique Universe...

You are experiencing your own personal play...your own Maya Verse...existing among infinite multi maya verses... the Sanskrit word for this is Maya Brahmand Ananta...meaning infinite illusionary multi universes...

What was not experienced...cannot be your universe...if it was...you would experience it in totality existent duration...from its beginning till its end...you however only experience an episode existence of your personal mayaverse...

Parallelly Merged Amongst All...

"Often I experience...
 Existence is...
 Parallelly merged amongst all...

 Where one's existence resides...
 In a timeline era...
 In an energetic aura...
 In an entire stage opera...
 All completely separate from...
 Parallelly merged amongst all...

 Often I experience...
 Existence is...
 Parallelly merged amongst all..."

Hugh Shergill

Maya Verse...
Multi Maya Leela Plays...
On Multi Maya Stages...

Multi-Verse...
Maya Brahmand Ananta...

Just like multiple different movies are playing in a multiplex cinema simultaneously...multiple universes are playing the multi maya leela play simultaneously...

Maya Leela

"Just as multi layers emerge out
  From inside of the banana stem…
  Even further exists…
  An infinite sequence of universes…
  Within each universe…"

Goddess Saraswati
(Divine Shakti Energy of Wisdom)

Vedas and Puranas…
Very first Scriptures ever known…
Made infinite Multi-Verses known…

The concept of multiple universes is mentioned numerously in Vedic Vedas and Puranic scripts, especially in the very first scriptures ever known to humankind…the Vedas and Puranas…especially the respective Bhagavata Purana… Fascinatingly…what now conventional modern science has just opened to slowly romance…has already been involved in a Love affair through Vedic scriptures 15,000 years plus…

It is clearly mentioned…that the visible universe is a bubble that consists of seven layers…from earth, planets, constellations, to galaxies…and there are an infinite number of these universes…just imagine one universe existing within a single atom…there are infinite atoms existing in infinite universes…

To conceptualize…each universe is encapsulated in a bubble…a very micro bubble…equivalent to a just a single atom in human experiential existence…to put that into relative scale perspective…only one single grain of sand consists of more than 1000 plus atoms…this single micro atom bubble of universe is just one of infinite multi-verses bubbles coexisting as infinite parallel universes…

Bhagavata Purana gives clear explanation in detail of parallel multi-verses…this sacred puranic vedic literature became documented more readily available just before common era CE…Vedic literature as Indian culture emphasized oral tradition over written…passed on generation to generation for centuries…Vedic literature was spoken numerous centuries long being written documented…with historic puranic references running back 15,000 year BCE…here are some compelling documented puranic revelating excerpts on multiple parallel universes:

"Every universe is covered by seven layers: earth, water, fire, air, sky, the total energy and false
ego. Each ten times greater than the previous one. There are innumerable universes besides this
one, and although they are unlimitedly large,
they move about like atoms in you.
Therefore you are called unlimited"

Bhagavata Purana 6.16.37

"Even though over a period of time
 I might count all the atoms of the universe,
 I could not count all of my opulences
 which I manifest
 within innumerable universes"

Bhagavata Purana 11.16.39

"What am I,
 a small creature measuring
 seven spans of my own hand?
 I am enclosed in a potlike universe
 composed of material nature,
 the total material energy,
 false ego, ether, air, water and earth.
 And what is Your glory?
 Unlimited universes pass through
 the pores of your body
 just as particles of dust pass through
 the openings of a screened window"

Bhagavata Purana 10.14.11

"Because you are unlimited,
 neither the lords of heaven
 nor even you yourself
 can ever reach the end of your glories.
 The countless universes,
 each enveloped in its shell,
 are compelled by the wheel of time
 to wander within you,
 like particles of dust blowing about in the sky.
 The śrutis, following their method
 of eliminating everything separate
 from the Supreme,
 become successful
 by revealing you
 as their final conclusion"

Bhagavata Purana 10.87.41

Maya Leela

"The layers or elements
  covering the universes
  are each ten times thicker
  than the one before,
  and all the universes
  clustered together
  appear like atoms
  in a huge combination"

Bhagavata Purana 3.11.41

"And who will search through
  the wide infinities of space
  to count the universes
  side by side,
  each containing its Brahma, its Vishnu, its Shiva?
  Who can count the Indras in them all
  Those Indras side by side,
  who reign at once
  in all the innumerable worlds;
  those others who passed away before them;
  or even the Indras who succeed each other
  in any given line,
  ascending to Godly kingship,
  one by one,
  and, one by one,
  passing away?"

Brahma Vaivarta Purana

Black Hole is the Universe Bubble Hole…

"The illusion of space expansion
  Is actually suction…
  The illusion of suction…
  Is actually deflation…"

The illusion of space expansion is actually suction…the illusion of suction is simply deflation… Imagine being in an air bubble that gets punctured…all of a sudden everything within the bubble air space will gravitate deflate out with tremendous pressure release out of the punctured zone…illusionary appearing as suction within the air bubble…yet in reality it is movement of deflation…

These infinite multiverse bubbles exist in the canvas of the Divine darkness of Turiya…often giving sneak glimpses that are referred as the black hole…what seems to illusionary vacuum in the visible universe…

is simply a deflating puncture in a particular universe bubble...deflating submerging with tremendous pressure into the canvas creation of Divine dark matter Shakti...

"My brain is only a receiver,
 in the Universe
 there is a core from which we obtain
 knowledge, strength and inspiration.
 I have not penetrated
 into the secrets of this core,
 but I know that it exists."

Nikola Tesla
(Renowned Scientist / Discovery Inventor)

Multi-Verses Mergence...
Merging of Multi-Verses...
Sharing Space with Multiple Timelines...

"The space we are sharing...
 It may not only have one timeline...
 It is possible to share same space...
 With merged multiple timelines..."

Space and time are fluctuations of illusion...placing...twirling...interacting...crossing with each other... same space can be occupied by different timeline spaces merging together...same timeline can present merging of different timeline spaces into the same exact space...this is the infinite illusion...Maya illusion of infinite co-existing multi-universes...Maya Verses...Multi-Verse...
Maya Brahmand Ananta... One individual's co-existence of their particular 3D three dimensional existence among another individual's 5D fifth dimensional existence...an interaction that places both their distinct existences onto the same stage space...

The stage platform remains established...yet each actor performing on the stage also holds a particular space...space upon the stage space...a particular vantage point...interaction of each actor with both the platform stage and other unique actor's particular space that represents their particular level credentials and experiences as an actor...all interacting simultaneously on the same stage platform...yet all in their own particular unique experiential space...this is Maya space...Maya Verse...Multi-Verse...Maya Brahmand Ananta...

There are moments in one's lifetime...where one either feels totally foreign in a familiar locale and amongst familiar people...or feels immediately at complete soul ease by instant connection to the foreign locale and amongst complete strangers... These moments are so profound that one experiences epiphany existence on a different level...different place...different timeline...than what is being perceived in the immediate... either completely connected or completely rejected... This experience is just not a passing thought...it is multi-verses mergence...it is a mergence phenomenon of alternative time and space into the immediate illusion of being present on the Maya Leela play stage... A unique existence...a unique experience...a unique universe...amongst other universes...all present in the illusionary immediate present... This multi-verses mergence is Divinity's synchronicity serving as a major script shift in your Leela play... Miracles... Caution... Divine intervention... Divine protection... Synchronicities... Immediate help from angelic souls... In retrospect...one is left fascinated by what actually happened and how it actually happened... leaving one amazed...as these moments never again get repeated...nor will you ever cross paths again with those particular individuals ever again... Often where one states..."That individual was an angel sent at the right place and time just for me..." Indeed one agrees...the right place and time for the multi-verses mergence...

"We both occupy this space...
 Is it actually one space?...
 Energetically I feel around you...
 Being completely out of space...
 Our timelines differ by birthdate...
 Is it actually our only time date?...
 We seem to be in close proximity...
 Yet deeply feel separate by eternity...
 Crossing of paths...
 Establishes distinct paths...
 Merging is its experience...
 Yet not the same space presence..."

Hugh Shergill

"Anything further...
 Perhaps would require to write...
 Another book on this further..."

EPILOGUE

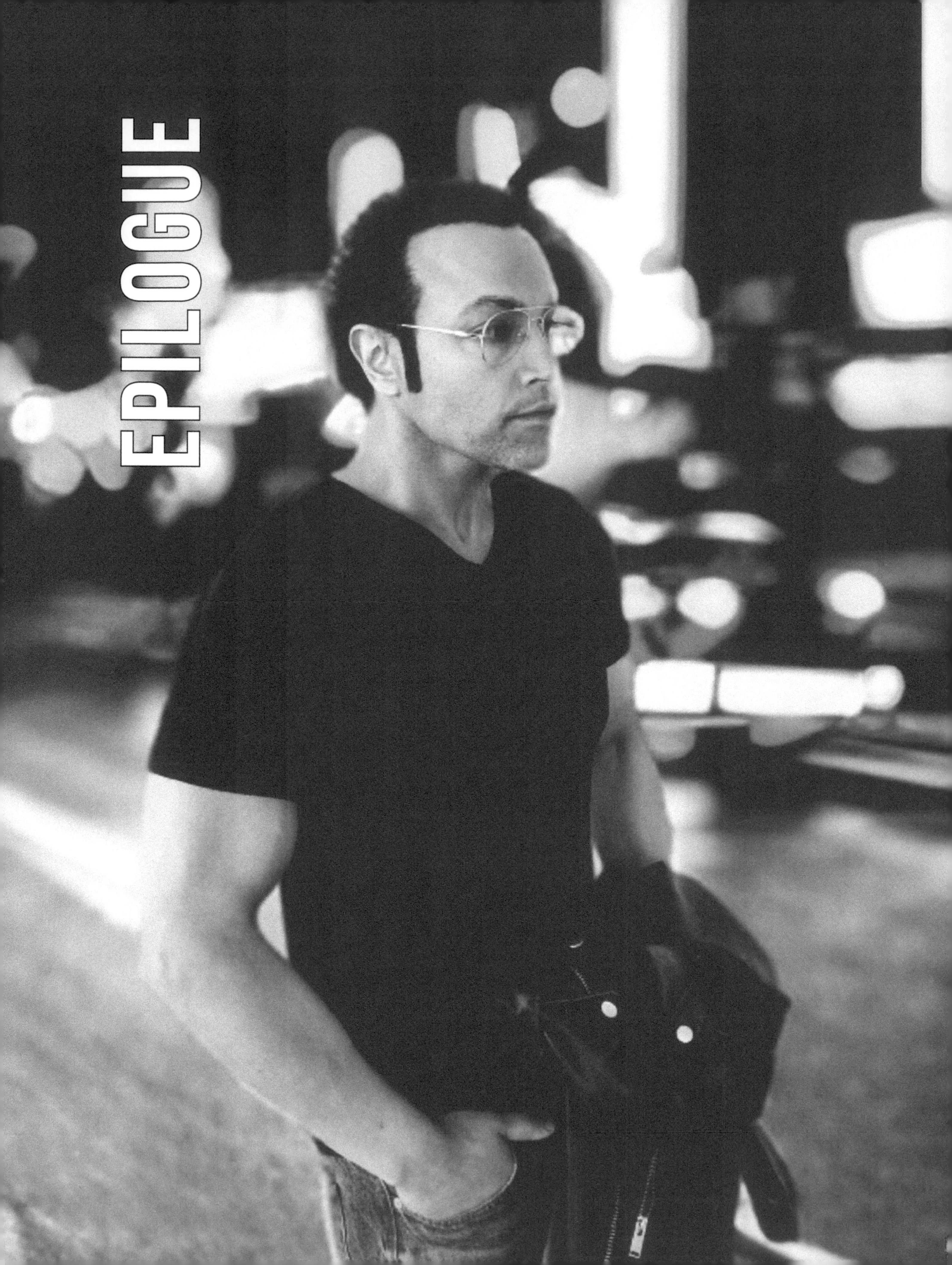

"Awareness is being aware…

Both of the knowing…

And even more so…

Of the unknowing…

Unknowing is never the end…

Absolutely the start…

For the continuous…

Indulgence for knowing…"

Hugh Shergill

Now…as one concludes the Maya Leela play study guide…lights on…curtains closing…getting up and heading towards the exit door of the Maya theatre…one continues to walk on the dedicated exit path… walking is movement…movement is seeking…seeking is exploring…exploring is continuing…as one may never conclude with the existence of the unknowing…spiritual seeking is as infinite as the spirit itself…

All existence is the art of the artist…one is in immense appreciation awe being in existence as the art of the Divine artist…being the art…that utmost humbled privilege…the art absolutely shall be appreciatively explored further within…as all existence is within…all questions and answers are within…with further infinite reveals yet to be revealed lies within the art itself…as art never reaches a conclusive point… always further existing as further seeking…the depth of the art is dependent on the depth of the gaze… as more depths emerging as discovering…therefore seeking continues and must continue…as one continues moving on performing…as its created creation…still perceived as an active participant in the illusionary play of Maya Leela…but participating by seeking…as seeking is a continuous movement process of continuing, never an achieved destination…

As in movement…admittingly…a continuing urge exists…to reveal further revelations of consciousness that shall test utmost processing capacity thresholds…reveal of the unreveal…the unentered realms on the other side of the Maya theatre exit doors…the exhale experiencing the inhale…where the escapism of illusion exists… Well for now…in this illusionary Maya Kaal time being…one shall leave with a ridling hint…

"Look into your own Eyes…

The..Unseen..Riddle..Itself..You've..Answered…"

Her Deep Lion…

Love…

Hugh Shergill

REFERENCES

ochs.org.uk/library/

vedicheritage.gov.in

sacred-texts.com

bl.uk

goodreads.com

conference-oxford.com

lib.cam.ac.uk

oxfordvisit.com

experienceoxfordshire.org

library.sriaurobindoashram.org

shakespeare.org.uk

londonlibrary.co.uk

britannica.com

archive.org

azquotes.com

folger.edu

rekhta.org

brainyquote.com

parade.com

jashnerekhta.org

yourquote.in

parade.com

stardustmagz.com

cineblitz.in